HISTORY AND PHILOSOPHY OF SPORT AND PHYSICAL ACTIVITY

R. Scott Kretchmar, PhD
Pennsylvania State University

Mark Dyreson, PhD
Pennsylvania State University

Matthew P. Llewellyn, PhD
California State University, Fullerton

John Gleaves, PhD
California State University, Fullerton

HUMAN KINETICS

Library of Congress Cataloging-in-Publication Data

Names: Kretchmar, R. Scott (Robert Scott), author. | Dyreson, Mark, 1959- author. | Llewellyn, Matthew P., author. | Gleaves, John, author.
Title: History and Philosophy of Sport and Physical Activity / R. Scott Kretchmar, Mark Dyreson, Matthew P. Llewellyn, John Gleaves.
Description: Champaign, IL : Human Kinetics, 2017. | Includes bibliographical references and index.
Identifiers: LCCN 2016044768 (print) | LCCN 2017000749 (ebook) | ISBN 9781450424202 (print) | ISBN 9781492548553 (e-book)
Subjects: LCSH: Sports--History. | Sports--Philosophy. | Exercise--History. | Exercise--Philosophy.
Classification: LCC GV571 .H57 2017 (print) | LCC GV571 (ebook) | DDC 796.01--dc23
LC record available at https://lccn.loc.gov/2016044768

ISBN: 978-1-4504-2420-2 (print)

The web addresses cited in this text were current as of January 2017, unless otherwise noted.

Acquisitions Editor: Myles S. Schrag; **Developmental Editor:** Melissa J. Zavala; **Managing Editor:** Kirsten E. Keller; **Copyeditor:** Tom Tiller; **Indexer:** Susan Danzi Hernandez; **Permissions Manager:** Dalene Reeder; **Graphic Designer:** Dawn Sills; **Cover Designer:** Keith Blomberg; **Photographs (interior):** © Human Kinetics, unless otherwise noted; **Photo Asset Manager:** Laura Fitch; **Photo Production Manager:** Jason Allen; **Senior Art Manager:** Kelly Hendren; **Printer:** Sheridan Books

Printed in the United States of America   10   9   8   7   6   5   4   3   2   1

The paper in this book is certified under a sustainable forestry program.

Human Kinetics
Website: www.HumanKinetics.com

United States: Human Kinetics
P.O. Box 5076
Champaign, IL 61825-5076
800-747-4457
e-mail: info@hkusa.com

Canada: Human Kinetics
475 Devonshire Road Unit 100
Windsor, ON N8Y 2L5
800-465-7301 (in Canada only)
e-mail: info@hkcanada.com

Europe: Human Kinetics
107 Bradford Road
Stanningley
Leeds LS28 6AT, United Kingdom
+44 (0) 113 255 5665
e-mail: hk@hkeurope.com

For information about Human Kinetics' coverage in other areas of the world, please visit our website: www.HumanKinetics.com

E5657

CONTENTS

History and philosophy can teach us a great deal about sport and physical activity. These lessons are both theoretical and practical, and both kinds matter. Good theory, the best ideas, conclusions that lie closest to the truth—these are important in their own right. If we care about sport, exercise, health, recreation, and other aspects of physical activity, we should want to understand them more completely and see them as they truly are. Good theory should also work in the marketplace; in other words, it should lead to good practice. Sometimes the process even works the other way around. That is, good practice can provide clues about good theory. This book is intended to be practical. Therefore, it is designed to close, or at least reduce, any gap that may exist between good ideas and sound professional behavior.

Many of you are headed into a health-related profession and working toward a career such as a physical therapist, physician assistant, physician, or chiropractor. Others will look to make a living in (among other possibilities) physical education, coaching, athletic training, corporate fitness, the recreation industry, sport management, or personal training. Whatever path you choose, you will want to be accomplished at what you do. Therefore, you will want your college education to lead you to new insights that you can apply in the setting of a hospital, clinic, rehabilitation center, exercise facility, gymnasium, recreation facility, or athletic field.

A Blended Approach

Much of your education is grounded in the sciences—for instance, chemistry, biology, physiology of exercise, biomechanics, and motor control. These courses should strike you as having clear connections to profes-sional practice, and they do. You cannot be a good health and activity professional without knowing these things.

The same is true for history and philosophy. Any worker in kinesiology, health, or recreation who is not equipped with information from these two areas will be less effective than he or she could be. More specifically, if you cannot reason ethically, describe the value of health and physical activity, see how movement has been used in different cultures and at different times, and evaluate current cultural trends in leisure behavior, athletics, health care, and attitudes toward the human body, then you will likely *not* have all of the professional resources that you will need.

The practicality of this text is related to its features. It is designed to be a cross-disciplinary book, to break down potentially harmful walls that have been constructed between the humanities and the sciences, between and within our many silos of kinesiology research, and even between history and philosophy. Accordingly, you will find no chapters and very few subheadings in this text that announce the initiation of a history lesson or a philosophical analysis. Nor will you find language suggesting that one can be done in the absence of the other. To be sure, some sections are more historical and others are more ethical or philosophical, but neither type has been produced in isolation from the other; in other words, neither type has been written to stand alone.

The four authors of this text (two of us trained more in philosophy, the other two more in history) worked with one another *before* we started writing. We talked. We shared different models for the book. From our different perspectives, we identified significant

eBook
available at
HumanKinetics.com

topics and events, as well as methods for jointly addressing them. Thus, philosophical ideas affected the historical content we decided to include, and history returned the favor by influencing the choice of what philosophical and ethical issues to feature. The result, we hope, is a unique book, a history~philosophy text. The tilde, or squiggle, in this term is intended to indicate mutual influence, integration, seamless transitions between ideas that are more embedded and context specific (the historical bent) and ideas that are more logical, idealistic, or principled (the philosophic bent).

This approach differs from much kinesiology that you will encounter in your studies. In your own major, you undoubtedly take classes that are discipline specific—for example, one related to chemistry and nutrition, another focused on biology and physiology, and yet another based on math and mechanical systems. Typically, you would be left on your own to make connections between these fields, to make sense of the whole. You would be asked to grasp the separate puzzle pieces you received in each class and somehow put them together to produce a coherent picture.

Unfortunately, such synthesizing is very difficult to do, which may be one reason that your professors do not often model this behavior themselves. They are more comfortable in their separate silos, doling out facts, theories, and other insights produced by their own respective disciplines. Nonetheless, we believe that the future of kinesiology and health- and leisure-related studies lies more in integration than in division, more in working together than in working alone, more in collaborating *before* we conduct research and teaching than in doing so afterward, when it is already too late. If this theory is valid, then we will *all* be further ahead if we integrate the available insights, all the way from the molecular and submolecular levels to the realms of culture, ethics, and values.

Even as this text emphasizes perspectives provided by the humanities, it is grounded in science—in elements such as the facts of anatomy and physiology, theories of evolution, and realities of motor learning. It must be grounded in the sciences as well as the humanities because most of you are preparing to enter professions designed to study or help people—people affected at once by molecules and meanings, by physiological states and cultural conditions, by chemicals and ethics. According to theories of holism (about which we say much more later in the book), we never get the one without the other. If that is the case, then we are far less likely to get to the full truth of any matter if we abstract these elements and study them out of context, apart from their natural relationships with one another. Some would even argue that it is dangerous to do so.

Understandably, movement and health professionals focus on the bodily processes that scientists explore—processes that range from chemical reactions to electrical impulses, from increases in bone density to the enhancement of oxygen uptake. Human bodies, however, do not move in vacuums, nor only in laboratories or on force plates. They move in family settings, with friends, in political systems, at certain points in history. In other words, human bodies move within a variety of cultural, social, and moral environments. In this text, we explore ideas about how and why the human environments we inhabit shape our understandings of our movements. We also assert that these ideas constitute both a key component and a practical necessity in the quest to understand the meaning of physical activity in the real lives of humans. We trust that you will enjoy the historical~philosophical~scientific journey you are about to undertake.

Organization of the Book

This text is organized chronologically in order to produce a coherent story. We begin with our early ancestors, chronicling the lives of hunter-foragers and exploring the transition of our ancestors to farming cultures. We proceed through the ancient world, focusing primarily on Western civilization but also highlighting key developments in Asian, African, and American civilizations. We move through classical Greece into the Roman Era and survey the similarities and differences in global patterns of physical culture through the Middle Ages.

We make the transition to modern history circa 1500, when a new global system began to emerge. We chart the effects of the Renaissance, the Reformation, the Scientific Revolution, and other events that laid a foundation for our modern world. We examine the British roots of modern sport and explore their diffusion around the world, as well as sporting traditions in diverse cultures. We look at the interrelationship of games and empires and examine sport as a tool of imperialism. We trace sport and physical activity into the contemporary world through the revival of the Olympic Games, the emergence of World Cup soccer, and other international developments. We also touch on growing pains experienced by international sport, including problems with gender and racial equity, the onset of televised sport, and issues related to commercialism. We bring our story to a close by speculating about the future of sport, health, and physical activity.

This historical chronology is accompanied by philosophical analyses. We attempt to find natural and complementary connections between historical accounts and potential philosophical contributions. Some of these relationships have to do with the nature of things. For instance, when our ancestors first played games, what exactly were they doing? What was the nature of a game? Other relationships have to do with questions about the value of a historical occurrence. For instance, we might wonder whether the lives of farmers were better or worse than those of hunter-foragers, as well as what the grounds might be for making such an argument. If new health risks were encountered by our more sedentary ancestors, we can ask how important health is. For instance, are longevity and safety more important than quality of life? Some historical events also prompt questions about ethics. For example, when we notice certain brutal forms of sport in antiquity—for example, chariot races and gladiatorial contests—we can ask whether they are morally defensible. Much later in history, questions arise about the ethics of technology. Is it right to use pharmaceuticals to enhance performance? What about prosthetics, such as the "blades" used by some athletes as artificial limbs? Do they provide an unfair advantage?

Other historical events raise questions about the theory of knowledge. The East has a long and distinguished history of physical activity—one that emphasizes intuitive ways of knowing. Thus, we might want to ask how the knowledge of Zen masters or followers of Confucius compares with more Western approaches to understanding. Are there different ways of knowing that deserve respect? Finally, some historical events raise questions about our appreciation of things. For instance, Britain exported soccer, the so-called "beautiful game." In what sense is it beautiful? More broadly, what is the relationship between physical activity and aesthetic appreciation?

These joint analyses point out the fact that without information provided by philosophy, history can be incomplete. Similarly, without a grounding in history, philosophy can be disconnected, overly abstract, and not very useful. Their combination in this book, we believe, provides unique insights about our storied journey from the origins of our species to the present time—and into the future.

Key Features of the Book

A variety of Historical Profile and Philosophical Application sidebars are included throughout the book to highlight important people, events, ideas, and other items of historical and philosophical note. These features provide more depth to our analyses and offer engaging anecdotes about the people and events of a given era. Another key feature of this textbook is the promotion of student activity. Each chapter includes exercises that enable students to apply new information, solve problems, and answer questions. Some of them can be used for in-class discussion or debate. Many of these exercises do not have final, authoritative answers; however, the positions that students take in answering them can be supported by arguments that are more or less persuasive. In effect, they enable students to practice historical reasoning and philosophical analysis.

Instructor Resources

Prior sections of this preface explain how this book is useful for students. There are also three available ancillaries for instructors: test package, instructor guide, and presentation package. The test package contains a mix of multiple choice, fill-in-the-blank, true/false, short answer, and essay questions designed to encourage students to think critically about the concepts presented in the text. The instructor guide includes a sample syllabus, an introduction to each chapter, tips for instructors that underline key points, guides for student exercises, and suggestions for further reading. The presentation package includes slides presenting the most important points discussed in the book; it can be used to customize class lectures.

Ancillary products supporting this textbook are available at www.humankinetics.com/HistoryandPhilosophyofSportand PhysicalActivity.

Introduction

HISTORY, PHILOSOPHY, AND KINESIOLOGY

Chapter Objectives

In this chapter, you will

1. review the evolution of kinesiology and appreciate the distinction between the discipline and its associated professions;

2. examine historical tensions and recent theories of complementation between the humanities and the sciences in both kinesiology and the academy at large;

3. identify the characteristics of history and philosophy and examine their similarities and differences;

4. see how history and philosophy complement one another and thereby provide more complete answers to movement questions than either one can produce on its own; and

5. look ahead to other chapters and learn that the simple act of running can be used to unlock some of the mysteries surrounding human development and its importance in promoting human well-being.

This book's historical~philosophical analyses of physical activity take place in the context of modern kinesiology, and this context bears on the book's content. In other words, if such a book had been written 40 or 50 years ago, it would not look anything like the one that you are reading now. Thus, we begin with an analysis of who we are as kinesiologists, what our subject matter is, and how the modern kinesiology major came to be.

The Evolution of Kinesiology

Modern kinesiology is both like and unlike its predecessors. Similarities can be found in the values and purposes assigned to physical activity, and one set of such values and purposes relates to utility. Moving skillfully is useful for any number of reasons, ranging from fitness for war to healthful living and enhanced longevity; in addition, some research now links physical activity to improved cognition and academic performance. In short, our field has been, and continues to be, shaped and defined by utility. Moving can also be playful, enjoyable, delightful—an end in itself. Thus, across history, we see movement in the form of frolic, dance, sport, and various kinds of celebration. Similarly, many exercise psychologists today argue that people should move for intrinsic reasons; in this view, activity should not be something that we *have* to do but that we *want* to do. Thus, our field has been, and continues to be, shaped by the joy of movement. You will find many other threads of similarity as you journey through this text with us.

These similarities notwithstanding, modern kinesiology also differs from its predecessors. In the United States, what is now referred to as kinesiology originated in 1886, when the academic study of human movement was first organized in the form of the Association for the Advancement of Physical Education. This organization brought together scholars from a wide variety of fields, including medicine, the sciences, and even philosophy and history! The association sought to improve U.S. society by promoting the spread of physical education programs in U.S. schools and championing a focus on fitness in U.S. medicine. For more than a century, the organization, now known as SHAPE America, helped build departments devoted to the study of health, physical education, recreation and dance.

More recently, during the last half century, our field has experienced dramatic changes in who we are and what we call ourselves. For starters, the current name of our field, "kinesiology," is relatively new. In the first half of the 20th century, most of our programs continued to be referred to as "physical education," and most students during those years planned to become teachers and coaches. Many programs combined studies in physical activity with courses in health education, so that graduates held dual certification in physical education and health. Thus, when you graduated, you would take a job in a school system and teach activity classes, perhaps teach a health class or two, and coach one or more sports after school. During this period, "physical education" was an appropriate title for the field because it described the profession that most majors entered. In the 1960s, however, the educational landscape changed—and quickly.

Just after the middle of the century, it became apparent that "physical education" no longer described who we had become. In effect, the term put us in a straitjacket that was uncomfortable for two reasons. First, many of our majors were finding work outside of teaching and coaching—in the fitness industry, in sport administration, and in the burgeoning allied health field. Second, a number of professors, led by Franklin Henry at the University of California, Berkeley, argued that the field should be identified with what we studied—that is, not with any particular movement-related profession but with human movement per se. Consider that even though some English students and math students go on to teaching careers in their respective fields, English students study literature and math students study such things as equations and numerical relationships. Analogously, it was suggested, our students study exercise, sport, dance, and other forms of physical activity, even though some of them go on to teaching and coaching careers. Based on this reasoning, the search was on to find a new name for our field.

A bewildering array of candidates emerged—for example, sport studies, exercise science, sport and exercise science, human movement, sport and physical activity, human physiology, human movement, and physical education. Some interested parties even coined humorous terms, such as "biomovemental sciences." A degree of confusion followed, and our colleagues in higher education complained that they could not find us because we were called different things at different institutions. Indeed, three neighboring colleges might offer virtually identical curricula, but students like you would be majoring in sport studies in one location, exercise science at the second school, and physical education at the third institution.

This situation persists to this day. In fact, you may be taking this class in a major program that is called something other than kinesiology. Nevertheless, a degree of consensus formed around this term in the 1990s, and it appears to be gaining increased currency. One can now find kinesiology departments at universities in English-speaking countries including the United States, Canada, and the United Kingdom, and other universities throughout Europe, Africa, Asia, and Latin America. Thus, for better or worse, we are now generally identified as kinesiologists—that is, as individuals who study human movement.

As a name for our field, "kinesiology" gives us a more comfortable set of clothes than did the straitjacket provided by "physical education." The term *kinesiology* was built from the ancient Greek *kinesis* (movement) and *ology* (subject of study or interest). Because human movement is an inclusive concept, it accommodates such diverse activities as sport, dance, exercise, work, and play. It can also serve as a foundation for a variety of professions, including teaching and coaching, provision of health care, fitness instruction, athletic training, provision of leisure activities and recreation, premed and pre-physical therapy education, and research in movement- and health-related institutions and businesses. In addition, some leaders in the field argue, only half-jokingly, that *kinesiology* is an ideal term because nobody knows what it means yet it sounds impressive! Indeed, some of you, when you decided to become "kines" majors, may have had to tell your own parents what this strange term means.

Terminology aside, the key to the evolution of modern kinesiology lay in the separation of the discipline from the profession, both conceptually and curricularly. That is, after the middle of the 20th century, the subject matter of our field would be taken more seriously. It would begin to attract top scholars; it would be grounded in the best research available; and, particularly important, human movement and related health issues would be showcased as the important elements of human existence that they are. Nothing in this shift was intended to denigrate the professions of physical education and coaching. They were, and remain, important options for some kinesiology graduates. But the shift liberated the subject matter from a single professional context at the same time that people increasingly understood the importance of human movement in a widening array of professions. Today, you can study physical activity and healthful living without the assumption that you will spend your life in a high school gymnasium or on an athletic field, as enjoyable and rewarding as those places can be.

Formal recognition of kinesiology as an academic field was achieved in 2006, when it was included for the first time in the taxonomy of the National Research Council (NRC). This council, populated by highly respected gatekeepers of higher education, agreed that kinesiology deserved to stand shoulder to shoulder with other academic disciplines, such as philosophy, history, English, chemistry, biology, and physics. As we told the NRC during the petitioning process, we already *were* these other disciplines all wrapped together in a single multidisciplinary unit. Our uniqueness, we said, lies in the fact that we study different things than those other disciplines do. Specifically, we are interested in physical activity, sport, the human body, movement, healthful living, and well-being as they relate to various forms of movement.

Kinesiology in the 21st century is still evolving. Indeed, as explored in the chapters that follow, our field is defined by a variety of tensions. Some believe that we should cast our lot with education and its values. Others in our field think that we should focus on more limited objectives, such as exercise and fitness. Some believe that sport is the most important subject matter and that competitive excellence is a central value. Others prefer more artistic movement activities, such as dance, or even spiritual practices, such as yoga and tai chi. Some believe that physical science is sufficient, or largely so, for understanding human movement. Others, like the four of us, see equally important insights coming from the humanities and social sciences. Some argue that health should define our field, particularly in light of current problems related to health-care costs, chronic illnesses linked to sedentary behavior, and excessive obesity. Others argue that health is only one issue among others and that our subject matter should be shaped more by the spirit of play than by utility. Some believe that major programs should emphasize academic subject matter. Others think that more time and credits need to be allocated to professional preparation and hands-on experiences in the workplace.

A number of these points of contention are summarized in the following list:

Tensions in Kinesiology

- Which professions should be featured—physical education and coaching, or others?
- Which activities are most important—exercise and physical fitness, or sport?
- Which kinds of intervention work best—therapeutic movements or cultural activities?
- Which values deserve top billing—public health and the utility of movement, or play and the joy of movement?
- What kind of knowledge is most important—theories of movement, or movement skills themselves?
- What curricular emphasis is most useful—academic subjects or clinical practice?
- Which disciplines deserve the most support—those in the science of physical activity, or the humanities and social sciences of movement?
- What contributes most to good living—spiritual exercises, aesthetic movements, a sporting quest for excellence, or some other emphasis?

This list is not exhaustive, but these items suggest the most prominent diverse emphases currently embraced by professionals in our field. Many of your own teachers are likely to have strong feelings about where our field should go and thus which emphases should carry more weight. It is important that you not only see these perspectives but also begin to form your own views based on informed consideration.

Your professors, your fellow students, and you yourself will help determine which points of view carry the day. In all probability, the future of kinesiology will be shaped by blending these various interests and purposes. What that blend will look like, however, no one knows for sure.

We hope that the study of philosophy and history will provide important insights into the forces that have shaped our field and, in some cases, continue to influence who we are and who we want to become.

The Humanities and the Sciences

History and philosophy are both humanities. Thus, they are often grouped with classics, foreign languages, literature, law, religion, and the performing arts; sometimes this category also includes the visual arts, media, anthropology, and sociology. These different disciplines are held together by two things: subject matter and methodology. As for subject matter, in one way or another, the humanities all address culture and the variety of symbolic behaviors and meanings that bring it to life. Symbolic behaviors include, for example, speaking, writing, painting, and playing musical instruments. Symbolic meanings are found in art, religion, rituals, family traditions, novels, poetry, and—important for us in kinesiology—games, play, sport, dance, exercise, and other movement forms.

The second distinguishing feature of the humanities is found in its methodology. Most humanities research is not empirical. In other words, scholars in the humanities do not typically measure things, assess their physical properties, look for underlying causal mechanisms, or report their findings in terms of percentages or "p values." Instead, investigations in the humanities are more likely to be descriptive, intuitive, logical, reflective, reasonable, speculative, interpretive, and creative. In this context, some observers have pointed out that most of mathematics, which uses abstract numbers to reflect on theoretical relationships, is better situated next to philosophy than with the natural sciences. In the humanities, we analyze texts, observe behavior, take surveys, listen to people's stories, and reflect on values. We write poetry, paint pictures, produce logical treatises, and speculate about why certain historical events happened the way they did. People in the humanities often resist reductive methodologies that would, for example, measure the joy of movement merely through degrees of excitement found in the prefrontal cortex. Instead, scholars in literature, history, and philosophy take the joy itself seriously and use methodologies that shed light on the lived experience.

We wish to avoid the common mistake of associating the sciences with the physical world and, in that sense, "real" things, while associating the humanities with fictitious or ethereal things. It is equally important not to assume that scientific methods are rigorous and destined to produce facts whereas methods in the humanities generate little more than opinions or wild speculations. In fact, the split between the so-called "bench sciences" and the humanities is one of the more unfortunate divisions in higher education.

This point was made by the English chemist and novelist C.P. Snow (1905-1980) in his classic book *The Two Cultures: And a Second Look*. Snow argues that people in the sciences and humanities hold a "curious distorted image of each other" and that, as a result, they "can't find much common ground." Snow claims that this lack of understanding and respect is both dangerous and destructive.

For instance, some scientists argue that those working in the humanities are slow to change and are pessimistic about the human condition. These critics also hold that the humanities lack rigorous methods of inquiry and therefore produce many claims that are fallacious, useless, or both. In this view, since the humanities do not collect data, their claims cannot be validated. Conversely, some scientists think that their own research is sufficient—that is, that they can discover everything knowable about the world and about human existence through their own methods. As a result, they posit, science and science-based technology will—given enough time and resources—solve all problems and guarantee a good life for everyone.

For their part, some in the humanities carry their own biases and view scientists as ignorant specialists. These critics consider scientists to be ignorant because they do not understand the cultural contexts of their work. Furthermore, they view scientists as not sufficiently aware of art and literature and therefore tending to ignore much of what makes life worth living. Snow noted, however, that many people in the humanities who offer "a pitying chuckle at the news of scientists who have never read a major work of English literature" could do no better if they were asked, say, to "describe the Second Law of Thermodynamics."

A narrow focus makes anyone, in an important sense, uneducated. Thus it puts scholars in any discipline at risk both of becoming blind to the triviality of some of their work and of failing to recognize weaknesses in their own research protocols. For instance, the scientific and medical "facts" of one decade may become fallacies in the next, and even valid findings may work only in artificial laboratory settings. In short, science sometimes lacks the tools and perspectives necessary to understand complex, idiosyncratic people embedded in a unique time and culture.

Attitudes that value one discipline over all others have negatively affected kinesiology, even if each may contain a kernel of truth. This is the case because our field has traditionally been more closely aligned with medicine and the sciences than with the humanities and the arts. This tendency has impeded creative, collaborative teamwork. It has resulted in asymmetrically staffed departments with

Looking for Evidence of Interdisciplinary Collaboration in Kinesiology

Student Exercise

Go online or visit your library to find concrete examples of collaboration between the sciences and the humanities. Here are some key words that you can use in your search:

- Holistic medicine, holistic coaching, holistic teaching, holistic leadership
- Healing and culture, folk medicine, alternative medicine
- Interdisciplinary, cross-disciplinary, or multidisciplinary research
- Hug therapy, play therapy, healing touch, pet or dog therapy
- Meaning and medicine, the placebo effect

After you have examined several sites relating to one of these sets of terms, write a one- or two-page report in which you do the following:

- Identify the two or more disciplines that have combined forces (e.g., biology and philosophy; or chemistry, psychology, and history).
- Describe how and why insights from these disciplines are expected to provide better answers or better practical outcomes than would findings from one discipline alone.
- List the conclusions or outcomes of the project or study.
- Comment on the validity of the conclusions. For example, were they produced by a controlled study involving large numbers of subjects? Is there a need for further studies or replications of results? What is the reputation or credibility of the individual or group reporting the information?

few or any faculty qualified to teach in the humanities. Similarly, it has produced an asymmetrical curriculum in which few if any courses are devoted to history, sport literature, philosophy, or dance. Indeed, for some of you, this is the only humanities-based course you will take in your entire program.

Many of these harmful attitudes are changing—in kinesiology, across higher education, and in culture at large. First, we are seeing many similarities between the humanities and the sciences. Moreover, most now believe that the best work in both areas is required in order to solve various human problems. Funding agencies, such as the National Institutes of Health, are currently asking for studies that combine the micro and the macro—in other words, studies that help us solve *human* problems. Perhaps most important, we are seeing more clearly how interrelated we are. For instance, good science is integrated with and dependent on good ethics. And sound ethical theory requires an understanding of human evolution, history, biology, and neurophysiology. Good clinical practice in physical therapy, for example, requires an integration of information related to the cell, the muscle, the person, and the culture in which that person lives.

These are sweeping, optimistic claims about new attitudes and activities in the sciences and humanities. If they are on target, you should be able to locate examples of such trends yourselves. Therefore, see if you can find evidence of this integration by completing the student exercise titled Looking for Evidence of Interdisciplinary Collaboration in Kinesiology.

The Nature of History and Philosophy

Although many students of kinesiology (and quite a few other majors) think of history and philosophy as less practical than other areas of study, we consider these subjects to be essential for success-

ful everyday living. In making the case for the practicality of history, imagine trying to function without any understanding of the past, from our own individual pasts to the collective past of humankind. If we entirely lacked memories or understandings of previous events and patterns, we would not know how to perform the simplest daily tasks, such as deciding what to wear based on the weather or season or determining what is safe or healthy or enjoyable to eat. Indeed, some people do suffer from memory disorders that inhibit their ability to perceive the world historically and make connections between past and present events, and as a result, they face enormous difficulties in navigating everyday tasks. Thus, both as individual beings and as members of communities, we experience reality historically. We remember the past and use it to understand our current dilemmas while also employing it as a fundamental data set to help us make decisions about future actions.

Therefore, memory and historical knowledge form crucial parts of human consciousness for both individuals and groups; in other words, we are wired to think historically. In addition, history does not consist simply of studying everything that happened in the past but hinges on selecting particular sets of information that can inform present actions and allow for the possibility of forecasting the future. Thus history seeks to understand the past in order to comprehend the present and shape the future. Mere study of the past for the sake of the past is antiquarianism, not history. In order for the past to have any meaning, historians must connect it to the present that people inhabit and the futures that people imagine. Viewed in this way, history represents an important human endeavor shaped by many of the characteristics that make us human.

Historians sift through the past for information, exploring everything they can find—in sources as varied as written documents, artistic depictions, human-made structures, and genetic markers of disease—in order to construct coherent stories about the past. In creating the most accurate and coherent stories that they can, historians generally rely on chronologies; in other words, they chart change over time and look for connections between past and present through causal sequences. As noted in the preface, this principle informs our organization of this book. Our 12 chapters begin with our prehistoric human origins—specifically, with questions about why our hominid (humanlike) ancestors were physically active and, even more specifically, why they were runners. Our final chapter looks at contemporary kinesiology and what sport and other forms of human movement might look like in the future. We have chosen this strategy because we want our human story of sport and other forms of physical activity to cohere, to make sense. The discipline of history asks us to start this journey at or near the beginning and then travel forward from that point.

Another useful distinction in understanding history involves the particular nature of historical "facts"—the basic "data" that historians use to craft coherent stories. Historical "facts" often differ from scientific facts in that they frequently consist of human memories and interpretations that are open to a vast array of analyses rather than the concrete physical and material properties that constitute scientific reality. For instance, if you ask 10 chemists to describe the properties of methane, all 10 would agree that CH_4 (one atom of carbon combined with four atoms of hydrogen) adequately represents the scientific fact of that substance. Ask 10 historians, however, for even a seemingly simple historical "fact"—for example, the date of the Declaration of Independence, which announced the birth of the United States—and you will get multiple answers and interpretations. Although July 4, 1776, the date placed on the document itself by the printing company that produced the paper version, has long been accepted as the factual date of independence, the vote declaring independence actually took place on July 2. In another wrinkle, most of the delegates did not sign the document until August 2, and some signed even later. One delegate, John Adams of Massachusetts, wrote his wife at the time that the world would remember July 2 as the day of American independence. Adams was, of course, wrong about that. He was correct, however, in predicting that American independence would be remembered in the future with "illuminations" and "sports," as is the case, for example, in the fireworks that now routinely follow Fourth of July baseball games.

The existence of differing sets of historical "facts" about the Declaration of Independence—combined with the reality that these facts do not speak for themselves but require historians to weigh, analyze, and interpret their data—reveals that the task of telling coherent stories about the past is a complex endeavor in which human perspectives and judgments inevitably play a crucial role. Historians can never collect all relevant data about the past, nor can they ignore the competing and contested facts that make up their database. Their task, therefore, is to create the best stories they can about the past based on the information they can excavate, knowing that their evidence is always incomplete and frequently a product of human perspectives, which are never infallible.

This interpretive process that lies at the heart of the historical method cannot be easily explained, but it must be employed rigorously. It must be clear, logical, reasonable, plausible, and, of course, consistent with what historians understand as facts. If an interpretation is speculative, it must be identified as such. If two or more interpretations are plausible, they should be acknowledged. Historians must also be open to the reality that people in the past have offered multiple answers to a great variety of questions, some of which still resonate in our contemporary world. In fact, many historians recognize that, in addition to chronology, the questions that cultures ask provide another set of coherences for structuring historical narratives. Answers vary over time, but humans have historically wondered in many times and many places about the proper relationship between individual liberties and the good of the community, about what constitutes the good life, about the purpose and meaning of human existence, and about a host of other issues. Many of these questions involve physical activity in a variety of ways, including questions about the relationship of body and mind, the role of sport and exercise in living a meaningful life, and the potential connections between play and ethics.

Indeed, history and philosophy overlap, both in their focus on enduring questions and in their insistence on interpretive processes that employ clear, logical, and rigorous reasoning. Scholars in both fields work with ideas. Both examine particulars and make broader or more abstract claims that they think are true. This practice can be referred to as good logic, right thinking, insightful intuition, effective reasoning, or, as Aristotle put it, "practical wisdom." Most philosophers and historians believe in the power of intelligence to ferret out generalities (inductive reasoning); to draw proper conclusions from premises (deductive reasoning); or to simply see relationships, differences, and similarities (intuitive reasoning).

Like history, philosophy is a reflective discipline. Unlike history, philosophers do not need to examine documents or interview individuals with special information about a person, time period, or event. Instead, they examine things with the mind's eye. This does not, however, give them license to make just any claims they wish; rather, they believe that philosophy, when done well, possesses rigor.

This is the case because from a philosophical perspective we live in a mostly common world. That is, we experience life in similar ways. As a result, we can check someone else's philosophical claims against our own experience. To be sure,

idiosyncratic perspectives produced by language, education, culture, and custom can get in the way of seeing things more or less correctly. But this fact does not prevent progress; rather, it urges caution and humility. Philosophers, like historians and scientists, must hold many of their claims tentatively and look for their studies to be replicated. They must have others examine the same things and see if they come to the same or similar conclusions. Good and clear thinking should allow us to slowly circle in on the best answers for the riddles of nature and human existence.

As you will see in detail in chapter 3, philosophers ask several kinds of questions:

- What things are (metaphysics)
- How we know (epistemology)
- How reasoning works (logic)
- What counts as beautiful or pleasing (aesthetics)
- How we should behave (ethics)
- What is valuable or what constitutes the good life (axiology)

Philosophers work in the domain of intangibles—of ideas, values, purposes, motives, emotions, logical relationships, and the like. Most philosophers think that intangibles are real. That is, intangibles such as love and anger are commonly experienced, they have causative power, and their features can be described. In this view, any research on human existence and behavior that does not take intangibles into account would be incomplete. Thus, philosophers see themselves as complementing the work of researchers in other disciplines. Microscopes and petri dishes, for instance, are not well suited to the task of examining intangibles; reflection and "practical wisdom," on the other hand, do fill the bill. For instance, no one will ever understand fully what love is merely from looking at a brain wave.

Philosophy and history complement one another too. As we have already noted, history helps to pull philosophy out of the clouds and bring it back to earth. It provides context for ideas and values. It also provides a kind of intellectual cold shower for any philosophers who would argue that nothing ever changes or, alternately, that everything always changes. Without context and the wisdom that comes from understanding history, the engine of philosophy could easily run off the tracks.

Here is an example. One line of reasoning in philosophy describes competition as a cooperative venture, one that often leads to friendship—even between opponents. There is a certain logic to this argument that makes sense. But history would have us think again. In certain contexts—under certain political regimes, within certain economic systems, in certain historical eras—those friendly relationships have not emerged. Thus history reminds philosophy that a logical possibility does not always turn out to be a historical reality.

Philosophy complements history in the other direction. It provides vision, possibilities, and ideals that may or may not have historical precedents. In the view of philosophers, the fact that something has never been done does not mean that it cannot or should not be done. Philosophy can also provide principled conceptual clarity to historical interpretations that lie too close to the action.

Here is another example. Historians have noted that in certain cultures sport involves an ethos or spirit in which athletes follow both written and unwritten rules. Any victory achieved by violating this ethos is viewed as unworthy or "cheap." Some educators during the 19th and early 20th centuries argued that this kind of fair-play ethos should be applied not just to sport but to all of life. In this view, sport can and should play a pedagogical role in culture.

While this historical fact is interesting in its own right, philosophers would be inclined to address broader philosophical issues in it. What, they would ask, is the relationship between games and rules? What is fair play? Is fair play a prerequisite for valid sporting competition? This decontextualizing move is done in hopes of finding larger answers to larger questions. Any conclusions reached as a result of this move would not contradict historical analysis, but they would transcend it.

We hope you enjoy the interplay of context-specific and transcendent analysis that you will find in the remainder of this text. We believe that the two approaches need each other; indeed, in a sense, they ask for each other. This is the way it is, or at least should be, with cross-disciplinary studies in kinesiology.

The Subject Matter of Kinesiology

We have already hinted that little consensus has been reached about our subject matter, and it may be counterproductive to argue that our content has to be one thing rather than another. The four of us prefer to take a more inclusive approach that appreciates the many values associated with human movement and with an active lifestyle. Thus, when asked if kinesiology focuses on sport, or exercise, or games, or play, or dance, or training, or health, or leisure, or recreation, or rehabilitation, or prevention, or athletics, or gardening, or practicing tai chi, or walking one's dog, we are inclined to say yes! It can focus on all of these things. If nothing else, this conclusion stands as a tribute to the significance of physical activity and, particularly, to the importance of skillful movement in human existence.

Those of us in the humanities are inclined to see this significance in the relationship between movement and the *quality* of life. Traditionally, our colleagues in the sciences are thought to focus on the biological or physiological benefits of activity, or life *itself*. But once again, these reified positions carry more than a modicum of bias and, as C.P. Snow told us, are potentially harmful.

It might be better, then, to view quality of life and life itself as interrelated. The reasons are not hard to see, particularly at the extremes. Without purpose, love, or meaning, life itself might not be worth living; this view is borne out by many studies of mental disease, depression, and alienation. Conversely, a life defined by disease, pain, and severe disability might lack quality. To be sure, many strong individuals maintain a healthy existence without much meaning or joy in their lives, and many individuals with disability live a good and meaningful life. The fact remains, however, that quality and quantity—meaning and health—are not independent elements in the whole person. They typically intermingle and affect one another. Much current work on aging populations shows how difficult it is to preserve quality of life, particularly under the strain of dementia or Alzheimer's disease. Similarly, much current research on mental disease shows that often it leads to, or is accompanied by, a variety of health problems.

Thus, we might conclude that kinesiology focuses on the physically active lifestyle as it affects (on one hand) health and life itself and (on the other hand) the meaning or quality of life. Because we focus in this book on lived experiences and cultural settings for physical activity, much of our analysis involves the forms of movement that we find in society—for example, sport, intercollegiate athletics, games, aerobic exercise, weightlifting, children's play, and dance. Such activities attracted the attention of our ancestors and continue to call to us today. They affect both life itself and the quality of that life.

In order to appreciate the range of interest in specific cultural activities, and to better see the interplay of life and quality of life, complete the student exercise titled Investigating the Importance of Play for Children.

From this exercise, it should be clear that physical activity and play are closely related. It should also be obvious from the historical research that valuations of play rise and fall depending on a number of cultural factors. You should see that play can be studied from the micro level to the macro level. Finally, you should be able to see and feel the philosophical tension between using play for other ends and allowing play to be an end in itself.

Investigating the Importance of Play for Children

Student Exercise

Suppose that you work with young children and are considering the proposition that play is good for children. You have been asked to list all of the reasons for promoting physically active play experiences for this young population. Because you are a kinesiology major, you already know many of these reasons.

1. List as many benefits of physically active play as you can think of; try for at least 10. (If your class works in groups, this would be a good group brainstorming exercise.)

2. Conduct online research to identify a historical period or culture in which play was emphasized and one in which it was suppressed. Give at least one reason for each.

3. Continue your online research to look for at least one study in biology, neuroanatomy, psychology, growth and development, anthropology, education, or sociology that would support the importance of play for children. Describe the significance of play articulated in the study and identify the discipline or disciplines from which its claims about play emerge.

4. Reflect philosophically on your analysis. Do you see enjoyment as one of the most valuable benefits of play? Do kids have a right to have fun? Do movement activities successfully induce children to play?

Wrapping Up and Looking Ahead

In chapter 1, we begin at the origin of our species with a practical philosophy and history of a fundamental form of human movement—running. Of course, we examine a wide variety of physical activities in the chapters that follow, but running serves both historically and conceptually as a very basic and important kind of human movement.

Our analysis of running highlights many of the ideas mentioned in this introduction. More specifically, in chapter 1 we consider the evolutionary and biological factors that made human running one of the key elements in the origins and survival of our species, turning us into what some scholars have referred to as "super-endurance predators"—as the naturalist Bernd Heinrich labeled our ancestors. We also examine how human cultures have valued running and other physical abilities and skills differently in different historical epochs. For example, our hunting and foraging ancestors viewed running, as well as throwing objects and carrying heavy objects, as essential and practical abilities. In contrast, some cultures in later periods viewed running and certain other physical activities as a waste of time and energy that could better be put to more productive uses, such as agricultural and industrial labor. Indeed, just a little more than a century ago, when endurance running became a modern, organized sport, those early racers who wanted to train in city streets or urban parks often had to do so surreptitiously in the middle of the night. Otherwise, they might be labeled as mentally disturbed nuisances or criminals fleeing from the authorities, since "normal" adults would not waste time or energy running in public. Now, we have a billion-dollar industry dedicated to outfitting the mass public in running gear and a chorus of experts who tell us that running, and other forms of cardiovascular exercise, can increase our life spans and make us happier and even better citizens—whatever that may mean.

The field of kinesiology has contributed a great deal to explaining how we run and what running means in terms of our physiological and biological composition. Our contribution here is to explore not just the whats and hows of running but *why* we run and, more broadly, why we move. Over the course of the book's 12 chapters, we explore the reasons for which people run and engage in a wide variety of other physical activities—as well as why they sometimes do *not* run or engage in much other purposeful movement—as a way to introduce you to both the theoretical and the practical sides of the history and philosophy of physical activity.

Study Questions

1. How and why has kinesiology been shaped both by utility and by serendipity? Are both influences worthy of support? Explain your reasoning.

2. What conceptual shift accompanied the change from "physical education" to "kinesiology"? Did this shift influence your own decision to major in this field? Why or why not?

3. What distinguishes the humanities from the sciences? What is the source of the tension that often exists between these two domains in higher education?

4. Why are both history and philosophy identified as humanities? In what important ways do they differ?

5. How are history and philosophy complementary and interrelated? How are the study of health or life itself and the study of quality of life complementary and interrelated?

BODIES, BRAINS, AND CULTURES

Human Origins and the Riddles of Why People Run

Chapter Objectives

In this chapter, you will

1. learn about our human origins and about current health problems related to those origins;

2. reflect on the vast expanse of geological time, the recent emergence of the human species, the brief duration of individual life spans, and the implications for our personal values and choices;

3. review a chronology of key events that mark the human story and note that evolutionary change is uneven and unpredictable;

4. see how evolution has created a need for movement, health, and leisure professionals;

5. consider speculations regarding how bipedalism, running, and other forms of physical activity may have stimulated human evolution;

6. consider the significance of social cooperation in human evolution and whether sport activities require cooperative agreements and promote mutual support;

7. examine the daily lives of our ancestors and identify the roots of sport and physical activity in hunting, warfare, and religion; and

8. determine how our ancestors worked and played, analyze differences between these two kinds of activity, and describe practical applications for motivating contemporary clients to adopt an active lifestyle.

In our contemporary world, which is now inhabited by more than seven billion humans, two major factors contribute to serious maladies that increasingly afflict vast numbers of people. For one thing, many of us move too little; we do not walk or run nearly as much as our forbearers did. Many of us also consume too many calories; we eat more, and more frequently and more consistently, than our ancestors did. According to a multitude of scientific studies, these two interconnected changes in the way that most of us live have produced a well-documented epidemic of diseases, including obesity, heart disease, cancer, and depression. These modern realities derive from the fact that we live in environments built with our own ingenuity in the setting of highly technological societies with mechanical transportation systems and industrialized agricultural practices. To our benefit, these conditions produce steady and abundant food supplies; to our detriment, they can also lead to physiological, psychological, and social problems.

Humans evolved over vast periods of time for very different environments than the ones we now inhabit. In the environments in which our ancestors emerged, survival required a reliance on the power of one's own locomotion in order to gather and hunt. Survival also privileged the genetic ability to hoard calories from infrequent times of plenty for long stretches marked by uncertain food supplies. Thus, our ability to navigate long distances under our own locomotive power and to store fat through occasional overconsumption constituted crucial adaptive strategies. In short, we were designed to run. We were also designed to eat, and sometimes to eat more than we needed in order to store calories for the inevitable cycles of scarcity that characterized our environment. Indeed, many scholars of human origins now contend that we were born to lope and gambol over vast distances and to eat a lot when we had the opportunity to consume food.

Today, however, modern transportation systems and technological developments mean that we no longer need to use our own locomotive systems as much as we did in the past. Similarly, modern agricultural processes mean that we have consistent access to more calories than our ancestors could have imagined. Yet we still have their genetic programming to overconsume in order to store fuel for periods of scarcity, which, for the vast majority of us, no longer exist. Combined, these two profound changes in the environments that we inhabit have produced conditions which, according to many experts, have created the foundation for a variety of health and wellness problems faced by modern humans.

The fully modern human species to which we belong, Homo sapiens, first appeared on the savannahs of East Africa about 150,000 to 200,000 years ago. Their ancestors (and ours), a variety of hominid species, had inhabited the savannahs for six to eight million years before the appearance of the species to which we belong. Our ancestors shared these vast grasslands with a wide range of other species adapted to the hot, dry plains that put a premium on movement for both predators and prey. In this environment, hominids gradually emerged as the dominant predators. Their human descendants would eventually migrate from the East African velds into every other ecosystem on earth, including harsh polar ecosystems. This human evolutionary trajectory—from savannah-dwelling hominids into the species with the largest range and greatest impact on global systems—requires some explanation. This is particularly true given that, from a variety of perspectives, our hominid ancestors did not appear to possess the capabilities necessary for the extraordinary evolutionary success that they, and now we, have enjoyed over the course of millions of years.

Making Sense of Our Story

Many modern-day scholars argue that we cannot understand who we are now without knowing who and what we were then. In other words, we need to get back to the start of the human story in order to get clues about how we think and act today. Our evolutionary history even offers information relevant to our current health problems, contemporary difficulties in promoting active lifestyles, and our fascination with sport. Many perspectives on human origins have been developed, disseminated, and debated. Our explanation of human history draws on theories proposed by scholars who work in the field and synthesizes the best current knowledge of human origins.

Many texts that offer a history of sport begin with the rise of Western civilization in Mesopotamia 7,000 to 10,000 years ago. A few offer brief commentaries on other ancient civilizations that developed at about the same time in various locations in Asia, Africa, and the Americas. Sometimes these books even include brief overviews of the hunter-foragers who populated the globe for tens of thousands of years before what has been termed the "rise of civilization." In this text, we encourage you to go back even further to get a feel for the vast expanses of time (often referred to as geological time) that allow us to trace the history of the earth. This journey allows you to see that humans are newcomers to the planet—in fact, incredibly recent newcomers! Still, we are the product of a chain of events going back millions of years. This is a remarkable, slow-moving, life-supporting story line that eventually produced smart, large-brained, handy, two-legged runners like us.

Existential thinkers are well known for reminding us that we are on the earth for only a short time. They suggest that authentic living requires an acknowledgement of death, of the fact that our existence is very temporary. This, they believe, adds urgency to our choices, makes it less likely that we will blindly follow the crowd, and encourages us to actualize our freedom.

Developing a Brief Chronology of Our Story

Over three billion years ago, one-celled organisms initiated an evolutionary journey that continues to this day. These simple forms of life, in their own primitive ways, needed to interact with their environment successfully in order to survive. In other words, they had some work to do. They had to find and metabolize food, rest and regenerate, locate an environment that was conducive to their survival, and reproduce.

Of course, we do these same things, albeit in vastly more complex and meaningful ways. Our work, our food gathering, and our survival needs are nothing like

Developing a Historical Timeline

Student Exercise

Look up world history timelines on the web and print out the most interesting one you find. Imagine the minutes, hours, days, years . . . and then millions and billions of years that it took to generate humankind. Offer a few thoughts about the significance of time, the appearance of Homo sapiens near the end of this expanse of time, or the importance of using time wisely. Do you find it unsettling to realize that our life span is but a blink of an eye in geological time? What is an appropriate response to a realization of your mortality? Live for today? Eat, drink, and be merry? Find religion? Exercise your freedom? Be yourself?

Seeking Authenticity in a Time-Limited Existence

Student Exercise

Look up commentaries on Leo Tolstoy's *The Death of Ivan Ilyich*. This classic novel engages issues related to the brevity of life and the significance of authentic living. Ilyich lived a carefree life but one that he eventually came to describe as "most simple and most ordinary and therefore most terrible." See if you can find out why he came to believe that his life had been a waste. When he lay on his deathbed and thought back to his youthful hopes and dreams, why did he see less and less of himself—less of who he, at one time, wanted to become?

Have you come to grips with the twin facts that time flies and life is short? Did you *choose*—freely, authentically, and courageously—to major in kinesiology, allied heath, leisure studies, or another activity- or health-related field? Or did you follow the crowd and gravitate to a program merely because you heard that it would lead to a job? Are you existentially awake, or are you more or less drifting along half-asleep like Ilyich? These are difficult and potentially threatening questions, but they are important ones for all of us. It is better that you deal with them now than when you are 40, 50, or 60 years old.

Write a short (300-word) essay about why you have chosen your major, why you are called to your intended profession, and what in the profession excites you. Are you in the right place? Does this profession fit your story, your values? Have you made an authentic choice? Or, in all honesty, did you merely follow the crowd?

---

those of our primitive one-celled ancestors, except for one crucial thing—we still have to pay them their due. Fundamentally, we are every bit as constrained in our own high-tech era as were our ancient cousins. If we do not work and rest (or receive the benefits that go with work and regeneration), we become weak and vulnerable. If we do not find conducive environments in which to live, and if we do not procreate at certain rates, we will eventually become extinct. Primitive life was embodied then, and we are embodied now. Existence was temporary billions of years ago, and we have a limited life span today. Primitive species, according to one of the pioneers of evolutionary theory, Charles Darwin, had to adapt to new survival pressures then, and that rule remains in effect today.

These similarities between human and nonhuman life should give us pause. As capable as we human beings are, and as remarkable an evolutionary journey as we have had, we are still grounded. In fact, the term *human* comes from *humus*, meaning "of the earth." Thus it is somewhat ironic that, in spite of the fact that we now exercise dominion over the earth, we carry our fundamental and self-effacing credentials on our person and even in our name. If we were to forget this and try to fly to the sun as the mythical Icarus did, we would receive a rude reminder of our human (or *humus*) nature and fall back to earth.

There is an important lesson here for us as professionals in physical activity, sport, health, and leisure. If, like Icarus, we forget who we are by nature and where we came from—in other words, if we suffer from developmental and evolutionary amnesia—then we might try to enter waters where we, our clients, and our students are not built to go, at least not easily. At best, we would be swimming against the current. Indeed, many utopian, scientific, perfectionist, and idealistic schemes have died because they ran contrary to the characteristics and tendencies of the people they were supposed to serve. That is why a careful historical and philosophical study of human beings can be helpful. As noted in the introduction, we can help ourselves avoid this common pitfall by heeding the practical implications presented in this book.

This trip back through history reminds us not only of our embodiment and the limitations~opportunities it carries. (You may recall from the preface and introduction that the tilde or squiggle signifies difference by degree and interpenetration, in contrast to hard and fast dualism.) It also raises questions about how we got from there to here. What happened? What steps

CHARLES DARWIN: ARE GREAT ATHLETES BORN OR MADE?

Historical Profile

Darwin may never have had to answer the question of whether great athletes are born or made, but he probably would have argued that the answer is both. That is, great athletes are born *and* made. Because the fitness of our ancestors affects who we are today, and because that fitness is transmitted genetically, our capabilities are, at least in part, inherited. We cannot take credit for the blessings of the genetic lottery. On the other hand, what we do with our potential is up to us. An understanding of Darwin's theories will help you see why this is the case.

Charles Robert Darwin was born in England in 1809 and died in 1882. He spent much of his life as a naturalist on the study of marine biology, including a five-year voyage on his famed HMS *Beagle*. His seminal work on evolution was published in his 1859 volume *On the Origin of Species*; in 1871, he expanded his theory to include human beings in *The Descent of Man*. Darwin's theory was controversial because it suggested that human existence resulted from natural events rather than supernatural activity

Library of Congress LC-USZ62-52389

Charles Darwin: biologist, scientist, originator of the theory of evolution.

or design. He posited that all life is related and that humans and apes share a common ancestor. This did not mean, as Darwin's critics often scoffed, that modern humans evolved from modern chimpanzees, gorillas, and orangutans but that at some point in our evolutionary past all four of these species shared a common parent before each took a divergent evolutionary path.

The mechanism that explained this evolutionary development is called natural selection. It is based on variation from generation to generation and the survival benefits that some variations confer. Offspring with beneficial traits live to reproduce more often than their less advantaged kin do, and they pass on their particular characteristics to their own offspring. Over many generations, Darwin asserted, the population shifts in the direction of individuals with the more beneficial profile. In other words, natural selection eliminates weaker species over time. Darwin insisted that natural selection was a powerful force but not the sole determinant of evolution, which he characterized as also being affected by both sexual selection (mating choices) and artificial selection (human engineering in creating domesticated plants and animals). In the ensuing years, more elaborate ideas about selection have been developed by contemporary evolutionary scientists.

From the vantage point of contemporary science, you may be surprised to know that Darwin developed his theory of natural selection without the benefit of genetic science. Indeed, the Czech scientist and Catholic priest Gregor Mendel (1822–1884) published his work on genetics in 1865, six years *after* the appearance of Darwin's *Origin*. Even then, Mendel's findings were largely ignored for decades, but they would eventually provide important support for Darwin's concepts.

In order to properly understand natural selection, we must realize that it does not require what scholars refer to as biological determinism. To explain by way of example, the remarkable eyesight of Ted Williams, one of the greatest baseball hitters who ever lived, and the remarkable physiology of John Elway and Jim Brown, two of the greatest athletes who ever played American football, did not guarantee or determine their success as athletes. Rather, they had to build on their good genetic fortune through untold hours of practice and training.

were taken? For what adaptive purposes did we eventually become beings who are bipedal, upright, reflective, language capable, self-conscious, spiritually interested, and ethically sensitive?

This complex story of transformation is not even close to being fully worked out or understood. In fact, Darwin and others have argued that we will never generate a complete account because of difficulties associated with getting evidence in the absence of written records. Still, we do know some of the broad outlines, a few of which are listed in table 1.1. Perhaps some of these advances were included in the time lines that you and your fellow students found in doing this chapter's first student exercise.

These time lines are still being worked on by anthropologists, evolutionary biologists, and others. Revisions are likely.

However, the broad outlines presented here show a holistic development of physical~cognitive advancement, from lower to higher capability and from lesser to greater complexity. Our ancestors became more fit, in Darwinian terms, because they evolved into increasingly clever and more capable embodied agents. In many ways, they could do more than infrahuman animals, and they could do it better.

These changes, however, did not necessarily signify that we were making regular progress as a species toward some fixed goal or telos. Evolution, according to most scientists today, is chaotic, uneven, and frequently unpredictable. Changes that promote survival today may end up inhibiting survival in the future. For all we know, the development of greater intelligence may be one of those things. Although improved cognition allowed us to be more

Table 1.1 A Brief Chronology of Life on Earth

3.7 billion years ago	First microbes (first life) appears.
400 million years ago	Fish (tetrapods) move to dry land.
60 million years ago	First primates appear.
8 to 5 million years ago	Bipedalism develops (apes emerge from the trees).
3.4 million years ago	First tool use is evident (in the use of natural objects such as sharp stones).
3 to 2 million years ago	Our species (Homo) emerges.
2.5 million years ago	Brain size begins to expand.
2.5 million years ago	Scavenging, hunting, and gathering behaviors are established.
1.8 million years ago	Our ancestors begin migrating out of Africa.
1.5 million years ago	Protein-rich diets are adopted, and meat eating is common.
1.5 million years ago	Stone tools are refined (tools are now designed, shaped, and built).
700,000 years ago	Fire is harnessed.
200,000 years ago	Anatomically modern humanlike hominids emerge; the appearance of some language and culture is probable.
50,000 to 30,000 years ago	The "great leap forward" takes place; evidence of modern behavior exists (e.g., cave painting, symbolism, ritual burial).
12,000 years ago	Agriculture begins to replace hunting and gathering.
10,000 to 7,000 years ago	The first cities are built.
150 years ago	The Industrial Revolution takes place.
25 years ago	Computing microprocessor revolution changes life.

efficient hunter-foragers, develop language, interact socially, and produce something called the technological revolution, it has come at a cost. We now deal with a sense of meaninglessness, boredom, depression, anomie—four conditions tethered to higher levels of intelligence. Thus, while we generally think that smarter is better, the unpredictable pathways of evolution raise an unsettling question: Is it possible to be too smart for our own good?

Similar questions can be raised about our anatomy. As noted earlier, all of us essentially still have hunter-forager bodies that require regular exercise for their maintenance, but we live in a push-button world where such bodies are no longer needed. It appears that evolution did not anticipate modern farming, grocery stores, fast food restaurants, current forms of transportation, and jobs that rarely require us to leave our chairs and computers. Is it possible that evolution threw us a curve ball by providing bodies that now have very little work to do? This chaotic, uncertain, and potentially negative direction of evolution was lampooned a number of years ago, as shown in figure 1.1.

This line of questioning provides those of us in the activity, health, and leisure professions with another important take-home message: Our professional worth or significance depends, at least in part, on potentially negative side effects of evolution. Our highly intelligent clients look for meaning, excitement, enjoyment, and other forms of stimulation outside work. We provide these things by introducing clients to challenging games, physical play, and a variety of adventurous leisure activities. Clients who suffer from chronic diseases related to sedentary living and overeating look for ways to move outside of work. Again, we provide these things, in this case by promoting exercise, supporting fitness facilities, and endorsing a wide range of physical play activities. In this regard, then, evolution has played directly into our hands! We do not need to be stimulated and move exactly like our ancestors did, but we do still need to find life interesting, and we still need to move.

Great Leaps Forward

At the start of this chapter, we asked an important question: How did we humans come to be the way we are today? This question is important not only because we all have a personal stake in the answer but also because it would have us seek answers to a fascinating mystery—one that might well be solved, at least in part, by better understanding physical activity, play, and other topics related to our own professional interests.

One version of the mystery story goes like this. As the evolutionary theorist Stephen Jay Gould observes, species can enter periods of equilibrium or stasis. During such periods, very little new adaptation occurs in generation after generation, but the species continue to survive, if not flourish, in some kind of environmental niche. Then, for some reason—and here is where the mystery comes in—this same species enters a period of rapid change. Why *this* change? Why now? Why so quickly? What is the stressor that, so to speak, upsets the previously stable applecart? These questions have been asked about some of the patterns shown in the chronology of life provided earlier, which ended (at least for now) with us.

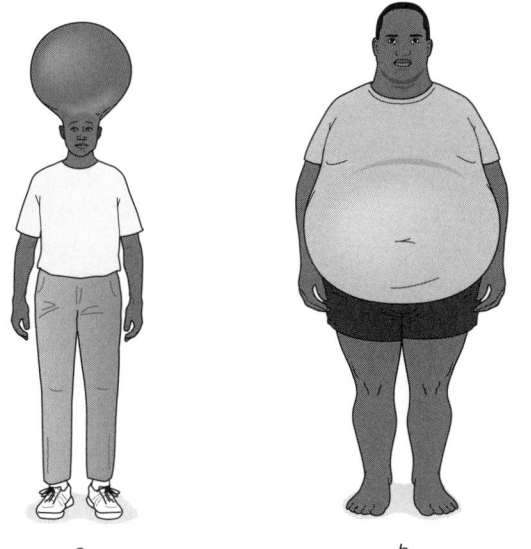

a   b

Figure 1.1 Uncertainties in evolution: *(a)* How evolution was supposed to go; *(b)* how it actually went.

Emerging Bipedalism and Related Advances

The first "great leap" identified by scholars of human evolution involves the move made by our hominid ancestors five to eight million years ago from the densely forested areas of Africa to the relatively open spaces of the savannah. These original bipedal hominids—they walked fully upright on two feet—entered a highly competitive savannah environment with what, at first glance, appeared to be few of the physical attributes necessary to compete for survival. Scholars who have studied the extraordinary ecosystems of the African savannahs have postulated that, over millennia, these environments produced an "arms race" between predators and prey that developed fast and strong species among both the hunters and the hunted. This context casts an intriguing light on the motto of the current Olympic games—*citius, altius, fortius*—which is a Latin (not Greek!) phrase that can be translated as "swifter, higher, stronger." It underscores our penchant for celebrating the power of our bodies in contests of speed, strength, and explosiveness.

Unfortunately, our ancestors on the African savannahs seemed ill equipped for this intense struggle for survival. They were neither swifter nor stronger nor able to jump higher than any of their competitors or even most of the prey they hunted. The speed kings and queens of this world—lions, leopards, cheetahs, and their kin—were far stronger and swifter than humans. The consummate pack hunters, such as African wild dogs, could also easily outrun hominids. Similarly, the favored prey in this ecosystem—a variety of fleet antelope species, zebra, and water buffalo—were much too fast for humans to catch. Meanwhile, large herbivores, such as elephants and giraffes, were far stronger than individual hominids. Some species inhabited niches where they scrounged the carcasses of prey brought down by swifter and stronger hunters, but hominids did not even have the speed or strength to compete directly with these hyenas, vul-tures, or other highly evolved scavengers. At first glance, our ancestors seemed to possess few capacities to compete in the "arms race" that shaped this world.

In this competitive environment, however, our ancestors eventually became the dominant predatory species through a combination of physical, mental, and social traits that allowed them to become, as physiologist Bernd Heinrich dubbed them, "super-endurance predators." The physical foundation for the emergence of these predators was provided by an interrelated set of attributes that began to develop roughly six million years ago, when our ancestors diverged from other apelike species. Hominids never evolved to outrun or outmuscle either competing predators or the prey that they sought over short distances—the typical pattern in deadly encounters on the savannah. Nor did they develop the capacity to outrun or outmuscle scavengers who survived on the kills of predators. Instead, hominids developed an enormous capacity for endurance. They could run—or walk, jog, amble, march, trot, or hike—over long distances, traveling for hours and even days in pursuit of prey. They could make these treks in all sorts of weather and at any time, including the heat of midday, when the competing predator species, such as the great cats and dog packs, hid from the intense African sun. Even hyenas and vultures fled from the sun in the hottest periods of the day, thus giving hominids, who could stand the heat, an important advantage in getting to carcasses.

One key attribute in this process was the development of bipedal locomotion, a trait that distinguished human ancestors from other species that evolved into modern apes. Bipedal locomotion provided an efficient gait for covering long distances. It also freed hominid hands to carry their young offspring, their captured prey, and their tools and weapons. In addition, their upright posture raised them above ground level on the savannah and helped them to see over longer distances. As compared with quadrupeds, bipeds also exposed far less surface area on their bodies to the sun, thereby increasing their capacity to work even in the heat of midday. Furthermore, the relative lack of fur or hair on their skin allowed these bipedal hominids to sweat in order to regulate heat, which gave them an advantage over competing thick-pelted predators that needed to rest in the shade during the hottest periods of the day.

Bipedalism provided hominids with advantages not only over other predators but also over their prey. Chasing antelope and other quarry in the heat of the day allowed hominids to use the evolutionary strengths of their targets against them. Antelope, for example, relied on massive bursts of speed to escape predators. They did not generally need to run for long periods—just for a bit longer than the cheetahs, leopards, and lions that pursued them. If these chases did not end quickly, the great cats lost interest and looked for easier game. In contrast, with the capacity to engage in long chases, the hominid hunters could repeatedly evoke the flight responses of their prey, using the high midday temperatures to make their quarry run over and over again until they were exhausted and became easy victims.

In summary, bipedalism made hominids the best thermoregulators on the savannah, and the interlinked physical attributes eventually made hominids the most successful predators in that environment. These physical attributes were also linked to a series of developments that increased hominids' intellectual and social capacities. For instance, bipedalism and upright postures widened the hips and allowed females to give birth to infants with larger cranial capacity. Bipedalism also freed the hands to carry infants, who were born at earlier stages of development than most other species and thus required more care but also had greater capacity for cranial growth after birth. Hands were also free to manipulate the environment and to carry and throw objects.

Success in the hunt provided regular sources of the protein necessary for physical and mental development. Crucially, the hominids were not solo hunters; rather, like other primates, as well as many other species, they lived in social groups and hunted together in common endeavors. Of course, team hunts required communication, a trait not unique to hominids but common to other species of social hunters, including the dog packs and baboon troops that inhabited the savannah alongside the hominids. The necessity of communication for survival led hominids to develop increasingly complex languages that privileged more complex and larger brains. In addition, the reality that hominid infants, like the newborn of later human groups, required long periods of intensive nurturing made food sharing a key social trait in hominid bands. All of these interrelated factors produced powerful forces that contributed to the growing intellectual and social development of our hominid ancestors.

Finally, and crucially, according to Heinrich—a leading scholar on human evolution and the complex interactions between our bodies, our brains, and our social worlds—our hominid ancestors developed "vision," the trait that transformed them into the super-endurance predators who eventually spread to every ecosystem and niche on the globe. By *vision*, Heinrich did not literally mean the mechanics of sight but rather the ability to picture things in the mind not immediately seen in the same temporal moment. This sort of vision allowed hominids to envision the end of the hunt, even if running an antelope to the ground in order to easily dispatch it might take days of persistent chasing. The capacity to set long-term goals and work to achieve them distinguished the hominids from most other species they encountered, both predators and prey.

Thus our evolutionary history as humans gave us bodies designed for consistent and regular locomotion over long distances. It made us into social beings who function as members of groups, and it made these groups essential to our survival. It provided us with powerful brains that can envision the future and hold distant goals in mind as achievable realities. In fact, some studies have shown

Looking for Cooperation in Competitive Sport

Student Exercise

As this chapter explains, social interaction and cooperation were among the key capabilities that led to many of the successes enjoyed by our ancestors. Accordingly, some contemporary critics of sport argue that it is ethically preferable to cooperate rather than to compete. Why, they ask, enter into a sporting competition that will produce losers and, potentially, generate hard feelings, disappointment, or worse? In this view, sport tears at the social fabric rather than mends it.

Apologists for, or defenders of, sport suggest that this criticism is unfounded, for at least two reasons. First, they contend that sport requires a considerable amount of cooperation—indeed, that games could not take place in the absence of cooperation. Second, they posit that competition can, in a spirit of mutual facilitation, build friendships and generate respect for one another.

For this exercise, choose one of these two lines of argument and use it to see how strong a case you can build for sport. If the critics are right, you should find it very difficult to rally a convincing argument. But if they are wrong, evidence in favor of sporting competition should not be hard to find. Alternatively, if you think both sides are right, depending on how a given sporting competition is organized or conducted, then you are welcome to develop that line of reasoning instead.

---

that humans and certain other primate species possess far more brainpower than necessary to merely earn a living from their environments. Some scholars have built on these studies to speculate that our powerful minds developed in order to help us navigate the *social* worlds that we inhabit. In other words, more than anything else, we need big brains in order to deal with other members of our species. In this view, we need the challenges and stimulations of the hunt, or other suitable endeavors, in order to engage not only our bodies but also our minds and our social inclinations.

Increasing Brain Size and Related Advances

The next great leap forward took place two to three million years ago and affected the brains that provided hominids with vision (in Heinrich's sense) and made them the dominant predatory species. The cranial volume of our hominid ancestors had been fairly stable for a long time, in the range of 400 to 550 cubic centimeters. Even with the gradual move to bipedalism and all that it meant—the freeing of the hands, the improved ability to carry objects, faster and more energy-efficient locomotion,

better visual perspective, and so on—brain size did not change appreciably during those years. In other words, the size of our ancestors' cranial cavities was in a condition of relative stasis. Then, for some mysterious reason, two to three million years ago, brains began to grow larger. Although brain size is not the only factor that influences intelligence, and though larger brains are not always smarter ones, this so-called "punctuation" changed our ancestors' physiology and their behavioral capabilities significantly in a relatively short period of time.

More specifically, the cranial capacities of the hominid species that evolved into modern humans grew rapidly and diverged dramatically from other hominid groups that are now extinct. Contemporary human cranial capacity runs about 1,200 cubic centimeters. Scholars puzzle over what happened to some hominid species that caused this remarkable, and remarkably fast, advance, which, in addition to being called a great leap forward, has been referred to as "a crossing of the evolutionary Rubicon" and as "the great brain race."

Nobody knows for sure what caused this leap forward to a more or less modern human existence. No one knows whether

BORN TO RUN

Historical Profile

Distance running: an asset in our ancestors' development as "super endurance predators."

Archaeological evidence suggests that about two million years ago, food supplies were scarce. At the same time, hominids had developed larger brains that were nutritionally costly organs; therefore, these individuals needed more and more calories, particularly in the form of protein. Because of this need, our ancestors had to become better hunters, and the adaptation that allowed them to meet this goal was distance running. Our ancestors could literally run their prey into the ground; alternately, they could compete successfully against other scavengers of already dead animals by covering longer distances more quickly. In short, distance running (especially in the heat) became adaptive. Those who had genes that favored running did better and thus reproduced at a higher rate than did their less mobile counterparts. Over many generations, the population shifted in the direction of capabilities for distance running.

Evolutionary biologists Dennis Bramble and Daniel Lieberman assert that evidence for adaptation from walking to running comes from both physiological and anatomical data. More specifically, the conclusion that our ancestors evolved into distance-running hominids during this period is supported by factors related to energetics, skeletal strength, efficient stabilization, and superior thermoregulation and respiration, as well as a considerable amount of archaeological evidence. Moreover, it may have been distance running, and the superior nutrition it enabled, that tipped the evolutionary scales in our favor and helped us separate from our nearest relatives.

The mystery of our origins is not likely to be solved soon, if indeed we will ever know what produced modern humans. Once again, however, an important take-home point can be found here for health and activity professionals. Although larger brains and intellectual development certainly had something to do with our great leap forward, it may well be that a simple physical action—perhaps running—also played a key role in this advance.

it resulted from an accumulation of factors that produced some kind of evolutionary tipping point or whether the cause involved adaptation to a particular stressor. Whatever the answer may be, those who are on the trail of such a stressor are in search of something now referred to as "the missing link." This is a puzzle worthy of any modern-day mystery novel and the talents of an anthropological Sherlock Holmes.

Many theories regarding this mystery revolve around language. Because language is our crowning glory, and because it is one of the things that most clearly separates us from other animals, some believe that it had to be involved directly in this leap forward. But nobody can be sure of this. In fact, as the linguist Michael Tomasello posits, there is much evidence to suggest that formal language came relatively late in the story. If that is true, then some other thing, or cluster of things, must have happened thousands of years ago to produce people like us. What could it have been?

Some of us who study the body, movement, sport, and play are inclined to think that this mysterious something had to be more fundamental and motor oriented than language. Because we humans are physical, earthy, and movement dependent, the stimulus for the "brain race" may well have emerged from one or more of these aspects of our existence.

Others have had the same thoughts. In fact, Darwin felt that the physical skills related to hunting played a major role in the unique evolution of humans. In *The Descent of Man*, he argued that stone weapons were used not only for purposes of defense but also for hunting—that is, for bringing down prey. Of course, the ability to be more efficient in capturing prey, and thereby in securing sustenance, would provide a huge fitness advantage. Thus, in this theory, clever and very physical methods of hunting were what made us human. Even today, scholars such as Douglas Carroll think that popular activities such as sport might be best understood as a kind of symbolic hunt.

Darwin, and many others since, have noticed particular qualities or capabilities of contemporary humans and then worked backward to develop plausible stories about how, why, and when these adaptations may have come about. This mode of inquiry is referred to as reverse engineering, and the accounts that emerge from it are often called "just-so stories." This is usually a pejorative label that references the 19th-century British novelist Rudyard Kipling's fanciful accounts, in *The Jungle Book*, of such things as how tigers got their stripes and how camels got their humps. The problem with just-so stories is that, while they may seem plausible and even attractive, they typically lack support from data and other forms of evidence. In addition, other accounts can be conjured up that seem equally plausible and attractive. Critics argue that, lacking conclusive evidence, whether archaeological or otherwise, there is no good way to choose between them.

However, at least one just-so story should attract our interest. Earlier in this chapter, we cited Heinrich's fascinating account of running. His speculations about the significance of this activity were given more credence a few years ago, when *Nature*, a very highly regarded scientific journal, published an article that provided additional scientific evidence in favor of running as a key stimulus in our human evolution.

Hunting, Foraging, and Related Advances

The next great leap took place approximately 150,000 years ago as the super-endurance predators that millions of years of evolution had created on the savannahs of East Africa evolved a new subspecies, Homo sapiens sapiens, the "family" from which the more than seven billion people now living on the earth are directly descended. The members of this new group quickly began to expand their territory, first to the rest of Africa, then to adjacent continents, and eventually to practically every bit of land around the world. They were fierce competitors and soon constituted the only remaining version of hominids on the planet. For more than 100,000 years, until about 10,000 years ago, they lived as hunters and foragers. (Scholars have recently decided that the term *forager* describes their lifeways more accurately than does the more traditional term *gatherer*.) Hunters and foragers roamed far and wide in the quest for survival while living in mobile units. The hunter-forager period represents by far the longest portion of the time span over which our particular subspecies, Homo sapiens sapiens, has inhabited the earth. It is also the historical period about which we know the least. Once again, much about the habits and practices of our ancestors remains clouded in mystery.

In Allen Guttmann's compendium of the history of sport over a period of 5,000 years, he skips over the first 140,000 or so years of human existence and begins his survey with ancient Western civilization. "The oldest sports about which we have reasonably reliable information are those of ancient Egypt," Guttmann asserts. His focus on "reasonably reliable information" is accurate, because we know very little about the sports, or anything else, of the hunting and foraging cultures that roamed vast swaths of the earth once they emerged about 150,000 to 200,000 years ago. Our recent ancestors have left us evidence of their hunting prowess in the form of stone tools and kill sites that span the globe. However, beyond those stone implements and artifacts manufactured from the bones of prey they killed or scavenged, as well as a limited collection of skeletal remains, little remains of the rest of their material culture (much of which, no doubt, was made of plant products or animal skins). They occasionally left us cave paintings and stone carvings, but their preliterate societies had not developed written languages that would offer us more detailed clues about their existence.

On the other hand, over the last few centuries, we have encountered a few remaining hunting and foraging societies as the industrial and technological societies that we label as modern have spread around the globe. Most of these remaining societies inhabit the environmental margins, where modernity has not yet wiped their cultures out—for example, the rain forests of the Amazon basin, the Pacific coast of North America and Asia at far northern latitudes, the Pacific Islands, and the deserts of Africa and Australia.

Scholars have studied these "vanishing" cultures for several centuries in order to find clues about how our ancestral hunter-forager cultures worked. At the same time, some critics have warned that the handful of hunter-forager cultures "discovered" in the past few centuries do not provide accurate information for speculating about the distant past. Their reasons include the fact that these societies have had contact, even if only periodically, with "civilization" for thousands of years and that some of these groups were even pushed out of "civilization," whereupon they went back to hunting and foraging in order to survive.

Another criticism has emerged in regard to the labeling of hunter-forager cultures as "primitive" in contrast to ostensibly more "sophisticated" modern societies. Experts have pointed out that while the material cultures of these groups may in fact be simpler and more limited than modern technologies, the political, familial, religious, and creative systems of hunters and foragers are every bit as complex as those found in modern societies. Therefore, given the paucity and reliability of relevant evidence, we can benefit from recalling Guttmann's warning that speculation about sport among the peoples who lived before the emergence of written language and monumental architecture is based on extremely limited and problematic data. Moreover, we can extend this warning beyond sport to every aspect of the lifeways of the hunters and foragers who lived tens of thousands of years ago. Thus, as in our earlier story of human evolution millions of years ago, we will have to make do here with just-so stories and speculative histories.

One thing we can be more certain about is that these societies were home to talented hunters. In fact, some scholars speculate that they were so effective in their hunts that they substantially altered their environments—for instance, by hunting into extinction the megafauna (large animals, such as mammoths and mastodons) that roamed vast regions of North America and Eurasia in herds until about 10,000 years ago. Though scholars debate whether these megafauna were destroyed by human depredation or by climate change or some other factor, the material record does provide reliable evidence of the hunting prowess of these human cultures. Therefore, hunting provides a good place to begin our speculations about the origins and development of sport in human societies.

Patterns of Culture in Hunter-Forager Societies

Before we develop a just-so story about the origins of sport and physical education, however, we need to briefly sketch the general characteristics of the hunter-forager societies that roamed the earth from roughly 200,000 to 10,000 years ago. These cultures created mobile communities that could follow animals on their migrations or arrive at key areas to gather plant foods when they were ripe and ready to harvest. In short, they traveled regularly to where their food sources were located. During these nomadic circuits, they built temporary shelters or used natural rock lodgings. They obtained the bulk of their diet by foraging for vegetables, grains, and fruits and also for edible insects, eggs, and carrion. Meat acquired through hunting provided essential supplements to their foraging, and success in the hunt conferred status on individuals and groups.

Thus, much of their lives centered on their quest to wrest a living from the environments they inhabited. Some anthropologists have suggested that these societies did not draw the sharp dichotomies between work and leisure that modern thinkers tend to establish. Still, many students of hunter-forager societies insist that they did not spend all, or even the vast majority, of their time working. In fact, in this view, although they did not possess the material abundance enjoyed by modern societies, they were "leisure rich." Experts estimate that they worked 20 hours per week, or less, on subsistence and therefore had an abundance of time for other pursuits.

Many scholars also speculate that a division of labor between men and women shaped social arrangements among hunter-foragers. Some students of these cultures draw stark lines between man as hunter and woman as forager and childcare worker that have seemed to some to justify gender divisions in modern cultures as being natural. However, more recent speculations based on the gender patterns of contemporary hunter-forager groups reveal a much more complex picture. In these groups, both men and women generally forage and carry responsibilities for child rearing. In a minority of cultures, women also hunt, sometimes more successfully than men. One possible explanation for the general pattern that men spend more time and energy on hunting than women do hinges on the fact that hunting is a dangerous occupation that increases the mortality rates of participants. Therefore, the practice of having men hunt could rest on a basic genetic logic, because, for the future evolutionary health of the species, men are much more expendable than women. In other words, a society with a few men and many women would have a better reproductive future than one with many men and just a few women.

Ancient hunter-forager cultures generally functioned in everyday life in small bands of roughly 25 individuals, many of whom were connected by close familial ties. Periodically in their nomadic travels, these bands would gather in larger groups (often denoted as tribes) of roughly 500 in order to trade and socialize. Scholars have argued that these two numbers, 25 and 500, represent important building blocks for developing social connections. The number of people with whom an individual can maintain deep and intimate connections seems to be about 25, and the number of people with whom an individual can form a less intense personal bond seems to be about 500. Above those limits, societies require bonds that go beyond the personal in order to forge community.

With some exceptions, hunters and foragers are thought to have had egalitarian social structures in which most individuals, and especially adults, were roughly equal. Leadership tasks were shared, as were the daily burdens of economic and social life. Kinship was often traced through the mother (the matrilineal line), and long-term monogamous relations between men and women were generally considered crucial to the stability of social relationships. When a man partnered with a mate, he often joined the band of his wife, perhaps to facilitate strong support for their offspring through the familial bonds that entangled the mother's group.

The Origins of Sport

As had been the case for our distant hominid ancestors, hunting required the use of complex physical, intellectual, and social skills. Some of these capabilities could be passed to offspring not genetically but through the sharing of hard-earned knowledge between generations—that is, through education.

Hunting and Foraging

Hunting and foraging cultures developed systems of education in which the physical, intellectual, and social skills required for survival were taught to children and youth. From this assertion, it is a short leap to imagine that tests of physical and mental prowess were crucial elements in these cultures. Such tests might have included endurance footraces, skillful use

of weapons, demonstrations of cunning and tracking, and even exercises designed to build teamwork. In turn, contests that taught and demonstrated the physical and intellectual abilities necessary for hunting formed one of the foundations of sport.

Religion

Many scholars have speculated that religion provided another foundation for human sporting contests. For instance, some researchers have proposed that primeval etchings and paintings of hunters pursuing animals—forms of artwork that dot caves and cliffs in various parts of the world—represent religious rituals designed to bring the hunters bounteous success. In addition, anthropologists and ethnographers have discovered that preliterate cultures frequently engage in sport as a part of religious rituals. For instance, ritualized relay races may be performed in order to bring rains from the heavens, wrestlers may grapple in order to win favor from the gods, and ball games may be used to recreate the creation myths of believers. In such ways, athletic contests can serve as symbolic ceremonies that animate the religious beliefs of practitioners.

Warfare

Along with hunting and religion, warfare completes the triad at the base of human sporting practices (figure 1.2). Just as sporting contests created suitable

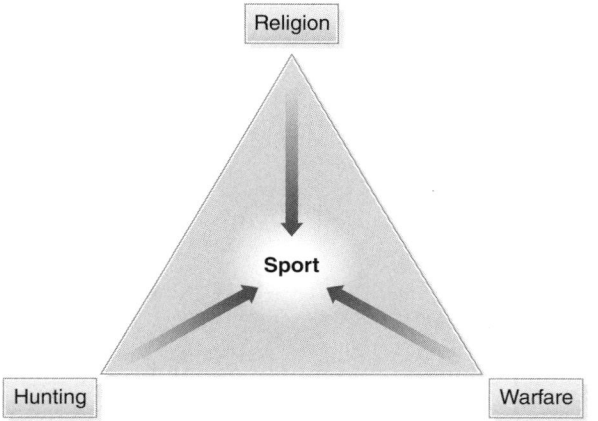

Figure 1.2 The triad of human sporting practices.

conditions for teaching and demonstrating the skills needed for hunting, they did the same for combat skills, such as accuracy with weapons, delivering and receiving blows, and engaging in teamwork to mount a successful mission. Thus, these skills could be practiced and proven not only in mortal combat but also in sporting con- tests; in other words, sport could be used to train warriors to defend their bands and tribes.

Some anthropologists have noticed a corollary between the type of warfare prac- ticed by hunter-foragers and some of the sporting behaviors exhibited in modern societies. Combat in hunter-forager cul-

Riddles of Human Violence and Warfare

A group of young males bonded by membership in the same group nurture a history of grudges against their counterparts in a neighboring group. Fueled by memories of slights to their honor, they plot revenge. They paint their faces, don tribal customs, and, encouraged by the con- sumption of alcohol or other mood-altering substances, seek out their enemies and confront them. Insults fly back and forth between the two rival groups, and soon projectiles are flying as fast as the epithets. A few of the young men attack one another and engage in unarmed hand-to-hand combat. Others wield weapons, either manufactured for violence or picked up on the spot, ranging from war clubs to tree branches. They swing wildly at their enemies, intending to inflict serious injury. After a short spasm of combat, each side retreats to its own territory. These encounters typically result in bruises, contusions, lacerations, and a few broken bones. On occasion, one or more of the combatants die in the fray, the victims of mortal blows. Anthropologists embedded with the groups write analytical accounts of these battles, seeking answers to the riddles of human aggression, violence, and warfare.

The preceding scenario describes how anthropologists have tried to make sense of both hunter-forager warfare in traditional societies and soccer hooliganism in modern societies. Such ethnographies serve as the foundation for famous studies—in some cases of traditional cultures, as in Jared Diamond's best-selling *The World Until Yesterday: What Can We Learn from Traditional Societies* (2012), and in other cases of modern phenomena such as hooliganism, as in Desmond Morris's groundbreaking *The Soccer Tribe* (1981).

How old, how deep, and how hardwired is human aggression? This question has fascinated many thinkers over the centuries. Some scholars see modern sporting habits as evidence of a universal human desire to watch and engage in aggressive, even violent, activity. Some even speculate that fan violence is a residual of much older behaviors, a trace of hunter-forager interactions that have survived into our modern, "civilized" era. Meanwhile, a debate also rages among researchers about whether violence and warfare in human cultures have increased or decreased since the time (7,000 to 10,000 years ago) when hunter-forager cultures mostly disappeared and "civilization" emerged (for more on that, see chapter 2). Research has been mustered to show that our distant hunter-forager ancestors were much more pacific than we are; in other words, "civilized" societies invented the massive killing fields that characterize modern war. Research has also been employed to argue the converse, that civilization has tempered the warrior urge embedded in human nature and that we are much less likely than our distant ancestors to perish in a battle.

These debates about the origin and nature of warfare, and about whether human aggression has declined or increased over the course of history, seem destined to continue to rage and to spur fascinating debates. In the interim, when you cross paths with face-painted, costumed-bedecked, insult-spewing fans of sport teams, you can speculate about whether or not your feelings match those of your ancient ancestors who wandered into the paths of their angry rival tribes.

tures generally involves groups that live close to each other and have developed some sort of intense rivalry. The warriors prepare for battle by decorating their bodies with paint and costumes, and the battles themselves involve a great deal of shouting, including threats of violence—but very little actual fighting. As a result, casualties are relatively minor, ranging from a few bloodied noses and broken bones to an occasional death. In both form and outcome, these hunter-forager wars resemble the clashes of football (soccer) hooligans in nations around the modern world. Adorning themselves in face paint and team colors, these hooligans to take to the streets, utter oaths and threats against their rivals, engage in some intense but brief hand-to-hand combat, and then retreat. Casualties are generally minor, although deaths do sometimes occur. What should we make of this symmetry?

The Complexities of Work and Play in Hunting and Foraging Societies

Hunting and foraging activities would typically be referred to as forms of work. The need for food imposes a recurring necessity on all animals, and this necessity provides sufficient reason for all of us to go to work. When our ancestors were tossing stones and spears at animals, or when they were running long distances after prey, they were presumably doing it for the meat and protein provided by a successful hunt, not for the fun of the challenge itself. In other words, they were at work. But as you have seen, this did not mean that they lacked time for play.

As Johan Huizinga, the Dutch historian and great student of play, was quick to realize, the same is true for nonhuman animals. Thus play (or something like it) affected creatures long before our hominid ancestors came along. In fact, some animal biologists suggest that play behaviors can

be readily observed in birds, reptiles, and even insects (such as bees). This may strike you as a bold claim. How do we know what play is for human beings, let alone for a bird or a bee?

This line of thought also raises an important metaphysical question—that is, a question about the nature of things. Can we reliably define the various things that populate our world, even fundamental things such as work and play? As we discuss in later chapters, philosophers and other scholars have not been of one mind in answering this question. Indeed, many skeptics doubt that much progress *can* be made in this regard.

Before drawing any hasty conclusions, however, we should try some definitions and see if they are helpful. We can start with the following common-sense hypothesis: Work is any behavior driven by needs. It is compelled, not freely chosen. Moreover, its success is evaluated on the extent to which it satisfies a need. That need might involve obtaining food or shelter, finding a mate, massaging one's ego, or fulfilling any number of other purposes. We work, in other words, for many reasons—some biological, some cultural, some personal or idiosyncratic, and most of them a mixture of all three.

The motives for work are prudential. It is good to work, it is important to work, and we have a duty to work in order to take care of ourselves and our loved ones. In one of Aesop's most well-known fables, the legendary ant is the hero because he plans ahead for the coming winter. He is the level-headed, responsible worker, the one who does not become a burden for his fellow ants when the weather turns cold and food is in short supply. The grasshopper, on the other hand, is the profligate, the playful wanderer, the fool, the one who can never get down to work. Of course, when bad weather arrives, he has to go to the ant for help.

According to many writers, work is activity that acknowledges deficiency, something that is needed. In this view, work is necessarily a means–end kind of behavior. It is a calculation that recommends putting up with a potentially distasteful process in order to secure a more important product. Thus, the mood or affect that characterizes deficiency-based behavior is anxiety. Will the means be effective? Will my efforts pay off? If not, what then?

Scholars have put a fancy label on this kind of human behavior: exotelic activity. This word comes from two roots—the suffix *telos* meaning "end" and the prefix *ex* meaning "outside," as in the *ex*terior walls of a house. Exotelic activity, then, is literally behavior whose end lies outside—that is, outside the doing, the effort, or the process that leads to success. As noted, even when the doing is not much fun, we put up with it because it gives us the product, the thing we want or need.

Analytic philosophers, unlike most skeptics, tend to be content with this kind of definition. Work is exotelic behavior conducted to remedy deficiencies. It is a domain of duty or obligation. People work because they have to, not because they want to.

This definition may be helpful as far as it goes. But other distinctions come to mind, and they muddy the definitional waters. Here is a common one with which all of you are familiar: Some necessitated behavior is enjoyable, even fun. For instance, some professional athletes love their sport and quite possibly would participate in it even if they were not paid to do so. In the same way, some professors truly enjoy being with students and helping them learn. For them, on some days, a class period seems to fly by. Similarly, some students "get into" a book that is required for a class. It moves them so much that they say they would have read it even if it weren't required. As a result, studying is enjoyable and perhaps even becomes a form of play.

What are we to make of these common experiences? For all three, the activity is necessitated. For all three, an important objective lies outside the doing. After all, athletes and teachers need to make a living, and students need to get degrees. In all three cases, then, the activity is fundamentally prudential, and these are classic examples of exotelic activity and of being extrinsically motivated.

The fly in the ointment, however, comes from the fact that all three groups of individuals enjoy the doing—if not always, then at least on occasion. Thus in a very real and concrete sense, the end for these folks, at least in these delightful moments, lies in the process itself. They seem to be intrinsically motivated, or at least partly so.

How then should we classify exotelic activities that are experienced, at least on occasion, as meaningful or otherwise enjoyable? Are we at work, at play, or involved in a combination of the two? We could say that we were at work when we started these projects but that, eventually, the play spirit took over. This solution has the advantage of keeping things simple, of keeping only two distinct and mutually exclusive entities on the definitional field—namely, work and play.

Another definitional option would be to divide work itself into two species. We might refer to them as dutiful work and enjoyable work. Both constitute work because both are exotelic. The dominant theme for both activities is one of getting an external prize—in our examples, the money for the athlete and teacher and the degree for the student. At the end of the day, it is the need for the money or the degree that determines the behavior.

Dutiful work is distinct from enjoyable work because it is done reluctantly, begrudgingly, only because it is necessary. It has few or no redeeming features beyond those promised by the prudential contract. This is the typical format for people who work out of a sense of duty or responsibility. In other words, it is rational to work even if it is not much fun. In the student exercise on authenticity earlier in this chapter, you may have decided that it is rational to choose a major in college for its good employment possibilities, even if you do not expect to enjoy the work.

Meaningful and thus enjoyable work, on the other hand, requires serendipity. It is a two-for-one kind of activity. We enter the work activity primarily for the external objective, but something else that is good (or even better) also comes along. Therefore, the doing, the pursuing, the process, turns out to be enjoyable as well; if we are lucky, it turns out to be as enjoyable as play activity. It is a kind of "as if" play. That is, it is almost as if we freely chose to compete, teach, or read simply for the sake of having the experience, even though we did not, and even though the primary objective remains operative.

This distinction between two kinds of work could be helpful for professionals in activity, health, and leisure who need to understand exercise and how to motivate people to adopt an active lifestyle. Specifically, we could categorize exercise as a fundamentally exotelic activity. It promotes health, increases one's energy, and extends one's life span, all of which are important ends. Thus, it is prudent to exercise, and it is rational to do it even if the activity is not much fun. Many of us take this very approach in promoting exercise in our clinics, schools, fitness establishments, and recreation centers. It may be particularly effective with adults, who should be able to understand the science behind physical activity and its relationship to good health.

However, if our distinction is valid, then dutiful exercise is not the only kind of exercise there is. We also have enjoyable exercise at our disposal. This brand of exercise still constitutes work because the health goals remain in place, but perhaps it can be converted into the sort of delightful experience described earlier for professional athletes, teachers, and students in their own work settings. In fact, many professionals today are experimenting with possibilities for infusing fun and meaning into exercise activities that clients have often experienced as boring or otherwise distasteful.

Later in this chapter, you will have a chance to wrestle with these distinctions in a practical setting, but first we must turn our attention to play. What is play? Can we define it? Those who are trying to understand the nature of play often cite Johan Huizinga. Here is his definition:

> *Summing up the formal characteristics of play, we might call it a free activity standing quite consciously outside "ordinary" life as being "not serious," but at the same time absorbing the player intensely and utterly. It is an activity connected with no material interest, and no profit can be gained by it. It proceeds with its own proper boundaries of time and space according to fixed rules and in an orderly manner. It promotes the formation of social groupings which tend to surround themselves with secrecy and to stress their difference from the common world by disguise or other means.*

Philosopher of sport Bernard Suits was among those who thought that Huizinga's definition was too broad—that is, that it allowed Huizinga to find play everywhere. Thus Suits argued that play has not just one defining feature but two. First, in contrast to the nature of work, and consistent with Huizinga's thoughts, play is *auto*telic. That is, the end, the satisfaction, the meaning of play lies in the doing. But Suits was aware that, as discussed earlier, one can also have this sort of encounter with many *necessitated* activities. Therefore, he realized that according to this definition some work would have to be called play. Doing so, however, would be confusing, and he was not sure that even intrinsically satisfying work was the same thing as play. It was this inclusion of enjoyable work that made the definition too broad. Thus Suits began searching for a second characteristic of play that would distinguish it from both kinds of work—that is, from both enjoyable and dutiful work.

JOHAN HUIZINGA: A CHAMPION OF PLAY

Historical Profile

Johan Huizinga (1872–1945) was born in Groningen, the Netherlands. He was well known as a historian of the Middle Ages well before he published *Homo Ludens* ("Man the Player") in 1938. He spent the majority of his career at Leiden University, where he was professor of general history. In 1941, during the war, Huizinga gave a speech in which he criticized the Nazis. He was imprisoned and later released, but he lived under detention until his death in 1945, shortly before the end of the war.

In *Homo Ludens*, Huizinga argued that culture arose in, through, and as play. Huizinga's doctoral training in comparative linguistics is evident in his analysis of world languages and their varied ability to capture what he saw as the universal existence and importance of play. The larger portion of his analysis is devoted to a sociocultural definition of play and a description of play in law, war, science, poetry, philosophy, and art. Huizinga was criticized for "finding play under every rock in the landscape" (his definition was, in some ways, too broad), for tying play too closely to ritual, and for ignoring gambling and games of chance (his definition was, in some ways, too narrow). But his analysis of play drew attention to a phenomenon that had been too long neglected and ignored. It is difficult, even today, to pick up any serious treatment of play and not find repeated references to Huizinga and *Homo Ludens*.

Johan Huizinga: Dutch historian who underlined the importance of play in the development of culture.

Photo by ullstein bild via Getty Images

He found this second factor in the concept of relationality or dependence. Play is essentially relational because it requires a reallocation of various resources from primary duties (utility) to secondary activities (serendipity). He attempted to make his case analytically by comparing play to the shadings of light and dark. Specifically, he claimed that we cannot understand one without the other. If everything were light, then the very intelligibility of light would be lost. Light needs the concept of dark in order to be appreciated. The color blue, by way of contrast, is not like that. Blue doesn't imply red or orange or any other color. And if the whole world were blue, it would still be blue (and not some other color). It would still be intelligible as blue.

Play, Suits concluded, is like light in contrast to dark. In other words, it stands in relationship. The time that play consumes stands in relationship to normal time that is used for good purposes. The space that play uses likewise stands in relationship to those places in which we complete important projects. Even new or reassigned functions stand in relationship to normal functions. Suits gave an example of a bored youngster at dinner who uses gravy and mashed potatoes to build lakes and rivers rather than to serve their normal function of providing nutrition.

Therefore, for Suits, enjoyable work or exercise is still work because no fundamental reallocation has taken place. The professional athlete and teacher need to keep their jobs; the student needs to pass the course and graduate; the obese individual in the fitness center who enjoys working out still intends (and needs) to lose weight. These objectives are still characterized by utility; furthermore, if the fun disappeared, the undergirding reasons for participation would remain. On the other hand, if any of them were to defect to the extent exemplified by the child building lakes and rivers in his mashed potatoes, then Suits would agree that the participants were truly playing. The reason is that the activity would now show the two necessary and sufficient conditions for play—autotelicity and reallocation. Of course, play would put these individuals at risk of either losing a job, failing to graduate, or failing to lose the desired weight because play motives would replace the previous prudential reasons for the activity at hand.

Although Suits' analysis is anything but foolproof, he emerged in largely the same place as a number of other play theorists who also argued that play is not only autotelic (constituting an end in itself) but also relational. For example, the German philosopher Eugen Fink described play as an oasis of happiness (such oases are intelligible only if contrasted with deserts of responsibility). Kenneth Schmitz, professor of philosophy emeritus at the University of Toronto, said that play involves a "suspension of the ordinary" in that it is temporary in relationship to other things that have first call, as it were, on our time and energy. Huizinga, as we saw in his definition, declared that play occurs in its own time and space—in, literally, a playground carved out of workaday time and space by free choice, joy, and fascination. When Huizinga argued that play "interrupts the appetitive process," he tacitly acknowledged that appetites are typically dominant and that play must often force itself into the picture. An interruption,

after all, is not a takeover. In another example, 18th-century German polymath Friedrich Schiller's classical work on play as aesthetic harmony is based on the idea that balance and beauty are unusual and stand in contrast to life, which is often distorted by the weight of rational duties on one hand and passionate emotions on the other. In summary, all of these theoreticians describe play as relational—as a kind of lovely, temporary, alternative experience that stands forever in contrast to the more mundane, common, normal, secular activities of "getting and spending," as the English poet William Wordsworth once put it.

Identifying Common Misconceptions of Play

Before moving on, we should alert ourselves to some common misconceptions of play. One of them is generated by Huizinga's ambiguous phrase "freely chosen." It could mean either of two things: doing *any old thing* that one wants to do or doing *some particular thing* that one wants to do.

Initial Misconceptions About Play

Which of the following two options sounds more like play?

> *Option A: In any play activity, the end no longer matters. Thus, whether I am involved in a computer game or playing soccer, I can do anything I want. This is why play is not serious. The outcome doesn't matter. If I fail miserably at the computer game or perform poorly in soccer, I don't care. In fact, it is better in true play activities not to have any outcomes in mind at all. They only limit you and the things you can do. It is better to be free of any constraints from rules and worries about objectives. Thus, play allows me to follow my momentary desires. While playing a game of soccer, if I want to kick the ball into a tree instead of the goal, I can do so.*

Option B: In most play activities, the end does matter. That is why I cannot do just anything I want. And that is why I choose to play my favorite computer game and then go outside and play soccer. Attempting to solve the problems offered by the computer game and by soccer is what makes these activities so much fun. That is why I seem to be so serious when I am at my computer. And that is why I pay careful attention to the ball and the positioning of my teammates when I play soccer. Most true play activities have objectives. Because their rules limit my behavior, they actually free me to improve, achieve, express myself, and have more fun than if I were simply lounging around doing any old thing I wanted to do.

Which did you choose? If we have read Huizinga and other play theorists correctly, and if our own reflections are on target, then the second option is the more faithful description of play. Although some forms of play are unorganized, most are goal directed and governed by rules. And even though some experiences of play fall into the categories of frolic, spontaneous dance, or free exploration, most are very goal directed. Indeed, it is the "tension" of play, as Huizinga put it, that captivates us. It is the attempt to meet the challenge—to solve the game problem, to win, to build the model airplane correctly, to stay in character in make-believe activities—that keeps us interested. Thus, most play, or at least most high-quality play, engages people completely and promotes intensity, even if the activity itself is not important. That is part of the magic of play. It invites us to take something that is not serious seriously!

So, can play be goal directed? And can play be experienced as serious or intense? The answer to both questions is yes. In fact, from an empirical standpoint, most play is goal directed, and most deep play absorbs us completely.

A second misconception relates to play and competition. Some people think that competitive activities are difficult, if not impossible, to experience as play. This position leads to the following practical recommendation: If you want to promote play, do not make an activity competitive.

Further Misconceptions About Play

Once again, look at the following two examples and decide which one better exemplifies play.

Play scenario 1: You have been bowling alone for about 20 years. You fell in love with the game as a child, have improved over the years, and are always trying to improve on your previous scores. Even though you have bowled for many years, you still find the game interesting. Among other things, you enjoy the drama of not knowing beforehand how well you will do.

Play scenario 2: You have been bowling alone for about 20 years. You still enjoy the game and appreciate the drama of not knowing, on any given day, how well you will do. But then a friend who has also been bowling for about the same amount of time approaches and says, "We've both been bowling alone for 20 years. Wouldn't it be fun if we challenged one another? Let's see who can bowl better this afternoon." You agree to do so and discover that competitive bowling contains not one drama but two. You still have the drama of not knowing how well you will bowl, and you also have the new drama of not knowing if you will bowl better or worse than your friend does.

Was the play spirit harmed or eliminated in the second scenario? Probably not. In fact, it appears that the activity took on new life. That is, the doing itself (the process of bowling) became not less but more enjoyable. Once competition is added to the mix, the delightful tension or drama that Huizinga found in play now has not one but two sources. In a sense, competitive bowling doubles the excitement and pleasure.

We also know, however, that competition can ruin a game. Thus, it is a bit like fire; it can either warm or burn. If competition turns from wanting to win to *having* to win, if egos are tender, if large extrinsic rewards go to the winner—then competition is often no friend of play. On the other hand, as shown in scenario 2, competition can be the salt that flavors the meat. It can produce interpersonal play that is even more "serious" and enjoyable than playing alone.

Finding Practical Applications for Philosophic Definitions

This exercise in distinguishing or defining things, as you learned previously, is called metaphysics. It can seem dry and academic, but newly discovered distinctions provide professionals with additional options and, hopefully, more effective interventions. We need to understand *why* the effort we put into identifying two kinds of work, as well as the nature of play, can pay off.

Our analysis of work and play has provided three fairly distinct possibilities for motivating students and clients to adopt an active lifestyle. We present them here with jogging or running indicated as the intended intervention. Specifically, we can present running to our clients . . .

1. . . . as work, as exotelic duty. Running is exercise. It is like medicine. It is good for you. If you have trouble getting motivated, remember that running will help you live longer, lose weight, reduce your bad cholesterol, and ultimately give you more energy.

2. . . . as work, as exotelic duty that is also enjoyable. Running is a health-promoting exercise that can also be fun. Run with a friend. Run in the woods or some other favorite place. Run with earbuds or on a treadmill in front of a television show. Set up an extrinsic reward for achieving your running goals; this will make it less boring and more enjoyable. Remember why you are running but try to keep it enjoyable.

3. . . . as play, as autotelic enjoyment. Running is an adventure. It can be exciting and meaningful. See how far you can go. Challenge yourself. Join a running club. Read running magazines. Take running vacations. Running may initially seem like a chore, but it will begin to speak to you. It may become part of who you are. Once running gets under your skin, you will not need any "good reason" to run, even though all kinds of healthful outcomes will come your way as a bonus.

Motivating Clients to Develop an Active Lifestyle

Student Exercise

Generate two strategies for a specific population, and list the strengths and weaknesses of each strategy for promoting persistence in an active lifestyle.

To see why it is so important to address persistence, look up statistics related to persisting in exercise and diet programs. You can do a web search for terms such as "exercise adherence," "attrition in exercise programs," "statistics on attrition in fitness clubs," and "persistence and success with diets." Some of the numbers you find may surprise you. Share them with others. This exercise highlights one of the most important dilemmas in the fields of activity, health, and leisure—the difficulty of motivating people to be physically active across the life span.

As a professional, you have a choice. Which is the best way to motivate the clients or students in your intended profession? Should you present exercise as dutiful work, enjoyable work, or play? Could the three approaches be combined, or could they be used in sequence? How might your strategies be affected by the age, gender, and other characteristics of your clients?

Play can be defined as a stance or approach to activity that is autotelic and temporary. In play, we stop the appetitive process, hold off on meeting necessity, and stop working—if only for a while.

Instead, we are captured by the meaning, the delight, and the attractive tensions of the doing. Although play behaviors may result in good things, such as health, good reputation, or fame, they are not designed to meet exotelic purposes. In contrast to intrinsically satisfying work, play behavior is not started, stopped, or modified for exotelic goals. In this sense, play is foolish. It takes us away from prudence, good purposes, and important duties. Players march to the beat of a play drummer—not necessarily that of prudence and common sense.

CHAPTER WRAP-UP

Wrapping Up and Looking Ahead

Our evolutionary history shapes how we march to the beat of our drummers, how we play, and how we work. Our origins gave us bodies designed for consistent and regular locomotion over long distances. They made us social beings that function as members of groups and made these groups essential to our survival. They provided us with powerful brains that can envision a future and hold distant goals in mind as achievable realities. Our brains needed challenges to develop cognitively, physiologically, and socially. Hunting and warfare provided complex challenges that fully engaged our super endurance predator ancestors and met those needs.

Our super endurance predator ancestors that millions of years of evolution created on the savannahs of East Africa began, about 150,000 years ago, to expand their territory. They migrated first to the rest of Africa and then to adjacent continents and eventually to practically every bit of habitable land around the world. Armed with powerful physiques, potent intellectual abilities, and formidable social networks, Homo sapiens sapiens would over the course of that time span become the most powerful factor not only in the evolution of their own kind but in the natural history of the planet. As we developed more complex social systems, evolved more sophisticated languages, and built more powerful teams, we profoundly changed the environments we inhabit. That did not mean, however, that we are not still born to run.

The first great challenge to our bodies, minds, and cultures that had been built for hunting, foraging, and running, would come about 10,000 years ago when we profoundly changed the way we lived. An agricultural revolution sparked by the human domestication of plants and animals (by human engineering of evolution) would generate the conditions for the emergence of civilizations and create a much more sedentary environment for us to inhabit. This raised important questions. With a lesser need to develop our physical assets, with fewer reasons to run, would we continue to do so?

Study Questions

1. How are current health problems among humans related to our human origins? Why is it important to run today, even though many of the ancient purposes for running are no longer necessary?

2. How does the perspective provided by geological time affect your perceptions of your own life? Why might the realization of your own mortality elevate the importance of your choices? Why did you choose to major in a field related to activity, health, or leisure?

3. What are some key events that led to the emergence of Homo sapiens sapiens and modern humans? Why are bipedalism and running thought to be important factors in our advancement?

4. How does sport relate to the lifestyles of our prehistoric ancestors? Where did sport come from? From what prehistoric activities did it borrow its characteristics and qualities?

5. Why is it reasonable to think that our ancestors experienced physical activity both as play and as work? What is the difference between these ways of moving? Identify two species of work and distinguish them both from play. Translate these three approaches to physical activity into distinct methods for motivating clients or students.

THE TRANSITION FROM ENDURANCE PREDATORS TO FARMERS

The Birth of "Civilizations"

Chapter Objectives

In this chapter, you will

1. learn about the Neolithic transition from hunter-foragers to cultivators of plants and animals and its implications for health and leisure time;

2. see the importance of the shift from a family- or tribe-centered community to the birth of the state and the rise of new cities;

3. learn about the utility of sport and other forms of physical activity for promoting health, affecting sexual selection, influencing religion in the East and West, developing leaders, and enhancing the unity and identity of the new city-states;

4. evaluate the importance of physical activity in terms of both its "tool value" (utility) and its "jewel value" (intrinsic worth);

5. examine the practical implications of promoting physical activity today as a means to an end or as an end in itself; and

6. debate some of the difficulties of interpreting the historical record and review a model of ancient sport and its cultural functions.

For more than 100,000 years, humans chased prey across landscapes all over the world, sometimes over enormous distances for days at a time. Their ability to run for long periods of time made them super-endurance predators (see chapter 1). In addition to following game animals, they foraged for seasonal crops at a variety of locations, living a nomadic lifestyle that put a premium on their mobility. Then, between 12,000 and 3,000 years ago, at a variety of independent locations around the world, a profound transformation began in the way humans lived. Hunting and foraging had provided a foundation for the development of elaborate and mobile cultures in which the development of the abilities needed to traverse long distances in pursuit of game represented a hallmark of human adaptation. Thus we humans began our sojourn on earth as super-endurance predators with bodies and minds attuned to what scholars of this vast span of human existence have dubbed the "long hunt." Then, over a period of about 10,000 years—a relatively short interval in the long span of human history—we would become much more sedentary creatures.

A Revolution in How We Lived

Scholars refer to these momentous changes in the patterns of human society and economics as the Neolithic (literally, "new stone") Revolution. In this period, our ancestors began to systematically domesticate plants and animals, an endeavor that produced more consistent and reliable food supplies and sparked dramatic increases in human populations. The Neolithic Revolution occurred not just in a single location but in multiple areas around the world. In the Mediterranean regions that scholars have dubbed the Fertile Crescent, people began to plant and harvest cereal grains, especially wheat and barley; they also domesticated sheep, goats, cattle, and pigs. In northern China, humans grew millet, rice, and soybeans as staple crops and bred cattle and pigs to provide meat. In Mesoamerica, people domesticated squash, beans, and maize and bred turkeys and dogs. In South America, they used the potato as a basic crop and domesticated llamas, alpacas, and guinea pigs. In various parts of Africa, humans grew sorghum, millet, and yams as staple plant foods and cattle as the main herd animal. On Pacific islands, in particular Papua New Guinea, people domesticated taros, yams, and bananas.

The Neolithic Revolution not only began in multiple places but also emerged from multiple causes. Although researchers continue to debate what factors moved human populations from hunting and foraging to agriculture and herding, most experts argue that different causes pushed human societies in similar directions in different locations. For example, the rise of farming economies in the Fertile Crescent of the Near East seems to have occurred when climate changes at the end of the last ice age led to the decline of the megafauna that hunters had long pursued and thus made the cultivation of wild cereals a priority for survival. In China, on the other hand, an increasing population seems to have put extreme pressure on traditional food sources and spurred innovations in the cultivation of plants and animals that led to the development of Asian agriculture.

The Consequences of the Neolithic Revolution

As human populations made the transformation from nomadic super-endurance predators to sedentary farmers and herders, their cultures and societies changed profoundly. The small, highly mobile bands typical of hunter-forager lifestyles gave way to settled communities that grew to incorporate much larger populations. In turn, this shift from more nomadic to more sedentary living patterns exerted a dramatic effect on the human species. Hunter-foragers had practiced various forms of population control to counteract periods of scarce resources and to maintain their essential mobility. In contrast, in this new stage of human development, permanent settlements and the domestication of plants and animals created more dependable resource supplies and sparked a dramatic increase in the growth of human populations. Human ingenuity soon created food storage systems that gave them a much more reliable caloric supply and allowed them to settle in a permanent location.

In addition, the size of human settlements increased exponentially. The small bands of 25 and the larger gatherings of 500 gave way to new settlement patterns in which thousands, then tens of thousands, and even hundreds of thousands of inhabitants gathered in close proximity. Thus the city came to form the fundamental economic, cultural, political, and social unit of the agricultural epoch; in turn, the rise of cities further transformed human cultures. Hunter-foragers had lived in relatively egalitarian communities, and their nomadic circuits meant that they could not accumulate large stores of material goods or food products. In contrast, in the new sedentary environments created by the agricultural and urban revolutions, the amount of property increased dramatically. As inequalities in wealth produced more stratified and specialized social structures, an elite governing class emerged to rule over a mass of agricultural laborers. Specialized classes developed to fulfill particular functions, including warriors, priests, civil servants, and other key groups necessary for managing and serving urban communities.

The Rise of "Civilization"

These new urban cultures left footprints that we can still see today, both in the material remnants excavated by archaeologists and, in many cases, in their own records using the representational languages (systems of writing) that they invented. Indeed, for centuries, scholars have argued that the invention of written language marked one key aspect of the "rise of civilization" (see chapter 1) and ushered in a new form of human culture. Although contemporary chroniclers of the urban transformation related to the Neolithic Revolution note an occasional exception, they concur that the development of a series of interrelated characteristics that generally includes the development of written languages defines these new forms of human society. Specifically, the "rise of civilization" is marked by a shift from hunting and foraging to systematic domestication of plants and animals and by a transition from nomadic to sedentary settlement patterns, population growth and the rise of urban centers, the development of record-keeping and writing, the emergence of food surpluses and the rise of trade and commerce, the appearance of monumental architecture, the intensification of complex religious practices, and the evolution of new forms of social and political organization.

Crucial social and political developments included a shift in the focus of human existence from family and kinship ties to urban identities, the specialization of roles into distinctive social classes, and the birth of the state and of well-organized central governments. Increasingly, human interactions focused on the abstract concept of the state rather than on the kinship ties and personal relationships that had marked older and smaller tribal affiliations. Amid these changes, sport and other forms of physical activity would play profound roles in defining social hierarchies, forging the identity of the state, and bonding the disparate populations of the new cities into functioning communities. Deeply interconnected with other human institutions that created communal connections, in particular with warfare, religion, and government, sport contributed to the social epoxies that bonded these new forms of society and culture into coherent entities.

For several centuries, historians, mainly writing from Western perspectives, argued that civilizations emerged first in the West, primarily in the Mesopotamian cities dotting the valleys of the Tigris and Euphrates Rivers of the Fertile Crescent in the Near East and in the Nile River valley in Egypt. Over the last century, however, most scholars have come to the conclusion that, rather than being constituted by a singular rise in the West, this development consisted of distinct civilizations emerging independently, and roughly contemporaneously, in a wide variety of locations around the globe. Key centers beyond Egypt and Mesopotamia included the Indus River valleys of present-day India, the fertile river systems of northeastern China, at least two locations in South America in what is now modern Peru, the fecund landscapes of Mesoamerica (present-day central Mexico and other Central American regions), and several places in sub-Saharan Africa.

The Emergence of Advanced Forms of Communication

As noted earlier, one of the most important developments during the Neolithic Revolution was the development of more sophisticated forms of communication, particularly the earliest forms of written language, which developed about 5,000 years ago in the form of Sumerian cuneiform scripts and Egyptian hieroglyphics. (Today, scholars estimate that more than 600 languages are spoken around the world.) Although we know that writing appeared relatively recently, we also know that sophisticated verbal languages preceded that event by thousands of years, perhaps even hundreds of thousands of years. The importance of communication in the Neolithic Revolution can hardly be overemphasized. The shift toward living in communities put a premium on cooperation and collaboration. Both of these aspects of human behavior presuppose communication that is clear and concise.

If effective communication was needed by hunter-foragers (and it was), it was even more needed by individuals who attempted to work out political, religious, military, and other social arrangements in larger communities.

We must remind ourselves, however, that much communication occurs in the absence of symbolic language, whether verbal or written. Recent studies of animal behavior show that many species of mammals, for example, communicate in surprisingly effective ways. For instance, animals can inform one another about dangers of different sorts, advertise mating opportunities, and issue warnings through the sounds they make and the gestures they use. Humans, of course, do much better than this. Our extensive vocabularies, rules of grammar, regulations of syntax, and the like allow us to say far more—and to do so with greater efficiency and, one hopes, very little ambiguity. Even so, we need to remember that communication transcends symbolic, verbal language. It transcended language during the Paleolithic and Neolithic Revolutions, and it transcends it today. We continue to communicate in many ways, and most of them involve the body and physicality.

Most fundamentally, we communicate with our posture, our gestures, the way in which we hold ourselves, and the ways in which we move. We "read" faces to determine whether a stranger is a friend or a foe. Our style of walking can communicate volumes about us and our self-image. People who stand erect and those who are bent over with their heads down send very different messages. In the realm of sport, many athletes play with a flair that communicates, without verbal or written supplementation, a great deal about who they are and what they value in life.

Our fine arts also serve as nonverbal means of communication that typically require high levels of physical skill. Music, painting, and sculpting often communicate ideas that are arguably difficult to

Communicating and Cooperating Without Using Verbal Language

Student Exercise

Your assignment is to invent a new game, communicate how the game is played to at least one other person, and, finally, turn that game into a contest. It could be a simple game of throwing a piece of paper into a waste basket while standing a certain distance away. You might award one point if the paper comes to rest within a foot of the basket and two points if it goes in. The game might consist of five tries. Can you communicate all of this using only gestures, personal modeling, and nonverbal sounds? Once the other person shows that he or she understands the game and has had a chance to play it, turn the game into a contest, again without using words. That is, challenge the other person to see who can score higher.

Was your communication and cooperation experiment successful? Were you able to teach a new game nonverbally? Try to give at least two reasons for your success or failure.

---

put into words. For instance, we can go to a concert or art museum and feel carried away without hearing or uttering a single word or sentence. In another example, mime is a current art form designed to communicate through gesture, suggestive movement, posture, and facial expression. To see how effective, and sometimes humorous, this form of communication can be, go online and view performances by Marcel Marceau.

As kinesiologists, you will need to be able to listen to your clients and students. The take-home point here is that this process may well involve not only hearing what they say but also reading between the lines. This "reading" may include interpreting their gestures, postures, eye movements, and multiple other cues. Some practitioners have even suggested that this kind of communicative sensitivity forms the basis for true expertise in kinesiology.

By now, the importance and power of nonverbal communication should be obvious. However, a simple exercise can drive the point home by showing you how much can be done through pointing and pantomime—that is, without using words.

We will probably never know exactly when formal languages developed. In all probability, they grew gradually over a period of more than a hundred centu-

ries. Undoubtedly, it took considerable time for our ancestors to transition from (more or less) hardwired animal sounds and postures to intentional pointing and pantomime and then to abstract symbols systems replete with rules of grammar, extensive vocabularies, and syntactic meanings. Whatever the specific facts of this story may be, it is clear that the Neolithic Revolution stood on the shoulders of enhanced communication and of the collaborative and cooperative cultural developments fostered by that communication.

The Impact of the Neolithic Revolution on Human Vigor and Health

For hundreds of years, historians considered the rise of civilization a key step in the unfettered history of human progress toward better lives for everyone. In the past few decades, however, more critical perspectives have been developed. First and foremost, the development of densely populated cities made life far more dangerous for humans due to communicable diseases. Viruses and bacteria that had failed to gain consistent footholds in the sparsely populated and widely dispersed hunter-forager bands found fertile ground among human hosts packed in close proximity in cities. Thus the rise of civilization increased human susceptibility to epidemic diseases.

Human bodies were also affected during this period by changes in diet. Hunter-forager diets, while not as dependable, were more balanced and diverse than the more abundant nutritional supplies provided by farmers. Archaeologists who study paleopathology (the study of diseases in the fossil record) have discovered that the average height for men and women declined among civilized populations as compared with their hunter-forager ancestors—from 5 feet 10 inches for men and 5 feet 6 inches for women to 5 feet 5 inches and 5 feet 1 inch, respectively. Indeed, human height did not

return to the earlier averages until the 20th century. Moreover, skeletal remains from the new urban-farming societies reveal that people were not only smaller in stature than their nomadic forbearers but also more prone to anemias, vitamin deficiencies, spinal deformations, and dental pathologies. In turn, the heightened effect of diseases in the rise of civilization led to a decrease in life expectancy. This decrease may also have resulted in part from the more rigorous demands of work in the agricultural economy. Whereas typical hunter-forager communities earned their livings with a 20-hour work week (see chapter 1), the new farmers worked far longer hours. At the same time, when the super-endurance predators who were

A Brief History of "Paleo" and "Neo" Diets

In the last few decades, as concerns about an obesity crisis and caloric overabundance have plagued contemporary societies, a few nutrition scholars, and legions of zealous dieters, have articulated the idea that, since our bodies were designed for the Paleolithic universe of hunting and foraging, our eating habits should return to the distant past as well. Advocates of the "caveman" or "Paleo" diet argue that the Neolithic Revolution was the worst thing that ever happened to human nutrition because it unleashed the evils of dairy products, milled grains, refined sugar, starchy legumes, processed oils, added salt, and fermented alcohol on an unsuspecting humankind. Proponents of the Paleo diet insist that these products of systematic plant and animal cultivation, along with the methods used to store and preserve food surpluses, have been the bane of human health ever since they appeared. In their view, bread and beer, milk and cheese, and sugar and salt are not what humans were meant to eat and have done enormous harm to human vitality over the millennia. Instead, promoters of the Paleo diet insist that we should return to simpler, more natural, and less-processed food products typical of the hunter-forager epoch. In other words, we should eat more meat (including organ meat); more fresh fruits and vegetables; and more nuts and roots.

Contemporary nutritionists would certainly agree that health and nutritional concerns arise with excessive consumption of processed foods and overindulgence in salt, alcohol, and sugar. They also acknowledge that some dietary benefits are conferred by consuming fresh fruits, vegetables, nuts, and roots. The Paleo diet's meat prescription remains more controversial among nutritionists. Overall, in examining these claims about what sorts of nutrition best suit human needs at this moment in our history, we should remember that the Neolithic Revolution, and particularly the food-processing practices spawned by it, provided a far more reliable food supply to human populations that had regularly faced serious periods of malnutrition and starvation. On the other hand, this steadier and more abundant supply of processed and preserved foods came at a price—a hard reality indicated by the evidence of high tooth-decay rates, bone disease, and shrinking stature that archaeologists have uncovered among the remains of Neolithic populations. These dietary and nutritional conundrums remain with us today.

our ancestors domesticated plants and animals and moved into cities, they created more sedentary lifestyles that, albeit perhaps more secure, were by some measures less healthy. Thus, as more and more people populated the earth, they were not necessarily healthier or more vital than their ancestors had been.

"Civilized" Physical Activity and Sport

As humans became more sedentary creatures, their lifestyles changed dramatically, but physical contests (sports) and organized systems of physical activity (including physical education) remained important components of human culture. Contests designed to publicly demonstrate skills—physical, intellectual, and social—no doubt originated in hunter-forager societies during the many millennia that preceded the Neolithic Revolution and the rise of urban civilizations. More specifically, individual or corporate success in competitions of endurance, strength, skill with weapons, and fortitude in the face of pain won accolades and admiration both from one's own tribe and from outsiders. Prowess, the public display of skills and abilities, could be won or lost in sporting competitions. Most historians contend that men used such contests to earn status and even to gain advantages in mating rituals and marriage customs. However, some anthropologists have pointed out that footraces, wrestling matches, and other quests for prowess are not entirely restricted to male participants. Some cultures also feature such contests for women, especially for young girls who were reaching sexual and social maturity.

Evidence from ancient agricultural societies reveals that public demonstrations of prowess through sport continued to flourish in the new social climate. Demonstrations of endurance, strength, and fortitude impressed agricultural laborers as much as they had dazzled hunter-foragers.

Though hunting no longer represented the center of the human economy, it remained a popular pastime for farmers. In addition, as many scholars have observed, the rise of cities increased the frequency and intensity of human warfare because communities now fought to protect or plunder property and wealth. As a professional military class emerged to defend the new urban centers, physical education systems proliferated to train warriors in the martial arts.

Prowess, Warfare, and Communal Solidarity

Sport and physical education have deep connections to warfare in human history. In fact, the ancient Greeks used the same term—*agon*, the root of the modern English term *agony*—to refer both to the struggles of athletic competition and to those of mortal combat. War games, which trained soldiers for the rigors of battle, proliferated in the new urban civilizations, helping soldiers develop physical and psychological stamina and training them to use the increasingly sophisticated weaponry that characterized "civilized" warfare. In particular, the ancient warrior classes in Western, Chinese, Indian, African, and American civilizations competed in combat sports, such as wrestling and boxing, thus giving these sports a seemingly universal presence in human history. They also engaged in archery, swordplay, and throwing competitions involving spears, javelins, and other tools of warfare. Equestrian sports played an especially prominent role, showcasing skills in charioteering and horseback riding (except, of course, in the American civilizations that did not have horses).

In the small communities of hunter-forager cultures, communal identity had depended on the bonding agents of personal relationships and kinship connections, but individual ties could not bind the thousands of inhabitants who made

ORIGINS OF SPECTATOR SPORTS AND STADIUMS

Historical Profile

A reproduction of ancient Rome, with the Circus Maximus (the large oval structure) in the center and the Colosseum (the large circular structure) in the upper right.

The first sporting events to draw thousands of spectators and necessitate the creation of permanent seating facilities in ancient societies were not contests pitting humans directly against one another but races involving horses piloted by humans. These horse races and chariot races took place in monumental structures that constitute the oldest dedicated sporting architecture in world history. Greek hippodromes—from the Greek *hippos* (horse) and *dromos* (course)—generally used hillside topography next to a flat raceway in order to provide seating areas for spectators; later additions included stone seats and platforms.

The Roman Empire outdid the ancient Greeks in building massive monuments for chariot races. The Romans built hippodromes in every part of their far-flung empire, from the British Isles and the Atlantic coast of western Europe to eastern Europe, the Middle East, and North Africa. These edifices were often adorned by the Latin term for a horse-racing spectacle: *circus*. When the Romans built the largest stadium in ancient Western civilization for equestrian contests, they named it the Circus Maximus. Conservative estimates indicate that it could hold at least 150,000 spectators, and some scholars argue that as many as 360,000 partisans could be crowded into this giant facility. (For more on Greek and Roman chariot racing, see chapters 3 and 4.)

up "the masses" of the new cities. They needed other epoxies to provide common experiences and beliefs that would bind them to their fellow citizens. To this end, in addition to training the warrior classes, sporting contests provided ancient civilizations with venues for creating communal solidarity in their new urban settings. For example, scholars have speculated that Mesoamerican ball games, which flourished in various forms for thousands of years, served a variety of purposes, from schooling warriors to creating surrogate mechanisms for conflict resolution to establishing sites for religious divination. Although the exact purposes of these games remain shrouded in mystery and speculation, the numerous stone ball courts built by Mesoamerican civilizations indicate that they were crucial elements of identity for these cultures. In the same vein, the athletic contests created in ancient Greek cultures served a variety of purposes, from religious pilgrimages to public displays of prowess and status for city-states. The construction of *stadia* (stadiums) throughout the Greek world highlighted the importance of these contests in shaping a particular Greek identity within the ancient West.

Sport thus enabled common experiences that helped shape the identities of urban civilizations, providing, along with warfare, a crucial element in binding these cultures into functional units. Stone relief carvings from ancient Mesopotamian cities illustrate this pattern. The carvings, designed to display the power of the ruling classes to the masses, depict fierce warriors engaged in military exercises, including boxing, wrestling, archery, hunting, and chariot racing. As the historian Richard Mandell has observed, the carvings highlight the ways in which "sport was intended to preserve the fitness of the dominant classes and to proclaim as propaganda their menacing power."

Prowess, the "Great Man," and the Rise of the State

Scholars posit that these new urban societies developed governmental structures that put an imperious "great man" (in the terminology of many ancient cultures) in charge. Thus chieftains, kings, pharaohs, and other autocrats dominated the political history of early human government. Abundant evidence from ancient Egypt reveals that the pharaohs who ruled this civilization for many centuries took pains to depict themselves as not only superhuman descendants of the gods but also superhuman athletes who could perform miraculous physical feats.

These amazing endeavors are recorded in the legacies they left, both in the form of stone reliefs and in the relics that filled their burial chambers. According to these depictions, they could run much longer and more swiftly than any of their subjects. Their massive musculature let them propel boats along the Nile at unbelievable speeds. They dispatched the most

Comparing the Circus Maximus With Contemporary Stadiums

Student Exercise

Take a moment to consider the Circus Maximus, which is discussed in the historical profile titled Origins of Spectator Sports and Stadiums. How does it compare with contemporary stadiums? Use the web to research the following questions: How many fans can be held in each of the 10 largest stadiums in the world today? Can any of them hold 150,000 spectators? How about 360,000? Do any single sporting events in the 21st century attract crowds larger than 360,000?

TOMBS OF BENI HASSAN AND OTHER SOURCES

Historical Profile

On the banks of the Nile River, about 150 miles (240 kilometers) south of present-day Cairo, ancient Egyptians built a complex of tombs that they named Beni Hassan. In these burial chambers, they deposited the mummified remains of provincial rulers and great warriors over a period of time that began some 40 centuries ago. (The necropolis was active from 2055 BCE to 1650 BCE during the Middle Kingdom period.) On the walls of these tombs, archaeologists have uncovered brightly colored paintings that constitute some of the oldest evidence of sporting cultures

Entrance to the tombs of Beni Hassan.

Library of Congress LC-DIG-ppmsca-0553

in Western civilization. The paintings depict generals and rulers and their subjects hunting in the surrounding deserts and engaging in numerous other sporting activities. One of the walls is adorned by a series of depictions of wrestlers using various holds. In other scenes, Egyptian soldiers train for combat by performing martial exercises, including javelin throws and archery contests. One set of portraits reveals Egyptian women engaged in acrobatic feats. Another group of paintings depicts an Egyptian stick-and-ball game that resembles an early form of field hockey. In other panels, Egyptian athletes swim or row watercraft in the Nile.

The paintings at Beni Hassan provide the richest trove of information about Egyptian sport, but artwork devoted to physical culture also dots many other sites left by ancient Egyptian civilization. Evidence from other Pharaonic monuments throughout ancient Egypt add to the portrait of early sports, revealing more exercises that trained warriors for combat, scenes of footraces, pictures of handball games and stick-and-hoop games, numerous depictions of boat races, and more frescoes of combat sports such as boxing and wrestling. Although the Egyptians did not leave extensive or detailed descriptions of their games and athletic exercises, their portraits of athletes and games provide one of the earliest records of human interest in sporting contests.

fearsome animals in their realms, even lions and elephants, in prodigious numbers. They shot arrows through massive sheets of copper with ease (and successive pharaohs bettered the marks of their predecessors in a progressive catalog of increasingly astonishing performances). As the historian William Baker has observed, an Egyptian inscription lauding the prowess of Amenophis II, king of Egypt from 1438 BCE to 1412 BCE, offers a striking example:

There was no one who could span his bow and none equaled him in running. Strong was his arm and he did not tire when he seized the oar and rowed at the stem of his boat as stroke for two hundred men. They stopped when they had only half a mile behind them. They were already exhausted and their limbs were tired and they were breathless. But his majesty was strong with his twenty-foot-long oar. He stopped and grounded his boat after he had rowed three miles without a pause. Faces beamed when they saw him doing this.

Certainly these records of athletic genius were not actual records of super-human accomplishment but exaggerations intended to gild the images of the immensely powerful Egyptian autocrats. That was the point of the game they were playing. The "great men" of ancient urban civilizations, in Egypt and elsewhere, spun legends of their athletic prowess in order to consolidate and burnish their political power. They served as the symbols of their cultures; therefore, the more powerful they seemed, the less likely outsiders were to seek to conquer their realms. In fact, in ancient Egypt, the mythologies of rulers' superhuman athletic powers extended beyond the boundaries of "great men" and applied not only to male members of the royal families but also to female pharaohs. Royal women in ancient Egypt garbed themselves in the same costumes of superheroic athletic prowess as their male relatives.

Prowess and Religious Practice

Even as sporting contests served to train warriors, unite the inhabitants of a city in a common culture, and promote the power of the state and its leaders, they also served as elements of religious belief sys-tems. Evidence from around the world con-firms the essential connections between the sporting events and the sacred rituals of ancient urban societies. Mesoamerican civilizations wrapped their ball games in the iconography of their cosmologies and linked them to their conceptions of gods. Jewish religious tradition employed ath-letic analogies to depict Jacob wrestling with God, who wrenches Jacob's hip out of his socket in order to humble him and then gives him a new name, Israel, which means "one who wrestles with God."

Other ancient Western civilizations com-peted to win the favor of their gods and to mark the passage of prominent citizens from earthly realms into the afterlife. For example, as early as 1829 BCE, the ancient Gaelic cultures of Ireland cele-brated the Tailteann Games, an athletic festival that, according to Irish mythology, served as a mourning ceremony for the mother (or stepmother, depending on the particular version of legend) of a powerful chieftain. A crucial part of the commem-oration consisted of the *Cuiteach Fuait*—games that tested mental and physical skills, including long jumps, high jumps, footraces, spear throwing, boxing, sword fighting, archery, wrestling, swimming, and chariot and horse races. The *Cuiteach Fuait* also featured hurling, a traditional Irish team sport played with sticks and a ball that celebrated warrior toughness. More broadly, the Tailteann Games also included singing, dancing, and storytelling contests; craft competitions for goldsmiths, jewelers, weavers, and armorers; and even mass marriages.

Perhaps the oldest written account of a sporting contest details another mourning ceremony, the funeral games honoring Patroclus as described by the Greek story-teller Homer (who lived in the 8th century BCE) in his epic known as the *Iliad* (circa 750 BCE). Homer's lyrical explanation of these funeral games provides one of the earliest written accounts of the meaning of sport in human history (for a fuller discussion, see chapter 3) and depicts the gods of Greek mythology as spectators who not only watch but sometimes intervene in order to aid their favorite human athletes. The funeral games of Patroclus showcase not only the religious dimensions of ancient sport but also the other components, especially the demonstration of warrior prowess and the expression of the bonds of cultural (in this case, Greek) identity.

Another ancient religious tradition involving physical prowess is associated with Eastern philosophy and the martial arts. As the term suggests, the martial arts derive their name from military, or martial, activities. References to the martial arts are found in the Vedas of India dating back to approximately 1700 BCE and in the *Yoga Sutras* published in the 3rd century BCE. Most scholars believe that martial arts, in some form or another, existed as folk traditions for thousands of years prior to any written record and may have had common roots in Mongolian wrestling that developed during the Neolithic Era in northeast Asia. As was true in other parts of the world during this period, early martial practices served as preparations for hunting and warfare and also accorded special status to champion athletes, their lords, and their communities.

Early Eastern religions were primarily either shamanistic (focused on attempts to achieve altered states of consciousness, interact with the spirit world, and use the results of this interaction to affect one's life for the better) or animistic (involving a belief that animals, plants, and inanimate objects have spiritual qualities and powers). However, the martial arts also evolved to carry religious significance for personal spiritual development, typically in the traditions of mystical religion, such as Buddhism, which originated in northern India in the 5th century BCE. The ultimate objective of sporting contests in Buddhism was not to defeat one's opponent but to achieve a kind of harmony or oneness with the environment, including the opponent and his or her hostile actions. The primary purpose of the contest, in other words, was to achieve enlightenment and tranquility. Today, we have any number of activities that find their origins in the Eastern martial arts, including judo, yoga, taekwondo, tai chi, kung fu, karate, aikido, and jujitsu. (For more on the martial arts religious tradition and its effect on Western sport, see chapter 4).

Physical Activity as a Tool and as a Jewel

The saga of human development from the dawn of Homo sapiens through the Neolithic Revolution highlights the centrality of physical capability for human well-being. However, we need to notice that this centrality is based on two distinct kinds of values—those of utility and work, on one hand, and those of intrinsic delight and play, on the other. This distinction is introduced in chapter 1, where we discuss metaphysical differences between work and play—or, more precisely, between two species of work (dutiful and enjoyable work) and play. With these distinctions in mind, we can ask a second kind of question: What is the value of physical activity as work and as play? This area of study is called axiology, or the theory of value.

Typically, axiology is preceded by metaphysics, because we need to know what things are and how they differ before we can assess their relative worth. However, metaphysics is no substitute for investigations related to value. Even if work and play are established as different activities, questions may linger about their worth or their rightful place in life. Therefore, we need to carry the analysis further—beyond metaphysics. Thus, in this chapter we investigate the relationship of work- and play-oriented physical activity to the good life, then use that information as a foundation for speculating about effective professional practices.

Much of our historical review to this point has underlined the undeniable utility of physical prowess. Some of this is obvious. Those with outstanding physical skills and strength do better at two activities with clear survival value—hunting and fighting, thus avoiding both starvation and death in combat. However, earlier in this chapter, you encountered other, more subtle utilities—for instance, those of providing a robust physical constitution that would be less vulnerable to disease, conferring advantages (possibly for both males and females) for sexual selection, promoting community solidarity and group identity, and developing respected leaders. You have also seen that physical prowess was useful in relationship to religious practices and spiritual development. In short, everywhere one looks in the Neolithic Age, one sees the importance of motor skill, strength, and physical ability. Thus, for purposes of simplicity as we begin our axiological journey, we identify these multiple functions as constituting the "tool value" of physical prowess. As with all tools, physical prowess can serve as a means to an end. In other words, this species of value allows us to answer the following question: What is skilled movement good for? The Neolithic answer is "lots of things."

A second question also needs to be asked: Is movement good in itself? Here too the answer is yes, or at least "it can be." We refer to this quality as the "jewel value" of physical activity. Chapter 1 reviews the characteristics of movement as play, as intrinsically valuable, as an end in itself. It describes play as a relational phenomenon, one that serves as a counterpoint to the more dominant themes of survival and work. In play, we go off-line, find a temporary "oasis of happiness," and "reallocate resources" normally used for workaday activities to other things that are simply fun.

Despite the arduous duties of farming and herding in the Neolithic Age, we can be assured that play found a way to show itself. Even today, when we live in what many social commentators refer to as a "workaholic" culture—in which some people hold two or three jobs, many citizens use free time for "self-improvement" activities, and many students (perhaps including you) take an overload of classes and hold down part-time jobs while in school—we find time to play. Undoubtedly, our Neolithic ancestors did too.

We can know that play is fundamental by observing children today and, as Huizinga did, noticing that play is universal among many species of nonhuman animals. As

Value of Play

Student Exercise

In cultures that value work, play is sometimes depicted as more appropriate for children than for adults. In other words, as we mature—when we graduate from school and go to work, and especially when we take on added responsibilities as parents or community members—play supposedly becomes expendable. It gives way and, in this view, *should* give way to more important duties.

Do you think these claims are valid? This book's introduction asks you to investigate evidence of the importance of play for children. But is play also valuable for adults? What pattern of play, dutiful work, and enjoyable work is best for building a good life? In searching for answers to these questions, interrogate your own experiences to determine how and when you play, as well as how important play is for your own well-being. You can also look into research on adult play and its relationship to overall physical and psychological well-being.

noted in chapter 1, play does not require human levels of intelligence, but it does require some ability to enjoy, delight, love, and appreciate. Fortunately, you and I do not need to worry about having this ability; it is a human birthright. We have played and will continue to play, even if, as sober and responsible adults, we now have to sneak it in. Once again, this is the jewel value of physical prowess and, as with all charms, it is appreciated for its own sake. It dismisses the utility-oriented question, "What is movement good for?" Indeed, players might answer "perhaps nothing." The experience of movement is good in itself. We move because we love to move.

The centrality of both work and play in human existence suggests that both are valuable. If this is true, you will not be choosing between work and play but rather examining times and places in which to honor them both. In fact, the degree to which you personally emphasize the tool or jewel features of activity may well depend on your current situation. If you are ill or hurting or need to lose some weight, then it may make sense to focus on the tool value of movement. If, however, you are run down from work responsibilities or burned out from too much studying, then play may be the more attractive option.

Likewise, the degree to which you emphasize the tool or jewel aspects of physical activity in your job may depend on context. If you have a youngster who hates to move, you may want to gear your interventions toward the jewel side of the equation. If, on the other hand, you have a senior citizen with various health problems, it may make sense to focus on the tool value of exercise.

Some scholars have argued, however, that it is not wise to consider play and work as alternatives or to focus on one in the absence of the other. These writers have claimed that it is impossible even to do so. In this theory, the professional question is not whether activity should be presented as work or as play, but rather, what emphasis or blend is appropriate, or what sequence of blends makes the most sense? This modern position is called holism, and you will learn more about this philosophical theory in chapter 10. For now, we analyze some of the implications of holism in relationship to the tool value and jewel value of physical activity.

We begin with the proposition that work and play are not mutually exclusive opposites but rather a complementary pair. Work includes elements of play, and play includes elements of work. Therefore, we exchange the notion of work versus play for the more homogeneous idea of work~play (figure 2.1); again, the tilde, or squiggle, symbolizes the interpenetration of the two. Extrinsically oriented work activities include intrinsically appreciated play

Holistic View

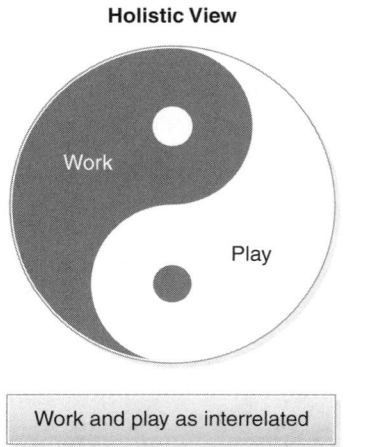

Work and play as interrelated

Dualistic View

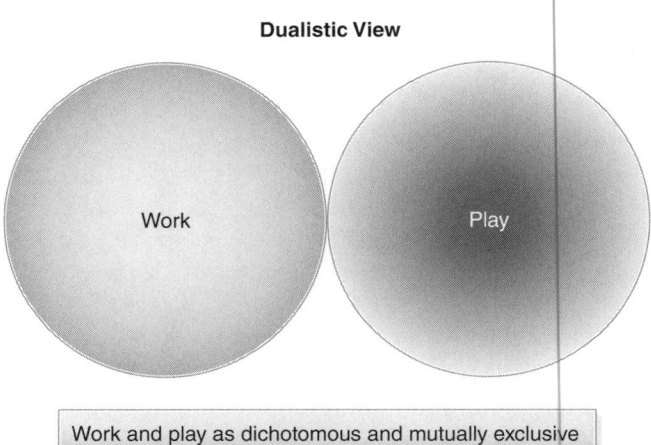
Work and play as dichotomous and mutually exclusive

Figure 2.1 Two conceptualizations of work and play.

elements. Focus on the end result (work), and focus on the process itself (play) shift back and forth in any number of variations with different degrees of intensity. Time and energy are allocated~reallocated. Most activity is rationally~irrationally motivated. Moving well is useful~enjoyable.

This does not mean that the blends cannot change—sometimes more in the direction of work, sometimes more in the direction of play—but it does mean that practitioners should not view utility and fun as opposites or as professional alternatives. Nor are different blends of these values inherently better or worse than others. Rather, the blend must fit the professional situation; therefore, it must change as the client's situation or your work setting changes.

The Tool End of the Spectrum

Even with this holistic approach, we must acknowledge the ends or extremes of the spectrum—that is, those blends that are mostly work or mostly play. We begin here with blends of work~play that emphasize utility. When we ask clients to move because it is good for them, we ask them to focus on the results—improved health,

Potential Tool Benefits of Regular Physical Activity

1. Physical activity increases life expectancy and can prevent or control heart disease, high blood pressure, abnormal blood lipid profile (cholesterol and triglyceride), stroke, type 2 diabetes, metabolic syndrome, and colon and breast cancers.

2. Physical activity has a beneficial effect on cardiorespiratory and muscular fitness.

3. Physical activity increases metabolic rates and helps individuals lose, or maintain a healthy, weight.

©davidf/E+/Getty Images

Physical activity is useful for the promotion of health and many other benefits.

4. Physical activity helps lower anxiety, stress, and depression; it can improve one's attitude or mood.
5. Physical activity helps older adults maintain mental acuity and decrease the rate of brain dysfunction.
6. Physical activity aids digestion and regularity.
7. Physical activity promotes bone calcification and improves bone density.
8. Physical activity helps a person maintain a youthful appearance and preserve youthful functions.
9. Physical activity helps a person sleep well.
10. Physical activity enhances overall quality of life.

Adapted, by permission, from SecondsCount.org. (Washington, DC: The Society for Cardiovascular Angiography and Interventions (SCAI). Available: http://secondscount.org/heart-resources/heart-resources-detail?cid=f32db674-f604-4483-a6fd-31081cf66065#.VbUg1E3JD5o reduced pain, or whatever other objective is desired. We even ask them to overlook the inconvenience or discomfort caused by the process. Although exercise and sweating may not be much fun, and although it can be costly and inconvenient to join a health club, it is worth the expense and the effort, or so we counsel our clients and students. Thus, even though we try to inject enjoyment into exercise, we require persistence even if it is not much fun.

Persistence in the absence of fun is warranted because researchers in kinesiology, recreation, health studies, and related fields have produced a wealth of information about the good effects of exercise. More specifically, physiologists, chemists, cell biologists, and medical personnel have identified a remarkably broad range of good outcomes associated with movement. In other words, they have fleshed out the powerful tool value of physical activity.

The sidebar Potential Tool Benefits of Regular Physical Activity contains only a conservative list. Studies have also been conducted that attempt to show causal relationships between exercise and academic performance in school, ability to concentrate, success in stopping bad habits such as smoking, and lowering the prevalence of teen pregnancy, among other benefits. It is likely that some of these claims will be substantiated in the years ahead and that yet others will be identified as potential outcomes deserving further study for possible confirmation. In light of this growing scientific information, it is not an exaggeration to claim that exercise is one of the strongest elixirs known to humankind. Thus the American College of Sports Medicine's well-known slogan—"exercise is medicine"—carries an important and valid message. Along with nutrition and safety, exercise promotes health and longevity.

The Jewel End of the Spectrum

Given the significance of physical activity as a tool, one might wonder why the jewel side of movement deserves much attention. If the theory of holism is correct, one answer has already been given—that is, it cannot be avoided, because utility and serendipity are not exclusive alternatives but a complementary pair. A second answer is provided in the sidebar titled Potential Tool Benefits of Regular Physical Activity. In that list, items 4, 8, 9, and 10 speak directly to quality of life and the importance of end values. As Aristotle argued centuries ago, ends carry more weight than means. He described this relationship as follows:

> *That which is sought for its own sake is more complete than that which is sought as a means to something else. That which is never sought as a means to something else is more complete than things sought both on their own account and on account of the former. By absolutely final, we mean that which is sought for its own sake, and never as a means to something else. Happiness seems to be something of that sort.*

Aristotle reminds us of one of life's truisms. We occasionally put up with discomfort and inconvenience in order to experience life at its fullest. To put it another way, activities such as studying hard and working out are valuable to the extent to which they promote what we really want in life—joy, love, meaning, friendship, excitement, security, peace, or, to use Aristotle's term, happiness. This logic places a priority on play.

Holism, however, suggests that intangibles such as happiness are also useful, whether or not the person who experiences such happiness knows of its utility. In other words, as already noted in the introduction, jewels have tool value, and tools have jewel value. For those of us in the health-related professions, this reciprocity means that a healthier person is likely to have a better quality of life. Conversely, and just as important, a person who has a better quality of life is likely to be healthier.

The first part of this equation is easy to accept. Those who work to maintain good health will have more energy and strength, less pain, greater flexibility and endurance—the kinds of things that allow us to play and generally enjoy life more fully. The second part of the equation may be harder to appreciate. How, we might wonder, can intangibles such as enjoyment affect health? Can love change blood pressure and body chemistry? Can happiness really enable us to live longer?

Some dualistic accounts make it difficult to understand how this could be true. Dualists such as René Descartes, who famously imagined an absolute division between bodies and minds, had a hard time explaining how ideas affect physical movements (for more on Descartes, see chapter 5). The problem for Descartes was this: Physical objects are affected only by other physical objects. That is, we cannot move a chair simply by thinking that it should move; we have to make physical contact. Similarly, in a dualistic account, it is hard to figure out how a mere idea or attitude can "move" or otherwise affect one's physical body. Although most dualists do accept the proposition that ideas effect physical changes, they cannot explain how this happens.

Contemporary materialists move even further away from holism. They do not even accept the proposition that tangible reality is affected by intangibles. In their view, the world is composed entirely of atoms and void; as a result, ideas have no efficacy. For materialists, only brain states affect health. Thus, ideas, values, and attitudes have no power to do anything. (For more on materialism and its effects on kinesiology, see chapter 5.)

Exercise is conceptualized in the materialist approach as a physical intervention. Like medicine, it is administered in doses, and its efficacy is measured according to the logic of medicine—that is, in terms of the minimal dosage for the desired health benefit. Therefore, efficient interventions (less time-consuming exercises) are preferred to their relatively inefficient counterparts, such as games and play. In addition, good-tasting medicine (exercise that is fun or at least tolerable) is preferred to its counterpart (e.g., painful workouts). Controlled dosages that can be monitored in laboratories or on treadmills are chosen in favor of less predictable interventions that may involve running in the woods or playing a game. This approach has been called the "medicalization of exercise." And like other forms of reductive medicine, it focuses on physical interventions and physical outcomes, on carefully measuring doses and benefits—in short, on fixing or maintaining the machine in scientifically measurable ways. This approach has led to the adoption of the popular "exercise is medicine" slogan mentioned earlier. It garners its popularity and effectiveness from an important truism: Tangibles affect other tangibles, and physical exercise affects physical health.

Holism, however, argues that any hard-and-fast distinction between tangibles and intangibles is a mistake. As difficult as it may be to understand, play, joy, and meaning are tangible~intangible at the same time. Because this is so, it is not unreasonable to think that *quality* of life affects *quantity* of life, that play affects health, that happiness changes both brain states and other aspects of body chemistry. Today, scientists are busy trying to tie down these relationships that move from values, affect, idea, and emotions to physically measurable changes, such as increases in epinephrine, dopamine, endorphins, and serotonin and decreases in blood pressure and resting heart rate.

Although more work needs to be done, the holistic theory of well-being leads to the following conclusion: play is medicine, and those who play will be healthier—psychologically, socially, and physically. Those who play are likely to live longer. This is the case not merely because some forms of vigorous play generate health-enhancing heart rates. Play is medicine also because meaning and other positive experiences affect us through and through—from our psychological outlook on life all the way down to how our genes express themselves. This insight requires that we rethink the nature and quality of our interventions. Our bodies are not just machines that automatically benefit from exercise. Although it is true that exercise of most types is medicine, it may also be the case that playful physical activity is particularly powerful medicine (see figure 2.2).

At the heart of this causal relationship between play and health lies an important professional paradox. You need to be aware of this paradox if you are to become a successful play promoter. The paradox can be stated as follows: play is important only when it is unimportant. That is, even if play-intensive blends of experience produce good spin-off health effects, people who play cannot do so for the express purpose of obtaining these effects. Doing so would compromise the joy of play and turn the activity into a duty, and when play becomes a duty, it loses some of its play value. In other words, play cannot become

Play + Exercise = Better health

Figure 2.2 Exercise is performed not just by bodies but by people; therefore, we might conclude that if (according to the popular slogan) "exercise is medicine," then playful exercise is better medicine.

a matter of prudence for the player; only when it is lived by the player as unimportant does it carry its full spillover benefits. Accordingly, play makers, or play facilitators, must keep the health agenda out of sight if play is to blossom. This is an agreeable bargain. If we generate play, we may be asking our students and clients to swallow the best-tasting medicine ever invented.

Before proceeding further with personal and professional implications, we need to clarify the kinds of values associated with physical activity as a jewel.

Professional Challenges

It should be clear by now that physical activity as a means~end can and should play a role in the good life. This role can carry a flavor of duty or responsibility; that is, exercise can be presented to clients as "good for you." This approach emphasizes the rational side of human nature. It suggests that people will not act unless they have good reason to do so. To put it another way, if people are convinced that a regular program of physical activity will help them live a longer, healthier life, then they will act accordingly.

This would seem to be a good strategy for adults who have reached the age of reason and are fully aware of health problems and risks. This prudential message should be particularly powerful for those who have had a health crisis, such as a heart attack, or who have seen a dramatically negative change in lifestyle because of physical infirmity or excess weight. Granted, children might be treated differently, but for sane, clear-thinking adults, the prudential approach might be the one to emphasize.

However, some scholars in the humanities have raised questions about this strategy, even for some adults, and recommend emphasizing the play strategy instead. Concerns about presenting movement primarily as a tool run in two directions. The first one questions an assumption about

Potential Jewel Benefits of Games, Sport, and Physical Play

1. Increased aesthetic pleasure (e.g., enjoying a walk in the woods, hitting the sweet spot on a golf club)
2. Increased tension or drama (e.g., the excitement of a close game)
3. New friendships (e.g., rewarding friendships with fellow exercisers, teammates, and opponents)
4. Increased sense of efficacy (growing range of "I cans," good feelings associated with competence)
5. Increased sense of freedom (more options associated with more "I cans"; ability to go more places, do more things, experience less constraint)
6. Greater sense of satisfaction (sense of accomplishment from learning skills that are challenging to learn, let alone master)
7. Increased feeling of harmony between self and world and between self and other (illusion of harmony created by higher skills) through loss of fear and increased confidence that accompanies skill development
8. Reduced self-consciousness due to enhanced health, fitness, and competence (the experience of better days when we do not have to worry about ourselves)
9. Decreased fears (reduction in fears related to many physical tasks thanks to increases in physical skill; e.g., reduced fear of water thanks to swimming ability)
10. Increased sense of coherence and stronger personal identity (development of stories about our play activities, our improvements, our successes and failures; e.g., "becoming" cyclists or saying we "are" cyclists)

the nature of human beings. Although we are, to a degree, rational animals, it is clear that we are also irrational animals. In other words, we do what we like to do, and we copy what others have done even when, from a more objective perspective, it may not be the best thing to do. Existentialists are famous for emphasizing the freedom of human beings to go against the grain of reason and tradition. In other words, we are not programmed to do what is safe, reasonable, rational, expected, or logical. Nor do we always have to act in accord with our own best self-interest. Many of Albert Camus' heroes, for instance, acted absurdly and put themselves in harm's way, in part to emphasize and actualize their freedom.

If Camus and others who follow this line of thought are right—if conscious, reflective human beings are not merely predictable machines that march automat-ically to the drumbeat of progress and self-interest—then we should find that rational, prudential approaches to exercise reap only limited returns. A similar conclusion presents itself when we consider a second problem highlighted by some scholars. Many scientifically grounded philosophers and psychologists have argued that we become, in part, what we practice. In other words, what seems rational or normal is variable depending on such factors as our environment and the influences of our parents and teachers—that is, what we have encountered and repeated over and over again. In short, we are creatures of habit. Of course, in this push-button age, many of our habits are sedentary. We take the car when we could walk, step into elevators when we could use the stairs, turn on the television or computer when we could ride a bicycle, and eat more than our bodies need. These habits are quite familiar to

ALBERT CAMUS AND THE MYTH OF SISYPHUS

Historical Profile

Albert Camus was born in 1913 in Algeria into a working class family of meager means. He attended the University of Algiers, where he played goalie for the football (soccer) team until an illness required that he refrain from further athletic activity, though he remained a staunch sport fan throughout his life. A novelist and playwright himself, he was once asked if he preferred theater or football. Reportedly, he quickly replied, "Football!"

A Nobel Prize–winning author, journalist, and philosopher, Camus is often classified as an existentialist even though he did not think of himself as one. His primary philosophical contribution lay in his theory of the absurd, perhaps best exemplified in his portrayal of Sisyphus, who was the embodiment of the absurd hero, the individual who affirms life without theological or metaphysical promises, assurances, or comforts—that is, without hope of accomplishing anything. According to myth, Sisyphus was condemned by the gods, for eternity, to push a heavy rock up a mountain only to stand at the top and watch it roll down the other side. As Camus (quoted in Kaufmann) wrote,

The "absurd hero" celebrates the irrationality that is a component of human existence.

Fine Art Images/Heritage Images/Getty Images

> *"It is during that return, that pause, that Sisyphus interests me. . . . I see that man going back down with a heavy yet measured step toward the torment of which he will never know the end. That hour like a breathing-space which returns as surely as his suffering, that is the hour of consciousness. At each of those moments when he leaves the heights and gradually sinks toward the lairs of the gods, he is superior to his fate. He is stronger than his rock. . . . [The decision to press on] crowns his victory. . . . The struggle toward the heights is enough to fill a man's heart. One must imagine Sisyphus happy."*

those of us who are practitioners in kinesiology, health, and recreation. We tell our students, athletes, and clients that they need to change their habits—often, unfortunately, to little avail.

Socialization is powerful, and habits resist modification. It takes years for unhealthy habits to form, and it may well take a long time to replace them. Therefore, the rationalist, exercise-is-good-for-you approach requires health and activity professionals to climb a very steep behavioral mountain by becoming, in a sense, enculturation and habit exorcists. In other words, old habits need to "come out" in order to be replaced by better choices about activity, recreation, and lifestyle. These reflections are supported by the findings of a number of exercise psychologists who have documented the limitations of rational, short-term interventions. Many studies show, for instance, that 50 percent or more of individuals who begin exercise programs for reasons related to health or appearance drop out within a year. Like many New Year's resolutions, intentions are good. But follow-up is poor!

Similar problems can be encountered when physical activity is presented more as a jewel. Many people, particularly adults in poor health, do not much like to move; in fact, that may well be one of the factors that sent them our way in the first place. Thus, to suggest that physical activity is a potentially rich playground may strike them as odd, if not absolutely absurd. Therefore, whereas most children have no trouble with this approach, adults habituated to sedentary living may resist. Those who have been habituated away from play may find it difficult to recapture their play impulses, particularly in sweaty, physical settings.

If a revitalization of play could be effected by merely introducing clients to a special playground, then the play-oriented approach would be easy to use. However, the discovery of movement playgrounds is typically not so easy to accomplish. Introductions to playgrounds do not typically produce "love at first sight." To the contrary, durable playgrounds, those that will provide pleasure for years to come, are usually grown patiently. You may know this from your own experiences of cultivating playgrounds that were perhaps introduced to you by your parents when you were young but have been expanded and shaped by you in the ensuing years. In other words, it takes time and effort to develop a would-be love affair between a mover and a movement environment. As a result, it is unlikely that movement and recreation professionals can merely present clients with a list of playground options and expect them to pick one that will provide long-lasting joy. Introductions are necessary but not sufficient; follow-up, cul-

tivation, and persistence are also required.

Paradoxically, this need may involve a move in the direction of work. Why? It is difficult to enjoy certain movement playgrounds if one is not fit, knowledgeable (of relevant rules, strategies, and culture), and reasonably well skilled. All of these elements are, in a sense, prerequisites for deeper experiences of movement pleasure. This reality suggests that admission to many movement playgrounds does not come quickly or cheaply. Therefore, a movement professional may aim at generating play but must sprinkle in heavy doses of duty and work along the way.

Final Thoughts on Holistic Work~Play Interventions

This analysis of problems with both work-tending and play-tending interventions leaves us with a provocative professional dilemma based on the realization that it can be difficult to promote lifestyle change. Behavior modification requires persistence and creativity. Professionals likely need to be not just mechanics but artists; that is, they must intuit the right moves, the right incentives, the right blend and sequence of tool and jewel approaches for each client. Of course, this endeavor takes practice and talent, and it is far easier said than done.

Our own preference falls in line with Aristotle's argument and with the knowledge that those who love to move are likely to persist in doing so. Thus, we hold that priority should be put on the jewel side of the equation for motivation and behavior modification. Here, in a nutshell, is the argument from our axiological findings: Movement as a jewel carries more axiological weight than does movement as a tool. This is the case because we do not just want to find means to the good life. We want to *live* the good life itself! In short, we want to spend our days experiencing love, knowledge, joy, friendship, adventure, and any number of other things that are good in themselves. When we help clients

Where Do You Stand On Exercise and Play?

Student Exercise

Much professional success depends on how well we can sell the "products" of our profession. Given your own personality and values, do you think it will be easier for you to convince your students or clients to become active by emphasizing the "exercise is medicine" strategy or the "activity is play" strategy? Or might some combination of the two be the best approach for you? Develop arguments for your conclusion.

---

find meaningful recreation in movement activities, we have made their lives not just healthier but richer. We have contributed not merely to quantity but to quality of life.

This may not sound like good advice for those who are employed specifically as health professionals. Many clients come to us in hopes of improving their health. Concerns about quality of life may come later and, perhaps, lie more in the province of counselors, psychiatrists, and spiritual leaders than of kinesiologists, health professionals, or recreationists.

However, here is where holism once again comes into the picture. In this theory, the development of playgrounds and the cultivation of a love of sport, dance, physical recreation, or another form of activity provides a three-for-one health benefit.

1. The playground itself may require the expenditure of effort and other health-promoting behaviors. Focusing on fun and enjoyment does not prevent high heart rates, for example, from providing the benefits they provide.

2. Those who love to move are more likely to persist, and those who persist in physical activity will be healthier. In short, play is one of the best motivators known to humankind.

3. Joy, pleasure, happiness, and overall zest for life are themselves preventive and medicinal. People who play improve their health holistically—with higher heart rates *and* higher

degrees of joy. Physical play positively affects both muscle and meaning, and both kinds of effects contribute to longer, healthier lives. This fact suggests that professionals should support holistic philosophies and shape their programs accordingly—even if the primary goal is improved health.

Our Neolithic ancestors did not face the same kinds of health problems that we encounter today, but in many ways they worked~played like we do in the 21st century. Physical work and play stand as universal themes in the development of our race. Utility and joy, in some form or other, were present in the long evolution of the human species. Both were and still are important; both were and still are valuable. However, the ways in which our ancestors worked and played were also, at least to some degree, different from our ways. The meanings associated with their work and play were, at least in part, different from the meanings associated with our own. Such meanings even differed between city-states in various parts of the world during Neolithic times.

These facts lead to problems of interpretation. As we address in the next chapter, two city-states in ancient Greek civilization came to epitomize the classical debate over the value of sport and physical education as utilitarian instruments for producing power and as moral components ennobling the quest for the "good life." In particular, Sparta became the symbol of physical culture as a tool, whereas Athens became the symbol of physical culture as a jewel.

The Difficulties of Interpreting Ancient Sporting Cultures

Careful examination of the depiction of Sparta as a tool and of Athens as a jewel reveals that such concepts are idealized archetypes that sometimes mask deeper complexities. For instance, ancient Spartans sometimes exercised to experience the joy of movement rather than as ceaseless preparation for combat. Similarly, ancient Athenians sometimes found sport a useful tool in training citizens for the mundane duties of war and commerce rather than always practicing athletic habits as deep philosophical commitments. Thus interpretation of ancient sporting cultures requires careful analysis and must often go beyond simple acceptance of evidence at face value.

Ancient cultures certainly provide both archaeological and iconographic evidence of the tool and jewel importance of sport in the civilizations that developed during the Neolithic Revolution. We have sporting implements from ancient games, such as the *halteres* (hand weights) used by ancient Greek long jumpers. We have the remains of monumental structures devoted to sporting contests—the hippodromes and stadiums of Western civilization and the ball courts of Mesoamerican civilization. These material relics comprise the archaeological record. We also have depictions, etched into stone and painted onto pottery, of sporting contests from all corners of the ancient world that demonstrate their connections to the development of warrior skills and the expression of religious convictions. These relics comprise the epigraphical record. We even have some early writings about sporting contests, culminating in Homer's *Iliad*, the earliest well-developed literary account of the meaning of sport in ancient culture. We have other remnants in the legends, sagas, and myths not only of Western cultures but also of other centers that led the "rise of civilization."

Still, in contrast with the massive amounts of data we have about sport in the past few centuries, we must make bold interpretative speculations based on our limited ancient evidence from literary, epigraphical, and archaeological sources to explore and explain their sporting worlds. Moreover, accounts from ancient civilizations are often swaddled in their own cultural, political, and religious contexts and should not be interpreted through simple literal logic, as demonstrated by the stories of pharaohs performing superhuman athletic feats.

A Model of Traditional Sport

The vast and diverse array of sporting customs and systems of physical activity that we find in the Neolithic Revolution seemingly defies categorization. These games and activities varied immensely from city to city and from civilization to civilization. Still, on close inspection, a few general patterns emerge. Sport and physical activity during this long period of human history were deeply intertwined with religious habits, the art of warfare, and the formation of communal identity. From some perspectives, these patterns appear to highlight the universal dimensions of the history of sport—the concept that certain basic features have characterized sport at all times, in all places, and in all cultures. In our own world, sport remains a crucial element in the creation of communal identities, and on occasion, it is still used in training soldiers and even manifests a few connections to religious practices. In addition, we still practice some of the same skills as our ancient forebearers in our modern sporting contests, including footraces, jumping and throwing events, combat sports such as boxing and wrestling, and even horse racing.

Much more important from the historical perspective, however, are the particular characteristics that differ between ancient and modern sporting practices—that is, the ways in which sport varies over time, across place, and between cultures. Focusing specifically on the contrasts across time—the comparisons between what one of the world's leading sport scholars, Allen Guttmann, has simply dubbed "*then* and *now*"—is essential to understanding the history of sport (for more on Guttmann's model, see chapter 6). How different was ancient sport from our modern forms of sport? We can build a model of ancient sporting traditions that reveals some broad generalities that differ significantly from modern sporting customs. Although multiple exceptions to some of the characteristics appear in the historical record, ancient sport manifested five unique characteristics that appeared with considerable frequency and that provide us with lines of demarcation between ancient and modern conceptions of physical activity. The following two lists summarize the difference:

A Model of Traditional Sport: Key Characteristics

Sacred

Local

Martial

Durable

Unequal

Allen Guttmann's Model of Modern Sport: Key Elements

Secularism

Equality

Rationalization

Bureaucratization

Specialization

Quantification

Quest for records

Sport in traditional societies was frequently a sacred practice, and ancient sporting customs were often connected to religious rituals in ways that modern sports are not. Although some contemporary commentators describe sport as the modern world's "new religion," they are generally seeking to describe the passion with which we embrace sport, a trait that they think was reserved for religious faith in earlier human epochs. They do not mean that sport has become a system of beliefs explaining the cause, nature, and purpose of existence. However (as we address in chapter 3), the fundamental purpose of the athletic festivals staged by the ancient Greeks was to honor their gods—not, as in the modern version of the Olympics, to celebrate human athletic excellence. For the ancient Greeks, athletic contests served not only as tests of human prowess but also as religious rituals.

Ancient sport was also consistently martial—that is, connected to the art and practice of warfare. Accordingly, it involved much more accurate and realistic simulations of combat than does modern sport. Ancient war games taught weaponry skills, schooled participants in the fundamentals of hand-to-hand engagement, and inculcated the psychological skills necessary to withstand the rigors of battle. Ancient Greeks sometimes argued vociferously over whether athletic contests were in fact the best methods for teaching warcraft (as we discuss in chapter 3). Nevertheless, even though modern militaries around the globe sometimes still use sport in training exercises, the ancient contests were much closer approximations of human experiences in war than are modern sports.

Ancient sports were also quite durable. The festivals and games created by ancient cultures often persisted for thousands of years and remained remarkably stable and unchanging over these enormous spans of time. Century after century, Mesoamericans played ball games, Irish clans celebrated the Tailteann Games, and ancient Greeks conducted hundreds of athletic festivals, foremost among them the Olympic Games, which lasted for 1,170 years (776 BCE–394 CE) with relatively little fundamental change in the nature of the contests. For comparison, the modern Olympics, which began in 1896, would have to endure until 3066 to equal the duration of the ancient Olympics.

From this perspective, modern sports are quite new and may yet prove to be relatively ephemeral. Indeed, the modern Olympics showcase some sports that are only a few decades old, such as mountain biking, triathlon, snowboarding, and freestyle skiing. Even if we push the notion and argue that these new "action" sports are really just evolutions of older forms of cycling, skiing, and multi-event endurance racing, we have to admit that these broader categories have existed in their modern forms for less than two centuries. Even basketball, which may strike you as an "ancient" pastime since it was invented in 1891, is just a little more than a century old—and thus a flash in the pan in the historical long view.

Ancient sports generally involved local customs and practices. They were rooted in particular places, unlike modern sports, which frequently have universal rules. For example, for the most part, basketball is basketball and soccer is soccer around the world, and similar rule books apply regardless of place or culture. In contrast, the Mesoamerican ball game should really be understood as a family of games with similar features but also with significant variations from city to city and from culture to culture. Most ancient sporting competitions were similarly rooted in local communities. Athletes rarely traveled great distances to play competitors. Local customs and traditions were generally passed down orally rather than through written documents. Thus, in contrast to the national and international dimensions of modern sporting practices, ancient sporting traditions were rooted in local communities.

On one level, some of the ancient Greek athletic festivals might be thought of as exceptions to this pattern. The games at Olympia, Delphi, Nemea, and Corinth (the latter known as the Isthmian Games) were clearly Panhellenic and drew athletes from thousands of miles of territory beyond the Grecian isles—that is, from the vast empire that made up the greater Greek world of antiquity (for more details of these games, see chapter 3). At the same time, however, the athletic festivals on this circuit were each deeply rooted in their own particular locations because they were tied to the geography of Greek religion and to the shrines, which honored particular gods, housed in each place.

Finally, ancient sport was fundamentally unequal, whereas equality lies at the core of modern ideas about sport (for a modern model of sport, see chapter 6). Equality suffuses modern sport in two basic ways. First, modern sporting customs hold in high regard the ideal of equal opportunity to compete, even if in some cases our sporting institutions do not always live up to that ideal. More specifically, in modern sport, the opportunity to compete and to have one's performance judged fairly is supposed to be determined by talent and accomplishment—not by economic class, racial heritage, ethnic background, gender, religion, or any other social category. Modern sport also values the ideal of equality in the conditions of competition, which can involve, for example, creating weight classes in combat sports in order to balance matches or including the same number of players on each team in order to construct equal barriers for each athlete to overcome. In contrast, we would find it strange, even unfathomable, to see goals of two different sizes in hockey or unequal distances set for competitors in footraces because such conditions would violate the central role we assign to equality in our games. Not coincidentally, equality stands as one of the dominant ideals in modern world views.

CHAPTER WRAP-UP

Wrapping Up and Looking Ahead

For many ancient cultures, a fundamental inequality rather than equality reflected their perspectives on social order and their sporting habits reflected their perceptions of who got to compete and how contests were structured. For instance, most ancient cultures excluded women from many sporting endeavors. They also excluded those who did not share their ethnic or religious backgrounds, and it was rare for a sporting activity to include members of different social or economic classes. For example, as shown in chapter 3, the ancient Greeks restricted participation in their Olympics to freeborn male citizens of Greek city-states; all others were barred from the sacred stadium at Olympia. The inequality embedded in ancient sport sometimes extended to the conditions of competition as well. For instance, weight classes were unknown in ancient combat sports. In addition, early ball games often featured teams of unequal sizes playing on fields of unequal lengths and seeking to score into goals of unequal dimensions.

In short, ancient sport reflected and reinforced the unequal social worlds that people inhabited. It also reflected and reinforced the dominance of religion in ancient cultures, as well as the martial ethic, the durable nature of institutions and customs, and the local focus of everyday life. The model of ancient sport as sacred, martial, durable, local, and unequal provides an important juxtaposition to modern ideas about sport, thus reinforcing the reality that for all the similarities in human physical activity across time, the differences between *then* and *now*—between *them* and *us*—are profound.

Study Questions

1. What were the most important changes in lifestyle ushered in during the Neolithic Revolution?

2. Did most of the changes work for the better or for the worse for our Neolithic ancestors? How did these changes affect nutrition, activity, and human health and vigor?

3. What role did sport, and particularly prowess in physical activity, play in the development of Neolithic societies? How does that role differ from the role played by similar activities in Paleolithic societies?

4. What does it mean to envision physical activity as a tool or as a jewel? What is added to this interpretation by holistic philosophy? Why does it make sense to consider the importance of play in exercise?

5. Why, and on what grounds, was sport in the Neolithic era both different from and the same as the sport we experience today?

ANCIENT GREECE AND THE SHAPE OF MODERN SPORT AND PHYSICAL EDUCATION

The Power of the Past in the Present and Future

Chapter Objectives

In this chapter, you will

1. learn about the importance of sport to ancient Greece's religious and cultural practices;

2. examine Greek contributions to the birth of philosophy, including its founders and intellectual foundations, as well as its main branches and one of its major ethical theories;

3. discover the Panhellenic sporting festivals and the place of athletes in Greek society;

4. explore methodological considerations related to historical evidence and philosophical inquiry;

5. compare various philosophical interpretations of physical education and consider the role of physical education in the 21st century.

The Neolithic Revolution generated profound transformations in human societies as sedentary farming communities and powerful city-states replaced the nomadic hunting and foraging tribes of old. In these new human societies, sport and physical activity provided common experiences that helped foster a sense of community and shape civic identities. Sport served particularly important social functions in Greece, perhaps more than in any other ancient culture. Specifically, it promoted Greek cultural and ethnic unity while providing a platform for both individual and civic displays of skill, athletic prowess, wealth, and ingenuity. Sport also reflected and reinforced the dominance of religion in ancient Greek culture, as well as its martial ethic, the durable nature of its institutions and customs, and the local—and eventually Panhellenic (all-Greek)—values of everyday life.

The Foundation of Western Civilization

Perhaps no civilization has influenced Western culture more than ancient Greece has. From the Archaic period of the 8th to 6th centuries BCE to the end of antiquity (the end of the 5th century CE), the ancient Greeks presided over a vast empire that spanned the western Mediterranean into central Asia and North Africa. Although Greek civilization flowered more than 2,500 years ago, the ideas of the ancient Greeks continue to influence modern Western culture, particularly in politics, art, theatre, philosophy, and science. Such contributions to humanity's intellectual life are among the ancient Greeks' greatest legacies. Key words such as *democracy* and *atom* trace back to ancient Greece, and entire academic disciplines—such as philosophy, biology, medicine, and even kinesiology—took shape from Greek antecedents. In fact, so much of ancient Greece remains present that if one transplanted the ancient Greek philosophers

Socrates, Plato, and Aristotle into a university's introductory philosophy seminar, they not only would be comfortable joining in a discussion about justice or beauty but also would recognize many of the sporting activities taking place in or around the *gymnasium*—another Greek word that survives today.

Such parallels illustrate ancient Greece's seminal influence on the history and philosophy of sport and physical activity. In fact, the story of organized sport in the ancient world is primarily the story of ancient Greece. The Greeks were the first to organize play at the cultural level. For more than a thousand years, hundreds of athletic festivals were held across the ancient Greek world, including the Olympic Games. Greek athletes dedicated their lives to the pursuit of athletic excellence and the rewards of fame, wealth, and prestige. The male athletic body was celebrated in Greek art, literature, and practice. The Greeks studied its anatomical structure and physiological function and provided regular training in physical education. At the gymnasium and the palaestra (wrestling school), ancient Greek boys and men cultivated their physical and mental skills under the watchful eye of a *paidotribes*, the world's first physical educator (kinesiologist).

Ancient Greece, however, did not spring forth as a fully formed culture. Understanding how it changed and developed can provide us with important lessons for interpreting the past and many of its features, and the debates the ancient Greeks generated offer useful lessons for us in the 21st century.

Myth, Religion, and the Origins of Greek Physical Culture

The origins of Greece's rich and vibrant sporting culture are difficult to discern. Who taught the Greeks to play? Why did the Greeks elevate sport, the body, and physical education to such a prominent position in their society? Scholars have found partial answers to these questions in Greek literature. The earliest and greatest literary depictions of Greek sporting competition are found in Homer's epics, the *Iliad* and the *Odyssey*. As we briefly discussed in chapter 2, Homer's poetic accounts of the Trojan War and of Odysseus' long and arduous journey back home from Troy following a Greek military victory depict a Greek world familiar with athletic contests. Homer tells of a mighty Mycenaean civilization (1600 BCE–1100 BCE) in which Greek social elites performed heroic deeds both in battle and in athletic contests. The Greeks created an agonistic culture, one dedicated to elite demonstrations of military and physical skill, prowess, and competitiveness. Homer sung of mighty Greek kings, princes, and generals striving to acquire *kleos* (glory and reputation) and to display and reaffirm their *arete* (excellence or virtue) through competitive endeavors, including athletics.

The *Iliad*

The description of the funeral games of Patroclus (for more on this, see chapter 2) in book 23 of the *Iliad* provides detailed insight into early Greek sporting culture. When Achilles, the great warrior-hero of the Trojan War, learns of Patroclus' death at the hands of the Trojan prince Hector, he arranges a funeral celebration to honor the life of his fallen friend. Homer's epic demonstrates that funeral games—athletic contests held in memory of a dead hero—were an integral feature of Mycenaean culture. As part of the funeral festivities, Achilles organizes athletic contests in chariot racing, running, boxing, wrestling, archery, javelin, weight throwing, and dueling with weapons. He displays his patronage to the social elites that competed in these contests of athletic skill and prowess by offering a valuable *athlon* (prize). As Homer noted, sport and

religion in the ancient Greek world were inextricably linked. The Greeks saw an intimate connection between the natural and spiritual realms. Accordingly, victors in the funeral games of Patroclus were often depicted as triumphing not by physical skill alone but through divine intervention. The goddess Athena, for example, ensures that the pious Diomedes wins the chariot race, retrieving his whip and later breaking the chariot yoke of Diomedes' rival, Eumelos. Similarly, when Odysseus prays to Athena for enhanced speed, the goddess honors his request, even going so far as to trip the younger, fleet-footed Ajax and forcing him to land in a pile of dung.

The *Odyssey*

In the *Odyssey*, Homer's romantic tale of wonders and wandering, sport continues to occupy a position of great importance. In book 8, the great warrior-hero Odysseus, king of Ithaca, washes ashore on the mythical island of Phaeacia. Exhausted and unrecognizable as a social elite due to his unkempt appearance, Odysseus first encounters a young princess, Nausicaa, playing with a ball to the rhythm of music. Taking pity on the bedraggled stranger, she invites him to the palace, where he is greeted as a guest of king Alcinos and treated to a royal banquet. Homer's poetic accounts describe local Phaeacian men attempting to impress their mysterious guest by competing in running, wrestling, boxing, and discus throwing.

Unwilling to reveal his true identity, and embarrassed by his ragged appearance, Odysseus spurns requests to compete against the best men of Phaeacia. Only when a brash young wrestler, Euryalos, challenges Odysseus' manhood and *arete* with the words "you must not be an athlete" does the mighty Greek king enter the fray. With the poise and strength befitting a warrior-hero, Odysseus hurls a giant *diskos* (discus) so far that the Phaeacians cower in admiration. Throughout the remainder of Homer's episodic tale, Odysseus competes in other contests of physical skill and athleticism. He defeats a beggar in an impromptu boxing match, and in the final scene (in book 21), he strings his great bow and fires an arrow through the sockets of 12 axe-handles as part of a contest to win back his wife, Penelope, after spending more than a decade away, initially at war and then adrift at sea.

Odysseus and Virtue Ethics

The accounts provided by both the *Iliad* and the *Odyssey* tell us a great deal about the ethics of the ancient Greeks. For example, Homer's hero Odysseus embodies the Greek notion of virtue. This quality would later form the centerpiece of one of ancient Greece's significant ethical theories, known as virtue ethics. In ethics, philosophers attempt to systematize, defend, and recommend concepts of right and wrong actions. Ethical systems help provide frameworks for navigating moral problems as they arise. Though virtue ethics would not receive its full development as an ethical system until Aristotle, its central tenets are embodied by Homer's hero Odysseus.

Unlike consequentialist or deontological theories of ethics (see chapters 6 and 7, respectively), virtue ethics emphasizes a person's character rather than the good consequences of the person's actions or the person's duty to certain ethical principles. In other words, rather than working to find the right principle or the most beneficial outcome, virtue ethics seeks to cultivate virtues. In this view, once people improve their virtues, they naturally do the right thing. Odysseus, for example, had cultivated the virtue of courage, which he demonstrated in various situations, such as fighting a Cyclops or convincing the witch-goddess Circe to change his men

VIRTUE ETHICS IN THE CONTEMPORARY WORLD

Historical Profile

Virtue ethics dominated Western moral philosophy from ancient Greece until the Enlightenment (and it has even deeper roots in Chinese philosophy). However, it later fell out of favor as deontology and utilitarianism began to offer promising alternatives. This trend was reversed in the 1950s, when first Elizabeth Anscombe and later Alasdair MacIntyre, revived interest in virtue ethics.

MacIntyre was born in Scotland in 1929 and was educated in London. He pursued a historical method of philosophy that rejected idealistic, phenomenological, and relativistic methodologies. While not claiming absolute truth or certainty, he identified the virtue ethics of Aristotle as offering the best insights into moral action for determining ethical behavior. Perhaps more than any other single contemporary philosopher, MacIntyre is responsible for the revival of virtue ethics and its continuing popularity.

MacIntyre and other contemporary virtue ethicists continued to draw on Greek ideals of *phronesis* and *eudaimonia*. Much like Homer, they situated ethics in social practices, such as educating, parenting, fighting, governing, and competing in athletics. In this view, virtues are required in order to realize the excellences that are available in these demanding practices. Thus athletes need to play honestly (a virtue) in their sport (a social practice) in order to realize some of the excellences that are available there (the internal goods of the sport). Regarding life in general, MacIntyre concluded that integrity or consistency was the virtue that transcended specific social practices and formed the basis for living the good life.

back from swine. Greek expositions of virtue ethics assumed that a person with good virtues will identify the right ethical action, much like the movements of a good compass will always find north.

The Greek emphasis on virtue ethics can be seen in ancient Greece's veneration for *arete*. This emphasis was apparent in Greek sport, which allowed individuals to cultivate and display virtues such as courage, strength, intelligence, and justice. Odysseus illustrates his *arete* at numerous points throughout Homer's epic, especially when impressing the Phaeacians by hurling the giant discus. This internal excellence guides Odysseus to right actions regardless of the setting. In another example, in the funeral games of Patroclus, Athena helps Diomedes win the chariot race because of his internal virtue; in turn, his publicly displayed success provides outward evidence of his internal *arete*.

Virtue ethics was formulated in part by the ancient Greek philosopher Aristotle (384 BCE–322 BCE). He concluded that a person becomes virtuous by practicing right actions. In order to practice right actions, Aristotle concluded, individuals must use moral wisdom (*phronesis*) to identify the ultimate aim (*telos*) of good actions—those that promote happiness or human flourishing (*eudaimonia*). Hence Aristotle concluded that ethical reasoning follows from two pressing questions: What is the good life? How do I live it?

Beyond Myth and Mystery

In the Mycenaean Greek world depicted by Homer, aristocratic funeral games and sport and athletic contests took place regularly in social and religious settings. This fact might seem to suggest that the earlier, Bronze Age Mycenaeans were the inspiration for the development of a later Greek sporting culture. However, many scholars strongly disagree. After all, Homer's epics blend fact with fiction, mixing historical events with myth and mystery. Moreover, although the *Iliad* and the *Odyssey* have their basis in the realities of the Mycenaean era (1600 BCE–1000 BCE), they were composed between 750 BCE and 725 BCE and better reflect the Archaic Age (800 BCE–480 BCE) in which Homer lived. For example, archaeological evidence proves the existence of Mycenaean funeral games in which competitors boxed and drove chariots, but it does not support Homer's claims that earlier, Bronze Age Greeks were skilled athletes who threw javelins and discuses, wrestled, and ran footraces. It appears, then, that Homer projected the athletic contests of his own day onto a murky and distant past in order to highlight the drama and personalities of his epics.

Whether or not Homer's accounts were grounded in historical fact, his contemporary (and later) audiences felt a great sense of cultural obligation to preserve these funeral sporting rituals. If Achilles and Odysseus were great athletes who enjoyed heroic status, then future generations of Greeks should also be inspired to train, strive, and compete. But scholars agree that early Greek sport did not have a single origin or a linear development. Rather, Greek sport emerged out of a confluence of social and political changes that occurred during the Archaic Age.

Even as Greeks sought to keep alive the funeral traditions of old, they reorganized their lands into independent political units, each of which was referred to as a *polis* (city-state). Each polis had its own religious temples and altars, *agoras* (marketplaces) gymnasia, theaters, and monetary currencies. As ambitions and competition for resources grew, ruling elites in these self-governing city-states slowly embraced organized sport as a means to measure and proclaim wealth, power, and status. As a result, civic expenditure on sport, physical fitness, and military

Archaeologists have uncovered pottery from the Archaic period, in which Homer lived, depicting runners much like those described by the poet. Physical evidence does not, however, indicate that these running events were practiced by the Mycenaean Greeks of Odysseus' era.

preparedness soared, and athletic talent became a precious commodity. Political leaders dedicated considerable resources to sport by sponsoring, establishing, and even reforming athletic contests. The mere act of hosting and administering sporting festivals was deemed a platform for demonstrating civic pride, ingenuity, and vitality.

In their quest for resources and recognition, rival Greek *poleis* (the plural of *polis*) eventually sought opportunities for land and trade overseas. They spread throughout the Mediterranean world, establishing colonies (each one a new polis) in such faraway regions as southern France, North Africa, and the Black Sea. In these foreign lands, Greeks fought to preserve and celebrate their ethnic identity in the face of competing local traditions. Scholars assert that sport served as a vessel for ensuring cultural integrity by binding remote Greek colonies to the motherland. Thus sport served an even higher social and cultural function in archaic Greece in that activities such as running, jumping, boxing, and wrestling represented Greek identity. In this way, sport functioned as a culturally unifying bond.

The Birth of Philosophy

Ancient Greece was not, however, just a culture in kinetic motion. In spite of (or perhaps because of) the culture's frenetic mixture of sport, war, and politics, an unprecedented intellectual revolution also swept through ancient Greece. Scholars have labeled this revolution the Ionian Enlightenment, and it fundamentally changed how people understood the world. It began around the city-state of Miletus in the 6th century BCE, where a handful of intellectually minded Greeks began to see the world as something governed by natural and rational causes that could be explained via observable phenomena. Previous civilizations had assumed either that the natural world lacked order or that supernatural forces governed every natural phenomenon, from weather to earthquakes. For instance, if an apple fell from a tree, the cause was held not to be gravity but Athena or some other anthropomorphized god.

Thales and the Ionian Enlightenment

This attitude began to change thanks to Thales of Miletus. Regarded by many, including Aristotle, as the first philosopher, Thales lived on the coast of Asia Minor in what today would be part of Turkey. Curious as to why natural objects behaved in certain ways, he rejected the prevailing belief that supernatural forces caused natural events. A student of mathematics, Thales used geometry to accurately predict a solar eclipse. Rather than claiming that it was a divinely inspired event, he argued that an unseen set of rational principles or laws governed the natural world. Moreover, he asserted, the power of human reason made these principles knowable. Therefore, by applying reason, humans could figure out how the natural world operated.

Today, we take such basic assumptions for granted because we live in a universe where humans have walked on the moon and split the atom. But for the ancient Greeks, the Ionian Enlightenment ushered in a revolutionary change in perspective, such that the natural world now had order, which was governed by a handful of principles or laws that could be understood through reason. The physicist and philosopher Gerald Holton labeled the emergence of this new attitude the Ionian Enchantment because it was as much a conviction as it was a discovery (without the belief, one would not even be able to talk about the notion of discovery). Arguably, this Ionian paradigm shift in human thinking eclipses more famous examples of scientific revolutions that revealed, for instance, that the world was a sphere or that the earth orbits the sun. With the adoption of this attitude, forms of human discovery became possible. Thus everything from philosophy and formal logic (e.g., if A equals B, and if B equals C, then A must equal C) to physics and biology owe their existence to the discovery that reason can identify natural laws to explain natural events. Imagine trying to understand how a cell works or arguing why slavery is unjust without using reason. When an e-mail arrives on a computer or a plane lifts off of the ground, we assume that these events are based on valid principles, even if we cannot personally explain the binary system or the tenets of aeronautical engineering.

The Ionian shift in how humans thought about the world, and about what was knowable, ushered in a flood of discoveries during the 5th and 4th centuries BCE. This period is known as the Classical or Hellenic period in Greek history. Applying *logos* (reason), Greece nurtured scholars such as Hippocrates (the philosopher and medical physician who established the Hippocratic oath), Pythagoras (the mathematician who provided proof of the Pythagorean theorem), Democritus (the physicist who believed that the world was assembled of small "atoms" that could bind together), Parmenides (the epistemologist who showed the difference between truth and opinion)—among many others, whose discoveries collectively shaped the trajectory of Western thought. By explaining the complexity of the natural world through rational laws rather than supernatural myths, humanity embarked on a project of discovery that continues to this day. When physicists smash protons and electrons, and when space probes send back evidence of salt crystals from distant planets, humanity continues a tradition of inquiry initiated by a handful of Ionian philosophers in ancient Greece.

The Ionian Enlightenment illustrates an important point that contemporary society often overlooks. Behind scientific inquiry rest philosophical premises. These premises—that the natural world has order, that this order is knowable, and that it can be described with basic principles—can be identified only through reason. They cannot be empirically shown. In other words, science cannot prove itself. To justify scientific enquiry, science depends on rational arguments about the nature of truth, objectivity, and reason derived from philosophical inquiries. This is just one more example of the humanities and the sciences working together to support human discovery, a saga that traces back to Thales and his intellectual descendants.

Socrates, Plato, and Aristotle

Even as the Ionian Enlightenment gave rise to a number of insights about the physical world, it also gave people permission to question widely held beliefs, even though some communities were not ready for the results. This critical form of inquiry provided the fertile ground that generated three of the most significant philosophers of Western thought: Socrates, Plato, and Aristotle. It is hard to overestimate the scope of the influence exerted by these three thinkers on Western culture. Consider how global religions such as Christianity and Islam trace their lineage to Jesus of Nazareth and Muhammad, respectively, and thus also to Greek thinking. These religious figures occupied a world in which the philosophy of Socrates, Plato, and Aristotle was already widespread. Plato's

dialogues were written almost 400 years before Jesus walked the earth and nearly 1,000 years prior to Muhammad's birth. Hence religious scholars have noted Greek philosophy's presence in many of Western civilization's religious texts alongside Hebrew, Babylonian, and Egyptian influences.

Such outsize influence stems from outsize characters, and Socrates was such a person. Not only does the modern philosophic world consider Socrates the first philosopher of any significance (apologies to Thales), but it also measures philosophical progress against his contributions by labeling all philosophers before him as "pre-Socratic." Born in 470 BCE, Socrates lived before good records or other historical accounts were common; thus, little is known of his life. In several places, however, references indicate that Socrates served with some distinction as a hoplite (foot soldier) in the Athenian army during the Peloponnesian War. He is also depicted as a person who constantly provoked the citizens of Athens with questions and conversation. He claimed that he asked so many questions because he could not find any answers. More often than not, however, his conversations exposed how little others knew about the world. In practice, his question-and-answering provided a useful method (known today as the Socratic method) for inquiry by using critical thinking to illuminate ideas or expose flaws in reasoning.

Eventually, in 399 BCE, tiring of Socrates' constant questions, the citizens of Athens put him on trial for corrupting the youth with his controversial ideas. Many suspect, however, that the real reason behind his trial may have been his willingness to expose the ignorance of prominent leaders. After refusing to recant his teachings, Socrates used his trial to further provoke the audience by pointing out that philosophy begins with ignorance, a quality which he argued that his accusers possessed in abundance. Unpersuaded by his arguments, the judges found Socrates guilty. Following the tradition of Athenian courts, they then allowed the accuser and the defendant to each propose a punishment for the judges to consider. The accusers proposed the death penalty, whereas Socrates suggested he should be "punished" with free meals for life paid for by the citizens of Athens, a prize normally awarded to Olympic champions. Weighing the two options, the judges sentenced Socrates to death by drinking poisonous hemlock.

For whatever reason, Socrates never wrote anything down. (Perhaps, true to his word, he thought he never knew anything worth recording.) Thus, much of what we know about his thought (and his life) comes from his student Plato, who lived from 429 BCE to 348 BCE. Plato was the child of an aristocratic Athenian family and received some of the best education available in Athens before becoming a devoted student of Socrates. Inspired by his mentor's life and death, Plato created a series of written works called dialogues, in which the character of Socrates typically asks questions of a cast of rotating characters as they explore topics such as love, beauty, truth, and justice. Among his notable contributions, Plato puts forward an explanation of knowledge in his dialogue *Theaetetus*. He argues that knowledge is justified true belief. That is, in order to know something, a person must *believe* something is true that actually *is* true and be able to justify that belief's accuracy.

Running throughout Plato's work is the idea that every material object or quality is an imperfect reproduction of its true form or essence. Coming to understand an object's essence would let us correctly identify it in the world. For example, understanding the essence of sport would help explain why we consider baseball, wrestling, and tennis to be sports but not ballet or chess. Though many philosophers have revised, amended, or abandoned some of Plato's positions, even more agree that he asked the right questions. This agreement prompted a famous 20th-century philosopher, Alfred North Whitehead, to assert that the "safest general characterization of the European philosophical tradition is that it consists of a series of footnotes to Plato."

The first philosopher to offer those footnotes was a pupil of Plato named Aristotle. Born in 384 BCE, Aristotle joined Plato's Academy at age 18 and stayed there for nearly 20 years before embarking on travels throughout Greece. In 343 BCE, Aristotle became tutor and advisor to Alexander, the son of Phillip II of Macedon. Alexander later became known as Alexander the Great and led Greek conquests of Persia, Asia Minor, and North Africa. During Alexander's conquests, Aristotle returned to Athens and started a rival school called the Lyceum.

Unlike Plato, Aristotle did not use dialogues in his writing, which covered many subjects in philosophy as well as early investigations of physics, biology, and zoology. His work on logic and ethics proved to be among his most durable contributions. In *Nicomachean Ethics*, Aristotle developed in detail the moral theory known as virtue ethics. Always focused on the practical, he systematically investigated reasoning, the results of which comprised his work *Prior Analytics*. In that work, he showed how logical argument could use deductive reasoning to go from premises (claims known to be true) to a valid conclusion. For example, the premise that all men are mortal and the premise that Socrates is a man can be combined to conclude that Socrates is mortal. Aristotle's work on reasoning also included several principles, such as the principle of noncontradiction (two contradictory statements cannot be true at the same time) and the law of the excluded middle (if A is either happy [H] or not happy [¬H], then A cannot be both positions at the same time, that is, both happy and unhappy—or written out in symbolic logic [H· ¬H]). Aristotle's work on logic forms the backbone of philosophical knowledge by showing how good arguments can be separated from bad ones.

The Branches of Philosophy

In addition to their own philosophy, Socrates, Plato, and Aristotle pioneered questions in what philosophers would later come to describe as philosophy's main branches or areas of inquiry. (For a brief overview of these branches, see this book's introduction.) Similar to the way in which natural science branches into biology, chemistry, astronomy, earth science, and physics, philosophy ramifies into metaphysics, epistemology, ethics, aesthetics, and logic.

These branches can help illustrate how philosophy works to produce a body of knowledge. *Metaphysics*, loosely translated from Greek as "beyond the physical," deals with the essence or nature of things. Thus Plato was doing metaphysics when he discussed forms and essences. *Epistemology* deals with knowledge and helps explain what is meant by truth, or how one can distinguish justified beliefs from personal opinions. To identify good actions, *ethics* attempts to systematize, defend, and recommend concepts of right and wrong conduct. *Aesthetics*, on the other hand, concerns itself with beauty, including how judgment and taste relate to works of art. *Logic* explores reasoning in order to determine whether a given conclusion follows validly from premises or other kinds of arguments. Its focus can range from fallacies in natural-language arguments to symbolic abstractions that use letters and signs to show connections. (The previous discussion of Aristotle's principle of noncontradiction provided you with an example of symbolic logic.)

Though philosophers often refer to these five main branches, the distinctions between them are not always sharp. Indeed, many philosophical questions draw on knowledge from multiple fields. For example, the question "How do we know that a painting is beautiful?" requires answers from epistemology and aesthetics. The question "What is the nature of the good life?" combines insights from ethics and aesthetics and is often referred to as a subbranch called *axiology*. At the same time, philosophy has also developed specialized topical branches, such as the philosophy of sport, the philosophy of science, and the philosophy of law, each of which draws on all of philosophy's major branches to examine its dedicated subject matter. You can examine table 3.1 to better understand philosophy's six branches and consider how they connect to the philosophy of sport—a topic that Socrates, Plato, and Aristotle certainly considered.

Table 3.1 Six Branches of Philosophy

Name	What it studies	Question it asks
Metaphysics	The nature of things	What are the defining features of a given action or object?
Epistemology	Study of knowledge	How does one know that something is true?
Ethics	Study of right actions	What should a person do?
Aesthetics	Study of beauty	What is beautiful?
Logic	Study of reasoning	Is a given line of reasoning valid?
Axiology	Study of value	What is the good life?

Kinds of Philosophic Questions

Student Exercise

Now examine table 3.2 and match each branch of philosophy to a question about the philosophy of sport. Then come up with a philosophy of sport question for each branch on your own. Finally, give a brief answer to each question in the table; provide reasons to justify your positions.

Table 3.2   Matching Branches with their Questions

Branches	Questions
Logic	What is the essence of play?
Aesthetics	Should professional female and male marathon runners receive equal prize money for winning a race?
Ethics	Do intentional fouls at the end of a basketball game harm the viewing experience for fans?
Epistemology	If a runner runs faster, he can win the race; but if every runner runs faster, can every runner win the race?
Metaphysics	Can a referee be certain that she has made the correct call, even if she uses instant replay?
Axiology	Is the length of life or quality of life more important?
Combination	How does sport contribute to the good life?

The Ancient Sporting Festivals

In their philosophical ruminations, Socrates, Plato, and Aristotle considered the role of physical activity and sport in human life. Specifically, they advocated physical education as a key component of citizenship in the polis, debated the connection between bodies and minds, and counseled balance in developing physical and intellectual skills. (For more on their thoughts, see the section titled Greek Recreation and Physical Education later in this chapter.) They turned to these subjects in part because they raised fundamental questions about the nature of human beings and in part because sport was a fundamental component of ancient Greek culture. In fact, sport grew sufficiently to become an integral feature of Greek culture both throughout the Greek mainland and in its distant colonial settlements.

The earlier aristocratic funeral games, famously described and embellished by Homer, persisted, but the Archaic Age also saw the emergence of religious and state athletic festivals, which transformed sport from an exclusively elite preserve into a popular pastime enjoyed by all levels of Greek male society. Over time, a Panhellenic athletic system took shape, in which Greek city-states and religious sanctuaries played host to a spectacular array of sporting festivals. The oldest and most prestigious of the Greek athletic festivals was the Olympic Games. The Greeks held their Olympics at Olympia, a remote religious sanctuary where, according to mythology, the gods and heroes mingled to accomplish feats deserving immortal praise. The ancient Olympics were held every four years without interruption for at least 1,170 years. With their elaborate program of running, equestrian, and combat events, as well as prayers, processions, sacrifices, and feasting, the Olympics constituted a sacred athletic festival in honor of Zeus, the king of the Greek gods.

The Panhellenic Festivals

The success and popularity of the Olympics inspired the creation of three other major athletic festivals also held at religious sanctuaries that belonged not to any polis but to the gods: the Pythian Games in Delphi, the Isthmian Games in Corinth, and the Nemean Games in Nemea. Along with the Olympics, these festivals formed a circuit (*periodos*) known as the Panhellenic Games (see table 3.3), which comprised the most important athletic events of the ancient Greek world. Reflecting the characteristics of ancient sport outlined in chapter 2, all four of these festivals shared a *sacred* context; each was dedicated in honor of a Greek god and claimed a foundational legend. Among many conflicting mythical accounts, the Olympic Games were instituted by Pelops in honor of his God-given victory in a chariot race against the father of a young woman he wished to wed. Also according to legend, Apollo established the Pythian Games after killing the great serpent (Pytho). Mythology records that the Isthmian Games were instituted in honor of Palaemon (also known as Melikertes), nephew of King Sisyphus, who drowned at sea and whose body later washed up on the Isthmus. Similarly, the Nemean Games were staged in remembrance of Opheltes, the infant son of King Lycurgus of Nemea who was killed by a snake.

Thus born of complicated mythological beginnings, the four Panhellenic festivals shared many common elements. They were known as *stephanitic* (crown) games because the Greeks crowned the winners with the prize of a victory wreath. The Games were open to all freeborn Greek males, and each festival boasted athletic and religious events. They were carefully arranged in sequence, with at least one of the great festivals held each year, culminating with the Olympics every fourth year.

The athletic festivals held at the great Panhellenic sanctuaries provided structure, regularity, and a religious context for increasingly popular ritualized athletic contests. Despite their many similarities, however, these festivals also displayed some distinctive elements. For one thing, reflecting the characteristics of ancient sport, the Panhellenic Games—while drawing athletes from thousands of miles of territory throughout the Greek world—were *local* in nature. Tied to the geography of Greek religion and the shrines and temples of particular gods, the four Panhellenic festivals were deeply rooted in particular locations. For example, the Pythian Games—second in prestige to the Olympics—took place during the Pythian festival honoring Apollo at Delphi, a remote mountainous sanctuary believed to be the navel (center) of the ancient Greek world. Home to the mighty Oracle (*Pythia*), the Pythian Games at Delphi established their own identity by staging both musical (singing and fluting) and athletic contests (including a larger roster of events for boys) on a quadrennial basis.

In contrast, the Isthmian Games, in honor of Poseidon, were held every two years in Isthmia, a religious sanctuary near the bustling coastal town of Corinth, which was renowned for its wealth, trade,

Table 3.3 Panhellenic Crown Games

Festival	Year founded (BCE)	Site	God	Crown	Frequency
Olympic	776	Olympia	Zeus	Olive	Every 4 years
Pythian	582	Delphi	Apollo	Laurel	Every 4 years
Isthmian	582	Corinth	Poseidon	Pine or dried celery	Every 2 years
Nemean	573	Nemea	Zeus	Wild celery	Every 2 years

and lively entertainment scene. The Isthmian Games offered an expansive cultural program that included contests in music, recital, writing, and painting, along with a full schedule of athletic events. The Nemean Games—the least prestigious of the crown festivals—were held in honor of Zeus on a two-year rotation at Nemea, a relatively nondescript region of the northeastern part of the Peloponnese. Using the Olympics as inspiration, the Nemean Games rejected musical and artistic events in favor of athletic contests. However, with their provision of athletic contests across three age categories (boys, youth, men)—as opposed to the standard Panhellenic categories of boys (*paides*) and men (*andres*)—even the Nemean Games found a way to distinguish itself among the crown festivals.

CHREMATITIC GAMES

Historical Profile

Aside from the great Panhellenic festivals, Greece also staged hundreds of local or regional games in city-states and local religious sanctuaries. The variety of these games, and of the deities they honored, is simply astonishing. The program of athletic contests differed widely from location to location. Indeed, athletic, musical, artistic, and dramatic events were held alongside contests in dancing, wine drinking, cheese stealing (a bizarre Spartan contest in which young male participants would vie to steal blocks of cheese from the Altar of Artemis Orthia without being caught by guards armed with whips), male beauty, and even torch relay running. Civic leaders expended enormous state and personal funds in staging these local games as a way of promoting their respective *poleis* and winning political and public favor. Perhaps inspired by Homer and the aristocratic funeral tradition of awarding valuable prestige goods to contestants, some civic leaders distributed extravagant cash or material prizes in order to demonstrate their conspicuous wealth and generosity.

Known as the *chrematitic* ("valuable-prize") games, these local contests widened social access to sport in Greece. Through their victories, working-class athletes suddenly possessed the financial means to dedicate their lives to training and competition. Also, in a contrast with the distant and expensive journeys by land and sea to the Panhellenic festivals, these games could be attended by spectators with relative ease.

Black-figure Pseudo-Panathenaic Amphora, The Walters Art Museum.

The Athenians awarded decorative amphoras filled with sacred olive oil to victors at the Greater Panathenaic games. First awarded 566, in the amphoras held both symbolic and monetary value: a victor in the men's stadion won 100 vases of oil, worth the equivalent of $135,600 in modern U.S. currency.

The Greater Panathenaic Games

More than any other Greek polis, the city-state of Athens dedicated considerable resources to staging athletic contests. Known for flourishing commerce as well as democracy, philosophy, and a series of remarkable cultural achievements, Athens also served as the locus of Greek sporting culture. The city hosted a wide variety of festivals, the most prestigious of which was the Greater Panathenaic Games. Although the Games never acquired Panhellenic status, the Panathenaea became the greatest of the *chrematitic* athletic festivals. At the Greater Panathenaic Games, all of the people of Athens—political leaders and humble citizens, men and women, young and old—assembled every four years to honor their city's patron goddess, Athena, over nine days of conviviality, worship, and athletic competition.

The Greater Panathenaea athletic festival was instituted in 566 BCE by Solon—an Athenian lawgiver who passed systematic reforms promoting civic responsibility and legislated against political, economic, and moral decline—to celebrate his constitutional accomplishments. Athenians offered lavish prizes to victors in the form of large and beautifully decorated amphoras of sacred olive oil. According to scholars, these large vases held significant financial worth and functioned as a form of currency. For instance, a victor in the men's *stadion* (sprint) event won 100 vases of olive oil, worth the equivalent of $135,600 U.S. dollars in modern currency. Prizes of various values were awarded to winners who competed in a dizzying array of musical, dramatic, gymnastic, and athletic contests, including equestrian and cavalry contests that were unique to Athens. For instance, the *apobates*, a chariot-dismounting contest, as well as a military-styled event in which a contestant threw a javelin at a target from horseback, illustrates the broad variety of athletic contests that had emerged in Archaic Greece.

The Olympic Games

Away from the bustling streets of Athens, in a remote religious sanctuary in the northwestern Peloponnese, lay Olympia, the home of the grandest athletic festival in ancient Greece: the Olympic Games. The commonly accepted starting date for the Olympics is 776 BCE; however, the origins of the Games are shrouded in myth and mystery. Over the centuries, the ancient Greeks fashioned a wide array of legendary tales to explain how the Olympics came into existence. While some clung to the legend of Pelops, others insisted that the Games were instituted in honor of Zeus' dominance over Cronus. Other yarns told of Herakles establishing the Olympics after completing one of his many labors. Like much of ancient history, the precise origins of the Games are irretrievable.

Modest, local athletic contests likely first emerged in Olympia as part of an existing religious cult of Zeus, perhaps even centuries prior to the first recorded festival in 776 BCE. Eventually, Greek pilgrims were gathering every four years at Olympia under the second full moon of the summer solstice for five days of worship, carnival celebrations, and athletic contests. The Greeks held the Olympic Games without interruption for more than 11 centuries until their eventual dissolution in 394 CE. As a testament to the durable nature of ancient sport, the Olympics survived times of famine, disease, natural disaster, civil war, and foreign invasion.

The Olympic Program

Little is known of the early Olympics, and Homer makes no mention of the Games in his epic accounts, thus suggesting that during the 8th century they constituted only a minor festival still in its infancy. Certainly, the Olympics were not born fully developed. Rather, they evolved slowly, over many centuries, from small-scale religious and athletic displays into the largest sporting event in the ancient world. This evolution is evident in the changing athletic program staged at Olympia over the years (see table 3.4).

For the first 52 years of recorded Olympic competition, contestants competed in just one event—the *stadion*, a roughly 200-meter sprint on foot. As growing numbers of Greek pilgrims descended on Olympia, organizers added more running events to the Olympic program, followed by contests in wrestling, pentathlon (a five-event contest including a *stadion* race, a javelin throw, a long jump, a discus throw, and a wrestling match), and boxing. In the 7th century BCE, the introduction of chariot and horseback races signaled the beginning of aristocratic patronage at Olympia. Using their wealth and social power, Greek aristocrats helped transform the Olympics over the succeeding centuries. In 648 BCE, Olympic organizers added the *pankration*—an all-out form of combat in which opponents kicked, punched, elbowed, butted, and grappled their opponents into submission. More than a century later, the program expanded to include the *hoplitodromos*, a footrace in armor. The addition of footraces, boxing, and wrestling events for boys (*paides*) between the ages of 12

and 17 marked the further expansion of the ancient Olympics as they evolved into a major religious and athletic festival.

The Olympic Sanctuary and Athletic Facilities

Like the athletic program, the religious and athletic facilities at Olympia also developed slowly over many centuries. The *Altis* (grove), the sacred precinct of Zeus, stood as the religious heart of Olympia. From the 7th century on, the stewards at Olympia gradually embellished this sanctuary with temples, altars, shrines, votive victory statues, stoas (covered walkways), and treasuries. The Temple of Zeus—constructed by Libon of Elis from 470 BCE to 456 BCE and adorned with sculptural scenes from the myths of Pelops, Herakles, and Theseus—became the crown jewel of Olympia. Housing a giant (40-foot, or 13-meter) wooden, seated sculpture (plated in bronze and ivory) of Zeus—heralded in ancient times as one of the Seven Wonders of the Ancient World—the Temple represented an architectural masterpiece. Beyond the *Altis*, construction continued

Table 3.4   Evolution of the Olympic Program

Date introduced	Athletic event
776 BCE	*Stadion* race
724 BCE	*Diaulos* (double *stadion* race, back and forth)
720 BCE	*Dolichos* (roughly 20- to 24-*stadion* race)
708 BCE	Wrestling and *pentathlon* (including *stadion* race, javelin throw, long jump, discus throw, and wrestling match)
688 BCE	Boxing
680 BCE	Chariot racing (four-horse, 12-lap)
648 BCE	*Pankration* (all-out combat) and *keles* (horseback riding)
632 BCE	Footraces and wrestling for boys
616 BCE	Boxing for boys
520 BCE	*Hoplitodromos* (footrace in armor)
408 BCE	*Synoris* (two-horse chariot race)
396 BCE	Contest for heralds and trumpeters
384 BCE	*Poloi* (four-colt chariot race)
268 BCE	*Poloi* (two-colt chariot race)
200 BCE	Boys' *pankration*

throughout the Classical era (in the 5th and 4th centuries BCE) and even into the 2nd century CE. The athletic stadium, with its sloping grassy embankments, housed the athletic and combat events, and the hippodrome hosted contests for horses and chariots. Olympia eventually grew to accommodate gymnasia, palaestra, offices for the council and magistrate, storehouses, a hostel, and banquet halls.

Despite its many adornments, Olympia never contained a modern-style Olympic village or comfortable facilities or accommodations for spectators. The Olympics were designed for worshipping the gods and celebrating individual feats of athletic excellence; meeting the needs of spectators was a distant afterthought. Indeed, a pilgrimage to Olympia proved to be a rather uncomfortable experience. The routine sacrificial slaughtering of animals brought hordes of insects and noxious smells. Many other factors—for instance, overcrowding, noise, poor sanitation, theft, water shortage, and lack of shade to protect from the searing summer sun—all took their toll on the estimated 100,000 dedicated pilgrims who made the long voyage to Olympia by land and sea. A popular joke from the ancient world neatly captured the hardships experienced by spectators at the Olympic Games: A slave owner would threaten unruly slaves not with a beating but with a trip to Olympia!

Administering the Olympics

Although rival city-states had long laid claim to the religious sanctuary at Olympia, the city-state of Elis generally administered the Olympic Games. Staging a religious and athletic festival of this magnitude constituted a considerable financial and logistical burden. The Eleans, however, proved themselves consummate organizers. They began by selecting Olympic judges—known initially as the *agonothetai* and, beginning in 580 BCE, as *Hellanodikai* ("Judges of the Greeks")—from among the elder statesmen of Elis. Distinguished

by their purple robes and forked sticks, the Elean judges governed the Olympic contests, fining and even expelling athletes for cheating or lying. The judges also supervised the training of Olympic athletes for a month prior to the commencement of the Games; all prospective athletes were also required to undertake 10 months of rigorous training in their respective city-states. If they possessed the requisite talent, they traveled to Elis, where the Elean judges put them through a series of trials and tests. The slower and weaker athletes were gradually weeded out in order to ensure that only the best athletes in Greece were granted the opportunity to display their *arete* before the eyes of the gods on the sacred sands of Olympia.

Months prior to the start of the Olympic festival, *spondophoroi* (heralds) from Elis traveled throughout the Greek world proclaiming that the Games were coming. These proclamations constituted a warning to athletes and spectators to begin making the necessary preparations. The *spondophoroi* also announced the *ekecheiria*, a sacred truce sworn in honor of Zeus. In effect, the *ekecheiria* guaranteed safe passage for all athletes and spectators traveling to and from Olympia; it also forbade armies from entering into Elean territory throughout the duration of the games. Contrary to contemporary interpretations, the truce did not stop wars. For example, Greeks competed at the Olympics in 480 BCE even as Xerxes' massive Persian army was busy laying siege to Athens. Later, the *ekecheiria* later failed to stem the Athenian and Spartan bloodshed during the Peloponnesian War (431 BCE–403 BCE).

With the preparations complete, a large procession of judges, athletes (typically accompanied by their fathers and brothers), trainers, spectators, and state officials made the roughly 37-mile (60-kilometer) journey by foot from Elis to Olympia. On arriving at the sanctuary, athletes swore an oath to Zeus that they would "do no evil" against the Games, and civic leaders filled treasuries with valuable gifts (typically, booty acquired through military conquests) and dedicated them to the gods. Over the following five days, mainland and colonial Greeks came to together to celebrate their shared ethnicity; worship their deities through prayers, oaths, and sacrifices; and watch the best athletes in the ancient Greek world vie for Olympic glory.

Greek Sporting Culture

The Olympic Games represented the pinnacle of Greek athletic competition. However, contrary to claims made by some later scholars, the Olympics were hardly a showcase for democracy and equality. In fact, social *inequality*, as exemplified in the model of ancient sport described in chapter 2, reigned at the Games. An exclusive affair, the ancient Olympics openly discriminated against people on the basis of ethnicity (as defined by the ability to speak Greek), gender, social status, and skill level. Eligibility was reserved exclusively for freeborn Greek males (without criminal records) who underwent sufficient training and displayed the requisite skill. In the equestrian events (chariot and horse racing), eligibility was reserved for wealthy Greek aristocrats who could afford the exorbitant costs of rearing and transporting horses. Although slaves drove the chariots and rode the horses, the social elites received the praise and recognition that accompanied victory.

Olympic Eligibility

The Olympics reflected the broader social hierarchy of Greek society. Women, in particular, occupied an extremely low rung on the social ladder. They were excluded from most social life, and their primary role was to care for their children and run the home. With some exceptions, women were excluded from gymnasiums as well as the punishing world of Greek athletics. For the purpose of the Olympic Games, the Eleans imposed an old, sacral law that prohibited women from attending. The punishment outlined in Elean law for violating this ban was death; specifically, though no records exist of women suffering this fate, offenders were to be thrown off the cliffs overlooking the Olympic sanctuary. Thus the Olympics represented a male social space, reserved exclusively for men.

Some ancient authors argue, however, that fathers brought their virgin daughters to Olympia in search of husbands. Others tell of Kallipateira of Rhodes, who disguised herself as an athletic trainer and snuck into the Olympic stadium to watch her son compete. When she was discovered, the Eleans spared her from death but instituted a new rule that trainers had to enter the stadium *gymnos* (naked). Still others point to the *Heraia*, a religious festival for women held at Olympia in honor of Hera, the goddess of women and marriage. Composed of a footrace for virgin girls, the *Heraia* has been presented as evidence of a strong female presence in ancient Greek athletics. In reality, these claims simply do not fit with the bulk of archaeological and written evidence. In the case of the *Heraia*, scholars argue that the footraces were religious rather competitive in nature; specifically, they were a symbolic, prenuptial rite of passage.

Amid the general exclusion of women from the ancient Greek Olympics, the story of Kyniska of Sparta stands as a famous aberration. Records show that in 396 BCE and 392 BCE, a Spartan princess, Kyniska, entered and won the four-horse chariot race in absentia. In ancient equestrian events, as noted earlier, Greeks proclaimed as winners the owners of the winning chariots rather than the lowly slaves who drove them. Thus, as a chariot owner Kyniska achieved Olympic victory without ever violating Elean law by stepping foot in Olympia during the duration of the Games. In the centuries following her victories, Kyniska has been seized upon as a female sporting hero—an icon of liberation in an oppressive, patriarchal world.

In truth, her victories reveal an important political and personal Spartan agenda.

Kyniska's Olympic successes occurred at the end of decades of increasing strife between Sparta on one side and Elis and Athens on the other. Fierce military conflict led to Sparta's exclusion from the Olympic Games. In Sparta's absence, the ruling elites of Athens dominated the equestrian events. Alcibiades, an affluent and extravagant young Athenian, entered more chariots and won more races than anyone before him. The young braggart loudly interpreted his victories as proof of his own *arete*, as well as that of Athens. Alcibiades originally served as general in the Athenian army during the Peloponnesian War (434 BCE–401 BCE) that pitted Athens against Sparta. He later changed sides and served as military advisor to the Spartans before betraying their cause and rejoining the Athenian forces. The Spartans loathed the inconstant Alcibiades and sought to discredit him. Indeed, some ancient sources claim that the Spartans eventually assassinated him. Whether or not those accounts are accurate, scholars contend that the King of Sparta, Agesilaus, entered his sister, Kyniska, into the four-horse chariot race in order to deliver an insulting, symbolic message to Sparta's rivals (Alcibiades in particular and Athens in general)—that victory in the Olympic equestrian events was guaranteed not by merit but by wealth. The victory of a woman made a mockery of Alcibiades' successes and his boastful claims of athletic excellence.

The Real Olympians

For the Greek men eligible to compete, sport was a zero-sum affair. There was one winner, who was perceived as divinely favored. The Greeks viewed the Olympic victor in an almost luminous light. He wore his olive crown as a symbol of *arete*, prestige, and even divinity. For the Greeks, the successful Olympic athlete transcended his mortality and occupied a position just below the gods. On his homecoming, civic officials embraced him with triumphal parades and showered him with lavish cash prizes and free meals. In some cases, shrines and temples were erected in honor of Olympic victors. The losers received an entirely different reception. They were mocked and disgraced. Ancient texts describe athletes who snuck home by back alleys following a defeat at Olympia. Others tell of mothers feeling ashamed of their sons' failures at the Games. In contrast to the modern era, the ancient Greeks did not award medals for second and third place finishes, and they refused to bestow recognition on athletes that achieved a personal best despite falling short of victory. Greece was a culture dedicated to the attainment of excellence. Winners were celebrated, and losers were shamed.

With such lavish rewards at stake, Greek athletes went to great lengths in pursuit of victory. They engaged in regimented, systematic training; they understood the principles of resistance exercise; and they were formidable competitors. Reflecting the martial nature of ancient sport, the Greeks viewed athletics as an *agon*—a battle, a life-or-death affair. In this context, the Greek athlete subjected his body to excruciating pain and suffering in the quest for an Olympic crown. The contests themselves were violent and combative. Ancient texts tell of boxers delivering such powerful blows that they bore down to the bone, charioteers being crushed under the weight of a rival chariot, as well as *pankratiasts* who wrenched an opponent's ankle joints out of their sockets and snapped fingers.

In short, these contests were not the gentlemanly "amateurs" of the Victorian imagination. As we discuss in chapter 9, 19th-century European social elites—such as Baron Pierre de Coubertin, founder of the modern Olympic Games—mistakenly believed that ancient Greek athletes competed purely for "love of the game." Like many of his contemporaries, Coubertin insisted that the ancient Olympians had shunned material prizes, fame, and recognition in the pursuit of fair play and gentlemanly competition.

In contrast to the view from the rose-tinted lenses of modern European elites, ancient Greek athletes were hardened professionals. Sport was a serious pursuit. In fact, Olympic victory was elevated to such a high plain that some Greek athletes were driven to violate the sacred oaths and break the rules. Evidence reveals, for example, that athletes occasionally false-started, disemboweled their opponents, and used lead curse tablets in an effort to hex their rivals; some also attempted to bribe their way to victory. For those who were caught cheating, their punishment was public humiliation. Their names were inscribed on *Zanes*, which were bronze statues of Zeus erected and paid for by the fines imposed on those who broke the sacred rules. For centuries, visitors to Olympia read the inscriptions on the bases of the *Zanes* that lined the entrance to the athletic stadium, thus learning of transgressions such as that committed by Calippus the Athenian, who plotted to bribe his way to victory in the pentathlon.

The Games as Meritocratic Competitions

This historical evidence illustrates an important philosophical and political point. Although Greece's social hierarchy shaped much of Greek society, including parts of the Olympic Games, elements of a more democratic process also emerged. Greece's increasing emphasis on equality and merit ties into an important cultural shift in how people considered sport and interpreted a person's virtue. Scholars argue that in a society in which status roles were strict and clearly defined, Greek sport served as a mechanism for developing citizenship and promoting greater equality. These effects developed as sport became

increasingly meritocratic and democratic. Though we often think of democracy as a political system, a democracy is in fact a society where a spirit of social equality leads to an equality of rights or privileges. This dimension of equality is often combined with meritocracy, a system in which those who are talented receive rewards based on personal achievement.

This progress came slowly. In much of Greek society, sport was reserved for the elite. For instance, citizens in Mycenaean Greece emphasized tribal, familial, and religious aspects of sport. Homer illustrated these practices in the funeral games of Patroclus when Achilles declared King Agamemnon the winner of the javelin contest even though the aging chieftain had not thrown a spear.

Such deference to members of the aristocracy was not characteristic of the Olympic Games. To the contrary, although social privilege and its attendant wealth provided advantages to certain athletes in training and preparing for their contests—particularly in high-cost activities such as chariot races—the races still had to be run. Even though the owners, and not the lowly slaves who raced the chariots, received the laurels, the owners had to earn their victory in the sporting arena. The emphasis on earning victory reflects the general trend toward sport as a meritocracy in which individuals earn their victories by talent rather than privilege. Accordingly, athletes were stripped naked to prevent any display of wealth through the possession of fine clothing or jewelry. In the competitive events, efforts were made to ensure that no athlete received an unearned advantage. For instance, new starting mechanisms (*hysplex*) ensured that everyone in a running event started at the same time. Similarly, boxers rotated sides so that neither gained an advantage from the sun glaring in the opponent's eyes.

In the end, the Greeks wanted athletic prowess—not aristocratic titles—to

Is Modern Sport a Meritocracy?

Student Exercise

Sport is often seen as the great equalizer—an activity that provides the true measure of a person's physical ability. Though some people receive a head start in life by inheriting wealth or having family members in positions of power, the sporting world cares only about what a person can do in the gymnasium or on the athletic field. This emphasis on ability has led some to consider sport a true meritocracy.

The ancient Greeks embraced the idea that the Olympic Games constituted a meritocracy. Athletes could neither buy their way onto the starting line, nor could they buy victory through bribery. Still, the chariot and horse races clearly favored the wealthy, who could own expensive horses and fast chariots. Even the running and combat events required money to support the travel and time necessary for training. Therefore, while the Greeks believed that all athletes were equal, some clearly had a head start in their journey to glory.

This insight raises an important question for sport ethics: Is modern sport a meritocracy?

Although it is easy to see the hypocrisy in ancient Greece, philosophy is also a useful tool for reconsidering our own biases and assumptions. Consider the modern Olympic Games. On one hand, the Games do not discriminate based on race, religion, politics, or wealth; thus, in theory, anyone can become an Olympic champion if they possess the requisite talent. On the other hand, athletes from some nations seem to have advantages that promote success. For example, they may have better training or access to more resources because they were born in a wealthy nation that values their chosen sport. They may also have geographic advantages or simply superior genetics. These examples point to the existence of some unearned advantages that benefit certain athletes.

Based on these considerations, discuss whether contemporary sport lives up to its meritocratic principles or whether it is still structured in ways that benefit the wealthy or those who are privileged.

- Are there other ways, in addition to those mentioned in the introduction to this exercise, in which sport is not purely meritocratic?
- What techniques does sport typically use to level the playing field?
- What additional steps could be taken to promote the meritocratic ideals of sport?

---

determine their Olympic champions. Regardless of one's status by birth, his athletic talents could raise him to demigod status, thus illustrating the democratizing power of sport. Such democratization in sport reflected—or perhaps influenced—a larger democratic turn in Greek society. As the sporting festivals became democratic, so did Greek society.

Sources of Evidence for Ancient Greek Sport

As discussed in chapter 2, much of what we know about ancient sporting culture, and about the ancient Olympics in particular, has been informed by two broad categorizations of evidence: written and mate-rial. Both provide important resources for understanding the sporting life of ancient Greeks.

Written Evidence

The relevant writings take several forms, each offering a fascinating insight into the world of Greek athletics. The importance of sport in Greek culture was so great that some ancient authors regularly used athletic stories to make political or moral points. Others, such as Pindar and Bacchylides, recorded their celebrations of athletic victories in full poetic splendor. Perhaps the most vivid written account of ancient Greek sport comes from Pausanias, a Greek who lived during the Roman period (146 BCE–330 CE) and visited the Panhellenic sanctuaries and sporting festivals. His writings provide key factual information about Olympia and the Olympic Games, including, names, dates, events, and accomplishments. Other forms of written evidence are less descriptive but still help scholars of sport and physical activity in their efforts to construct and understand the past. Examples include epigraphical inscriptions (such as dedicatory texts carved into statue bases at Olympia and other athletic festival sites) and fragments of papyrus (listing Olympic victors or describing training techniques).

Material Evidence

The various written accounts of ancient Greek sport are supported by a vast wealth of material evidence. For example, scholars can use the archaeological remains of ancient Greek stadiums—including the dressing rooms, entrance tunnels, starting lines (*balbides*), and turning posts (*kampteres*)—to visualize where the ancient athletic festivals took place. In addition, ancient Greek athletes are depicted running, jumping, boxing, and wrestling in a considerable array of marble reliefs and an even larger collection of vase paintings, most dating to the 6th and 5th centuries BCE. Others capture heroic performances or regulatory transgressions, including wrestlers biting and gouging their opponents. Although rarely fully preserved, marble and bronze statues bring us face to face with ancient Greek athletes. These sculptural masterpieces reveal the size and musculature of Greek runners and wrestlers and offer fascinating insights into the techniques used by ancient discus and javelin throwers. Perhaps the most important of these works (though the original bronze statue has been lost to history) is Myron's *Discobolus*, which depicts an ancient Greek discus thrower in a tightly wound pose prior to release.

Ancient Sporting Equipment

Preserved among the vast body of material evidence from ancient Greek antiquity are some pieces of the actual equipment used by athletes in practice or competition, including *diskoi* (discuses) and stone *halteres* (hand weights used in the long jump). In particular, the *halteres* (as supported by visual evidence) reveal an important technical difference between the ancient Greek long jump and the modern event practiced today. Carrying the roughly 7- to 9-pound (3- to 4-kilogram) *halteres*, one in each hand, ancient Greek long jumpers ran toward the sand pit (*skamma*), leapt into the air, and then discarded the weights at the highest point of the jump. The Greeks, it is assumed, believed that the release of the extra weight would help propel the athlete forward.

A drawing of Myron's Discobolus.

© Ivan Burmistrov/iStock/Getty Images

Nude Athletes

Archaeologists have also discovered among the possession of ancient Greek athletes an *aryballos* (jar of olive oil). Prior to competition, the Greek athlete massaged oil into his skin in order to protect it from the radiating heat of the sun, to limber up the muscles, or perhaps to ensure an aesthetically pleasing and desirable complexion. Herein lies another important departure point from our modern sporting world: The ancient Greek athlete competed in the nude—that is, he went *gymnos*.

The origin of and reasoning behind Greek athletic nudity have been the subject of many theories over the centuries. Some have argued that it reflected the egalitarian impulse in Greek society by removing the appearance of wealth and status, thus ensuring that all athletes were equal under the eyes of the gods. Others maintain that nudity represented a state of religious purity or even purportedly offered athletes a form of magical protection from pernicious spiritual forces. Scholars have also contended that athletic nudity simply reflected the homoeroticism and bisexuality that was commonplace in ancient Greek society. Some Greeks considered the naked body of a young, well-proportioned athletic male to be a visual delight for the gaggles of male spectators in attendance. The Greek athlete certainly went to great lengths to enhance his physical appearance, sprinkling a light yellow powder (*konis*) over his oiled skin prior to competition. He would later remove the excess powder, oil, blood, sweat, and tears with a *strigil*, a carved bronze or iron tool. This accumulation of waste (*gloios*) removed from a healthy fit body was believed to possess medicinal and magical properties and was sold to cure skin diseases and inflammation.

The rich body of written and material evidence just outlined affords students of sport and physical activity a fascinating source of insight into the world of ancient Greek athletics. However, scholars issue an important note of caution. In history and philosophy, as in the scientific subdisciplines that are part of our field of kinesiology, we must closely scrutinize and verify evidence. We must apply critical standards in order to ensure validity and confirm that what is written or depicted is historically accurate.

Greek Recreation and Physical Education

Ancient Greek culture teemed with opportunities for entertainment, exercise, and recreation. Away from the hypercompetitive world of athletics, most Greeks (both young and old) engaged in mild and entertaining forms of physical activity. Adults hunted,

Weighing the Evidence

Student Exercise

An ancient inscription tells of Phayllus of Crotona, a highly decorated Greek naval commander and pentathlete, who reportedly jumped an astonishing 55 feet (17 meters) in the long jump at the ancient Olympic Games. In modern context, Phayllus' purported performance is simply staggering. The modern world record for the long jump is held by Mike Powell of the United States, who, at the 1991 IAAF World Championships in Tokyo, Japan, clinched the long-jump gold medal by leaping 29 feet 4 1/4 inches (about 9 meters).

Applying critical standards of historical analysis, consider whether or not it was possible for an ancient Greek Olympian to jump more than 25 feet (7.5 meters) farther than our leading modern-day athletes, who have the advantage of modern knowledge in sport science, coaching, technique, and nutrition. How can we rationalize or make sense of this ancient claim? In small groups, work together to see if you can generate 5 theories that argue either for or against accepting this incredible feat at face value.

swam, rowed boats, and performed acrobatic feats. Children played dice, amused themselves with yo-yos, juggled, and rolled bronze hoops. Both children and adults also practiced a variety of ball games using their hands and sometimes sticks. Examples include *aporrhaxis*, a popular game in which contestants vied to bounce a ball successfully, and *episkyros*, a team-based game in which players strategically threw a ball into an opponent's territory. These games were part of a long list of popular pastimes enjoyed by Greek males and, in some instances, females.

Exercising the Mind and Body

The gymnasium and palaestra were among the defining features of city-states across the ancient Greek world. Constructed, organized, and administered by the state, these institutions served as the centers of Greek physical and intellectual education—the training grounds for every male child and youth in every aspect of manhood. Greek males came to the gymnasium and palaestra on an almost daily basis to train for athletic competition, to exercise, and to study. In most Greek city-states, all 18-year-old males (*epheboi*) spent an additional two years at the *gymnasia* and the *palaestra* undergoing citizenship training.

The *gymnasiarch*, the leader of the gymnasium, took charge of the facility and drafted the educational program. *Didaskalos* (teachers) offered classes in a wide variety of academic disciplines, including music, dance, writing, grammar, and infantry training. *Paidotribai* (physical educators)—the original kinesiologists—put their students through a series of exercises and physical contests. As salaried employees, they constituted part of the staff of the Greek gymnasium. Yet little is known of these early kinesiologists other than the fact that they were men, mainly from the lower social ranks, who had experience in athletics. City-states charged the *paidotribai* with developing formal and systematic training regimes to build healthy and productive citizens. They promoted beauty, strength, agility, and grace in motion. Some even prepared athletes for competition, accompanied them to athletic festivals, and worked with them during mandatory training periods. Throughout the Archaic Age, *paidotribai* were responsible for their students' health, exercise, and dietary needs. They offered dietary advice—often recommending meat- or cheese-heavy diets—and even proscribed sexual activity. Scholars believe, however, that the *paidotribai* were later stripped of some of their responsibilities due to medical advancements and increasing specialization in Greek sport.

Philosophers and Athletes

Given the close association in ancient Greece between physical education, mental education, and overall health, the gymnasia became hubs for scholarship and discovery. These tree-shaded facilities were not only useful for training athletes but also served as ideal venues for public lectures and debates. By the 4th century BCE, Plato and Aristotle established schools at two of Athens' most famous gymnasia. Indeed, Plato's Academy (*Akademy*) and Aristotle's Lyceum (*Lykeion*) perhaps best illustrate the fusion of Greece's education, sport, and inquiry. Imagine the atmosphere as Plato or Aristotle trained alongside aspiring Olympians, budding poets, politicians, and playwrights—a fusion of Arnold Schwarzenegger's Muscle Beach and Albert Einstein's Institute for Advanced Study. For that reason, the gymnasia happily supported such scholars while citizens paid taxes and membership fees to subsidize these public institutions.

Still, philosophers such as Plato and Aristotle did not always see eye to eye with Greece's sporting culture. Though both philosophers embraced athletic training and competition as useful tools for educating and preparing youth for their future civic obligations, they criticized the imbalance and excess that marked the athletic culture of their day. Plato believed that students should receive a balanced education of body (gymnastics) and mind (music). Students who developed only their muscles would become harsh and savage, while those who developed only their minds would be soft and useless. Aristotle also viewed the ideal approach as consisting of balanced education, which would combine reading and writing, athletics, music, and drawing. By attaining balanced education in each of these four areas, a person would achieve the desired *arete*.

Some philosophers also criticized Greece's practice of idolizing its athletes. For example, Xenophanes, a philosopher in the 6th century BCE, criticized the honors and prizes bestowed on athletes. In an argument that some might also apply to contemporary sporting culture, he asserted that athletes did not contribute anything to society and thus did not deserve to be treated as heroes. The real heroes, in Xenophanes' mind, were philosophers such as himself, whose wisdom was "better than the strength of men and of horses." Whether philosophers were really worth more than Olympians can be debated, but Xenophanes' point illustrates just how highly athletes were regarded in ancient Greece.

An Ideal Education

Contemporary Western culture often assumes that physical strength and intellectual intelligence are mutually exclusive. If a person has a strong body, so culture tells us, then he or she must have a weak mind, and vice versa. This conception culminates in the stereotypes of the dumb jock and the weak nerd, which seems to drive a wedge between athletes and "mathletes."

Although many contemporary values and beliefs would be familiar to the ancient Greeks, this division of brains and brawn would not. To the contrary, the Greeks viewed physical education and sport as a means for nurturing an individual's *arete* and creating a physically fit citizen capable of performing productive labor and defending his polis in war. Though philosophers debated the ideal balance between *arete* and civic fitness, they generally agreed on an approach to education known as *paideia*, which combined the study of writing, grammar, and arithmetic with training in gymnastics, wrestling, singing, and music. The expectation was that such education formed ideal members for the polis who were equally prepared to fend off foreign invaders, manage trade, and hold public office. In addition, many of Greece's brightest thinkers showed evidence of being practiced athletes and lovers of sport. Consider the following examples:

- Thales of Miletus (624 BCE–546 BCE), a philosopher and mathematician considered one of the Seven Sages of Greece, reportedly died in Olympia while watching the Games of the 58th Olympiad.

- Pindar (522 BCE–433 BCE) was a legendary poet whose most famous works are victory odes devoted to Greek champions. Pindar must have known something of sport in order to write eloquent lines such as "Creatures for a day! What is a man? / What is he not? A dream of a shadow / Is our mortal being. But when there comes to men / A gleam of splendour given of heaven, / Then rests on them a light of glory / And blessed are their days" (*Pythia* VIII, lines 95–97).

- Diogenes of Sinope (412 BCE–323 BCE), founder of the cynic movement, rejected human convention, custom, and morality and chose instead to live like a dog (*cynic* is derived from the word for dog in ancient Greek). At the Isthmian Games, he declared that his own struggles against hunger, thirst, cold, and pain were nobler than the struggles of the athletes and characterized their prizes as trivial tokens as compared with his lifelong happiness and *arete*.

Proper Role of Physical Education

Student Exercise

In most schools today, basic academic subjects such as math and science are prioritized over curricula in music, driver education, nutrition, health education, theater, physical education, and other supposedly nonessential areas of study. Therefore, when budgets are cut, these latter courses, along with athletics, are often the first to be dropped or scaled back. Some educators argue that these decisions are wise; others disagree. As you have seen, many ancient Greek philosophers and educators believed that balance was an important educational concept. Is this idea still valid today? Discuss the following specific questions:

- Should physical education still be an important component of a student's education? How important is physical education as compared with traditional subjects such as math, science, history, and English?
- If we take physical education seriously, should schools require students to achieve a standard of physical literacy much like they enforce standards in math, reading, and writing?
- Student-athletes are ruled ineligible for school sports if their academic grades are too low. Would it be right to prevent a student from participating in after-school activities such as theater or government if he or she is failing physical education?

- Socrates (470 BCE–399 BCE) received his physical education while serving as a hoplite in the Athenian military. Though he never wrote anything down, Socrates is quoted in Xenophon's *Memorabilia* as arguing that all people should maintain a high a state of physical fitness and asserting that "it is a disgrace to grow old . . . before seeing what manner of man you may become by developing your bodily strength and beauty to their highest limit."

- Plato (428 BCE–348 BCE) distinguished himself during his early studies as a wrestler and may even have competed in the Isthmian Games and Pythian Games before going on to become one of the most distinguished philosophers of Western thought.

- Aristotle (384 BCE–322 BCE) established his school at the Lyceum upon arriving in Athens in 335 BCE. The Lyceum was a gymnasium that included a running track and wrestling school for training Athenian athletes, as well as space for learning, reading, and debating.

The Spartan Model of Physical Education

The ancient Greek warrior society of Sparta has long fascinated scholars and students (including Plato), in part due to its regimented system of physical education (*agoge*) and the training opportunities it afforded to females. Spartan males were culled by the state from their homes at age seven and forced to participate in rigorous exercises, paramilitary contests, and violent games. In effect, the *agoge* served as a vehicle for male socialization, initiation, and military preparedness. It fostered hypermasculinity, celebrated male bonding and fraternity, and idealized supreme physical fitness. The state magistrate (*paidonomos*) organized Spartan boys into "herds" (*agelai*), supervised their training, and enforced discipline among them. The boys underwent frequent physical inspections in the nude, whereupon those who were weak or out of shape were flogged and shamed. Spartan boys were trained to hunt and scavenge for food and resources, to fight, and to defend their city-state with honor and bravery. Those who dropped out of the *agoge* were excluded from citizenship and labeled *hypomeinoes* ("below-dwellers").

Spartan leaders intended their educational system to promote and maintain the well-being of the polis. As a result, even women in Sparta engaged in daily physical education; specifically, ancient Spartan beliefs about eugenics meant that women were encouraged to train their bodies for marriage and childbirth.

Although their training was less rigorous than that administered in the male *agoge*, Spartan females still exercised, ran footraces, wrestled, and threw the discus and javelin. However, contrary to popular visions of liberation and female empowerment in the ancient world, the Spartans designed female physical education to promote optimal breeding and ensure healthy (preferably male) offspring.

CHAPTER WRAP-UP

Wrapping Up and Looking Ahead

Despite their advances, constant infighting and political divisions left the ancient Greeks vulnerable to conquest by a rising civilization to their west, namely Rome. Following the Roman victory over the Greek city-states at the Battle of Corinth in 146 BCE, most of Greece fell under Roman rule. Even so, much of life in Greece, including the Olympics, continued under the Roman Empire as it had been conducted before. In fact, Greek language, philosophical thought, literature, art, and architecture profoundly affected Roman culture. As addressed in chapter 4, Romans also borrowed heavily from Greek ideas concerning medicine, health, exercise, and the human body. In particular, the Greek notion of mutual dependence between a sound mind and a healthy body persisted in Rome throughout its republican and imperial periods. However, beyond the favorable effect of physical training on general health and aesthetics, the Romans were intent on making practical use of it—that is, training men for military battle.

Greece's sporting legacy persisted into the Roman era and beyond. Even today, much of what forms our modern sporting world, as well as our field of kinesiology, has been informed or influenced by the ancient Greeks. Specifically, the lionization of successful athletes, the organization and administration of sporting festivals such as the Olympics, the specialized pursuit of sporting and physical excellence, and debates about the proper methods for educating mind and body—all of these elements remain important in the 21st century. The ancient Greeks were the first culture to truly organize and rationalize their human impulse to play. Therefore, those of us working today in the modern field of kinesiology have inherited much from this remarkable ancient civilization. As you will see in chapter 4, much of this inheritance was both spread and challenged by Roman modifications. Beyond the borders of Western civilization, a vast variety of other ideas and practices about physical activity emerged, some of which resembled Greek conceptions—and many of which did not.

Study Questions

1. What explains the emergence of a rich and vibrant Panhellenic sporting culture in ancient Greece?

2. What philosophical ideals and values drove physical activity in ancient Greece?

3. In what ways do modern kinesiology and its subdisciplines trace their origins back to ancient Greece and its many influential thinkers?

4. How, and in what ways, was Greek sport closely associated with, or even inseparable from, religion? In what ways were the ancient Greek Olympics discriminatory? How were they meritocratic?

5. How has ancient Greece affected both the modern sporting world and our modern field of kinesiology?

6. What parallels exist between philosophical debates about physical activity in ancient Greece and those in contemporary society?

CONTINUITY AND CHANGE IN PHYSICAL CULTURES

From the Maturation and Decline of Classical Civilizations to the Middle Ages

Chapter Objectives

In this chapter, you will

1. analyze the development of sport during the 3,000-year period from 1500 BCE to 1500 CE in cultures and civilizations around the globe;

2. compare brutal sporting spectacles in different parts of the world, including the Roman Empire and Mesoamerica;

3. review religious and philosophical opposition to brutality in sport and speculate about whether progress has been made in reducing violence and brutality, both in society in general and in sport in particular;

4. examine martial arts traditions in the East and around the world while noting the close connections between sport and military virtues;

5. review differences between world views in the East and in the West and their effects on the purpose and meaning of competition and prowess; and

6. study the recreation and sporting traditions of the peasants and the ruling classes who populated the world during this period of time.

When the Roman Empire conquered Greece in the 100s BCE, it guaranteed not the extermination but the preservation of Greek ideas about human nature and physical activity, as well as Greek styles of sport and physical education. The Romans, especially the ruling classes, adopted many of the practices of Greek culture. As a result, gymnasia, hippodromes, and *stadia* (stadiums) proliferated in Western civilization as the Romans conquered and ruled vast swaths of the Mediterranean world and pushed northward across Europe. Hadrian's Wall, begun in 122 CE under the edict of Emperor Hadrian (76–138 CE), marked the northernmost border of the vast Roman Empire at its apogee. Just 75 miles (120 kilometers) south of the wall, in the city of Isurium Brigantum, the Romans built a hilltop amphitheater that housed the many species of the *Ludi Romani* ("Games of the Romans"), including chariot races and gladiatorial combats.

Monuments to Sporting Spectacles

At the center of the empire, in Rome, massive monuments testified to the prominence of the *Ludi Romani* and ranked among the architectural marvels of the ancient world. The Circus Maximus, a chariot-racing track initially laid out in the 500s BCE and improved constantly over the centuries that followed, seated more than 150,000 spectators. The Colosseum, built from 72 to 80 CE, held as many as 80,000 fans, who watched gladiator combat in this marble and concrete edifice. Though it lacked the monumental scale and permanence of its more famous cousins in Rome, the rudimentary stadium in Isurium Brigantum at the northern end of the empire revealed that the taste for spectator sports had spread throughout Western civilization during the Roman epoch.

Stadiums also served as central features of urban civilizations located thousands of miles to the west, across the Atlantic Ocean in the jungles of the Yucatán Peninsula and the fertile valleys of central Mexico. Like the Roman stadiums, these monumental edifices were built of stone and accommodated thousands of spectators. The largest of the more than 1,300 stadiums discovered to date in these regions is the Chichén Itzá Grand Ball Court, built between 1050 and 1200 CE. This I-shaped structure (a common feature among Mesoamerican stadiums) measured 554 feet (169 meters) long and 231 feet (70 meters) wide. As with Roman amphitheaters, less elaborate versions of Mesoamerican ball courts have been uncovered thousands of miles away from the core of their civilizations, including among the urban centers of the Hohokam cultures near present-day Phoenix and the Mound Builder cultures of the Ohio River Valley and Great Lakes region near present-day Pittsburgh and Cleveland.

The cultures that built these stadiums—the Olmec, Maya, Toltec, Mixtec, Zapotec, and Aztec foremost among them—did not stage *Ludi Romani* in their sporting complexes. Indeed, horses had become extinct in the Americas long before the Neolithic Revolution (see chapter 2), during which humans domesticated horses and some other animals. Without horses, hippodromes were clearly an American impossibility. Archaeological evidence reveals that while the I-shaped stadiums probably staged a variety of religious and political events and sometimes housed wrestling matches, Mesoamerican cultures built them mainly to showcase ballgames.

Rubber was an indigenous product of the Americas, and Mesoamerican cultures developed several forms of a game played with rubber balls. Some of the variations required players to hit balls with sticks and other implements; in others, players used the hands, feet, head, hips, and various other body parts to direct the ball.

Thus, the Mesoamerican ball game is best understood not as a specific brand of game played in precisely the same way throughout the region but as a generic family of games played with a rubber ball and characterized by differing local customs. Mesoamerican cultures played these games for the same reasons that most traditional societies have engaged in sporting contests—for fun and amusement, to demonstrate prowess, and as a featured component of religious rituals.

Comparing Mesoamerican and Roman Spectacles of Blood

The particular brand of ball game played by the Mayans at Chichén Itzá's Grand Ball Court might well have appealed to the Roman spectators who turned out in droves to watch the most violent of the *Ludi Romani*—namely the *munera*, which featured gladiatorial combats that sometimes ended in the deaths of one or more "players." Only limited archaeological evidence has been found regarding the particular details and rules of these Mesoamerican ball games. The records we do have reveal that, in their stone stadiums, the Mayans played a "classic" version of the ball game that pitted teams of two to four players against one another. The rules prohibited touching the ball with the hands or feet, thus requiring participants to use mainly their hips in order to direct the ball where they wanted it to go. The evidence suggests that teams scored by advancing the ball to the back wall of their opponents' side of the I-shaped court. Some courts also had small stone rings placed on the side walls. A player who could direct the ball through such a ring scored an outstanding goal, which was worth more than the points garnered by pushing the ball into the opponent's rear wall. The rings at Chichén

Itzá are more than 24 feet (7 meters) off the ground. Directing a ball through any of these rings with just one's hip would be a truly astounding feat.

Mesoamerican ball games were furiously violent affairs. Players donned leather protective gear that covered the knees, arms, hands, and chests. Indigenous accounts and later Spanish chronicles describe commonplace injuries ranging from contusions to broken bones. In addition, human sacrifice often accompanied the game. The specific pattern of the executions varied from culture to culture. Some Mayan accounts describe death penalties carried out immediately after a game concluded—sometimes for the captain of the losing side, sometimes for the entire losing squad, sometimes for the captain of the winning side, and even occasionally for the entire winning team. The limited nature of the available records leaves a shroud of uncertainty about the details of many aspects of the game, including which body parts players could use to advance the ball and when and why certain players were selected for sacrifice.

We have much more extensive records about Roman gladiatorial contests, in which the combatants fought either as individuals or, sometimes, as teams. The Romans created a wide variety of classifications for the types of weapons and armor used by fighters in the arena. To perfect their deadly arts, Roman gladiators trained in schools run by superintendents, many of whom were former gladiators. In addition to training their charges, they served as agents who sold the services of their gladiatorial teams to stadiums throughout the Roman Empire. Amphitheaters located in the hinterlands, such as the one at Isurium Brigantum in the British Isles, often operated as minor-league development circuits. Meanwhile, the Colosseum in Rome served as the primary showcase for the most talented gladiators. Constantinople, the city that became the capital of the Roman Empire in the east,

THE COLOSSEUM AND THE GRAND BALL COURT

Historical Profile

The Colosseum in Rome and the Grand Ball Court at Chichén Itzá represent two of the architectural wonders produced by the civilizations of classical antiquity. The Colosseum was built by the Flavian dynasty of Roman emperors (which ruled from 69 to 96 CE) as a showcase in the center of the empire to stage the *munera*, the gladiatorial combats that drew enormous crowds of spectators. Completed in 80 CE and known officially as the Flavian Amphitheatre, the Roman emperors financed the project with the treasure and slaves they exacted from crushing the Jewish rebellion against their occupation of ancient Israel. More than 100,000 Jewish slaves labored on the massive stone and concrete project.

The largest amphitheater the Romans ever built was the Colosseum, and its architects lavished a variety of flourishes on the structure, including elaborate decorative murals and a canvas roof called the *velarium* (sail or curtain in Latin) that could be stretched over the massive arena to protect spectators from sun or rain. A hole in the center of the *velarium* allowed sunlight and rain to fall onto the unfortunate gladiators fighting on the floor, thus reinforcing the boundary between players and spectators in these Roman games. Ancient sources indicate that the stadium had a capacity of 87,000 spectators, though archaeologists have calculated that a range of 50,000 to 60,000 is a more accurate accounting of the seating. Whatever their specific number, the seating arrangements reflected the rigid class structures of ancient Rome. The emperors and the patricians sat in the lower tiers with the best views, whereas the plebeians congregated in the "nosebleed" sections high above the action. The Colosseum primarily hosted *munera* but was also used to stage *naumachia* (mock naval battles), public executions, wild animal hunts, and dramas based on Roman mythology.

Similarly, in the midst of the temples and palaces of the classical Mayan city of Chichén Itzá, the Grand Ball Court occupied a central position. Housing a playing field more than twice the size of an American football field, the I-shaped stone stadium featured massive murals of ball players in action and carved stone decorations evoking the pantheon of Mayan divinities. Because the Grand Ball Court is so much larger than any other stadium uncovered by archaeologists in Mesoamerica, some scholars speculate that it was not used to stage actual ball games but instead constituted a gigantic monument to the game. Other researchers, however, think that it served as the central site for the most important Mayan ball games.

The Mayans built the Grand Ball Court about a millennium after the Romans completed the Colosseum—that is, between 1050 and 1200 CE. The scant sources from Mayan records provide us with far fewer details about how and why the Grand Ball Court was built than we have for the famous Roman stadium. At one end of the Grand Ball Court, the Temple of the Bearded Man (so named for its stone carvings of bearded men, a rarity in Mayan art) provided vantage points from which the nobility watched the games. On one side of the structure, the Temple of the Jaguars rose above the walls and offered an additional viewing area for the rich and powerful. In contrast, Mayan commoners took their places on the remaining spaces around the court, thus replicating the Roman pattern in which the lower orders of society were given the poorest views. Estimates vary widely as to how many spectators the Grand Ball Court accommodated, but certainly thousands and even tens of thousands may have crowded into the available viewing spaces.

and other major Roman cities joined Rome to form a "major-league" circuit.

Gladiators fought to either incapacitation or death. Losers who did not die often faced a judgment from the sponsor of the contest, who sometimes sought input from the crowd as to whether the incapacitated opponent had fought bravely and should be granted a chance to fight another day or whether the winner should dispatch the loser with a kill shot on the spot. Thus, as with the Mesoamerican ball game, human sacrifice in front of thousands of spectators constituted an essential element of the Roman gladiatorial spectacles.

Roman *munera* and Mesoamerican ball games also shared many commonalities. They both drew spectators from all ranks of society, from the common peasants (*plebeians* in Latin and *elemicqui* in Nahuatl, the Aztec language) to the religious and political rulers of their respective empires (*patricians* in the Latin lexicon and *pipiltin* in Nahuatl). Members of the ruling elite sponsored these games in order to garner influence and reinforce their status, both among their fellow patricians and in the eyes of the plebeian masses. The elites made political and commercial deals at the contests, while the masses enjoyed a brief respite from their daily routines of grueling labor by feasting and watching the spectacles. Food and alcohol fueled these events, and both the masses and the aristocrats gambled with abandon. During the contests, religious leaders performed rituals to honor the gods and to celebrate communal solidarity. Thus the games provided a mechanism to highlight the political and religious traditions of each civilization and served as one of the most important components for reinforcing the common culture shared by both the rulers and the masses.

Roman *munera* and Mesoamerican ball games also revealed clear differences between the two civilizations. Mesoamerican societies played a ball game (albeit a violent one) and then sacrificed players at the end. The Romans staged ritualized and stylized versions of combat itself which often resulted directly in death among the "players." The religious ceremonies celebrated different gods, different cosmologies, and different religious traditions. Spectators ate different foods and imbibed different beverages.

The most startling difference, however, consists of who played the games. The Mesoamerican ball games drew participants from the upper ranks of their societies. Warriors and nobles clashed in the I-shaped stone courts in a struggle to win the adoration of their fellow citizens and the admiration of their gods. In contrast, in most circumstances, Roman citizens did not clamber into their arenas to fight to the death. Only a handful of thrill-seeking Romans, dubbed the *auctorati,* chose careers as gladiators, and the general consensus among the Romans was that these volunteers were not of sound mind. Instead, Rome drew its gladiatorial participants from among war captives, slaves, and criminals sentenced to death and therefore looking to avoid a quick and painful execution. A criminal who "volunteered" to become a gladiator had his death sentence suspended and was required to serve a stint in the arena. The vast majority of gladiators did not survive their three-year terms.

Opposition to Gladiatorial Contests

Groups within the Roman Empire whose members suffered in the gladiatorial amphitheaters offered impassioned opposition to these cruel spectacles. The Greeks, who during their conquest were sentenced in large numbers to the *munera,* had their own category of gladiator, the *hoplomachus* (a combatant armed in the Greek fashion). Greeks complained loudly when the Romans staged gladiator contests in Greece, even rioting on occasion to protest the events. Early Christians, who sometimes faced public execution in the arenas for refusing to bend their beliefs to Roman dictates, also decried the *munera.* "We see little difference between watching a man being put to death and killing him," declared Athenagoras, an early Christian leader in Athens. "So we have given up such spectacles." Another early Christian philosopher, Tatian, described the spectacles as a "cannibal banquet for the soul." Tertullian, another leading early Christian

Voices of Opposition to Brutal Sporting Spectacles

Student Exercise

Based on the critical comments provided by Roman citizens in table 4.1, answer the following questions:

- What does patrician opposition to the *munera* reveal about how the Romans viewed gladiators?
- What does it reveal about the crowds who flocked to the arena?
- What insights do these sources provide regarding why the Romans staged such brutal gladiatorial games?

Table 4.1 Critical Comments From Roman Citizens

Source	Comment
Cicero	"Just look at the gladiators, either debased men or foreigners, and consider the blows they endure! Consider how they who have been well disciplined prefer to accept a blow than ignominiously avoid it! How often it is made clear that they consider nothing other than the satisfaction of their master or the people! Even when they are covered with wounds, they send a messenger to their master to inquire his will. If they have given satisfaction to their masters, they are pleased to fall. What even mediocre gladiator ever groans, ever alters the expression on his face? Which one of them acts shamefully, either standing or falling? And which of them, even when he does succumb, ever contracts his neck when ordered to receive the blow?"
Seneca	"There is nothing so ruinous to good character as to idle away one's time at some spectacle. Vices have a way of creeping in because of the feeling of pleasure that it brings. Why do you think that I say that I personally return from shows greedier, more ambitious, and more given to luxury, and, I might add, with thoughts of greater cruelty and less humanity, simply because I have been among humans? "The other day, I chanced to drop in at the midday games, expecting sport and wit and some relaxation to rest men's eyes from the sight of human blood. Just the opposite was the case. Any fighting before that was as nothing; all trifles were now put aside—it was plain butchery. "The men had nothing with which to protect themselves, for their whole bodies were open to the thrust, and every thrust told. The common people prefer this to matches on level terms or request performances. Of course they do. The blade is not parried by helmet or shield, and what use is skill or defense? All these merely postpone death. "In the morning, men are thrown to bears or lions, at midday to those who were previously watching them. The crowd cries for the killers to be paired with those who will kill them, and reserves the victor for yet another death. This is the only release the gladiators have. The whole business needs fire and steel to urge men on to fight. There was no escape for them. The slayer was kept fighting until he could be slain. "'Kill him! Flog him! Burn him alive!' (the spectators roared). 'Why is he such a coward? Why won't he rush on the steel? Why does he fall so meekly? Why won't he die willingly?' "Unhappy as I am, how have I deserved that I must look on such a scene as this? Do not, my Lucilius, attend the games, I pray you. Either you will be corrupted by the multitude, or, if you show disgust, be hated by them. So stay away."
Roman literary exercise included in a fictional account of a gladiator's "eyewitness" vision of the arena	"And so the day arrived. Already the populace had gathered for the spectacle of our punishment, and the bodies of those about to die had their own death-parade across the arena. The presenter of the shows, who hoped to gain favor with our blood, took his seat. . . . Although no one knew my birth, my fortune, my family, one fact made some people pity me; I seemed unfairly matched. I was destined to be a certain victim in the sand. . . . All around I could hear the instruments of death: a sword being sharpened, iron plates being heated in a fire [to stop fighters from retreating and to prove that they were not faking death], birch-rods and whips were prepared. One would have imagined that these were the pirates. The trumpets sounded their foreboding notes; stretchers for the dead were brought on, a funeral parade before death. Everywhere I could see wounds, groans, blood, danger."

theologian, characterized the brutal contests held in the arena as a "misuse of God's creation by God's creatures."

Gladiators themselves, as prisoners of the system, could rarely protest. One exception occurred from 73 BCE to 71 BCE in the form of an uprising led by a band of gladiators who escaped from the gladiatorial training school at Capua. The escapees were commanded by Spartacus, a Thracian warrior sentenced to the gladiatorial arena, and their numbers were swelled by slaves emboldened by the gladiators' bold uprising and hopeful of ending their bondage. With Rome's main army away in Spain to fight new wars of conquest, Spartacus won several victories over local militias and small cohorts of Roman legionnaires and gathered more than 70,000 slaves into his crusade. Whether Spartacus and his colleagues were trying to overthrow slavery in the Roman Empire or simply escape Rome's grasp and return to their homelands remains lost in the mists of history. When Rome's legions returned from their Spanish conquests, they brutally destroyed the rebel army. Roman officials ruthlessly condemned Spartacus and the other leaders to horrible deaths, crucifying them upside down and leaving their bodies as reminders along the highways leading to Rome as a warning to other slaves who might entertain dreams of rebellion.

Even Roman citizens, many of them patrician leaders, sometimes voiced their discomfort with the *munera*. As the Roman philosopher and politician Cicero (107 BCE–43 BCE) pointedly asked, "What entertainment can possibly arise, to a refined and humanized spirit, from seeing a noble beast struck to the heart by its merciless hunter, or one of our own weak species cruelly mangled by an animal of far greater strength?" The Roman philosopher Seneca (4 BCE–65 CE) added his doubts about the spectacles in a letter to a friend: "I came home more greedy, more cruel and inhuman. Man, a sacred thing to man, is killed for sport and merriment."

The Ethics of Brutality in Sport

The historical record underlines the brutality that characterized some early versions of sport. This portrayal is ironic because sport is advertised today as a safe place in which to compete. Most sport organizations take aggressive steps to ensure that physical risks are minimal, serious accidents are rare, and fatalities are virtually nonexistent. For example, sport governing boards have, among other steps, changed rules to reduce dangerous actions, increased penalties for excessively rough play, improved equipment safety features, and provided medical support at competitions. Even in rough-and-tumble sports, such as American football, the losers generally live to play another day, usually without serious injury. We would probably count this civilizing process of sport as moral progress, and it would be hard to find anyone today who would seriously argue that we should return to the "good old days" of chariot races, gladiatorial contests, or games in which contestants literally lost their heads.

This observation raises two sorts of provocative questions about what counts as moral progress. First, are there any objective standards for claiming that one culture is superior to another? That is, can we confidently judge the Roman and Mesoamerican cultures as morally bankrupt? Second, over the course of human history, have we made demonstrable moral progress? Can we document the assertion that we are kinder and gentler than our ancestors? Have violent acts around the world decreased over time?

The first pair of questions falls into the philosophical domains of axiology and epistemology (for more on these branches of philosophy, see the introduction and chapter 3). As you have learned, axiology is the study of value, and it asks questions about the nature of the good life. Epistemology, on the other hand, is the study of methodology, of how we come to know, of whether or not we can approach or reach certainty about our truth claims. The truth claim at issue here addresses moral progress—specifically, the hypothesis that we are objectively better moral agents than were most of our ancient kin, and that we live in a better world than they did. The philosophical goal here is to provide criteria for such a claim. Can we identify what counts as better and obtain agreement on these standards from all, or at least nearly all, thoughtful people?

The second series of questions is empirical in nature. Questions about actual moral progress can be answered only if we have some way of measuring or assessing the ethical status of a culture. As you learned in the introduction, philosophers typically do not tend toward measurement. Even so, they may view the information that results from accurate measurement as complementing their own research. We will consider how this combined philosophic and empirical research can lead to intriguing claims about moral progress.

Philosophers who believe that values and other intangibles can be identified by those who reflect carefully and skillfully are called realists. Those who believe, on the other hand, that reflection produces no such valid outcomes include relativists and nominalists. These latter two groups would argue that any value claims are strictly opinions. That is, they hold that no persuasive evidence can be brought to bear on claims that one style of living is better than another—for example, that we are any better than the Romans or the Mesoamericans. More specifically, relativists doubt that reflection can uncover the truth because, as they claim, we are all embedded in cultures that bias or otherwise distort our thinking processes. That is, no Archimedean point exists from which to see the world clearly. Nominalists, on the other hand, believe that we construct the world to our own liking. That is, we divide up values in ways that suit ourselves and then give these artificial categories names—thus the term *nominalists*.

In other words, the way in which we divide up, conceptualize, and symbolize the world of value in language is a product of our own thinking, *not* the way the world really is.

In this text, we take a position of cautious or critical realism. Although we agree that nobody enjoys access to any Archimedean perspective—and that our enculturation often frustrates our attempts to identify solid values—we believe that progress is possible. As a result, we might also be called epistemological optimists.

This optimism stems from several factors. One is the demonstrable power of reason, particularly when examining extreme positions. For instance, it is difficult for anyone—regardless of religion, education, or enculturation—to argue persuasively that it is acceptable to torture innocent children, abandon a good friend in time of need, or hoard food in a time of famine. Our human reasoning capabilities help us identify these acts as wrong, and we have a great deal of confidence in these judgments. This capability supports realism because different people in different cultures have independently come to similar conclusions on such matters. Such consensus would be wildly improbable if relativism or nominalism were true.

Another supporting factor is our inability to change our minds about certain moral issues that were, at one time, controversial but now have been resolved, at least in most of the civilized world. This resolution includes rational consensus on such things as the practice of slavery, the denial of women's right to vote and to receive an education, the use of duels to settle disputes, and the application of the death penalty for petty crimes. In fact, the consensus on such matters is so strong that it seems inaccurate to refer to it as mere opinion; to the contrary, we see such practices as *objectively* improper, retrograde, unjust, and uncivil. As a result, we do not expect to have to revisit these issues or debate them again in the future. Moreover, we regard any culture that currently embraces such outmoded practices as behind the times, and we hope that someday they will see the light of reason and change their ways accordingly.

Similarly, we would not expect to see a revival of the brutal games of the Mayans, Aztecs, or Romans. In fact, we would be appalled if anyone were to recommend that we should add excitement to next Saturday's football games by executing the losers on the 50-yard line. It is a moral truth, we might conclude, that such brutish and uncivil behavior in sport is simply and objectively wrong—perhaps as wrong as the errant mathematical claim that 2 + 2 = 5.

It must be granted, however, that moral claims cannot be proven, at least not in

IS MIXED MARTIAL ARTS A BRUTAL SPORT?

Philosophical Application

Mixed martial arts (MMA) has proven to be controversial because it is a full-contact sport allowing a number of combative techniques that range from grappling to punching to choking. Much like the ancient Greek *pankration*, it is designed to test overall fighting capability and therefore has few rules. Although a number of safety regulations have been added to MMA in recent years, some fatalities have been reported, along with a variety of serious injuries, including lacerations and broken bones. Moreover, the injury rate is two to five times higher in MMA than in other martial arts and combat sports, such as judo, taekwondo, and boxing. The most common area for injury, as in boxing, is the head. Techniques commonly used in MMA include "sprawl-and-brawl" (e.g., kickboxing), "ground-and-pound" (taking an opponent down, securing top position, and striking the opponent with the fists or elbows), and "submission seeking" (using a painful or dangerous hold to force the opponent to admit defeat). One common way to win a match is to render the opponent unconscious.

A number of MMA organizations—including the World Mixed Martial Arts Association and the International Mixed Martial Arts Federation—have been formed to better control the sport, improve its safety regulations, and assure its future. Although some countries have restricted or banned MMA, it is gaining popularity in many parts of the world. It is even said to be challenging boxing and professional wrestling in terms of overall popularity. If anything, this increasing popularity has heightened the controversy about its moral status.

© Ginger Monteleone//Dreamstime.com

Ethical controversy surrounds high-risk, combative sports such as mixed martial arts, boxing, and even American football.

any strict sense. If someone were to ask us to literally demonstrate through logic that slavery is wrong, we would lack the resources to do so. Rather, moral conclusions rest on rational judgments that must be accepted. Thus intelligent discernment, using arguments about rights, freedom, and suffering, permits us to judge slavery as wrong and to be confident in that claim.

It must also be granted that many moral dilemmas are less clear cut. In contemporary culture, for example, we are still arguing over such issues as abortion, physician-assisted suicide, gay marriage, capital punishment, animal rights, environmental protection, disparity in wealth, and a variety of other topics. In the world of sport, people argue over the ethics of "flopping," the use of performance enhancers, and the proper reach of Title IX and other methods for supporting girls' and women's sporting opportunities. We are also facing new ethical questions raised by evolving technologies, such as genetic engineering. Should we allow parents to engineer an athletic child? Many ethicists today would argue against this practice, but they would also say that it is difficult to come to firm conclusions. This does not necessarily mean, however, that solid judgments on these issues will always remain beyond our reach. It means that *today* we cannot identify compelling arguments for one side over the other.

Philosophers who are cautious realists might conclude, then, that efforts to identify characteristics of ethical living, the good life, human flourishing—whatever we want to call it—are not futile. On the basis of intelligent discernment, we support freedom over slavery, love over hatred, justice over special privilege, fair play over cheating, life over death, friendship over alienation, knowledge over ignorance, peace over war, joy and delight over pain and suffering, and civility over brutality. These distinctions speak to our earlier questions about our ability, philosophically, to identify standards of progress.

Our tentative conclusions are that ethical insight is possible, that our ethical knowledge has improved over time, and that we can be reasonably confident that we have identified at least some characteristics of the good life.

This line of thought leaves us with the second set of empirical questions about actual improvement. Are we moving in the right direction—say, toward less violence and more justice? Can sociologists and other students of culture point to facts showing that the human race in general, and the rich variety of cultures around the world specifically, are on a positive ethical trajectory?

Some of you may be skeptical about empirical claims that moral progress has been made across the broad sweep of human history. You would have good reason to harbor such doubts because the ills of the modern world are not hard to identify. We still have war. We still have cases of ethnic cleansing. We still have slavery in parts of the globe. Acts of terrorism are far too common. Girls and women are treated as second-class citizens or worse in many countries. We still see religion used to justify horrible crimes. We still witness intolerance in many places for people who are "not like us." Perhaps it is more accurate, then, to conclude that brutality, injustice, and disregard for human rights are as prevalent today as they were in ancient times.

Similar skepticism may seem to be warranted in the world of sport. Scandals are common at all levels of athletics, from youth leagues to intercollegiate programs to professional sports. Systematic cheating still takes place. Injured athletes are returned to games. Coaches and parents berate young athletes. Drug use and other means of illegal performance enhancement have been difficult to control. Women still have not reached parity in terms of athletic opportunity. Overtraining and long schedules lead to a variety of crippling disabilities. Incredible sums of money are

IS IT ETHICAL TO PLAY OR WATCH AMERICAN FOOTBALL?

Philosophical Application

More than a century ago, in the early 1900s, in the wake of crippling injuries and even deaths among players, a large number of critics called for a ban on American football. Obviously, their arguments failed to persuade most of our ancestors. Today, a new campaign (which began in the early 2000s) seeks to address similar concerns, either by appealing to our reason or by legislating the sport out of existence. These efforts rely increasingly on medical data, as well as tragic anecdotes. Even a few of the most dedicated football insiders have begun to wonder about their own sport. One such person is Mike Ditka, the Chicago Bears legend and Hall of Fame player and coach. Having personified football toughness for decades, Ditka has proclaimed to the national media that if he had an 8-year-old son, he would bar the boy from playing football. In another example, a recent best-selling book, Against Football: One Fan's Reluctant Manifesto, chronicles the struggles of a lifelong fan who gave up his passion for the game when he came to view it as a morally indefensible pastime.

More generally, a growing chorus of voices discourages the American passion for football, seeking to persuade us to voluntarily surrender our interest in the game. Some even argue that we should outlaw it, in part because it is a brutish activity. Here are some of the more common arguments supporting this line of thought.

- Football involves hurling one's body against an opponent's body in order to administer potentially harmful blows, sometimes to the head. Indeed, doing so is a crucial element of the game—and sometimes a necessary means to winning. Thus, although intent to harm may not be present in most football players, collisions that could potentially harm another person are inherent in the structure of the sport.

- Although much scientific work remains to be done, researchers are increasingly discovering that the risks of concussion and traumatic brain injury are greater than previously believed at every level of football, from youth leagues to the college game to professional contests. Moreover, dramatic evidence has begun to emerge showing long-term brain damage resulting in depression, dementia, and death among professional football players. Meanwhile, the list grows longer and longer of players whom we once cheered but who have succumbed to early deaths and whose autopsied brains show evidence of chronic traumatic encephalopathy.

- The violent collisions that so many fans enjoy in football sometimes result in broken bones and torn ligaments. For some players, they permanently damage joints and bones, producing crippling post-career challenges that can potentially diminish quality of life and even contribute to early death. Brain injuries leave less immediately observable damage but can result in even more dire health consequences than destroyed knees and shoulders. Such costs are morally indefensible.

- Football can promote unethical attitudes among fans—for example, cheering "savage" hits. Some critics suggest that football and other combat sports celebrate a form of violence and make it more acceptable in society at large. (This same argument is used against some types of graphically violent movies and computer games.)

- Demographic studies indicate that fewer Americans are willing to let their children play football. In particular, parents who fit the category of what economists dub "knowledge workers"—that is, well-educated people in high-salaried professions—steer their children away from football due to fear of brain injury. As a result, many observers think that football may go the way of professional boxing, a sport in which the vast majority of athletes come from the lower socioeconomic rungs of society, where people perceive that they have few choices for escaping hardship. As with boxing, then, some individuals may perceive football as their "only way out." Thus, like some boxers, those who strive to play professional football in the future may not freely choose it so much as feel effectively coerced into entering a dangerous occupation.

lavished on coaches and athletes. Brutality still exists in certain sports. Many citizens in Western democracies are far more likely to attend the "big game" than to vote in a national election. And this list could be continued. Perhaps, then, we are no better than our seemingly more brutal ancestors. Perhaps we have just sanitized our brutality and injustice to make them look better.

Many scholars of culture disagree with the pessimistic view that "nothing ever really changes." One example is Steven Pinker, who argues that across the many centuries of recorded history, violence has declined considerably; moreover, he thinks that his claim is supported by persuasive evidence. Using historical accounts and data, he traces reductions in many brutal practices, including, among others, war, cruel and unusual punishment, genocide and terrorism, lynching, sexual abuse, fighting, various nonfatal crimes, cruel treatment of animals raised for meat, and gay bashing.

To support many of his claims, Pinker provides data related to improved attitudes, more exacting values related to life and the evils of suffering, and statistics showing reductions in virtually all forms of violence. Although he notes that this progress has not been even or linear from culture to culture, he tries to show that overall the progress is both unmistakable and dramatic. In qualitative terms, he suggests that we are kinder and gentler people than were many of our ancestors—or, if we are not better per se, at least we control our baser impulses more effectively and adopt more tolerant attitudes. In other words, he argues, we are more effective at developing and cultivating the "better angels" of our nature—a phrase that Pinker adopted from Abraham Lincoln's first inaugural address. For example, we abhor forms of violence that were commonplace and even celebrated in previous cultures. In Pinker's heralded yet controversial book *The Better Angels of Our Nature: Why Violence Has Declined*, he characterizes his findings as follows:

The problem I have set out to understand is the reduction in violence at many scales—in the family, in the neighborhood, between tribes and other armed factions, and among major nations and states. If the history of violence at each level of granularity had an idiosyncratic trajectory, each would belong in a separate book. But to my repeated astonishment, the global trends in almost all of them, viewed from the vantage point of the present, point downward.

Across human history, from our days as hunter-foragers to the present, Pinker documents a decline, both in violence itself and in our tolerance of brutality, through six trends: the pacification process, the civilizing process, the humanitarian revolution, the long peace, the new peace, and the rights revolution. The rising opposition to blood sports, documented in this chapter, belongs to Pinker's second chronologically ordered trend—the civilizing process. As you saw earlier in the chapter, this process can be traced to two sources—religion and secular ethics. Religion, and particularly Christianity in the Western world, played a role in criticizing brutal sporting games and helping to eliminate them. Secular scholars also made arguments to the effect that brutality and sport should not mix. These early ethicists believed that our leisure-time pursuits, and particularly our sporting activities, should be safe and civil.

Chapter 3 addresses one line of secular reasoning that can lead to more civility—namely virtue ethics, which connects the right and the good. If the good is understood to include the pursuit of fair and honorable athletic victory, the display of excellent motor skill, and the avoidance of activities that would maim athletes and their opponents, then the right—that is, moral virtue—might require that one be honest and follow the rules, be respectful and treat opponents and officials properly, and be careful to use strategies that do not impose significant harm or high risk on oneself or one's opponents. The virtuous athlete, therefore, is honest, respectful, and careful—all of which promote civility.

The same is true for utilitarian ethical systems, which are addressed in greater detail in chapter 6. Briefly, utilitarians believe that behavior should be guided by promoting the greatest balance of good over harm. Of course, brutality in sport produces pain, suffering, loss of life, and other harms. Thus, most utilitarians see the minimization of brutality as an important feature of their ethical calculations. Here again, maximizing pleasure over pain promotes civility.

Chapter 7 introduces a third major ethical theory, which is often referred to as deontological or rule ethics. Immanuel Kant believed that ethics should not be a matter of calculating maximal benefit or choosing which pleasures to privilege. Rather, it should be based on treating people with respect or, as he often put it, regarding others as ends, not as means. In contrast to this approach, brutality in the quest for victory treats others as means rather than ends. It fails to respect the rights of others.

These three lines of ethical thinking—the virtue, utilitarian, and deontological approaches—have been used to argue against brutality. Along with theological values related to humility, kindness, love, and the sanctity of life, such thinking began to expose brutish practices in life and in sport for what they were—ethically unacceptable behaviors!

Even so, questions related to civility and gentility are still with us, even in the world of sport. For example, we still see rough play and fighting in the sport of hockey and argue over the degree to which this kind of behavior is acceptable. In other examples, soccer and American football have been identified as sports that cause concussions, and some parents are reluctant to allow their children to participate in them for fear of serious injury. In addition, we still wonder if so-called "blood sports" such as boxing are morally acceptable (recall the earlier sidebar about mixed martial arts). In addition, critics of some forms of hunting argue that it is brutish to kill animals (and, in some cases, to cause them to suffer what appear to be slow and painful deaths) primarily for recreational pleasure.

Drawing Conclusions About the Ethical Status of Football

Student Exercise

Review the arguments presented in the sidebar on the ethics of playing and watching American football, then use them as a starting point for defending one of the following three positions.

1. These arguments are persuasive. Football should be outlawed. Although football injuries are not usually fatal, the game is an unfortunate holdover from our less civilized history when many sports were brutal and often lethal. Quality of life is often compromised for football players, and their life spans can be shortened. These costs are too high.

2. These arguments carry some weight. Football can be supported, but only with additional safety precautions, better equipment, and rule revisions. (Some forms of football have moved in this direction—for example, the intramural flag football found on many campuses.) In short, the costs of football need to be minimized.

3. These arguments are not persuasive. Professional football in its current form is morally defensible, both for informed adults who choose to step onto the gridiron and for parents who allow or encourage their children to play football. Our society is becoming too safe, too sanitized, too tame. Football is rough, but that is part of its charm. Rough is not the same thing as brutal. The costs are acceptable.

Contrast and Continuity

Our "civilized" debates about combat sports (such as boxing) and collision sports (such as American football) often center on concern for the health and welfare of participants, as well as uneasiness about the entailed violence and brutality. Comparable concerns rarely surfaced in the 3,000-year period from 1500 BCE to 1500 CE. As revealed earlier in the chapter, in the comparison of the Roman gladiatorial games and the Mayan ball game, cultures in this period of human history engaged in a variety of sporting traditions that displayed both remarkable similarities and profound differences. A catalogue of those differences would produce an enormous compendium of diverse local, regional, and even continental variations that would dazzle the imagination. These civilizations, and the multitude of cultures that inhabited them, displayed an amazing variety of unique sporting and recreational patterns. Instead of chronicling this enormous diversity, however, this chapter focuses on the broad similarities. Certain common features appeared in the sports and games, the physical education traditions, and the philosophies of embodiment in all of these cultures during the 3,000-year period immediately preceding the birth of the modern era.

The model of ancient sport that we introduced in Chapter 2 provides a template for these contests. The traditional patterns of sacred, martial, durable, local, and unequal characteristics continued to structure their games and contests over these many centuries. In our survey of the sporting habits of Western, Asian, American, and African civilizations, we will trace the similarities in the martial arts methods that developed in each of these cultures, compare and contrast how religion shaped their visions of sport and the body, and examine how sporting institutions and physical education practices reinforced the unequal social hierarchies that dominated these civilizations—marking distinctions between rulers and the masses, priests and warriors, religious and ethnic groups, and men and women. We will also examine the political and cultural dimensions of the festivals that featured sporting contests, seeking to make sense out of how these civilizations understood and explained their devotion to sporting spectacles.

The Enduring Martial Traditions

Agriculture provided the foundation for traditional ancient civilizations. In turn, protecting arable lands and the wealth built from farming surpluses required powerful armies. Some ancient empires, including the Roman Republic, used regular citizens as the foundation of their military might. Even in Rome, however, as imperial demands grew ever more intense and the republic gave way to the age of emperors, a professional class of warriors developed to protect, defend, and expand the empire. Freed from constant agricultural demands, these soldier castes spent their time training for war. The Roman Empire and medieval Europe; traditional China, Japan, and India; the urban empires of Mesoamerica and Peru; and the kingdoms of Africa, central Asia, and the Middle East cultivated regular cadres of fighters who devoted their lives to warfare. Each of these cultures developed elaborate systems of martial arts in which participants trained for hand-to-hand encounters and drilled with the tools of their craft.

Asian Martial Arts Traditions

More than 10,000 years ago in East Asia, along the fertile valleys of the Yellow and the Yangtze Rivers, Chinese cultures began to domesticate crops and animals, especially millet, wheat, rice, and pigs. They faced formidable environmental barriers in controlling their flood-prone rivers; eventually, however, they planted the foundations for robust agricultural economies, built cities, and developed written languages. Thus Chinese civilization is one of the oldest and most vibrant in human history. In spite of wars and the cyclical rise and fall of dynasties, Chinese civilization was remarkably successful at providing general governmental stability for an enormous population spread over an immense territory. As a result, China represents the most secure and durable of the globe's ancient civilizations.

China's relative stability commenced after a period of metropolitan autonomy when the early Chinese cities organized themselves into a powerful and wealthy empire known as the Xia dynasty (circa 2070 BCE–1600 BCE). After dominating China for centuries, the Xia rulers weakened, and China split into multiple warring kingdoms. Eventually, a new empire emerged in the form of the Zhou dynasty (1046 BCE–256 BCE), which ruled for centuries until it also declined and China again fractured into multiple regions ruled by warlords. This pattern of the rise and fall of imperial dynasties interspersed with periods in which regional kingdoms dominated the landscape characterized Chinese civilization into the modern era. In some cases, imperial collapse resulted from internal uprisings and power struggles. In other cases, imperial dynasties were toppled by invasions from outside of China's historic boundaries, particularly by tribes from the steppes of central Asia. When "barbarians" from outside conquered China, they were generally assimilated within a few generations into the patterns and traditions that continued to shape Chinese civilization as a series of dynasties waxed and waned.

Chinese sport and systems of physical education reflected the traditional characteristics that shaped ancient physical cultures around the world. In particular, the need to train warriors to defend empires against attacks, whether from inside or outside of China, produced well-organized agonistic contests and disciplines designed for combat training. Chinese soldiers exercised with weapons and also learned intensive systems of unarmed hand-to-hand fighting techniques. Collectively, these combat exercises became known as *wushu* (a generic term for martial arts). Specifically, records from the Zhou dynasty reveal contests in archery, sword craft, and chariot races that prepared the army to use the implements of warfare. Chinese warriors also ran footraces, wrestled, and engaged in jumping and throwing contests. By the Han dynasty (206 BCE–220 AD), cavalry mounted on horseback replaced chariots as the dominant military technology, and equestrian sports flourished among the warrior classes.

The unarmed versions of *wushu* proved especially durable and popular in Chinese culture and laid the foundation for the development of the elaborate martial arts disciplines that have evolved from ancient roots throughout Asia, including Chinese kung fu; Japanese *budo* (generic term for martial arts) disciplines such as karate, sumo, and judo; Korean *hangul* (martial arts) disciplines such as taekwondo; and variants in most other East and South Asian cultures, including India, Vietnam, Cambodia, Laos, Thailand, and even the Philippines.

Chinese civilization influenced the rise of other Asian civilizations, including flourishing cultures in Korea and Japan. Influenced by the traditions of mainland Asia as well as indigenous developments, urban civilization grew on the Japanese islands from about 1000 BCE. For many centuries, Japan divided into a myriad of kingdoms ruled by military clans and warlords Then, over several millennia, an imperial authority developed and slowly grew stronger. In both ancient and medieval Japanese history, military power played a decisive role. As in China, a military caste of professional soldiers dominated the political landscape.

Japanese warriors practiced martial arts that demonstrated their military craftsmanship. This military caste, which became known as the *samurai* by the

1100s CE, consisted of formidable soldiers and dominated Japan for two millennia, from the origins of urban settlements until the middle of the 19th century. In addition to the unarmed *budo* arts, Japanese warriors trained in sporting contests that displayed their skill with weapons. Archery initially dominated ancient Japanese warfare, and contests that demonstrated proficiency with long bows became popular events at both rural and urban festivals and in the courts of warlords and the imperial dynasty. Japanese archers stood and shot at fixed targets. They also practiced *yobusame*, a spectacular sport in which they demonstrated both their skill as cavalry and their shooting skill. Galloping down long tracks at full speed, *samurai* on horseback fired flights of arrows at tiny targets to prove their mastery of the bow.

Archery eventually declined as an effective military tactic due to improved armor, which made the *samurai* increasingly

Chushin gishi meimei den, The Walters Art Museum

Zen archery or *kyūdō,* (the way of the bow) and *kendō* (the way of the sword) were among the martial arts practiced by Japanese warriors called *samurai.*

impervious to even the most skillfully targeted arrow. Even then, however, it remained an important skill in contests of *samurai* prowess. In medieval Japan, *kyūdō*, "the way of the bow," developed as an organized discipline that every *samurai* needed to master, at least in contests if no longer in combat. Even though archery declined as an effective military technology, swordsmanship remained a consistently lethal practice. *Kendō*, "the way of the sword," offered warriors an organized system of killing techniques that eventually spawned fencing competitions as popular as the archery contests had been. Japanese swords were far sharper than European versions; therefore, in order to make fencing into a sport, the Japanese had to replace their steel weapons with bamboo substitutes. Even with wooden swords, serious injuries occurred frequently; therefore, the Japanese developed protective gear to cover the hands, arms, chest, and head. This equipment remains the fundamental gear for forms of *kendō* that have survived into the modern period.

Beyond China and Japan, flourishing martial arts traditions were also used to train Indian warriors, as is illustrated in lyric epics written over thousands of years (1400 BCE–400 CE) in Sanskrit, the ancient language of Hinduism. Indian warriors showcased their skills with weapons and proved their physical prowess in wrestling matches and footraces. Wrestling also flourished in Islamic regions of West Asia and in the Arab kingdoms of the Middle East. In fact, grappling in wrestling matches was the leading pastime of common folk in those regions. The ruling classes, on the other hand, flocked to archery and hunting in order to prove their prowess. Increasingly, from about 500 CE, they undertook these two pastimes on horseback. Similar patterns shaped the pastimes of ancient African kingdoms. Wrestling flourished throughout the African continent, and warriors also trained in archery and engaged in stick fights and other forms of weapons training. Hunting demonstrated prowess and showcased the martial spirit, particularly when Africans engaged the large predators that inhabited their continent.

Martial Equestrian Sports

After 500 CE, mounted warriors increasingly dominated warfare in Asia. In the 1200s CE, hordes of Mongol cavalry from the steppes of central Asia conquered China. Mongol emperors promoted the equestrian game of polo, which had long been popular in the Chinese army for training cavalry troops. Even Chinese emperors had been ardent players, and polo had flourished among China's warrior classes. Its popularity increased after the Mongol conquest. The game also arrived in India in the form of horse-mounted invaders, in this case the Muslim cavalry that conquered the northwestern territories of the subcontinent. Polo played a central role in the art and literature of India's Islamic Mughal Empire (circa the 1520s to the 1870s) and attracted an enormous following among Hindus as well. It also thrived in Turkey and Persia, kingdoms in which mounted warriors dominated the political and military landscape. Thus polo spread throughout Asia during these millennia and even made inroads in Africa. The Islamic conquests of the Saharan regions in East and North Africa brought the passion for polo to cavalries in those areas, though the taste for this equestrian sport seems not to have migrated to sub-Saharan regions.

Most scholars think that polo developed from early games played by the nomadic tribes of central Asia, who covered vast distances on horseback. One precursor game from Afghanistan, *buzkashi*, survived into the 20th century; in this game, hundreds of mounted warriors compete to commandeer a headless goat carcass. Emperors and warriors used polo to showcase their prowess on horseback for centuries, thus underscoring in the 1000s CE what a Persian poet once observed: "There are four things for kings to do . . . feast, hunt, play polo, and make war."

Roman Martial Sports

Invented in central Asia, polo trained cavalry forces and entertained emperors in China, India, and the Islamic kingdoms of western Asia and the Middle East. The game spread beyond Asia to Europe, at least to the borderlands between the West and the Islamic realms where the Byzantine Empire (330–1453 CE) carried on the legacy of the eastern Roman Empire. In Western civilization, however, polo remained solely in the Byzantine provinces and never spread to the rest of Europe. Not until the 1860s when British cavalry officers in India developed a fascination for the sport and began to found polo clubs in occupied South Asia did the sport return to the West. The British military imported the game back to their homeland. From the British Isles, they quickly expanded it throughout the world via their far-flung outposts that defended their global empire.

Although polo and other Asian pastimes did not invade the western half of the Roman Empire, Rome certainly developed its own martial and imperial sporting traditions. Even though Rome borrowed extensively from Greek culture, the Romans remained skeptical of the athletic contests and gymnastics codes that the Greeks had viewed as providing the foundation of Hellenistic military prowess. A minority of the Roman patrician ruling class did fall under the spell of Grecian lifestyles and sought to introduce Greek-style athletics and gymnastics systems to Rome, but these trends were dismissed by most patricians and by the plebian masses. For one thing, the puritanical Romans found Greek athletic nudity scandalous; even more telling, they found Greek athletic and gymnastics pastimes insufficient for the cultivation of effective warriors. The Romans preferred real military drills to Greek athletics and scornfully dismissed the spectacle of nude runners and long jumpers as unmasculine and unmartial silliness.

Romans created spaces for their martial exercises not in the gymnasia, which were built by Greek immigrants to Roman cities, but at the *thermae*, the public baths that served as the ubiquitous meeting spaces for all manner of social interactions. Roman bathhouses littered the empire and provided places where Romans of all classes could relax in hot and cold pools, play leisurely ball games, debate current events, make business deals, and engage in other forms of social intercourse. For martial activity, the Romans eschewed the Greek regimens and engaged instead in routine physical fitness programs and weapons training exercises that provided the military with a ready source of legionnaires to fill the Roman ranks.

The Romans also staged dramatic spectacles that they believed nurtured a martial ethos and linked war to civic cohesion and religious rituals. These festivals, called *ludi*, involved games, parades, and theatrical productions honoring the gods, celebrating Roman battlefield victories, and evoking the power of war as the fundamental force on which imperial might was built. The Latin term for participants in these spectacles was *ludiones*—literally, a player in a game or an actor in a stage show. The contrast between these terms and the Greek terms *agon* and *athlete* showcase a fundamental difference between Greek and Roman attitudes toward sporting contests. Whereas Greek culture focused on the experience of personal participation in the struggle for victory in contests of prowess, Roman culture focused on the experience of spectators who watched individuals viewed as actors or entertainers reenact the struggle for victory.

The term *ludi* also stood for the annual festivals and special spectacles that the Romans regularly staged. The *Ludi Romani*, or "Games of the Romans," referred specifically to three martial spectacles: circuses, *munera*, and *naumachia*. Circuses were the most popular and most common branch of the *Ludi Romani*; they featured chariot racing as the main event. Roman audiences also thrilled to the *munera*, or gladiatorial combats. Finally, the most spectacular and the rarest form of *Ludi Romani* were the *naumachia*—the mock naval battles celebrating special Roman victories or the anointing of a powerful new emperor.

On the surface, the *Ludi Romani* appear to be classical examples of the martial nature of ancient sport. On closer inspection, however, none of these contests directly trained Roman citizens for their military duties. For instance, chariots had been the dominant weapons (about 1700 BCE–500 BCE) on ancient battlefields hundreds of years before the Romans rose to power, but first the Greek phalanx and then the Roman legion had made coordinated infantry units the supreme force. Thus chariots represented an outmoded and archaic military machine by the time the Roman circuses flourished (200 BCE–400 CE). The *munera*, on the other hand, featured armed combat, frequently to the death, between individuals or teams of gladiators. Though this combat was contained inside the boundaries of arenas and staged to thrill the throngs of spectators who watched from the stands, it was indistinguishable from hand-to-hand skirmishes on the battlefield. However, with the exception of the handful of the aforementioned *auctorati* (drawn from ranks of thrill seekers and those who were delusional), the gladiatorial spectacles rarely included Romans as participants. In other words, Roman citizens did not fight to death in the *munera*; instead, they made their vanquished enemies, their convicted criminals, and their degraded slaves serve as the *ludiones* in these dramas.

The *naumachia* followed the same pattern, as the Romans forced small navies of war captives and convicts sentenced to death to fight in reenactments. These spectacles were rare and expensive, and Roman records indicate that fewer than a dozen were ever staged, though they often drew huge crowds. In 52 CE, the emperor Claudius staged the most lavish *naumachia*, which featured 100 ships and 19,000 combatants. Thousands perished as Roman spectators gawked from hillsides. Most of the victims drowned as their armor bore them straight to the bottom of the shallow lake used for the event rather falling in hand-to-hand struggle against their foes.

Although the *Ludi Romani* did not provide Roman citizens with hands-on lessons in warcraft, the games nevertheless fueled the martial ethic at the heart of Roman imperial power. The *munera*, and the occasional *naumachia*, reminded Romans that bloody sacrifices and military aggression created the empire and animated the Pax Romana. The gladiatorial spectacles reinforced the cultural tradition of Roman unity forged by a long history of wars for survival against powerful enemies. In addition, even as the *munera* and *naumachia* forged internal unity, they also served as warnings to the many peoples conquered and subjugated by the Roman Empire, and to the "barbarians" living outside of the empire's boundaries, that Rome was a cruel and bloodthirsty master. Indeed, the gladiatorial games were designed both to prevent rebellion by conquered tribes and to intimidate imperial enemies on the border into pacific relations.

Reflections on Why the Romans and Mesoamericans Staged Brutal Games

Student Exercise

The following list details the major reasons why, according to scholars' speculations, the Romans developed and promoted the *Ludi Romani*. Which of these reasons do you think best explains Roman motives? Might any of these rationales also explain why Mesoamerican civilizations staged their epic ball games? Construct a list of potential Mesoamerican motives that reveals similarities to and differences from the Roman profile.

- Roman unity was based on a long history of wars fought for survival against powerful enemies. As a result, fear of conquest by outsiders made Romans into aggressive conquerors. The gladiatorial games were reminders to a now-powerful Roman empire of the bloody sacrifices and military aggression that had created the Pax Romana.

- The *Ludi Romani* provided Rome with re-creations of war in order to build patriotism and loyalty. Not every citizen served in the army or fought directly in the wars of conquest, but every citizen could attend the games and get a taste of the violence that built the empire.

- Roman politics and social structures were shaped by the process through which the ruling classes (first patricians, then emperors) provided basic necessities and entertainment (bread and circuses) for the masses (plebeians). Thus the *Ludi Romani* constituted the cost of keeping the restless masses in their place.

- The *Ludi Romani* provided evidence to the poor masses that they were not at the bottom of the social structure. Specifically, they saw that they were better off than the sacrificial victims and disposable gladiators.

- Roman spectators were desensitized by the violence of the *Ludi Romani*. The power of violent images created a desire for ever-more violent entertainment.

- The Romans staged the *Ludi Romani* to warn both their conquered subjects and the "barbarians" who visited from outside of the empire that Rome was a cruel and bloodthirsty master. Thus the games were designed to prevent rebellion and warfare.

- The Romans staged the *Ludi Romani* to teach young citizens that the price of maintaining the empire was a willingness to shed blood. Thus the games constituted a lesson to future leaders that toughness and cruelty, rather than kindness and caring, kept the empire intact.

From the Fall of Rome to the Rise of Western Feudalism

In roughly the 400s CE, the Roman Empire in the West collapsed, and ancient varieties of Western sport fell with it. The spectacles of the *Ludi Romani* quickly withered into extinction, and the stadiums and chariot tracks fell into oblivion. In 393 CE, the emperor Theodosius (who reigned from 379–395) banned all pagan festivals in an effort to promote Christianity in the empire. Although Theodosius did not specifically target the Olympics, the ancient Greek athletic festival celebrating the power of Zeus did not fit into Christian cosmology. The imperial ban, in combination with "barbarian" looting of the site and a series of floods and earthquakes, effectively ended the durable athletic tradition at Olympia after more than 1,100 years. Theodosius' successor, Honorius (who reigned from 395–423), followed the same logic in passing laws that ended the *munera* in 399. After a Christian monk was martyred in Rome while trying to enforce the ban, Honorius reaffirmed it in 404. That year seems to mark the end of gladiatorial combats in the western Roman Empire (no later mentions of it exist in the historical records). Similarly, the year 549 marks the last recorded chariot race staged in Rome. By then, the Roman Empire had faded into oblivion and the ancient Greek athletic site at Olympia— covered by several feet of sediment from a series of floods and earthquakes—had disappeared, along with many of the traces of the ancient Western world.

After Rome's demise, Europe was divided into a patchwork of rival principalities that engaged in a constant series of wars. Power flowed into the hands of warlords who could field armies of mounted warriors—the knights of feudal tradition. During the millennium from the fall of Rome through the emergence in the 1500s of the modern world system, martial sports dominated the landscape of European pastimes. Indeed, the tournaments featuring contests between medieval knights blurred the lines between combat and contest more completely than had been the case with any other sporting custom. In one tournament held on the banks of the Rhine River in what is known today as Germany, as many as 60 combatants perished—a casualty count higher than the death toll in many medieval battles. Such tournaments consisted of jousting and melees. A jousting contest typically pitted two mounted knights wielding lances against one another. They charged down a course, and each sought to drive the other off of his horse. A melee generally pitted teams of warriors against each other, either on horseback or on foot, whacking away at one another with blunted weapons. The medieval tournament might well have developed from older Roman cavalry training practices, though concrete links between these traditions remain elusive, due in part to the lack of records from the 400s to the 700s.

Medieval warriors honed their combat skills in such tournaments for hundreds of years. As the tournaments grew more elaborate, they drew spectators from all classes. Monarchs and the nobility were seated in the best locations, in the stands, while peasants scrambled up trees to glimpse the action. By the 1300s and 1400s, the tournaments had become military anachronisms but remained powerful as political festivals and revealed the hierarchies of power that shaped feudal Europe. These hierarchies also affected medieval hunting. The best hunting grounds and premier game animals were reserved for the monarchs and nobles of Europe. For common folk, on the other hand, access to prime hunting grounds and preferred game was restricted by labyrinthine laws. However, as revealed by the large number of poaching cases that clogged medieval courts, peasants did not passively acquiesce to their exclusion from many venues and targets.

As in other civilizations, archery contests constituted an important component in the arsenal of martial sports. Although archery sometimes served the purpose of military preparedness, a significant recreational devotion to the longbow, and especially the crossbow, also developed in medieval Europe, most notably in the German-speaking regions of the continent. Archery contests were watched and sometimes sponsored by the feudal royalty and nobility, but the sport was controlled by the emerging middle classes (the bourgeoisie). Members of this new class occasionally used their skills in European armies, but they practiced archery mainly in order to garner status in recreational contests.

Beginning in the 1400s, archery began to be supplanted among the bourgeoisie by a burgeoning interest in court tennis, a game initially developed in medieval monasteries and then adopted by the royalty and nobility before spreading to middle-class enthusiasts. Tennis tournaments soon came to rival archery contests among the urban elites of European cities. A few steps up the social-status ladder, the aristocratic passion for tennis spread from its roots in France to England and then to the rest of Europe. Thus court tennis became a wildly popular game from London to Lisbon, from Versailles to Venice.

Religious and Intellectual Opposition to Martial Sports

The mayhem generated by martial sports sometimes offended the sensibilities of the religious leaders of ancient and medieval civilizations. The Catholic Church in the European Middle Ages issued numerous edicts, dictums, and appeals seeking to ban the jousts and melees that frequently wounded, and sometimes killed, the

knights who participated. The warriors mainly ignored the appeals of their religious brethren. Similarly, ancient Chinese philosophers, who were committed to cultivating the spiritual harmony sought by adherents of Confucianism and Buddhism, eschewed both the fierce contests celebrated by warriors and the violent pastimes of peasants.

The Chinese philosophers did not, however, entirely reject demonstrations of physical prowess; in fact, they championed archery as a mechanism for melding mind and body rather than for making war. They also developed the graceful exercises practiced in tai chi and other systems that promoted rhythmic movement for integrating the physical and spiritual components of human nature. Buddhist and Hindu devotees of these religious practices in other Asian cultures spread these sentiments throughout the Asian world. Their European counterparts, the priests and monks of Catholicism, exhibited similar sensibilities. Although the clerics criticized the sometimes deadly sports of the warrior classes, they nourished a variety of other traditional European games, including bowling and the forms of handball that eventually spawned tennis.

In Western civilization, Catholic clergy sustained the ancient Greek idea that a sound body provides the necessary housing for a sound mind. In so doing, medieval scholars blended the Greek rationalism of Socrates, Plato, and Aristotle with their Christian theologies. Specifically, the work of scholars such as St. Thomas Aquinas reveals a continuing Western dedication to both physical and intellectual education as requisite training for development of the "whole" person. Medieval Muslim scholars, such as Averroes and Avicenna, also kept Greek philosophy alive and sought to synthesize it with Islamic theology, incorporating ancient Greek ideas about sport, physical education, and embodiment into their cultural traditions.

Similarities and Differences Between Eastern and Western Sport

One of this chapter's major themes is the tension between the similarities and the differences in the development of sport and other physical activities around the world. As you have seen, much sport is rooted in martial or military activity. In addition, many sporting activities test common abilities, such as speed, strength, power, ability to ride and control horses, or ability to throw a spear or shoot an arrow. You have also seen that sport has served similar functions in different cultures—for example, to promote certain religious world views, to highlight and celebrate a culture's values, and to promote cultural cohesion.

At the same time, sport was organized, promoted, and experienced differently in different cultures. Indeed, in some ways, the purposes served by sport were notably different. This section of the chapter highlights some fundamental distinctions between the purposes, qualities, and conceptualizations of sport based on Eastern influences and of sport based on Western influences.

This is a dangerous exercise because geographically tethered influences are uneven and complex. For instance, Eastern cultures are themselves diverse; thus they cannot be captured accurately with broad-brush generalizations. The same is true for the Western world; no particular size or influence fits all. Moreover, Eastern and Western influences intermingled to some degree. Even so, it is useful to examine differences at the extremes and notice factors that influenced diverse cultural traditions. Thus, for purposes of simplicity and clarity, we examine on one hand sporting traditions influenced by Eastern world views, particularly those of Zen Buddhism, and, on the other hand, traditions influenced by Western world views, particularly those based on Platonic dualism as found both in some versions of Christianity and in secular culture.

More specifically, we consider four aspects of competitive sport in order to notice differences in how sport is understood and experienced.

1. Purposes of sport
2. Relationships between strategies and actions
3. Views of the opponent
4. Meanings related to winning and losing

Purposes of Sport

If you asked people influenced by Western cultural traditions about the goal or purpose of competitive sport, most would describe it in terms of victory, being recognized as the best, or seeking a championship ring. In fact, one of the typical ethical tenets of Western sport calls for "trying one's hardest"; after all, victory does not mean as much if an opponent is not trying to do his or her best. This view of sport assumes a zero-sum relationship between adversaries. That is, to the extent that my opponent succeeds, I fail, and vice versa. We each try to get more so that our opponent has less. Only one person or team wins.

Thus, winning and losing stand as contraries, opposites, mutually exclusive alternatives for sporting outcomes. In this paradigm, no one begins a game by trying to "sort of win"; in fact, there is no "sort of winning." One either wins or loses. This dichotomy frames our understanding of competition. It defines our purposes. We want to win, not lose. Because of this, ego is noticeably present, and part of the joy of competition comes with the attribution of merit: "*I* did it," says the victor. "*We* did it," reports the winning team.

In this view, ties are regarded by many as nonevents, even as failed contests. Logically speaking, a tie is a valid and entirely comprehensible outcome; it simply means that two teams scored the same, even though it was not the intention of either one to do so. Perfectly matched teams, in fact, would be expected to produce more ties and fewer blowouts than poorly matched teams. Yet in most sports, ties are not allowed to stand. Instead, extra periods, shootouts, and all other manner of tiebreakers are used to reach what is considered a "real" verdict in our dichotomous understanding of competition. Games apparently do not count unless they culminate in a victory for one side— and a defeat for the other.

This is not the case in many Eastern cultures. If you asked a person in the Zen Buddhist tradition about the goal of sport, the answer might surprise you. It would likely *not* be framed in dichotomous terms. Eugen Herrigel, author of the delightful book *Zen in the Art of Archery*, studied his subject for years in Japan, where he was told that the target in spiritual archery was not the object at the far end of the range but rather himself. In other words, Herrigel was supposed to develop new insights, a kind of enlightenment, with the assistance of the archery discipline. Of course, he had to develop techniques that produced good shots, but, more important, he was also taught to breathe, concentrate, and respect the equipment. Thus archery was framed not as a sport but as an art. Although victories might accompany perfection in the art, they were by-products of the mystical relationship between archer, bow, and target. Thus, after a successful competition, the archer would likely say, "The arrow shot itself." No ego. Just harmony. Therefore, Herrigel would be more likely to bow to "it" rather than pat himself on the back.

Relationships Between Strategies and Actions

In Western traditions, we often think of sporting success as the result of another dichotomy or dualism, this one involving thinking and doing. In other words, we make plans mentally, then carry them out physically. Mind first, body second. The mind is the pilot, and the body is the ship. Thus, in learning a skill, we think that we have to conceptualize proper technique first, imagine what a good movement looks like, and then try to act it out, practice it, and hopefully make it more automatic. Likewise, in competition, we assess the strengths of our opponent, put them up against our own abilities, formulate a rational strategy, and then (and only then) try to implement the strategy in the contest. This brand of sport is very cognitive. It posits that theory comes first and practice comes second. Moreover, it holds that the fastest route to good practice consists of sound insight, good propositions, and knowledge of how to play the game. In this schema, then, mind is superior to body.

In Eastern approaches, however, thinking and acting are not two distinct things. Instead, playing and competing well are all of one piece. You have already learned about complementation as an alternative to dichotomy in this book's introduction. Under the rubric of complementation, a martial arts practitioner would experience learning and competition as "thinking-doing" and "bodymind" or (returning to our earlier use of the tilde, or squiggle) as thinking~doing and body~mind. Thus apprentice learning would take precedence over cognitive understanding. More specifically, emulation, repetition, breathing exercises, work on concentration, and the development of "feel" would replace the two-part pedagogical strategy of planning and then doing. Intuition would take precedence over explanation. Words and theory could be used to explain fine performances, but in this tradition, they are no substitute for the concrete know-how of the intuitively insightful athlete.

Views of the Opponent

Another set of dichotomies is also at work in Western versions of sport—self versus other, me versus you, our team versus their team, and the "good guys" versus the "bad guys." Drama is added to the sporting experience by objectifying and sometimes demonizing one's opponents. They are not just opponents—they are enemies! They stand between us and the coveted championship. The fact that meaningful competition requires an opponent—as well as collaboration and cooperation with that opponent—is either overlooked by or lost on many Western athletes who are focused on winning at any cost. In their view, the opponent is not a collaborator but a hindrance. As in war, the opponent is seen as someone who wants to get exactly what I want to get. One of us will live; the other will die. This is hardly an exaggerated characterization of competition in the West. As a result, in many of our sporting venues, we have to work hard to promote civility—between opposing players, between fans and officials, and between fans of one team and fans of another. We are told to behave decently, but we know that our opponents are not us. They are the "other."

In contrast, the cosmology of Eastern thought is characterized less by difference and opposition and more by continuity. Moreover, the Eastern athlete strives to gain an enlightened experience of continuity. For Herrigel, this continuity occurred between himself, his bow and arrow, and the target—one harmonious whole. For those in judo, it includes oneself and one's opponent. Paradoxically, the opponent and his or her energy are encountered as continuous with one's own actions. Thus competition is not so much done against as done with. The movements of the opponent are incorporated seamlessly and harmoniously into one's own actions. It is a kind of mutual dance, a moving together. Such descriptions may not make sense to those of us from the West. They are, after all, not intellectual propositions to be accepted but rather spiritual or mystical truths to be encountered and experienced. This is why Herrigel spent years in Japan learning his art; it is also why many people today engage in Zen meditation and other spiritual practices for years on end. The eradication of ego-dominated living and dichotomous ways of thinking comes slowly.

Meanings Related to Winning and Losing

To reiterate, those of us raised in Western cultures are socialized to think of competitive outcomes in dualistic terms—as winning and losing. However, we all know intellectually that winning and losing

The Utility of Eastern Traditions in Medical and Sport Practices

Student Exercise

Many Western medical practitioners today use Eastern activities such as meditation, yoga, and tai chi as interventions to reduce stress and promote overall health. Meanwhile, some researchers are investigating these practices to determine the nature and degree of therapeutic value they may hold.

Likewise, some sport coaches and physical education teachers are adopting Eastern techniques to promote relaxation and focused attention as ways to improve performance. Some of these techniques have been popularized in such books as *The Inner Game of Tennis* (Gallwey), *Playing in the Zone* (Cooper), and *Flow: The Psychology of Optimal Experience* (Csikszentmihalyi). A number of sport psychologists have also been employing these techniques with both beginning and high-level athletes.

Your assignment is to pick one of these two areas—either medical practice or sport performance—and then search the web for current research addressing the utility of techniques inspired by Eastern traditions. Does the evidence suggest that they work? Support your answer with evidence-based reasoning.

occur by degrees. We can win and play well, or we can win and play poorly. We can win with an improved performance or without showing any improvement. We can win on the basis of luck, a referee's errant call, or a display of superior skill. We can win easily or win a very close game. Yet, despite these differences of degree, these variations in performance, the outcome is still identified as a "W." In short, we largely ignore one way of seeing or experiencing competition in favor of another way. We largely ignore the complexity of competitive experiences in favor of a dichotomous and more simplistic metric.

Those who compete from a Zen Buddhist stance might ask, "What is winning? What is losing?" It is their way of saying, "Who cares about this gross dichotomy?" Indeed, reality is far richer than that! For the Zen practitioner, no two victories and no two defeats are the same. Rather, they are intuited as the precise mixture of achievement and failure, of yin and yang, that they are. Because victory and defeat are continuous, there is no-thing, no reified object, to fear. The Zen question of "What is defeat?" is not merely a rhetorical question or a glib response. It emanates from a different way of seeing the world.

Global Continuities and Contrasts

Of course, the vast majority of people who lived in the cultures that flourished between 1500 BCE and 1500 CE were not scholars or clerics who explored ideas espoused by ancient philosophy. Nor were they monarchs or nobles who adored polo or hunting—or *samurai* or knights who devoted themselves to the martial arts. Rather, they were agricultural laborers who toiled in the fields and worked with livestock. In their traditional societies, they enjoyed little social mobility and generally could not hope that either they or their offspring would rise above the ranks of the vast peasantry that fed the world. Whether they lived in Asia, Africa, the Americas, or Europe, sport provided them with recreation and diversion—a temporary escape from the routine drudgery that marked their daily lives.

These individuals were generally untroubled by the presence of violence in their games. Indeed, routine violence marked their daily lives, including the slaughter of animals, the frequent cruelty meted out by the masters who directed their labors, the ever-present possibility of accidental injury or death in their agricultural occupations, the common scourge of disease that sometimes killed vast numbers among their ranks, and the blight of warfare that sometimes claimed them even though they were generally noncombatants. In this context, sport provided them not only with escape from drudgery but also with the chance, particularly for males, to garner some degree of status by demonstrating the forms of prowess that peasant life demanded—physical strength and endurance, dominance over animals, and hardiness and fortitude.

Peasant Sports

In most cultures, peasant sport featured contests showcasing the key attributes highlighted in the preceding section. Sports that involved animals, including cockfights, the baiting of bears, bulls, and other animals, as well as hunting, demonstrated the peasants' power over other creatures. Human sports, in contrast, including wrestling, feats of strength, footraces, and a multitude of ball games, demonstrated their hardihood, their muscular vigor, and their ability to both dish out and endure the violent conditions that often marked their lives. In particular, contests that featured wrestling, heavy lifting, and running formed universal patterns of recreation in peasant cultures. In these routine events, participants either won or lost status. The events in which peasants participated were often sponsored by the elites who ruled their kingdoms, the warrior class who fought to conquer or defend their lands, and the clerics who organized their religious rituals. As a general rule, those who inhabited the upper classes did not engage in athletic contests with peasants; indeed, doing so would have put them at risk of losing enormous amounts of status with nothing to gain if they won.

Festivals

Sporting contests thrived at times when the rulers of these civilizations declared interruptions of the normal routines of agricultural labor. More specifically, festivals flourished when official calendars set aside days for religious celebration, for commemoration of political milestones, or for other special purposes. Gambling and alcohol frequently fueled these sporting events. In fact, sporting habits, drinking traditions, and wagering customs evolved to form an intertwined triad at the heart of many festivals. As you may recognize, this relationship remains intact in many contemporary sporting practices in spite of more than a century of effort on the part of some interest groups to disentangle gambling and drinking from sport. The festivals also provided sites for economic exchange, thus creating spaces for entertainment and recreational markets to develop.

The Romans staged the *Ludi Romani* on the numerous public holidays when the empire celebrated its religious and civic ceremonies. In medieval Britain, Shrove Tuesday (the day before Ash Wednesday) was the occasion of riotous games of peasant football, a traditional team sport shaped by local customs that pitted church parishes or village neighborhoods against one another. In classical Mayan civilization, ball games were played during recurring religious celebrations. In ancient China, displays of fireworks and wrestling matches accompanied religious jubilees and commemorations of victories over invading hordes.

Like the ancient Olympics, these festivals highlighted the common religious, political, and social customs that united communities across class structures, thus linking peasants to ruling elites. Whether the festivals featured warrior games or peasant pastimes, they served as rituals of communal solidarity in which sporting events and other entertainments, including feasting on special foods and imbibing special beverages, created enduring bonds. The sporting practices that dominated these festivals varied widely, both within and between civilizations. The games people played, the foods they consumed, and the drinks they quaffed varied tremendously, based in large part on local tradition.

CHAPTER WRAP-UP

Wrapping Up and Looking Ahead

In spite of the enormous diversity of these customs, the general inclusion of sporting contests and recreational games as critical components of festivities that reinforced the mystic chords of cultural bonding constitutes one of the remarkable continuities between African, American, Asian, and Western civilizations. Diversity flourished in the particularities, but deep commonalities blossomed underneath the cornucopia of sporting practices that prodded these cultures to build stadiums at Chichén Itzá and Isurium Brigantum, to stage warrior games in the courts of feudal Europe and the courts of feudal Japan, and to celebrate athletic talents through Asian polo matches and French court-tennis tournaments.

In time, the dazzling diversity and broad commonalities of sport and physical activity in traditional and ancient cultures would be challenged by the emergence of new and novel patterns. More specifically, over the next several centuries, the sacred connections to sport would be severed by secular developments. Similarly, the martial traditions long embedded in sport and in systems of physical education would weaken and diminish. The structural inequalities embedded in traditional customs of physical activity would also be challenged by a new focus on equality and egalitarianism. In addition, the local sporting habits of cultures would increasingly be rationalized into universal global forms. The durable sporting habits that people had replicated in generation after generation, with little change or innovation over centuries or even millennia, would be confronted by new and novel habits that developed and spread rapidly—and sometimes disappeared just as quickly. A new, modern world would be born, and novel forms of sport and physical activity would soon emerge to dominate the present and to cast traditional pastimes into the shadows of an increasingly distant past.

Study Questions

1. In what ways did the Romans both preserve and change sporting traditions inherited from Greece?

2. How were the blood spectacles in Rome and Mesoamerica similar and different? What functions did they serve?

3. Can philosophers produce strong arguments against violence and brutality? Does history show any trends toward greater civility? Is brutality a moral issue in any contemporary sports? If so, which ones?

4. How did martial arts traditions affect sporting practices around the world? Specifically, how did Eastern traditions in China and Japan affect martial sports in the West?

5. How have Eastern and Western traditions affected the shape of sport, how it is played, and how it is experienced? What differences exist between Eastern and Western sport in purpose, strategy, attitudes toward opponents, and conceptualizations of winning and losing?

6. What functions did sport have for peasants and other elements of the working class? How was sport shaped to fit their agrarian culture? What kinds of sports were developed by these individuals?

THE EXPANSION OF THE WEST AND THE BIRTH OF THE MODERN WORLD

Global Transformations of Physical Cultures

Chapter Objectives

In this chapter, you will

1. explore the origins of modernization and globalization;

2. learn about the process of globalization and how it spread ideas about sport, physical activity, and the human body;

3. discover the Renaissance, which developed the notion of the "Renaissance Man," as well as philosophical theories about the human person that fall under the rubric of dualism;

4. study the Reformation, its views on the human body and the balance between work and leisure, and its influence on modern conceptions of physical activity;

5. examine the Scientific Revolution, including the philosophical development of the scientific method, scientism, and scientific materialism; and

6. begin to appreciate how modern societies differ markedly from their ancient predecessors.

The empires of Rome and of Mesoamerica (see chapter 4) fell thousands of years ago. The ruins of their stadiums remain and serve as gigantic stone reminders of the violent games that these ancient cultures once played in their monumental arenas. Today, rising on the rubble of these decayed empires, vast stadiums once again dominate the skylines of the world's cities. In Mexico City, over the ruins of the ancient Aztec capital of Tenochtitlán, Estadio Azteca (Aztec Stadium) now looms over the landscape where Aztec ball courts once stood. Fans of Mexico's national team wave the red, white, and green national flag, a banner emblazoned with a dramatic depiction of an eagle standing atop a prickly pear cactus with a serpent clasped in its talons. This symbol is derived from a legend dating back to the Aztec period in which the eagle and serpent represent the indigenous founding myth of Tenochtitlán.

From one angle, this confluence of ancient Aztec symbolism, modern urban architecture, and an enduring passion for sport that spans millennia seems to hint at deep historical continuities between past and present. However, in spite of some ironic similarities, what happens in the 21st century inside Estadio Azteca is not a re-creation of an ancient pastime but something quite new and distinct. Specifically, the *fútbol* matches played before roaring audiences in Mexico City's famous stadium are not modern versions of the ancient Aztec ball games. Moreover, unlike the games chronicled in chapter 4, these modern matches are *not* based largely on local traditions but represent instead a new global tradition that reaches to every continent on earth.

Estadio Azteca symbolizes the transformation from local to global that has taken place over the past few centuries, a process that has changed the world in profound ways, including the realm of sporting contests as well as ideas about the body and its purpose. From the beginnings of the agricultural revolution more than 10,000 years ago until about 1500 CE, geography and distance limited interchanges between civilizations and nurtured a dazzling diversity of sporting practices and physical culture traditions (surveyed in chapter 4). During this period, the civilizations of the Americas remained isolated from the rest of the world. Among African, Asian, and European civilizations, on the other hand, commerce, ideas, and beliefs drifted across cultural borders, but they did not erode the differences between the regions. Therefore, as in the Americas, sport, physical education, and ideas about the human body developed along insular lines.

Even when a custom did spread across the borders of a few civilizations, it did not permeate the entire "Old World,"—a region that spanned three continents. For instance, although medieval polo captured enthusiasts throughout Asia—migrating from its origins on the central steppes of the continent to China, India, and Middle Eastern realms—the game did not spread through medieval Europe or Africa. More generally, the intense and constant global interchanges that characterize the world today did not yet exist, nor did cultural practices enjoy worldwide popularity. Therefore, the possibility of a single game spreading across the globe remained beyond the reach of anyone's imagination.

That limitation began to change around 1500 CE, and in the five centuries since then the world has been fundamentally transformed. In the world we now inhabit, no part of the globe is totally isolated and no civilization or culture can remain completely insular. Commerce, ideas, and beliefs now flow back and forth in torrents all around the globe. Religious, political, economic, and social habits have global reaches and global impacts. As a result, we can now imagine a game that spans the globe. In fact, the sport that people in the United States call soccer and that the rest of the world calls football—or *fútbol* (in Spanish), *futebol* (in Portuguese), *fußball* (in German), and *le foot* (in French)—has reigned for close to a century as the world's most popular sport. *Fútbol*'s status as the world's most popular game was made possible by the historical processes unleashed by what scholars have called modernization or globalization, the momentous collisions that began around 1500 between Western civilization and the rest of the world and have continued ever since. Those collisions transformed the world.

The Birth of the "Modern World"

For thousands of years, the civilizations that emerged in Asia, Africa, and Europe enjoyed a limited but lucrative trade with one another. In particular, luxury goods such as spices, gems, and fabrics flowed overland from China to the rest of Asia and to Africa and Europe. Commerce in precious metals and human slaves also developed along this route, known as the "Silk Road." Ideas and free people flowed along the Silk Road as well. European adventurers, including Marco Polo, journeyed to Asia, while Chinese explorers ventured throughout Asia and into the Middle East and Africa. The route also facilitated the growth of some religions. Christianity, Buddhism, and Islam migrated into new civilizations via the Silk Road. From the 800s CE, the Islamic kingdoms of the Middle East served as the conduits for this trade route, controlling access from Asia into Europe and Africa. Eventually, European merchants grew disenchanted with Middle Eastern control over the Silk Road and sought to find new routes that would bypass the Islamic kingdoms' hegemony over the lucrative commerce.

Expeditions and Their Cargo

In the second half of the 1400s, explorers on voyages commissioned by Portugal began to sail down the Atlantic coast of Africa, around the Cape of Good Hope, and into the Indian Ocean. They followed the eastern coast of Africa to Asia, pioneering new routes to India and China. With Portugal dominating the African route,

explorers sponsored by Spain decided to sail due west into the open Atlantic in an effort to reach Asia. In 1492, a Genoese captain and merchant financed by the Spanish monarchy, Cristoforo Colombo (Christopher Columbus), led a tiny flotilla of three ships westward into the Atlantic. As an educated European, Columbus understood that the globe was spherical rather than flat. He planned his trip following the calculations of Western cartographers, who estimated that Japan was roughly 3,000 nautical miles from Spain. That distance represented the outer limit that European sailing vessels could venture without replenishing food and water supplies. It also represented a serious and potentially fatal miscalculation by European mapmakers as Japan lay more than 7,500 nautical miles away from Spain.

Fortunately for Columbus and his crew, other lands existed 3,000 miles to the west of Spain. When the fleet made landfall on a small island, they were convinced that they had reached the Far East—tellingly labeling the people they found on the island as "Indians." In 1493, Columbus returned to Spain and proclaimed that he had found a new route to Asia. He made three return voyages between 1493 and 1504, discovering more islands and a larger land mass. He died in Spain in 1506, still convinced that he had made it all the way to Asia.

In fact, Columbus and his sailors had voyaged to a region unknown to European mapmakers and in doing so, they inaugurated a globe-changing process. They established a permanent connection between the Americas and the rest of the world that changed the political, economic, and social fortune of every civilization on earth. When Europeans arrived in the 1490s, somewhere between 50 million and 100 million (scholarly estimates vary widely) people lived in the Americas. Over the course of the next two centuries, however, as they came into contact with European explorers and settlers, vast numbers of indigenous Americans perished. While some died from the violent encounters that accompanied contact and colonization, the vast majority perished from the importation of diseases from the Asia-Africa-Europe gene pool into the Americas. Specifically, smallpox, measles, yellow fever, influenza, bubonic and pneumonic forms of the plague, diphtheria, chicken pox, and several other infectious diseases created raging epidemics that entirely wiped out some American civilizations and devastated the vast majority of indigenous cultures.

These maladies were previously unknown among American populations, and they had no natural immunities to illnesses that in Europe, Asia, and Africa were certainly significant but to which, due to long exposure, "Old World" populations had developed considerable resistance. The vast majority of diseases traveled in one direction, from the Old World to the "New World." Researchers speculate that the only significant disease that passed the other way was syphilis, which was transmitted less easily and by much more intimate contact. Scholars estimate that these plagues killed between 60 percent and 90 percent of the American inhabitants of what Europeans called the New World. By contrast, the "Black Death," an epidemic of bubonic plague that swept down the Silk Road from Asia into the Middle East and Europe in the 1300s, has been estimated to have killed 25 percent to 50 percent of those populations—a horrific figure but not as devastating as the combined effect of the multiple New World plagues.

The singular direction of the vast bulk of this Columbian disease exchange was an accident of genetic fate that produced profound consequences. Ravaged by Old World plagues, American civilizations quickly crumbled in the face of European onslaughts. With tiny armies numbering in the hundreds, Spanish conquistadores defeated empires consisting of millions of citizens, including the Aztecs in central Mexico and the Incas in Peru. Other European nations, especially Portugal, France, Holland, and England, quickly joined Spain in subduing and colonizing the American continents. In short, after Columbus' initial voyages, Europeans soon realized that they had discovered what for the civilizations of the Old World were previously unknown lands.

Pushing outward from their new American bases, European explorers quickly pioneered routes between their New World colonies and Asia and Africa, as well as Europe. Their voyages laid the foundation for a global system of transportation and trade. People and products began to flow in larger and larger quantities between the Americas and Europe, Asia, and Africa. An international economy developed, linking the civilizations of the globe in an increasingly interdependent network. Thus the foundation was laid for a new world system that, over the next five centuries, would fundamentally change the political, economic, and social lives of the world's cultures.

Diverse Legacies of Globalization: Food Versus Sport

We can see the impact of centuries of globalization in our own daily experiences. Our diets and cuisines have been radically transformed as plants and animal species have crisscrossed the globe. Given that Columbus was born in Genoa, Italian cuisine provides a fitting example to illuminate the power of global biological exchanges. When we think of Italian food, we often conjure visions of tasty pasta and rich tomato-based sauces. That version of Italian food, however, combines staple products of other parts of the world far distant from Italy. Pasta originated in China produced through techniques for making wheat into an easy-to-use food. Tomatoes originated in the Americas. Before Columbus ignited globalization, the current version of Italian food would have been impossible to create.

With the new world-system that emerged, the Italian cuisine we recognize could spread everywhere, as could many other contemporary global cuisines from Mexican and Peruvian to Thai and Korean that reveal similar fusions of foods that arose from diverse places. Rice was an Old World staple, whereas beans originated in the New World. Most chili pepper varieties and many other hot spices originated in the New World, as did corn, squash, potatoes, and the turkey that stands at the centerpiece of many Thanksgiving feasts in the contemporary United States. Chicken, beef, and pork comes from animals that emerged in the Old World, as do bananas, broccoli, and onions. This diverse mixture that has enriched global diets could not have developed without the rise of globalization.

Whereas contemporary cuisines represent a true blending of influences that developed all over the world, contemporary sport does not. In fact, global sports spread

MYTHS AND REALITIES OF THE ORIGINS OF *FÚTBOL*

Historical Profile

When Spanish conquistadores seized central Mexico in the 1500s, the Aztec ball game fascinated them. In 1528, Hernán Cortés, the conqueror of Mexico, took a team of indigenous American ball players back to Spain, where they demonstrated the game, with its rubber balls, to the Spanish king and his courtiers. Based on this early interchange and a few other tidbits, legends have grown in Mexico and the rest of Latin America that the roots of *fútbol* reach back into the distant past of the Americas—specifically, to the invention of rubber balls (rubber trees are an American species) and the Mesoamerican spectacles (see chapter 4) that flourished for centuries before Europeans arrived and irretrievably altered the New World. In fact, some Latin American chroniclers of the game trace an unbroken lineage between ancient American ball games and the soccer-crazed masses in contemporary Latin American nations who live and die with the fortunes of their teams and stars.

Seeing modern *fútbol* as a product of ancient indigenous sport gives the game an attractive mythopoetic quality, but it does not match the historical realities of soccer's rise to its current position as the world's most popular game. The Aztec ball-game players that Cortés exhibited in Spain did not inspire a ball-playing craze in Europe that gave rise to modern varieties of football. Nor did rubber balls flood world markets and create new hybrid games that merged traditions from all over the globe into a novel form. Rather, modern football was born in the middle of the 19th century in Great Britain. From there, it spread through Britain's vast imperial connections to the rest of the world.

In spite of the historical reality that modern soccer emerged as a British game, not only in the Americas but also in other parts of the world, a variety of origin myths attempt, for nationalistic purposes, to obscure the British roots of the game. The claim that soccer emerged from ancient Chinese practices has a wide popular following. In Germany and Italy, arguments about soccer ignore the British connections and link the game instead to traditional Germanic and Italian folk games. In the 20th century, as soccer became the world's game rather than the sole province of Great Britain, the tendency to imagine alternative origin stories expanded in order to frame the game not as a product of the British nation but as a component of national experiences and identities in many other nations.

more like the bubonic plague than the burrito. They are global phenomena that emerged almost exclusively from Western civilization—from European nations and European settler societies—and spread to other parts of the world. Take, for instance, soccer (association football). Before European contact, ball games that limited or barred the use of the hands flourished in Mesoamerica. Today, *fútbol* ignites the passions of millions of Mexicans. Estadio Azteca has been filled to overflowing for two World Cup finals (1970 and 1986) and a multitude of other international matches. You might easily conclude that *fútbol* fused Mesoamerican and European sporting pastimes, much like pizza and pasta fused Old World and New World food. It did not.

Instead, the roots of *fútbol* reside in 19th-century Western civilization, specifically in Great Britain in the midst of the Industrial Revolution. From its birth in modern Britain in the 1860s, association football spread fairly quickly around the globe. Half a century later, by the 1920s, association football (by all its many names) already ranked as the world's game—the most popular sport not only in Great Britain but also in Europe, Latin America, Africa, and Asia. Over the ensuing century, the game has deepened its hold on the world (for more on the global spread of soccer, see chapters 7 through 11).

In stark contrast to the history of food and cuisine that reveals that globalization sometimes creates fusion, the history of the spread of soccer and other modern sports around the world reveals a different side of these processes—a side in which ideas, technologies, and cultural practices that originated in Western civilization dominated the interchanges. Although global tastes have profited from the fusion of cuisines from many civilizations, modern global sport has been dominated by Western games, Western attitudes, and Western ideas. Thus the great variety of indigenous pastimes that flourished before 1500 CE in the civilizations of Asia, Africa, and the Americas have, with few exceptions, faded into extinction while Western sporting habits and ideas have flourished.

The European Catalyst in Modernization and Globalization

Western sport has dominated the globe in large part because Europe served as the catalyst in the interchange. Europeans explored, conquered, and colonized the rest of the globe, while other civilizations sought to defend themselves against the Western onslaught rather than launch their own expansionist ventures. That the West pushed outward and led the transformation was not, as some assume, due to any innate superiority manifested in Western societies. Indeed, when viewed from the vantage point of scientific and technological achievements, or in terms of economic wealth and advancement, the West, circa 1500 CE, ranked behind many other civilizations. The Islamic kingdoms of the Middle East, the Aztec and Incan civilizations in the Americas, and Chinese civilization all enjoyed higher standards of living, built larger urban centers, and demonstrated greater technological and scientific acumen than did Europe. In fact, as the center of the Silk Road, home to the wealthiest economy in the world, and a hotbed of scientific and technical innovation, China reigned in 1500 as the globe's most advanced civilization.

Moreover, a review of the "tool kit" with which Europe conquered the world and created the foundations of globalization, reveals that most of the elements were borrowed from other cultures. The sailing equipment that allowed trips as long as 3,000 miles without resupplying had been developed in the Indian Ocean by Asian and Middle Eastern seafarers. The Chinese also invented the compass, gunpowder, the printing press, and paper—all key elements in Europe's global explorations and conquests.

Europe's expansionist genius manifested itself in borrowing technologies from other cultures and employing them in new ways, particularly in adapting these foreign tools to warfare. Gunpowder provides an instructive example. The Chinese inventors of gunpowder used it for artistic expression and religious celebration through colorful displays of fireworks. Europeans adapted the Chinese invention to push projectiles out of metal tubes, developing the handguns, muskets, and cannons that revolutionized modern warfare.

A variety of other factors also contributed to Europe's ability to push outward around 1500. For one thing, Europe's population had recovered from the demographic cataclysm of the Black Death two centuries earlier, and its increasing population densities fueled the impetus to expand. At the same time, Europe's role in the world economy impelled Europeans to seek new routes to the wealth of Asia that circumvented the Islamic kingdoms' dominion over the Silk Road. The rise of early modern financial structures, including banks, paper currency, and joint-stock corporations, instigated a market revolution that supported expansion into new realms. The rise of early modern nation-states along the Atlantic rim of Europe particularly Spain, Portugal, France, Holland, and England created rivalries for power and influence that generated expansionist adventures—as the Spanish crown's subsidy of Columbus' journeys testified.

In addition, three powerful intellectual movements that swept over Europe in a series of cultural waves beginning in the late 1300s and reaching full pitch by the 1500s encouraged expansive, outward-looking habits of mind. The Renaissance (14th century through 17th century), the Reformation (late 15th century through 18th century), and the Scientific Revolution (16th century through 18th century) generated new sensibilities in regard to questions and puzzles in philosophy and the arts, in religion and cosmology, and in logic and the sciences. Although each

WHY DID EUROPE RATHER THAN CHINA PUSH OUTWARD?

Historical Profile

At the risk of vastly oversimplifying complex historical developments, an illustration of the contrast between European and Chinese world views offers insights into why Western civilization became the catalyst for globalization and modernization and China did not. Among the grandest technological marvels built by China's world-leading engineers was the Great Wall, a massive project begun in the 200s BCE and constantly improved through 1500 CE. Over those centuries, Westerners built nothing that could remotely match the Great Wall. Significantly, the Chinese raised the Great Wall to keep the world out of their realm, especially the Asian "barbarians" who sought to plunder China's wealth. Chinese civilization thus remained content to inhabit what the Chinese considered the center of the world rather than pushing out into *terra incognita* (a Latin term for "unknown lands," frequently used in early chronicles of European exploration). In contrast, when the moment arrived for those in the West to expand and conquer, they seized it with a ferociousness that overwhelmed even more sophisticated and advanced civilizations. The Renaissance, the Reformation, and the Scientific Revolution not only encouraged Europeans to venture into *terra incognita*; they also created new attitudes toward sport and recreation, revived interest in systems of physical education, and reoriented European understandings of the human body and its potential for dynamic movement.

had a different focus, these three revolutions also displayed many interrelated perspectives. In concert, this trio of intellectual and cultural revolutions energized adventurous and inquisitive sensibilities in European cultures.

The Renaissance, Neoclassical Revivals of Sport, and the "Nature of Man"

The Renaissance, derived from a French term translated literally as "rebirth," marked the revival of formal systems of learning in the West, the rediscovery of classical Greek and Roman knowledge, and the flowering of new artistic and literary movements. The Renaissance began in the late 1300s in Italy with the emergence of republican city-states that promoted education, supported artistic endeavors, encouraged technological and commercial innovation, and renewed interest in ancient Greek and Latin learning and literature. The Renaissance blossomed in universities sponsored by the city-states. From the founding of the University of Bologna in 1088, education flourished in the region, and more institutions devoted to learning appeared during the 1200s and 1300s, including universities in Padua, Naples, Siena, Rome, Perugia, Florence, Camerino, and Pisa.

The Renaissance and Physical Education

As Renaissance scholars at these universities recovered the works of Homer, Plato, Aristotle, and others, they discovered the enormous significance of athletic competition and physical education in Greek civilization (see chapter 3). Although the restoration of the Olympics, or the rise of other forms of organized sport inspired by classical devotion to athletics, would not take place until the 19th century (see chapter 9), Renaissance thinkers began to build the case that engagement in contests of physical prowess produced superior citizens, particularly among the elites who ruled the Italian city-states. They reanimated ancient Greek arguments about the proper relation between the education of the mind and the body, about whether social programs to train bodies should be focused on the athletically gifted elite or on the general public, and about how cultures could use athletics and physical education to create ideal citizens to lead their cities. Like their ancient Greek counterparts—Socrates, Plato, and Aristotle—Renaissance philosophers pondered the role of athletics and physical education in training citizens as warriors who could protect their city-states. Renaissance scholars resurrected the classical concept of the gymnasium, the public site devoted both to training the body for rigorous contests and for imparting the wisdom of science and philosophy, mathematics and music, and literature and art.

Using the classical model as a foundation, Renaissance thinkers crafted a model of an ideal man who could be trained in new versions of the gymnasium to serve his city-state in every significant realm of endeavor, from politics and warcraft to the arts and letters. The "Renaissance Man," as this ideal came to be known, shared with the classical patriarchal ideal not only the investment of social power in men and manhood but also the Socratic commandment to harbor sound minds in sound bodies. The formula for the Renaissance Man detailed a long list of attributes that such a paragon of virtue, wisdom, and capability would need in order to serve his city-state. Renaissance Men, the recipe promised, were socially adept, skilled in the arts of war, politically astute, well versed in languages and literature, broadly educated in many disciplines, patrons of the arts, and devotees of physical fitness. Last but not least, they were pleasing to the eye—like the ancient Greeks, Renaissance thinkers believed that physical fitness and beauty reflected intellectual and spiritual virtue.

First in the Italian city-states and then in the rest of Europe, promoters of the ideal of the Renaissance Man wrote textbooks and developed schools modeled on the ancient Greek gymnasia to produce elite leaders for their communities. Following classical Greek models, these schools prescribed a mixture of both academic and physical training for their pupils. Inspired by classical concepts of the whole person as a manifestation of both body and mind, they championed intellectual development and physical education as complementary mechanisms that were each required for symmetrical human development. The concept of the Renaissance Man was cultivated for the elites by the elites. The new pedagogy mainly influenced the thinking of the ruling classes of Europe. The elite schools they envisioned, however, would eventually become the models for a mass educational system that would teach not only boys but also girls. That democratic development, however, would not materialize for several centuries.

Renaissance Schooling: Building Bodies and Minds

To produce the Renaissance Man, Europeans reimagined the Greek gymnasia. They wrote texts promoting "new" systems of education that melded the training of mind and body in the neoclassical tradition. They built schools devoted to producing "princes" and "courtiers" who manifested these qualities. These schools taught immersive Latin and included studies in history, moral philosophy, rhetoric, and literature that were balanced by a curriculum that required physical exercises and contests.

To cite one example, Petrus Paulus Vergerius, a scholar educated at the University of Padua, crafted a foundational text titled *The New Education* (circa 1400), a how-to guide for educating "princes." Drawing inspiration from a mix of Plato's works, particularly the *Republic*, as well as Spartan models, he focused his physical education system on training students in martial activities, including equestrianism, fencing, swimming, archery, wrestling, hunting, and even folk ball games. Another University of Padua scholar, Vittorino da Feltre, founded a school called La Casa Giocosa ("the House of Joy") in the small city-state of Mantua. It earned the nickname "School of Princes" for its role as the model for educating the sons of the elite to serve Italy as Renaissance Men. The school required two hours of daily physical activity. Like Vergerius, da Feltre focused especially on martial skills in the physical education curriculum, including equestrian training as well as long camping treks in the summer.

In their books and schools, the Italian Renaissance humanists sought to create the "guardians" of the social order that they so admired in Plato's imaginary utopian state as outlined in the *Republic*. An Italian soldier, diplomat, and politician, Baldasare Castiglione, codified the training regimen for "Renaissance Men" in *The Book of the Courtier*, published in 1528. Castiglione explained that the ideal courtier—someone who served in the personal retinue of the monarchs who had arisen to rule the city-states and nations of Europe—must be classically educated in Greek and Latin and should be handsome, fit, and well proportioned. He should also possess expertise in every martial skill, from swordsmanship to marksmanship to horsemanship. Courtiers, the early modern European versions of Plato's "guardians," required extensive physical and academic schooling in academies such as the one at Mantua, where Castiglione himself was born and grew up. Castiglione also elevated "court tennis," a popular pastime of the era's monarchs and aristocrats, by distinguishing it as the sport that every

Renaissance Man needed to master, not only for its intense physicality but also for the graceful movement and agreeable conviviality it inspired.

Translated into Spanish, French, and English, *The Courtier* became a Renaissance classic. As Renaissance ideas spread throughout Europe, Castiglione's concepts and the theories of other humanist pedagogues inspired imitators and sparked the creation of schools in Spain, Portugal, France, Holland, England, and other nations. In the British Isles, Thomas Elyot's *The Book of the Governor* (1531) drew heavily on Italian ideas, as did Roger Ascham's *The Scholemaster: Shewing a Plain and Perfect Way of Teaching Languages* (1570). Elyot and Ascham disliked common folk games, such as peasant football and bowling on village greens. Instead, they counseled gentlemen to follow the Greeks and Romans and take up running, swimming, hunting, fencing, equestrianism, archery, and sharpshooting. They also seconded Castiglione's endorsement of tennis.

Neoclassical ideas about the role of sport in education took hold as a new form of school appeared in the British Isles. The "public school"—public in the sense that it gathered boys onto a campus where they boarded together and shared teachers and classrooms, rather than being educated at home by private tutors—developed as preparatory institutions for sending elite children on to Oxford University or Cambridge University. Beginning with the 1440 founding of Eton, the original public school, dozens of competitors flowered and flourished over the next two centuries. These new academies nurtured the belief that sport and other physical activities prepared the ruling elites for their roles in societies, in particular, they fed the growing faith that military prowess initially emerged in schoolyard sporting contests. From such notions emerged the famous but probably apocryphal British maxim proclaiming "the battle of Waterloo was won on the playing fields of Eton."

The Emergence of "Modern" Debates on Human Nature

Renaissance thinkers resurrected the ancient tradition of educating the whole person, of cultivating both body and mind. Philosophers such as Marsilio Ficino (1433–1499) and Giovanni Pico della Mirandola (1463–1494) bolstered the ancient Greco-Roman conception of a "great chain of being" linking physical reality to a spiritual realm beyond the physical (that is, to a metaphysical realm). In this cosmology, humans represented the connecting point between the physical and the metaphysical, and bodies and minds were linked by the fundamental structure of reality. The schools that Renaissance leaders developed stressed this connectivity by promoting relatively equal doses of physical education and intellectual training. They thought that the proper cultivation of human nature required both books that challenged brains and games that challenged muscles. Games that challenged both muscles and brains, like tennis, were according to Renaissance thinkers the best recipe for stimulating human growth.

The relationship between bodies and minds, however, as in the classical philosophies so admired by Renaissance thinkers, remained a contentious subject. In spite of the general veneration in the Renaissance intellectual tradition for the great chain of being that linked bodies and minds, the revitalized spirit of inquiry and the rekindled interest in philosophical speculation spawned new ideas that would lead in very different directions. In fact, working from differing perspectives, a powerful group of thinkers was about to sever the great chain, to disenchant faith in connections between matter and spirit, and to drive a wedge between bodies and minds. These new philosophical perspectives were ignited by the processes of modernization that were transforming social, economic, and political institutions. What emerged would erode the centuries-old Western consensus regarding the connectivity of essential human parts, such as bodies and minds. In its place, several new and competing ideas about the fundamental nature of humans would usher in new dualisms, radical materialisms, and other innovative methodologies for exploring matter and spirit. In the process, "modern" philosophy would be born.

Varieties of Dualism

Before we tackle the details of these modern splits from tradition, let us set up an exercise to both review the older ways of understanding human nature and introduce some newer models. Arguably, philosophers' sustained interest in the nature of the human person constitutes one of their most relevant contributions for contemporary kinesiology. In part, this is so because we still think like the ancients in some ways and assert that any study of human physical activity starts with theoretical concepts about what makes a person a person. That is, our theoretical concepts are vital to our thinking and our actions; theories form the metaphorical glasses through which we see the world. For that reason, our theoretical concepts about the human person are also important for practical reasons. Since theories influence our practice, we must consider the practical implications of certain theoretical models. As modernity transformed the world, our metaphorical glasses changed.

One major change in the philosophical glasses of this period involves a major shift in the types of dualism that Western thinkers advocated. Dualism is based on a metaphysical claim that two different substances exist in the universe—the physical and the nonphysical. In the human person, dualism groups the physical substances together as the *body*, which includes everything that is material, from atoms to bones. If it exists in the physical

Creating a Concept Map of the Human Person

Student Exercise

Concept maps are diagrams that organize knowledge and illustrate connections. With a human person in the middle of your concept map, begin writing down characteristics of a person. For example, all people have bodies, so you can write *body* and draw a line connecting the word to the picture of the person. What else do people have? Think broadly. Then begin to add further components; for example, you might break the body up into DNA, muscles, and other components. Now try to connect the various characteristics that relate to each other. By the time you are finished, your concept map should look like a giant spider web of characteristics connected by lines.

Consider how messy and complicated the concept map looks—the more detailed your map, the more complicated it can appear. During the emerging modern era, philosophers who wanted to better understand the human person sought to create a theoretical model that could capture this complexity through metaphysical explanations.

For people in kinesiology, these theoretical models have practical applications. How we think about a person influences how we treat the person. As you can see by examining your concept map, people are complicated. As practitioners, if we fail to understand what a person is—if we fail to appreciate these complexities—then our work with people will likely suffer. If, for example, we ignore a patient or athlete's emotional needs and merely treat the body, then we reduce our effectiveness and may ultimately harm the person.

world, then it is considered body. On the other side of the divide is the nonphysical substance called *mind*, which includes everything that is typically assumed to be part of a person but is nonphysical. This category includes a person's thoughts, emotions, personality, or soul. Often, the mind (the nonphysical) is associated with the brain (the physical); hence philosophers sometimes refer to dualism as a divide between the mind and the brain in order to more clearly assert that the mind is nonphysical and thus not the neurons or electrical impulses that might be witnessed in the brain. Dualists would assert that although certain areas of a brain might process certain kinds of thoughts, the thoughts themselves are not localized in the brain. This view is further supported by evidence from muscle memory, a form of intelligence (the nonphysical part) that exists in other areas of a person's body such as muscles and nerves as well as their brain (the physical elements).

Dualism developed as a metaphysical explanation thanks in large part to Renaissance thinkers' veneration of the cultures of ancient Greece and Rome. The Greek and Roman texts not only shaped Renaissance education but also revived a fascination with the beauties of the human body and the pleasures of corporeal existence in art, medicine, and popular culture. Greco-Roman sculpture and painting had depicted athletic bodies as ideal forms, and Renaissance scholars returned to this classical aesthetic. A growing interest in depicting the body in exquisite detail in art also infused the study of medicine with a renewed focus on studying bodies directly rather than relying almost entirely on medical texts. Thus Renaissance medical schools developed the practice of dissection to cultivate empirical understandings of the body even as Renaissance painters studied bodies intently to reconstruct them more accurately on canvas and in stone. Moreover, these approaches sometimes merged in the work of a Renaissance scholar—for example, in the precise sketches made by the Italian polymath Leonardo da Vinci that inspired both artists and scientists to study the human form intently and intensely through direct observation and hands-on experience.

Substance Dualism

Such investigations also sparked further inquiries into metaphysics. Philosophers as far back as Plato had gone beyond physical drawings of the human body to discuss nonphysical aspects of human beings, including soul, mind, and spirit. In particular, René Descartes deserves substantial credit for creating modern ways of seeing the world and fracturing the idea that minds and bodies were inherently connected. In many ways, Descartes embodied the ideal of the Renaissance Man. He was educated in the classics and made contributions to mathematics, the sciences, and philosophy. He also developed an abiding interest in seeking absolute certainty in an era of rapid transition as the early stirrings of globalization and modernization revolutionized the world and created a climate of impermanence and uncertainty.

Descartes gave rise to a modern variation of dualism that stressed the separation of mind and matter rather than focusing on connections between the parts (as in the supposed great chain of being) that had been honored by Western thinkers since the time of ancient Greece. Descartes argued that there were two substances: matter, which takes up space, and mind, which consists of thoughts, ideas, and ideals. Descartes and other philosophers arrived at this stance, referred to as substance dualism, by first arguing that there is more to a person than just physical matter. It is obvious that a person has a physical nature, because bodies can be clearly seen and felt; their existence is not in doubt. But how to assert that there is more than just the physical? How to be sure that *I* exist?

In his work *Meditations*, Descartes sought to strip the mind of all physical inputs through a thought experiment. In his reflections, he imagined that an evil genius had concocted a grand experiment to fool his mind into believing that he had senses and even a body (a premise later borrowed in the classic 1999 science fiction film *The Matrix*). In this thought experiment, Descartes concluded that even if all of his physical senses betrayed him, he could be certain of one thing—that he was having a thought. Because he was having this thought, Descartes concluded that he could be certain he had a mind. This conclusion led him to write perhaps the most repeated line in philosophy: "I think, therefore I am" (*Cogito, ergo sum*). In short, Descartes realized that he could be certain that he was having a thought, and from

RENÉ DESCARTES

Historical Profile

"If you would be a real seeker after truth, it is necessary that at least once in your life you doubt, as far as possible, all things," urged René Descartes (1596–1650), one of the greatest minds of the Renaissance. In many ways, Descartes (pronounced like "day cart") embodied the ideal Renaissance Man even as he also stands as the grandfather of modernity. Born in La Haye en Touraine, France, Descartes eventually entered university to follow in his father's footsteps in law and politics. Like many students of his day, Descartes studied the classical Greek scholars Plato and Aristotle. He also discovered the works of Galileo, which inspired the curious thinker to pursue studies in mathematics and physics. After pioneering work in analytic geometry, Descartes became a "natural philosopher," or what we would today call a natural scientist. From his study of the natural world, Descartes graduated to philosophical inquiry. His scientific work led him to believe that the natural world contained both material and immaterial substances.

Library of Congress LC-US262-61365

René Descartes: mathematician, scientist, philosopher—called the "father" of Western philosophy.

Behind all of this inquiry, Descartes persisted in methodological doubt, which requires us to doubt things that we *believe* to be true and rebuild knowledge from what we *know* to be true. Such doubting led Descartes to assert that his only certainty was that he existed as a doubting or thinking being. This line of thought resulted in his pithy conclusion "I think, therefore I am." Descartes' interest in the mind and the laws that affect thinking, and in the body and the laws that affect physical machines, continued to fuel his interest in philosophy, anatomy and physiology throughout his life. If he were alive today, Descartes would likely find a comfortable niche in modern kinesiology departments. Indeed, darting between anatomy labs, field research, and philosophy seminars, Descartes' cross-disciplinary interests anticipated the route that contemporary kinesiology scholarship now travels.

that certainty, he concluded that *he* as a nonphysical mind must exist. Based on this realization, Descartes reasoned that two substances exist—a nonphysical mind and a physical body. The most important point to remember in regard to substance dualism is its assertion that the human person is comprised of two substances—mind and body—both of which are real substances, and each of which is radically distinct from the other.

Value Dualism

Like substance dualism, value dualism assumes that the mind and body are distinct substances. Where the two differ, however, is that value dualism claims that one substance is more important than the other. Which substance receives top billing? For value dualists, it is the mind. They justify this position with a number of reasons. First, in many cases, we can see that a person's body lives on but that his or her mind is not present, as in patients who are anesthetized or in a coma. Without the mind present, a person's body appears to be only a shadow of the real person. Second, many European philosophers associated the mind with a spiritual soul. As you will read later, Protestant reformers embraced value dualism's rejection of the body, which they viewed as a source of corruption, whereas the soul was eternal. Why spend time on the pleasures and pursuits of the body, an organism that will decay back into dust, when nonphysical substances will last forever? Moreover, philosophers could see how bodies break down with age and injury even as minds remain sharp. Thus, while eyes lose their vision or ears lose their hearing, the mind persists in its ability to reason and discern truth. Third, value dualists often identified the mind, with its capability for rational thought, as marking an important distinction between humans and animals. Though many animals possessed greater physical abilities, humans' minds allowed them to triumph over nature.

You may already see some flaws in this reasoning (a point we will discuss). At the same time, you must also realize how persistent value dualism remains—for example, in stereotypes about "dumb jocks," in praise for the intelligence of "rocket scientists," and in sustained emphasis on mind-based learning (such as math and literature) at the expense of body-based physical education and skilled artisanship. The orientation that produces such lines of thought stems from and reinforces value dualist claims about the human person. The most important points to remember in regard to value dualism are that it views the human person as consisting of two substances and that, although those substances are connected, it views one of them (mind) as more important than the other (body).

Behavior Dualism

Behavior dualism also assumes that the person consists of two separate if connected substances (mind and body) but emphasizes that the mind is the operator of the body. In this version of dualism, we can envision the body, composed of only physical material, acting like an automobile, in which various parts are capable of working together to form a machine that provides transportation. Though parts can break down or be replaced, this machine essentially performs all of its tasks in accordance with its own mechanical design. Alone, however, the car cannot go anywhere. It needs a driver. Here, behavior dualists insert the mind. The nonphysical mind can operate the body much as a driver can steer, accelerate, and brake an automobile. Without the driver, the car stays put. Similarly, without the mind, the body might continue to function (like a car engine idling) but can do little more. In this sense, behavior dualism does not *expressly* claim (as value dualists do) that the mind is more important than the body; it does, however, tacitly support overemphasizing the mind's importance by assigning

THREE KINDS OF DUALISM IN PROFESSIONAL SETTINGS

Philosophical Application

Dualism is a broad umbrella under which variations exist. Three of these variations are important for kinesiology, because they can affect your professional practice, the status of your profession, how you treat clients, and other matters. All dualisms share some features, but each also has unique characteristics. Knowing these characteristics will help you identify dualism in the workplace.

Name	Claim	Effects on kinesiology
Substance dualism	Divides the person into two separate substances—mind and body—each with radically different characteristics.	We treat the material body and the immaterial mind separately rather than treating the whole person; as kinesiologists, we tend to focus on the body—that is, the machine.
Value dualism	Places a higher value on the mind and a lower value on the body.	We work in environments where educating the intellect is perceived as more important than educating the physical intelligences; thus, as kinesiologists, or body experts, our work tends to be devalued.
Behavior dualism	Views the mind as the driver of the body; posits that thinking always precedes doing and that good ideas are always responsible for good actions.	We adopt two-part interventions that seek to have a patient's or athlete's thoughts precede and then affect his or her physical performances; as kinesiologists and movers, our excellence is always attributed to previous thoughts.

Though these three kinds of dualism overlap, it is common for one of them to come to the fore in certain professional settings. For example, coaches might exhibit a behavior dualist view of the human person as they use words to explain to an athlete how to execute a new skill. The assumption by the coach is that if an athlete's mind can understand the task, then his or her mind can make the body achieve it. Value dualism, on the other hand, might emerge through a teacher who places greater emphasis on chair-based learning in courses such as math or history than on physical education; indeed, the latter might even be excluded from the curriculum. This teacher assumes that educating the mind is more valuable than educating the body. Finally, substance dualism might appear in a physical therapy clinic where a therapist works to improve a patient's strength and flexibility apart from any psychological or emotional needs.

it a superior role in human functioning. Moreover, when it comes to motor learning, behavior dualism emphasizes the priority of the mind in acquiring new physical skills. When considering behavior dualism, the most important point is that it views the nonphysical mind as operating the physical body.

Theoretical and Practical Criticisms of Dualism

Dualism remains a popular view of the human person in Western societies, where the philosophical work of Descartes and other modern philosophers from Europe remains influential. In other intellectual traditions, especially in Asia, alternative explanations are available in the form of *materialism* (discussed later in this chapter) and *holism* (see chapter 10). Regardless of your personal experience, you have probably noticed the popularity of dualism. Thanks to the process of globalization initiated by European expansion, many people express a perceived dualistic divide between mind and body in their ordinary conversations. Examples include expressions such as "A mind is a terrible thing to waste!" and "Mind over matter!" More important, many people who hold dualistic views of the human person remain unaware that they have adopted a theoretical model of the person. Instead, they imagine the concepts of "mind" and "body" are facts rather than theories. Without their realizing it, this model shades their view of people like a metaphysical pair of sunglasses. The subtle tinting not only directs their attention to "minds" and "bodies" but also risks creating blind spots when dualists apply their theory in practice.

Dualism is a commonly held theory and one that is often applied in the kinesiology professions. Philosophers have identified, however, significant counterarguments that raise doubts about dualism's accuracy. In fact, objections to Descartes' brand of substance dualism troubled the French philosopher up until his death. Though his arguments were attractive, philosophers pointed out two fundamental problems. First, they asked how a nonphysical mind could interact with the physical body; this issue became known famously as the "mind–body problem." Descartes had defined the mind as nonphysical and as separate from the body. Now he faced the difficulty of explaining how this non-physical substance could act on physical substances without being physical itself. For example, it is easy to see how neurons and electrons coursing through the brain can stimulate the central nervous system to send signals to a person's legs, thus causing him or her to walk. But all of these processes are physical and contained in the body. Where in this system can a nonphysical mind step in and cause a person's electrons and neurons to start firing? Though Descartes feebly argued that perhaps the interaction occurred in the poorly understood pineal gland, a pea-sized structure located in the brain of most vertebrate animals, philosophers have continued to view the inability of dualism to explain how a nonphysical mind interacts with a physical body as a major theoretical flaw in dualistic explanations of the human person.

Second, we each experience our thoughts, our hopes, and our ideal as our own. That is, for each of us, they are part of the person that we are. But Descartes' insistence that these elements are nonphysical raised a puzzling question about their location "in" us. Only physical things can be located in places. Marbles, for instance, can be located in a jar. But how could mind, an entirely nonphysical substance, be located here in us . . . or anywhere for that matter?

For both of these theoretical problems raised by mind–body dualism, reason and theory find themselves at odds. Everyone knows that our thoughts affect our physical actions. And everyone knows that our

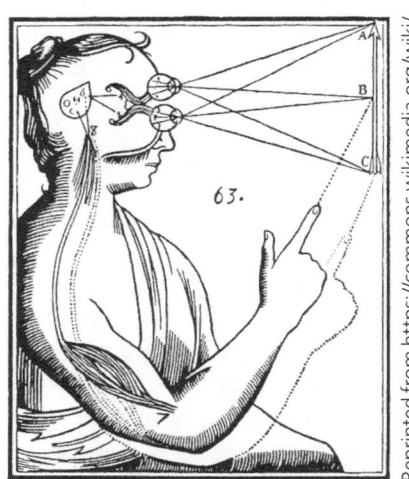

Drawing from René Descartes' *Treatise of Man* explaining his hypothesis regarding the function of the pineal gland.

thoughts are located in us or connected to us. But Descartes' theory could not account for these everyday facts.

Even if philosophers one day explain dualism's theoretical problems, practitioners, especially in kinesiology, have demonstrated dualism's problems in practical settings. These practical limits need consideration as well. For example, consider how value dualism places low emphasis on skilled movement and physical education in favor of mental intellect and learning, as if these two parts of us existed in independent realms. Now compare this imbalance with the growing body of evidence illustrating how physical activity plays a significant role both in increasing learning in young people and in reducing cognitive decline in older adults. Had value dualism not overemphasized the mind's value at the expense of the body, perhaps societies would have accorded physical activity a greater role in promoting well-being in years past.

A second practical limit of dualism emerges when practitioners note that we cannot administer interventions only on a person's body or only on his or her mind. If these were separate substances, we would expect that treatments could be restricted to the substance they targeted. However, our practical experience indicates that even localized treatments on a part of the body can alter a person's mental state. For example, consider how often an athlete carries psychological trauma, including a lack of confidence or increased fear following an injury, into a game. Or consider how a person's confidence or motivation can influence his or her ability to perform. Thus, rather than experiencing mind–body dualism in the real world, our practice often points out that mind and body are hardly the separate substances that dualism would have us believe they are.

The combined theoretical and practical problems with dualism illustrate two important points. First, theoretical flaws and practical problems combine to illustrate dualism's limits as a philosophical position. This point should reassure us that our philosophical reasoning is on the right track; if our theories contain flaws, we would naturally expect the practices

Removing Dualism From Our Thoughts and Language

Student Exercise

For each of the following statements, indicate whether it exhibits substance dualism, value dualism, or behavior dualism. Then rewrite the sentence to express the same idea without employing a dualistic view of the person.

Statement	Type of dualism	Rewrite
My mind keeps freezing when I try to serve in tennis.	Substance dualism	I keep freezing when I try to serve in tennis.
She is all brawn and no brain, so have her spend more time watching game film.		
He needs math more than he needs exercise; therefore, he can skip recess.		
To get out of a slump, just block out your mind and let your body do the work.		

that they influence to contain flaws as well. Second, philosophical theory influences practice, even when practitioners do not know the philosophical theory that they are using. By studying philosophy, you become better equipped to identify such theories in practice and reflect on their accuracy. Your ability to critically engage the underlying theoretical premises of many practices in kinesiology will help you later as you discard flawed strategies while innovating new ones. (For further reading on applying philosophy to practice, see chapter 10.)

The Protestant Reformation and Sport, Physical Education, and the Body

The early modern focus on matter and minds, on bodies and souls, profoundly impacted both theological and philosophical ideas in the West. Most Renaissance thinkers held dualistic positions that bodies and souls were distinct, if connected, components of a bifurcated human nature. While their Christian sentiments convinced them that the development of the soul ultimately paid a higher dividend than the cultivation of the body, their resurrection of the classical ideal that sound bodies harbored healthy souls led them to embrace physical activities and pleasures. The renewed focus on the corporeal as well as spiritual aspects of human being sanctioned the popular sporting habits of both the elites and the masses. The elites kept the pageantry of medieval martial tournaments alive even as the lances, swords, and crossbows that had formed the sporting equipment of the chivalric tradition gave way to firearms and artillery in actual combat. The aristocrats also patronized horse racing, reveling in the gambling and partying that flourished in conjunction with these events. Tournaments devoted to fencing and tennis also flourished on elite social calendars. Among the masses, the earthy and earthly pleasures of festivals that featured sporting contests that encouraged wagering and were built around the feasting and drinking rituals of the holiday timetables of the Catholic Church continued to make up the bulk of their popular leisure-time pursuits.

The earthy and earthly pleasures that the masters and the masses enjoyed soon came under an intense assault from religious reformers who launched a full-scale assault on every aspect of the Catholic Church's role in Western life. Over several centuries, a long series of schisms had developed in the Catholic Church on issues of theology, culture, and politics, revealing the fault lines that would eventually fracture the "universal" (the Latin translation of *catholic*) religious institution that had, since the fall of the Roman Empire, linked the diverse cultures of the West into a common faith. The Protestant Reformation reshaped the religious and national cartography of Europe, sparked widespread political and economic upheavals, and splintered Western Christianity into a myriad of diverse denominations and sects.

Although the grievances of Protestant reformers differed tremendously—some harbored deep theological objections to Catholic doctrine, others cited corrupt practices that had crept into the Church, while still others resented the political and economic clout wielded by the Catholic Church—their opposition to Catholic hegemony transformed Europe and, in tandem with the Renaissance, pushed European mentalities into expansionist modes. Indeed, a tremendous rivalry soon erupted between Catholics and Protestants in their efforts to convert nonbelievers to their respective brands of Christianity, first in the Americas and then in other non-Western parts of the world. Missionaries joined merchants and soldiers in the vanguard of European global expansion.

When it came to attitudes toward sport and the human body, Protestant factions were generally appalled by the traditional festival culture that had been endorsed for centuries under Catholic rule. In particular, Protestants disliked the gambling, drinking, and carousing that often accompanied sporting contests. They especially objected to rowdy sporting contests held on the Christian Sabbath (on Sundays)—a stance that earned them a generally deserved reputation as strict Sabbatarians (those who desire to keep the Sabbath "pure") who wanted all nonreligious behavior barred on Sundays. In addition, many Protestant groups took a different view from most of their fellow Europeans in regard to the relationship between labor and leisure. After centuries of inhabiting societies with extremely limited social mobility, in which hard work earned the masses little more than mere subsistence, a preference for leisure over labor had logically developed a strong hold on European world views. Europeans had traditionally "worked to live" and sought meaning in leisure, in their festival culture and religious rituals. Many Protestants adopted a different view and developed a puritan ethic, positing that one sign of divine favor was success in worldly affairs—a view that encouraged the elevation of work over play. Accordingly, Protestant Sunday schools inculcated children with the proverb that "idle hands" were "the devil's playthings," cementing the preference for labor over leisure.

In addition to their focus on labor as superior to leisure and their rejection of the popular pastimes of traditional Europe as wicked and wasteful, many Protestants embraced theological perspectives that countered the Renaissance endorsement of corporeal as well as spiritual pleasures. Embracing a form of value dualism, Protestants viewed the physical body as morally suspect. The Dutch protoreformer Desiderius Erasmus (1466–1536), who sought to reform Catholicism from inside of the institutional church rather than by joining the open rebellion, captured the Protestant unease with the world of

the flesh by warning that human bodies were "earthly, wild, slow, mortal, diseased, ignoble." His anticipation of the Protestant cleavage of the body from the soul and mind foreshadowed an enormous shift in Western thought. To the neoclassical ideal of the "whole man" who sought to develop both body and mind, Erasmus offered a clear rebuke: "We are not concerned with developing athletes," he declared, "but scholars and men competent to affairs, for whom we desire adequate constitution indeed, but not the physique of Milo"—a reference to the legendary ancient Greek athlete who won an astounding six Olympic wrestling crowns.

Given the typical Protestant rejection of the popular pastimes of festival culture, their elevation of work over play, and their theological convictions about the depravity of bodily existence, it is easy to see why many scholars have defined Protestant reformers as "frowning puritans" or, in the parlance of their own era, "spoilsports." That stereotype, however, does not fit neatly in terms of defining Protestant attitudes toward physical culture. Indeed, the German reformer Martin Luther, generally considered the original instigator of the Reformation, did not harbor the same animus toward festival culture as some of his Protestant colleagues. To the contrary, Luther enjoyed bowling, beer drinking, dancing, wrestling, fencing, and archery. Moreover, he accepted the neoclassical notion that sound minds needed sound bodies. At the same time, his emphasis on salvation by faith alone took the pressure off attempts to harness bodily pleasures, commit oneself to good works, and otherwise earn one's way to heaven.

If Luther offers an example contrary to the image of Protestant "killjoy" (another contemporary term for those who condemned earthly pleasures), the influential French Protestant firebrand John Calvin comes far closer to embodying the "frowning puritan" label. Calvin, perhaps the most influential theologian of his era, put his beliefs into practice by creating a model Protestant community in Geneva. Before Calvin and his followers "purified" the Swiss city, it held a well-deserved reputation as a hotbed of festival culture—a place where drinking, gambling, and sport attracted crowds of peasants and aristocrats from throughout central Europe who were intent on debauchery. From 1541 to 1564, Calvin instituted a theocracy (a government run by religious leaders) in Geneva and outlawed the many diversions of festival culture in the city. In the school he created for his followers, he instructed teachers to avoid "silly sports." Calvin's Geneva became a model of the Reformation's "purifying" wing and inspired puritan movements in Europe (especially in Holland, England, and Scotland) to imitate his methods of social control.

Protestant reformers were certainly not the first people to attack popular pastimes. A contingent of Roman philosophers decried the brutality of the gladiatorial arenas, and Confucian scholars had criticized what they perceived as the coarse martial exercises of warlords (see chapter 4). Still, where Protestants were able to exercise political power and cultural influence—particularly in Switzerland, Holland, Scotland, and England and its colonies—they sought to pass laws prohibiting gambling, drinking, and sport on Sundays, as well as discouraging horse racing, cock fighting, and a host of other recreations in which wagering played a central role.

Even so, though it is certainly fair to label them as adamant opponents of the sporting activities of festival culture, Protestants did not automatically line up against sport in all of its forms. Even in puritanical Geneva, Calvin advocated recreations that refreshed citizens in preparation for their Christian duties. Protestants engaged in all sorts of sports and recreations in which they could argue that these activities invigorated their calling to become better workers, better members of their church congregations, better members of their family, better members of their community, and better devotees of their faith. Protestants redefined sport and recreation in a very modern sense, marrying physical activity to personal and civic improvement. If running, or swimming, or playing folk football, or even racing horses improved one's well-being, nurtured bodily health, developed moral virtue, or expanded spiritual acumen, then it fit neatly into the Protestant world view. Wagering on the outcomes of horse races, however, remained a puritanical taboo in most Protestant denominations.

In fact, the older puritan ethic—that life should center on labor and not on leisure—has been secularized as the work ethic that many now consider essential to a modern social order. The puritan tradition of seeing sport and physical activity as useful mechanisms for building healthy societies has become a component of modern visions of the role of physical activity in our lives. Faith in the inherent value of play, fun, and enjoyment as the highest goods in our physical activities has given way to much more utilitarian outlooks in which we "work out" in order to prevent disease, to recharge ourselves to do better in our jobs, and to refuel ourselves for all the duties of modern citizenship. The ghost of puritanism lingers in our efforts to define physical activity entirely in the utilitarian rhetoric of the material improvement of our biological and sociological being. To put it in terms introduced in chapter 2, the ghost of puritanism is far more comfortable thinking of exercise as a tool rather than as a jewel.

The Scientific Revolution and Modern Attitudes Toward Sport, Physical Education, and the Body

The intellectual ferment created by the Reformation and the Renaissance, as well as the new data generated by the beginnings of globalization, ignited a new movement in Western civilization that historians refer to as the Scientific Revolution. From the 1400s through the 1700s, Europeans made enormous advances in every branch of the sciences, from mathematics, astronomy, and physics to biology, chemistry, and geology. Indeed, this "Age of Discovery," as these European ventures into "new worlds" have been labeled, required sophisticated mathematical and scientific tools for navigating the globe, for accounting for and tracking the vast new volumes of commerce, and for explaining the novel biological and cultural diversity that these ventures encountered. The Scientific Revolution altered Western

SCIENTIFIC METHOD

Historical Profile

Francis Bacon (1561–1626) was an English philosopher whose research developed the scientific method. Like Thales of ancient Greece, Bacon used inductive reasoning and careful observation of natural events to produce scientific explanations. Bacon also argued that a methodological approach employing skepticism could help scientists avoid biased observations and unwarranted conclusions.

Although the scientific method should not be mistaken for an inclusive definition of modern science, the methodologies adopted by early researchers did come to be understood as a general set of principles to which those who are engaged in the endeavor should subscribe. Bacon's scientific method counseled inductive approaches that began not with grand theories but with open minds free of suppositions and focused on rigorous empiricism—that is, with the proposition that knowledge begins with observation of the physical world through the human senses. The basic principles were soon joined by the strategy of designing repeatable experiments to test theories about one's observations.

Francis Bacon (1561–1626), the English philosopher who created the scientific method.

Though the scientific method continued to be refined, Bacon's reasoning about the epistemological framework in science improved scientists' ability to understand the natural world and laid the foundation for science to flourish. Today, physiologists, biomechanists, and even some psychologists employ this scientific method for conducting empirical research; meanwhile, philosophers follow Bacon's theoretical inquiry into the philosophy of science, one of the many smaller branches of philosophy that can be useful in kinesiology. Bacon's development of the scientific method is one more example of theory improving practice. More important, it illustrates how philosophical inquiry can produce insights that lead to practical application. By employing the scientific method, scientists have produced more knowledge much faster than was possible prior to the use of such techniques.

views of the universe, replacing the old Earth-centered model of the solar system with a Sun-centered paradigm, promulgating laws of nature that governed the physical movement of material objects, and classifying and organizing the enormous biological diversity of life forms that existed on the planet.

Europeans grounded their new scientific outlooks in what came to be known as the scientific method (see the historical profile titled Scientific Method). Whatever their nationality or their faith—Catholic, Protestant, agnostic, or atheistic—European scientists subscribed to the scientific method as the foundation of the new science and sought, if not always with complete success, to put it into practice in their work.

Scientism

Such faith in science has led some to note the rise of a position referred to as scientism, which includes the belief that science and scientific methods constitute the best (or only) ways to produce true knowledge. In this view, anything *not* based on empirical data amounts to nothing more than opinion or educated guesswork. Real knowledge, such advocates claim, requires facts and data that provide objectivity and certainty.

We live in an age in which many people consider scientific discovery to be the gold standard of human knowledge. These people point to scientific breakthroughs such as splitting the atom and splicing the gene as proof that the pace of scientific progress seems to know no limit. With headlines reporting promises of new cures for diseases and new discoveries with unimagined implications, many people's faith in science is stronger than ever.

Since the Scientific Revolution, however, scientism has produced two major effects that, arguably, have hindered scholarship and understanding. First, as noted in this book's introduction, scientism has led to the denigration of nonscientific fields. Because the humanities, including history and philosophy, do not rely on the

scientific method to produce empirical data, scientism would dismiss them as unworthy disciplines, as repositories for mere conjecture and opinion. This attitude has produced asymmetrical departments in kinesiology in which humanities faculty are invisible and humanities courses are few in number, if indeed they exist at all. Some departments of kinesiology do not support PhD programs in history or philosophy because, in their opinion, these areas do not produce real research.

Second, scientism has led some scholars to try to adopt (or adapt) scientific methods to nonscientific subjects in order to produce empirically defensible and supposedly more respectable claims. According to some scholars, such as Mary Midgley, this phenomenon has truncated and distorted research in such fields as psychology and sociology—two disciplines that might benefit from a blend of scientific methodologies and reflective, descriptive, or interpretive methodologies. Moreover, as discussed in the introduction, the extreme views of scientism helped fuel the divisiveness depicted in Snow's *Two Cultures*.

Fortunately, many modern scientists do not hold such a view, and there are good reasons for this. For one thing, science quickly falls under its own weight because it cannot answer all questions. Indeed, many of the most ardent physicists and neuroscientists admit to the inherent limits of science. These limits exist because science, by definition, applies only to natural phenomena, whereas some questions—such as the nature of love or how we should live our lives—cannot be explored through microscopes or empirical inquiries.

More often, important questions draw on findings produced by a variety of fields. In kinesiology, the focus remains on human physical activity, but understanding such a complex topic requires knowledge of human evolution, history, and culture, as well as motor learning, biomechanics, and human anatomy. Intuitively, we know that even an explanation of the endorphins associated with exercise cannot capture the passion that many of us feel for our various forms of meaningful physical activity. Therefore, rather than choosing sides in any debate about science versus the humanities, we believe that the future belongs to scholars who are multilingual in the sense of being able to speak the languages of various disciplines. As argued in the introduction, those who can interpret, analyze, and apply findings generated from one field to inform new questions investigated in another field can contribute to the large and complex inquiries that enable meaningful improvement in people's lives.

Scientific Materialism

As you now realize, the Scientific Revolution altered Western views of the human body and of its capacity for motion. Drawing on Renaissance thinkers' interest in detailed and accurate studies of human anatomy—including a commitment to the hands-on discoveries made possible by dissection—scientists and physicians came to understand the human body as a marvelous and complicated mechanism. Empirical methodologies dominated their approaches as they turned from a reliance on the ancient Greek wisdom of the physician Galen, whose models of human anatomy were built on animal dissections, to experimental studies of the human body itself.

In one notable example, the Italian medical researcher Andreas Vesalius (1514–1564) undertook extensive studies of human cadavers and concluded that Galen's ancient texts were fundamentally flawed. In 1543, Vesalius published *De Humani Corporis Fabrica* (*On the Structure of the Human Body*), a physiology and anatomy text grounded in the empirical and experimental approaches of the emerging scientific method that revolutionized Western comprehension of biology. Inspired by Vesalius, other medical researchers began to unravel additional mechanical secrets of human physiology. The English scientist William Harvey, for instance, discovered the workings of the circulatory system and depicted the heart as a mechanical pump. Other researchers probed the processes of respiration, describing them in terms of a mechanical bellows, and delved into the physics of human locomotion while characterizing the body's limbs as mechanical levers. Such mechanical analogies abounded in the new theories promoted by anatomical and physiological studies.

These advances stood in stark contrast to dualism's continuing mind–body problem. The Scientific Revolution increasingly considered the body as a mechanism governed by physical laws and forces discoverable through empirical observation and rigorous experimentation. These thinkers did not need, nor could they identify, any nonphysical mind at work in the human person. Inspired by the Scientific Revolution, philosophers began arguing that perhaps the "mind" that had given dualists so much trouble was a fiction. The person might more accurately be described in terms of physical substances—that is, as a complex machine. This position, which is known as materialism, holds that what people often refer to as "mind" is really a set of mental phenomena, a kind of sideshow, produced by material interactions in the brain and elsewhere in the body. Thus a person is a sum total of material parts, laws, and interactions.

Such a view of the person was at home in an age inspired by the exciting promises of science and empirical observation. Having jettisoned the mind, and therefore not needing to take seriously the subjective aspects of life—one's emotions, thoughts, beliefs, ideas, and attitudes—scientists were free to apply their empirical methodologies to the machine and figure out how it worked. This philosophy has produced mixed results. For reasons already mentioned, the hope of answering all questions has not been fulfilled; furthermore, holists (discussed in chapter 10) suggest that they never will be. But the debate goes on.

When materialists' lack of progress is criticized, they typically offer two rejoinders. First, they argue that the machine (the person) is more complex than originally thought. Although progress is evident, for instance, in the mapping of the human genome, more time is needed in order to truly unravel the material structures underlying reality. Second, the slowness of technological advances has impeded progress because it has been impossible to measure everything that needs to be measured; once again, they assert, more time is needed. In this view, then, the materialist dream of producing complete explanations of human nature and human behavior remains alive.

Monistic Materialism

Unlike substance dualism, monistic materialism (or monism) holds that a person is the product of one thing—namely atoms, or, as it is sometimes described, atoms and void. In this view, thoughts, emotions, memories, and any components of the nonphysical mind found in dualism are really chemicals, electrons, and neurons working in sequence to provide such perceptions. In this paradigm, then, they do not constitute a separate substance but rather another physical experience. The easiest way to apprehend how a monistic explanation of a person's perceived nonphysical experiences might be explained entirely in terms of the physical is to consider an experience of pain. Imagine stubbing your bare toe on the edge of a chair. The force of your toe connecting with the chair rapidly causes electrical impulses to travel from your toe to your brain via your central nervous system. Your brain rapidly translates the resulting signals into an experience of physical pain that you know is located in your toe.

The reliance on the physical in monistic materialism appealed to the philosophers of the Scientific Revolution because it relied on empirical methodologies. As scientists sought rational explanations of the natural world, they distrusted supernatural or mystical claims about reality. Descartes' nonphysical mind seemed to be one more relic from a prescientific world. Focusing only on the physical, relying on their senses, and measuring things carefully, these researchers believed that they could provide the kind of certainty promised by science. Though later inquiry revealed the limits of both science and materialism, scholars enamored with the new scientific world view adopted the monistic view of the human person.

Measurement Materialism

Measurement materialism emphasizes knowing the human person by quantifying or measuring important characteristics. For example, measuring a person's height, weight, and blood pressure offers insight into his or her health. The picture becomes clearer if we expand the measurements to address heart rate, lean muscle mass, chemical levels in the blood, and other measurable features. For measurement materialists, these numbers carry significant weight because numbers present the appearance of objective, hard facts. In contrast, perceived "feelings" are imprecise and difficult to compare from one person to the next.

Consider the difference between the subjective claim "I worked out hard" and the objective fact "I bench-pressed 135 pounds 10 times and burned 272 calories on the treadmill in 20 minutes of running." The former claim is variable, private, and personal; in contrast, the latter claim is fixed, public, and objectively verifiable. Thus, in measurement materialism, gaining knowledge about people through quantification provides seemingly objective insights into a person while allowing us to create standard ranges for vague terms such as "normal" and "healthy." In this view, since the person is entirely physical, all aspects of the person can be measured and recorded—even thoughts and emotions, as new technology allows us to quantify areas of brain activity. Any measurements that we cannot make, measurement materialists contend, are limited only by our inability to produce technology capable of capturing the phenomenon that we wish to measure.

Reductive Materialism

Reductive materialism, or reductionism, aims to know the person by examining the underlying smaller parts that make up the whole. For example, a person can be understood by examining the parts of his or her anatomy such as muscle fibers, organs, and bones. Anatomy, in turn, can be understood by examining each body part on the cellular level, and cells can be further understood by examining chemical interactions, which in turn can be understood by studying physics. You may be wondering if reductionists have to stop at some point. That is true, but it is also beside the point. Reductionists often stop at the first underlying cause that they are attempting to understand. Nutritionists, for example, do not typically reduce food to the point of physics, but they do often reduce it to its chemical level in order to understand, say, the glucose, amino acids, and fatty acids included in a person's diet. Thus reductionism often involves simply the disposition to reduce a phenomenon to smaller parts, and it need not be an absolute reduction to the smallest part.

THREE KINDS OF MATERIALISM IN PROFESSIONAL SETTINGS

Philosophical Application

Like dualism, materialism is an umbrella that covers various explanations of the human person as physical material. Though all materialism treats the human person as a sum of only physical substances, specific types of materialism differ on important points. Knowing these differences will help you identify materialism in practical settings.

Name	Claim	Effects on kinesiology
Monistic materialism	The person is a giant and complex machine composed only of matter.	Ignoring or diminishing the importance of thoughts and emotions in treatment
Measurement materialism	The person can be understood through quantified measurements of physical material.	Placing emphasis on knowing or treating only the quantifiable parts of people
Reductive materialism	The person is understood by reducing larger material (e.g., blood and bones) to their underlying parts (e.g., atoms and molecules).	Failing to include larger factors such as environment, culture, and power structure when studying or treating problems

Although these three kinds of materialism overlap, it is common to see different blends in different professional settings. For example, an exercise physiologist might exhibit measurement materialism by prioritizing measurements as a way of explaining a person; for example, measurement of $\dot{V}O_2$max and of muscle fibers can help explain a person's performance capacity. Monistic materialism, on the other hand, might appear in the medical profession if a surgeon frequently performs procedures to repair damaged joints or organs. Repeatedly treating people's anesthetized bodies can lead to a view of the person as an organic machine. Finally, reductive materialism might appear among nutritionists who view diet as a combination of micro- and macronutrients that can be reduced to chemical interactions. Such a view might miss how emotions, habits, and behaviors may influence a person's dietary choices. Perhaps you can identify other examples of these three facets of materialism in professional settings.

Theoretical and Practical Criticisms of Materialism

Scientific materialism appeals to some supporters (even among contemporary thinkers) because it presents knowledge as objective, empirical, and accurate. Numbers, so the thinking goes, do not lie. Nor does the physical material right in front of us, assuming that it is observed or measured accurately. Unlike the mind in dualism, which we cannot see or feel, the physical appears real—seemingly "out there" waiting to be examined, dissected, and understood. However, materialism also has both theoretical and practical drawbacks that should concern future practitioners in kinesiology.

Theoretically, materialism makes a big leap of faith that troubles many philosophers. Specifically, it assumes from the start that only physical things are real and then attempts to prove this claim by pointing to physical material as evidence. However, since materialists look only for physical material—and since their empirical instruments are set up to measure only the physical—their failure to find nonphysical substances such as "mind" hardly constitutes proof that such substances do not exist. Consider the example of a metal detector. Because it is set up to detect only metallic objects, we cannot conclude that its failure to detect anything metallic inside of a bag necessarily means that the bag is empty. Similarly, measurement materialists might inadvertently dismiss aspects of a person that cannot be detected through measurement. For instance, the feeling of love between a parent and a child will not register on their equipment: they can measure (and convert to numbers) only the changes in blood pressure or brain state that may accompany love.

Moreover, simply reducing a person to smaller parts might miss the influence

Removing Materialism From Our Thoughts and Language

Student Exercise

For each of the following statements, indicate whether it exhibits monistic materialism, reductive materialism, or measurement materialism. Then rewrite the sentence to express the same idea without employing a materialistic view of the person.

Sentence	Type of materialism	Rewrite
I need to see her slow-twitch muscle fiber count before I can see if she will do well on the cross country team.	Measurement materialism	I need to see her potential before I can see if she will do well on the cross country team.
An elite athlete is a finely tuned machine that needs premium fuel.		
To understand intelligence, we need to look at the brain, and to understand the brain, we need to understand the neurons.		
Judging by her height, weight, BMI, and blood pressure, I would say she is healthy.		

of broad factors such as environment, culture, and society on a person, too. Concluding that we can know only what we *directly observe* wrongly assumes that there is nothing we can know that is *unobservable*. Much of a person's inner life, including meaning, joy, anxiety, fear, and happiness, exist under the surface, and describing what it is like to live those emotions and experiences only through descriptions of physical material strikes us intuitively as unduly narrow. Numbers and measurements give us only part of the human picture.

In practice, we also see that such aspects of our inner life produce profound effects on our behavior. For example, consider how goal setting and visualization can help us improve physical performance through mental practices. In another example, when trying to help patients lose weight, a clinician would be unwise to look at obesity only as a matter of reducing caloric intake or increasing caloric expenditure. Indeed, attending to emotions, mental health, environment, and habits is likely to be more important than simply measuring "calories in" and "calories out." In fact, to be effective practitioners, we often want to use tools that scientific materialism disregards or deemphasizes in its focus on people's physical attributes.

The Scientific Revolution, the Social Order, and Physical Education

The Scientific Revolution spawned new conceptions of both the social and the biological bases of human nature. Inspired by the scientific method, European thinkers sought to apply what they believed were the "laws of nature" that governed human interactions to physical education. Enthused in particular by the work of the English philosopher John Locke (1632–1704), these "enlightened" scholars conceived of humans as naturally empirical creatures who begin to learn during infancy from direct observation of the world around them and use induction to gradually build theories about how the world works. In Locke's famous treatise, *An Essay Concerning Human Understanding* (1689), he argued that a human being is born as a "tabula rasa" (blank slate, without preconceived ideas) and is shaped almost entirely by his or her environments. Locke theorized that good environments produce good citizens and that bad environments produce corrupt citizens—a simple notion that has shaped much of modern social science since he first promulgated it. Actually, his ideas are more complex than that, because he also argues that humans are fitted to receive empirical data and shape it into meaningful ideas.

Locke's "environmental psychology," as it came to be known, reinforced earlier Renaissance contentions that physical education was essential to all other forms of human learning. Locke and his legion of disciples argued that initial learning for all humans emerges from their physical engagement with their environment. Working from that premise, human understanding begins not with books or in classrooms but from actual experiences with nature, such as running through the woods, hunting for plants and animals, and throwing stones into ponds. In this view, then, sport, exercise, and recreation serve as the starting point for making good citizens for modern societies. During the 18th century, the French philosopher Jean-Jacques Rousseau (1712–1788) took Locke's position to its logical extreme by advocating for physical activity in natural environments to replace schoolrooms as the foundation of education.

In Germany from the end of the 18th century through the beginning of the 19th century the employment of "scientific" physical education reached its apogee in the new gymnasiums (as the Germans called them following neoclassical tradition) that sprang up to train "guardians" of the new modern nation of Germany that was emerging out of a collection of provinces and principalities that had existed for centuries in the German-speaking areas of central Europe. These gymnasiums, or *Turnvereine* (Turner societies) as they were known in Germany, taught a form of physical education intended to prepare Germans for the duties of citizenship, especially for military service, in the long series of conflicts that marked the emergence of the modern German state. In the history of physical activity, the *Turnverein* represented one of the many fruits of the Renaissance, the Reformation, and the Scientific Revolution in molding modern ideas about the importance of physical education in modern societies.

CHAPTER WRAP-UP

Wrapping Up and Looking Ahead

The Renaissance, the Reformation, and the Scientific Revolution shaped Western attitudes about the human body as a machine and made the training of bodies through sporting contests or physical education programs an essential duty of modern societies. In these scientific theories, the human body constituted a useful tool that could be put to a variety of useful purposes. Well-trained bodies could serve in armies. They could work in factories. In order to function effectively, however, human bodies needed education, training, and "scientific" regulation. These new ideas would spread to every part of the globe through the new world-system created by the collision of the West and other civilizations beginning in 1500.

Five centuries later, when the Mexican national *fútbol* team faces off against teams from other nations at Estadio Azteca, the players who take the field have been finely tuned by the latest training methods developed by modern science. Their diets have been carefully programmed to maximize performance. Their physiologies have been tweaked by state-of-the-art training methods that include everything from sleeping in hyperbaric chambers to gain an advantage in processing oxygen at Mexico City's lofty elevation to participating in exercise programs prescribed to enhance their individual strengths and remedy their individual weaknesses. Their minds also reflect the work of psychologists, who have honed the athletes' focus or helped calm their anxiety. Sometimes the athletes even ingest chemical substances to enhance their capabilities.

When the action begins, billions of fans around the globe watch them play on television. At the highest level of competition, in World Cup matches, the number of people who tune in to watch represents, for 90 minutes, the largest shared experience on the planet. These athletes serve as icons of their nations, living symbols of their cultural and social identities. The processes of globalization and modernization created the conditions for these monumental changes in human cultures as well as the providing the foundation for philosophical world views developed by European scholars in the Renaissance, the Reformation, and the Scientific Revolution.

Modern systems of sport and physical activity would develop first at the center of Western society, in the nations where the processes of modernization rapidly transformed social and economic structures in profound ways. The intellectual transformations wrought by the Renaissance, the Reformation, and the Scientific Revolution ushered in a continuing series of interconnected revolutions—industrial, technological, commercial, social, and political. It was no coincidence that Great Britain, the heartland for these modern revolutions, also gave the world modern forms of football and other sports.

Study Questions

1. How and why did Europeans push outward after 1500?

2. What effects did globalization have on modern sporting culture? How does the world today reflect the processes of the past?

3. What is dualism, and what are the three kinds of dualism discussed in the chapter? Describe the theoretical and practical arguments against dualism.

4. What was the Reformation, and what philosophical perspectives did it develop regarding sport, physical education, and the body?

5. What was the Scientific Revolution? Describe the scientific method and scientism.

6. What is scientific materialism, and what are the three kinds of materialism discussed in the chapter? Describe the theoretical and practical arguments against scientific materialism.

GREAT BRITAIN AND THE BIRTH OF MODERN SPORT

Economic, Political, Social, and Cultural Revolutions

Chapter Objectives

In this chapter, you will

1. see how *Tom Brown's Schooldays* helped stimulate a shift from folk sport to its modern, rational foundations;
2. learn how sport was used as a tool for nation building and other important social ends;
3. identify the qualities and characteristics of rationalization, particularly as it applies to sport and its rules;
4. see why utilitarian ethics became popular during this period and examine its strengths and weaknesses in promoting ethical behavior in sport and other aspects of life;
5. learn about the rise of gambling and "deep play" and their effects on game rules and institutional control;
6. examine two distinct senses of fair play, see their relationship to gambling, and determine how the two notions can work together to promote "good games"; and
7. review new emphases on team sports and their role in making modern citizens.

The great British coming-of-age novel *Tom Brown's Schooldays*, first published in 1857, became an instant best seller in the Victorian world and has continued to influence modern culture ever since. Translated from English into a host of other languages during the 19th and 20th centuries, Thomas Hughes' enduring tale of the struggles between good and evil has sparked a host of famous imitators, not least among them J.K. Rowling's Harry Potter series. In *Tom Brown's Schooldays*, Hughes crafted an autobiographical tale, set in an English boarding school, chronicling a young boy's journey from childhood to manhood. Sports of all sorts (but not Quidditch!) play a key role in the novel, ranging from the exciting folk games that a very young Tom Brown adores during his visits to country fairs to the eponymous form of football that an older Tom falls in love with when he enrolls at Rugby School.

The novel highlights the modern notion that sport and physical activity play fundamental roles in the education of modern citizens. Hughes insisted that the lessons learned by young Tom Brown and his classmates on the playing fields of Rugby were as important, indeed, in some cases even more important, than anything else they learned in school. Engagement in sport curried the cardinal virtues that they carried over into their later lives when they became leaders of the globe-spanning British Empire. Sport served as an instrument for nurturing the qualities that the military officers, government officials, and commercial innovators who staffed the machinery of empire needed to complete their duties.

A scene near the end of the novel crystalizes the notion that sport amounts to far more than mere games; that it serves as a tool for creating modern citizens fit for the tasks of national and international leadership. Tom and his classmates prepare for a cricket match against the venerable Marylebone Cricket Club (MCC), a team that, since its founding in 1787, has ruled the game worldwide (and continues to do so into the 21st century) through the Laws of Cricket codified and published by its members. Chosen by his peers to captain Rugby's cricket squad for the match against the MCC, an honor that makes him the leader of his teammates in the contest against the most famous team in the world, Tom discusses the merits of cricket with his best friend Arthur and one of their teachers. The teacher, new to the intricate rules and tactics of the game, observes to Tom and Arthur that cricket is a truly magnificent game. Tom replies to their teacher, "Isn't it? But it's more than a game. It's an institution." "Yes," says Arthur, "the birthright of British boys old and young, as habeas corpus and trial by jury are of British men."

Sport as a Critical Modern Institution

For Tom Brown, and for his nonfictional fellow Britons who ruled the 19th-century's most powerful empire, sport did indeed amount to far more than a mere game. Sport served as a tool for teaching men—and, some insisted, women—the skills necessary to thrive in a modern society. Sport represented one of the key institutions for building a stable, prosperous, and dynamic nation. Sport had become a "birthright"—something that should be freely guaranteed to all citizens of modern nations. From this perspective, the rights guaranteed by constitutions included not only legal guarantees—for example, habeas corpus (a legal concept that required the government to demonstrate that it had lawful evidence of misconduct in order to arrest and try someone), trial by jury, and the other fundamental political and personal liberties enshrined in the British, U.S., and other constitutions such as freedom of speech, freedom of conscience and religious sensibility, freedom of the press, and freedom to assemble—but also a birthright guarantee to freely engage in sport!

The idea that sport was not just mere games but constituted a critical institution in modern cultures quickly moved beyond the borders of the English-speaking world. Translated into Japanese, *Tom Brown's Schooldays* exported the idea of sport as a tool for building a modern society into Japan during the Meiji Restoration (1868–1912), a period in which that nation transitioned rapidly (in the span of just a few decades) from a traditional, feudal, agricultural society into a modern industrial, technological, and urban power. As part of this transition, Westernized sport became an essential component in Japanese programs of modernization. The novel also captured imaginations in France, where it led one educational reformer who wanted his nation to keep up with Great Britain and the United States in the race toward modernization to spark a movement that created one of the most significant international sporting events in world history—the modern Olympics. That reformer, Baron Pierre de Coubertin, who ranked *Tom Brown's Schooldays* as his favorite book, led the movement to fashion a modern version of the Olympics inspired in part by ancient Greek ideas but also by modern notions of sport as not just games but also a critical institution for building healthy modern societies.

Modernization and the Transformation of Sport and Physical Activity

By the middle of the 19th century, when *Tom Brown's Schooldays* first intrigued readers, the processes of modernization rapidly transformed Great Britain and the rest of the world from the static societies of the medieval epoch into dynamic new patterns. The idea of "modernization" emerged fully in this period to explain the nature, directions, and interconnections of a series of revolutions that transformed the lives of people around the world. These revolutions altered how people thought and believed, how they worked and played, and how they organized and governed. Over the course of several centuries, this interrelated series of revolutions manifested itself in technology and innovation, in transportation and communication, in markets and finance, in agriculture and industry, in science and social thought, in urbanization and demography, in politics and government, and in social organization and social structures—all of which, taken together, profoundly changed the lives of most people on the planet.

From the 1500s to the present, these interrelated economic, social, political, cultural, and social revolutions have dramatically changed societies around the globe, in the process making them more similar and more interdependent. A new world economy centered on commerce and industry emerged. New technological innovations connected cultures across vast distances. New scientific ideas altered fundamental notions of how the world functioned. People migrated in huge numbers from rural farms to urban centers. New nations arose and remade the traditional political order. A new world-system emerged, unspooled by the processes of modernization.

Those processes including industrialization, technological innovation, and urbanization, surged in uneven but unceasing waves over every region of the globe. Western civilization, with its core in Europe and its new territories in the Americas, Asia, Africa, and the Pacific, served as the epicenter of modernization, the foundry that unleashed these cultural, commercial, industrial, technological, and urban revolutions. In Europe, Great Britain stood at ground zero of the surge toward modernity that emerged as early as the 16th century, rising through industrial and financial innovations to become, by the 19th century, the modern world's dominant power.

THOMAS HUGHES

Historical Profile

The author of *Tom Brown's Schooldays*, Thomas Hughes (1822–1896), went to the same Rugby School in which he set his tales of Tom Brown. Like his title character, Hughes made a stronger impression on Rugby's playing fields than in its classrooms. In spite of his average academic record, Hughes went to Oxford University, where he continued his stellar athletic career, starring for Oxford's cricket team and also earning a bachelor's degree. He then made a career in law, rising from barrister to county court judge.

Hughes also immersed himself in politics, joining the Christian socialist movement in Great Britain that sought to improve the lot of the working classes and condemned the excesses of capitalist entrepreneurs. He won election to the House of Commons in 1865 and kept his seat until 1874, when he made an unsuccessful attempt to win the borough of Marylebone, the district that contained the famous Marylebone Cricket Club that ruled British cricket. Both in and out of office, Hughes fought for the rights of laborers to organize trade unions, denounced the opium trade that had fueled drug abuse in the British Empire, and sponsored a utopian commune in Tennessee named Rugby.

Cover of a 1911 edition of *Tom Brown's Schooldays* by Thomas Hughes.

Thomas Hughes' book *Tom Brown's Schooldays*, illustrated by Louis Rhead, digitized by The Internet Archive, shared by Wikimedia Commons.

He did not achieve major success in his political endeavors, and his commune at Rugby quickly failed, but Hughes did make his mark in literature. He wrote widely, both nonfiction and fiction. His novels preached the gospel of "muscular Christianity"—the notion that sport could bolster the tenets of evangelical Protestantism and win new converts. Both *Tom Brown's Schooldays* (1857) and its sequel, *Tom Brown at Oxford* (1861), sold large numbers, and the former earned a place on reading lists for young boys in schools throughout the English-speaking world. Theodore Roosevelt, the American political celebrity who served as U.S. president from 1901 to 1908, proclaimed *Tom Brown's Schooldays* as one of two books that every boy should read. (The other book Roosevelt promoted, now long forgotten, was a Thomas Bailey Aldrich's 1870 novel, *The Story of a Bad Boy*, a tale heavily influenced by *Tom Brown's Schooldays*.) *Tom Brown's Schooldays* continues to serve as the formulaic foundation for every book and movie that portrays sport as a vehicle for turning rowdy children into upstanding young adults. Hughes and his fellow apostles of muscular Christianity inspired the flourishing of the Young Men's Christian Association, an institution that originated in England in 1844 and soon spread to global dimensions with powerful branches in the United States, Canada, and many other nations.

Modernization, Rationalization, and the Characteristics of Modern Sport

The concept of rationalization represents the foundation of modernization. Traditional societies relied on ritualized customs, kinship ties, personal connections, religious concepts, and charismatic authority to provide logics for behaviors. Modern societies rely on different instruments. In modernity (at least in theory), custom yields to calculation, bureaucracy replaces kinship, secular insights trump religious perspectives, and logical persuasion supplants charismatic evocations. Rationalization ranks order, structure, efficiency, and instrumentality as the chief aims of enlightened endeavor.

In Great Britain, evidence of the beginnings of rationalization in sport date back as early as 1618, when King James I had his government issue a "Declaration Concerning Lawful Sports." This document declared that British people had a "birthright" to play sport, thus establishing that proposition as a component of the nation's emerging constitution. James I issued the proclamation to win favor with the common folk in the midst of a battle with religious dissenters and political rivals over the fundamental nature of British culture. Among the many provisions of this declaration of sporting rights, the British monarchy endorsed the common folk's passion for archery, a sport that had proved extremely useful in filling British armies with experts in the longbow drawn from the masses. By making common citizens into soldiers, the monarchy reduced its dependence on the nobility to provide knights for military might, thus greatly strengthening royal power. In this way, the construction of a rational "right" to engage in sport served as a useful tool in the political struggles that shaped modernizing Britain.

Many scholars insist that rationalization bound together a variety of interrelated characteristics, outlooks, and attitudes that created the conditions for modernization and for the industrial, technological, and urban revolutions that it spawned. The sport scholar Allen Guttmann has linked seven fundamental characteristics of modernization to sport—foremost among them rationalization, as well as secularism, equality, specialization, bureaucratization, quantification, and the quest for records. Guttmann's model contends that rationalization stands at the center of these interconnected characteristics, linking them together in an intensely modern chain. The rationalization of modern sport—for instance, the British monarchy's endorsement of archery over other traditional games—replaced more traditional religious justifications for engaging in sport and marked the increasing secularization (separation from religion) of modern social logics. Rationalization also pushed sport toward equality in two ways. First, modern sports embrace equality in the conditions of competition, for instance standardizing and organizing contests to focus on pitting equal sides against one another in an effort to enhance the usefulness of competition. Second, modern sport encourages, at least ideally, equality of opportunity to compete, placing athletic skill or some other characteristic that all people possess at the heart of engaging in sport rather than using sport to demarcate the kinship or parochial connections so crucial to traditional sport.

Rationalization creates bureaucracies as rational instruments for organizing and promoting sport. Rationalization endorses specialization in sport, assigning specific and particular tasks to different players just as an assembly line in a factory assigns specific and particular tasks to different workers in order to promote productive efficiency. In addition, rationalization spurs the quantification of sport, not just in terms of simple scorekeeping but also in applying the arithmetic of human performance to every aspect of games, from the bodies of players to the tactics required to defeat opponents. In turn, quantification spurs the development of a quest for records. Keeping detailed accounts of sport allows for comparison of performances over not only large geographical areas but also vast spans of time. Records allow the comparison of the present with the past—a very modern habit.

For an illustration of how Guttmann's model of characteristics works in practice, we can consider the contrast between the folk football games of medieval Britain and modernized forms of the game, such as association football (what Americans refer to as soccer) and the rugby version codified at Tom Brown's school. Folk football, played for centuries by peasants in the British Isles, was sanctioned by the medieval Catholic Church, which provided both time to play during "holy days" (holidays) and spaces to play in the fields owned by the churches. Folk football pitted religious groups, such as church parishes, against one another. Players "made the team" based not on athletic skill but simply on their residency in the parish. Folk football teams frequently featured unequal sides, a few dozen players versus a few hundred, since the size of the parish, not the rational ideal of equality of the conditions of competition determined the structure of the game. Folk football players did not play specific positions but joined the general scrum, just as in their daily lives they did not perform specialized labor but engaged in the basic agricultural tasks common to all peasants.

Just as team size varied, so did the size of the field of play and even of the goals. Tradition rather than rational calculation set the spatial parameters of the game—the goal was the corner of the church and the main road for one team, the old oak tree and the new hedgerow for the other squad. In folk football, one team might even literally "play uphill" since the fields of play followed the contours of the landscape, unlike in modern contests where such claims are merely excuses made by players and coaches after a loss. Oral tradition and inherited custom provided the rules of the game, and disputes about

these vague regulations were not uncommon. No bureaucracies kept these codes. They belonged instead to the inheritance passed along by ancestors. Parishes kept score, but beyond those rudimentary numbers, folk football was thoroughly unquantified.

In sharp contrast, in 1863, a group of British gentlemen met in London and formed the Football Association (FA), a bureaucracy that quickly cobbled together a written rulebook for association football, or "soccer" (a term from British slang for the abbreviation of *association*). The FA's design rationalized several earlier sets of rules for football games into a standardized version. The rules demanded equality of the conditions of competition, with matched teams of 11 competing on level fields rather than having one side slog constantly uphill. Equality of opportunity to compete quickly followed, as the game expanded from a favored pastime of the elites who had created it into a passionate craze, first among the British and then among the world's teeming masses. Modern football quickly developed specialization, with goalkeepers defending their lines and strikers, midfielders, and defenders all performing intricate and precise roles. Quantification also developed quickly, as people counted not only goals but also touches, possessions, tackles, and saves. Eventually, trainers began to track all manner of physiological data about players' bodies, through microchips embedded under their uniforms, in an effort to build a quantified science of football performance. These contrasts between folk football and modern association football illuminate how modernization dramatically changed the fundamental nature of a game with ancient roots.

The Rationalization of Ethics Under Utilitarianism

These factors—the decline of religious influence, the rise of science, reliance on measurement and empirical facts, and belief in the powers of reason—also influenced ethical theory and practice. In particular, Jeremy Bentham (1748–1832) developed a system of ethics called utilitarianism, a no-nonsense approach to behavior that dispenses with unverifiable claims about humans as creatures of God or, in more secular terms, the bearers of special rights or privileges. Instead, Bentham argued that ethics is grounded in the most fundamental of human wants and needs—the desire to increase happiness and avoid pain and suffering—and called pleasure and pain our "sovereign masters." Bentham claimed that our life course

JEREMY BENTHAM

Historical Profile

Born in London in 1748, Jeremy Bentham was influenced by both his mother's pious beliefs and his father's enlightened rationalism. He attended Queen's College at Oxford University and studied law, though he never entered the legal profession. He devoted himself to an arduous schedule of studying and developing practical ideas for the reform of social institutions. He published little and, by most accounts, had relatively little impact during his lifetime. His original ideas about utilitarianism would be spread, and amended, by those who followed him, most notably John Stuart Mill, John Austin, and other consequentialists. Bentham's basic ethical concepts were published in 1789 in *An Introduction to the Principles of Morals and Legislation.*

Bentham is considered a hedonist because he championed a variety of pleasures that he collected under the generic term *happiness*. He favored reason over custom and tradition, tangible clarity over idealistic fictions, and concrete good (utility) over debates on human rights. He emphasized an ethics of individual behavior and regarded people as egoists—that is, as being fully under the influence of their two "sovereign masters"—pleasure and pain.

Bentham died in 1832, leaving behind a large quantity of unpublished manuscripts and a sizeable estate that was later used

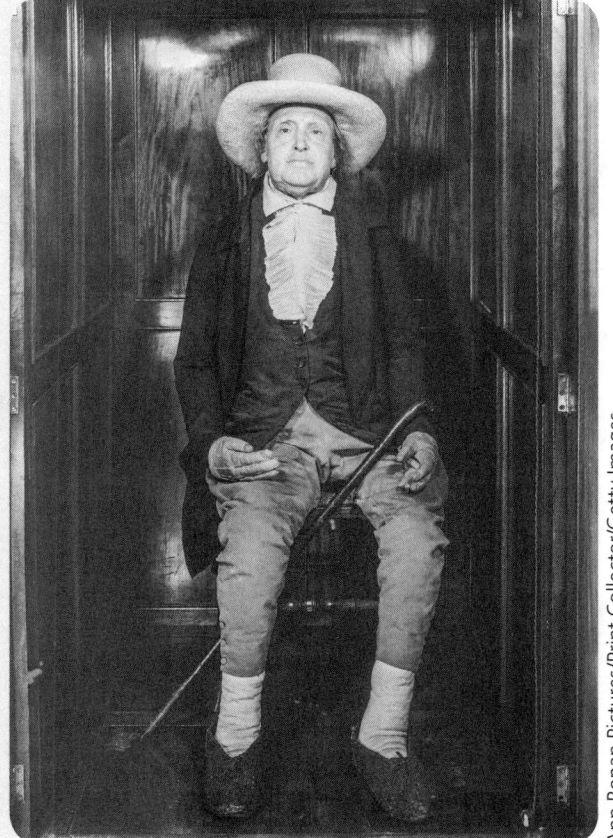

Jeremy Bentham: philosopher, jurist, radical social reformer, and utilitarian ethicist. His mummified body (pictured here) is on permanent display at University College London.

Ann Ronan Pictures/Print Collector/Getty Images

to establish University College London, a place where individuals who could not gain access to traditional universities (particularly Jews, Catholics, and political nonconformists) could study. His cadaver was embalmed, put in a chair, and placed in a glass cabinet as he had instructed. He remains seated in a hallway of the main building at University College to the present day.

is directed by those poles of attraction and repulsion and, even more important, that our moral obligations are directly tethered to responsibility for increasing the amount of happiness in life and decreasing anything that would detract from it.

Bentham modeled his version of ethics on the precision of science. Ethical decision-making, he argued, could be based on a type of mathematical calculus. All manner of human experience, he believed, could be put on a single scale and assigned a score for its relative contribution to the promotion of the greatest utility—that is, the most intense and durable satisfaction. Thus if two actions are possible, the one with the higher utility score is the morally right thing to do.

Such thinking is often used, for instance, as the basis for defending just wars. Although war brings much suffering to all, and though many innocent people may be inadvertently killed in the course of the fighting, the sum of the negative utility scores for these costs is still lower than the sum of the scores for the greater good that a successful campaign will bring. For example, most would argue that World War II and the defeat of the Nazi regime produced, on balance and in the long run, far more happiness than suffering and pain.

Advantages of Utilitarian Ethics

You may already be familiar with this brand of thinking. Whenever we say "the ends justify the means," we are giving some credence to the calculus of utilitarian thinking. Bentham's method has proven attractive and durable for a number of reasons. First, it is nonjudgmental about the great variety of human experiences and conditions that promote happiness. Many things bring satisfaction to human beings—knowledge, sensuous delights, peace, tranquility, security, fame, fortune, love, friendship, independence, and freedom, among others. Likewise, many things have the opposite effect—alienation,

physical pain, boredom, anger, ignorance, poverty, enslavement, and illness, to name only a few. No matter what our tastes and preferences may be regarding the pursuit of pleasure and the avoidance of pain, we can perform the calculations that provide guidance for ethical behavior. This flexibility fits nicely with the pluralism of the 21st century and with our current reluctance to impose on others our own opinions about how to live.

Second, utilitarian thinking can be attractive because it takes the promotion of the good seriously. Promoting enjoyable living, increasing lasting satisfactions, and reducing suffering would seem to be worthy goals for all of us. If they are important enough, then we should not necessarily let worries about violating rights, breaking promises, or even occasionally using other people as a means stand in our way.

For instance, policies regarding graduated income tax can be defended on the basis of utilitarian logic. Granted, the practice of taking money from individuals who have honestly earned it, taxing some people more than others, using money to help others when it could be used by the folks who earned it, and devoting some of those funds for purposes that might not be endorsed by the individuals from whom the money was taken—all of these practices are, at least from one point of view, unfair or otherwise harmful. In other words, they all have some negative utility. Bentham would assign a number or weight to that negative utility based on intensity, duration, certainty, proximity, and quality of the harm produced by the tax policy. He would then do the same thing for the benefits. If he came out with a positive number, and if that number were higher than the number for any other tax system, then imposing a graduated tax would be the most ethical policy to enact. It would be the ethical thing to do, once again, not because the poor have rights or because it would honor an abstract ideal of fairness but simply because it produces the greatest concrete balance of happiness over suffering or pain for the most people.

This power of utilitarian thinking has been recognized by many who have pondered Philippa Foot's well-known ethical dilemma about a runaway trolley car that is rumbling down the tracks toward five innocent individuals who are tethered to the rails. All five individuals will be killed by the trolley, but you happen to be standing by a switch that could send the trolley onto a siding where only one innocent person is tied to the tracks. In this hypothetical situation, Foot indicates that throwing the switch is the only lifesaving action available to you. There is no time to warn the individuals, stop the trolley, or save the five people in any other way. What would you do? Would you throw the switch or not? Would you do the rational thing and sacrifice one person in order to save five?

Most individuals presented with this dilemma say they would throw the switch. This action seems the morally right thing to do on utilitarian grounds. The happiness of five people outweighs the sacrifice of one. But the decision is not an easy one, and some believe strongly that throwing the switch forces us to use the sacrificed individual as a means to another end, even though it may be a rationally defensible end. As discussed in chapter 7, the philosopher Immanuel Kant argued that we are under an equally rational imperative not to do so. As tragic as the unfolding accident will be, it does not give us the right to cause the death of an innocent bystander. This line of reasoning suggests that something beyond utility informs (and should inform) our ethical thinking.

If you read about the trolley case on the web, you will find that the story does not end with the question of whether or not you would throw the switch. It proceeds to a second case where you would need to push a very large and unsuspecting person off a bridge and onto the tracks in front of the oncoming trolley. This individual's size would stop the trolley and thus save the five innocent individuals who are located farther down the tracks, but he or she would be killed. Thus, once again, you are asked to make a decision. Would you push this individual off the bridge (assuming that no other options for saving the five individuals was available to you)? You might be surprised to learn that many individuals who would throw the switch would not push the person off the bridge.

Some regard this difference as surprising because, in terms of utility, there would seem to be no substantial difference between the two cases. Each one requires you to sacrifice one person in order to save five. Moreover, because that individual dies instantly in both cases, there is no greater or lesser suffering imposed on that person. Thus the difference between throwing a switch and pushing a person would seem to be immaterial. You are equally responsible for the person's death either way. As with the first question, this finding suggests that something other than utility affects our moral responsibilities. We will return to these possible shortcomings of utilitarianism later in this chapter, after applying this method to a contemporary issue.

Test Case for Utilitarianism

Utility is often used today to justify the presence of intercollegiate athletics at colleges and universities. For large universities, the so-called "front porch value" of athletics is seen by presidents and others as extraordinarily important. Some have even argued that all "real" universities must have an American football team. Showcase teams are thought to attract large donors, keep alumni happy, increase applications, enhance pride in the university, and generate all the enjoyable social activities associated with "big game" weekends.

The smaller schools in the NCAA's Division III also support athletics for a variety of reasons, such as attracting applicants, providing healthful activities for a substantial portion of the student body, building campus pride and identity, and garnering alumni support. However, athletics is also regularly in the news for scandals ranging from academic fraud and the admission of unqualified students to all manner of misbehavior by athletes. This creates a dilemma. Is it morally acceptable to promote intercollegiate athletics on college and university campuses . . . or not? To pose the question in more specific terms, if a college or university president is faced with the prospect of dropping a football program that has been traditionally unsuccessful and routinely finished near the bottom of the league, what should he or she do? This very problem has been faced by some academic leaders and will likely be faced by others in the years to come.

In order to gain clarity about the right course of action, we can perform a quick utilitarian calculation of positive and negative satisfaction. Using a 10-point scale, the calculation might proceed as follows (the number of points assigned to each factor is indicated in parentheses).

Considerations That Favor Cutting the Team

1. The program has been costly, and the money saved could be put to better purposes, many of them related to core academic enhancement. (7)

2. The program has been unsuccessful—even an embarrassment to alumni, fans, and students—because of its poor record. After replacing several coaches and observing no improvements, there is little reason for optimism. (5)

3. A number of players have been injured, in part because they have been outmanned and outsized by their opponents. Recent research on concussions is also worrisome, and there is concern about sponsoring a program with such high risk factors. (4)

4. The school is located in an area where a number of other schools have popular and far more successful teams; therefore, the market is difficult and is unlikely to improve. (5)

5. There is some support among important donors and trustees for cutting the team; therefore, doing so may be politically feasible. (2)

Thus the total utility score for cutting the team is 7 + 5 + 4 + 5 + 2 = 23.

Considerations That Favor Keeping the Team

1. The stature of the school would likely suffer if the program were dropped, because there seems to be both symbolic and "front porch" value in having a football program. (5)

2. The school has been working for years to promote a good campus environment and to persuade more students to become residents rather than commuters. Football, even with its lack of success, has been one of the most important vehicles for promoting campus spirit, through parties, homecoming parades, and big-game weekends. (8)

3. Cutting the team would remove anticipated athletic experiences for more than 100 players. Many athletes, both in football and in other sports, have told the president that their experiences on the field or court have been as important as those in the classroom. (7)

4. Enrollments and applications might decrease if the football program were cut. (9)

5. It is difficult to predict how some donors, trustees, past football players, and other university supporters would react if the program were dropped. Some attempts to cut sports at other schools have not gone well. (8)

Deciding to Cut or Retain a Costly Athletic Team

Student Exercise

Your ethical dilemma is the same one faced by the college president as described in the main discussion. Should you cut the football team or retain it? First, identify at least three additional factors for cutting the team and three more for keeping it. Then assign utility scores to all of the factors—those from the main discussion as well as those you have added. See if you come out with the same decision we did. Here are a few suggestions for steps to take before doing the calculations.

1. You might want to identify a specific school before doing this exercise. The particulars of the institution will undoubtedly make a considerable difference in determining the utility of its football program.

2. You might also want to add some specific facts. For instance, how much money is being lost? How influential are the trustees and donors who support cutting the team?

3. Research the value of intercollegiate athletics in order to separate fact from fiction regarding the many claims (both positive and negative) made about sport. For instance, do applications and enrollments really go up when a school supports a successful football team?

Thus the total utility score for keeping the team is $5 + 8 + 7 + 9 + 8 = 37$, significantly more than the total of 23 for cutting the team. Therefore, on utilitarian grounds—that is, on the basis of providing the greatest good for the greatest number (or the greatest balance of good over harm)—the right moral decision is to keep the team.

It should be obvious from this example that such calculations are difficult at best. For one thing, you might well be asking yourself if additional factors not listed here should also be considered. In addition, are the utility scores assigned to the listed factors appropriate, or might they be too high or too low? How can anyone, for instance, reliably put a number on the significance of lessons learned on the football field?

Disadvantages of Utilitarian Ethics

Philosophers have a number of stock objections to utilitarian ethics. The first one, encountered in the runaway trolley case, is that utilitarianism may not take the rights of individuals seriously enough. We struggle, for instance, with the idea that any one of us or any one of our loved ones might be sacrificed or harmed for some greater good. A second objection is closely related to the first; namely, it is very difficult to put all experiences and all values on a single scale. How much worth does a human life have? Does it even make sense to compare life itself with such things as knowledge, aesthetic pleasure, peace, and happiness? Many also criticized Bentham for something that others counted as an advantage—specifically, his nonjudgmental claim that all pleasures are equally valid. Common sense would suggest that they are not, that the hedonistic joys of food and drink, for instance, should not be given equal weight with the satisfactions of helping others, reading a good book, or discovering new knowledge. Finally, the calculations required by utilitarianism can be time-consuming and thus unwieldy, yet some ethical dilemmas require a quick decision.

Even with its disadvantages, utilitarianism provided an alternate, rational foundation on which to make ethical decisions. Thus it provided our 18th-century predecessors with additional resources for determining right and wrong actions and good and bad social policies. These resources were much needed in regard to the rise of gambling.

Rationalization and Gambling

Utilitarian philosophy developed in rapidly modernizing Western culture as one of many thought systems designed to calculate methods for providing structure and order in an era of rapid change as traditional agricultural societies evolved into urban and industrial nations. As mentioned earlier, the concept of rationalization signified the underlying foundation of these modern thought systems that asserted that human intelligence and ingenuity could control and direct these dynamic modern changes. Rationalization thus stood as the key component of modernization, as the changes that altered traditional folk pastimes into modern sports reveal. The oral traditions that had provided guidelines for folk games gave way to specific and detailed written rules. Local customs and habits yielded to ordered and structured rulebooks that could be applied across regions, nations, and even continents. Written rules standardized and homogenized sports into similar formats wherever they were played.

Written sets of rules appeared first in horse racing, in the form of legal contracts between wealthy British aristocrats who wanted to rationalize the contests in order to protect the large wagers that they regularly placed on the races. Horse racing (as indicated in previous chapters) has a long history that stretches back into ancient cultures. Gambling on the outcomes has always been a central feature of the sport. Horse racing blossomed into the popular "sport of kings" in late medieval Europe as a traditional pastime in which the ruling classes demonstrated their equestrian prowess. Beginning in the 1600s, as new wealth from the global commercial system flowed into the pockets of the wealthy British entrepreneurs who engineered the early market revolution, gambling on horse racing flourished as a status symbol among the new industrialists who joined the ruling classes in the rapidly modernizing nation.

Gambling and Deep Play

From the perspective of some adherents of rationalism—including Bentham, who sought to apply rational principles not only to ethics but to every aspect of human society—the wagering of large sums of money on horse races seemed an utterly irrational endeavor. Bentham described the habitual gambling of his wealthy countrymen as "deep play," an activity in which the risks involved so outweigh the rewards that from a rational perspective the pastime has no useful purpose. Bentham contended that the "deep play" of gambling on horse races wasted resources, eroded fortunes that could otherwise be productively invested in the economy, and diverted the energy of business leaders from more important tasks. Bentham hoped that rational thinkers would avoid such behavior and suggested laws banning such wasteful practices for the less enlightened. In his view, "deep play" belonged to the less enlightened past and had no place in the calculus of modern rational societies. Most of his fellow Britons, however, simply ignored Bentham's advice and continued to merrily plunk large sums of money on the ponies.

Although his idea had virtually no impact in the short run on the gambling habits of modern societies, Bentham did uncover a key paradox in the history of rationalizing and modernizing sport. The original impetus for writing rules for sporting contests was the desire to protect what were, from a modern perspective, the irrational practices of gambling associated with sports that were inherited from traditional customs. Horse-racing contracts originally stipulated basic elements of the contests, including the parties making the bets, the horses and jockeys involved, the length of the course, the time and place of the contest, and the amount wagered on the race. Courts treated such contracts as legally enforceable agreements and thus gave "constitutional" protections to the rationalization of horse racing through written rules. Horse racing thus became an institution—not just a "mere" game.

The next step in the process of modernization was the emergence of communities of interest that took over the rule-writing tasks and promoted particular sports. Clubs, voluntary associations united by common interests, served as the original communities of interest and quickly established bureaucracies to give order and structure to the rule-making process. In 1750, British aristocrats devoted to horse racing founded the Jockey Club. Headquartered in the Pall Mall neighborhood of London, where a host of other "gentlemen's" clubs also took root, the Jockey Club had a misleading name. It was not an association of jockeys but an organization created by the owners of the horse-racing industry to promote their sport. The Jockey Club quickly became an effective bureaucracy that brought order to the British horse racing industry, establishing rules not only for the races themselves but also for documenting the genealogy of horses through bloodlines catalogued in the *General Stud Book* (first published in 1791), for standardizing the buying and selling of horses at Tattersalls auction hall in the Hyde Park neighborhood of London, for organizing a racing calendar so that racetracks throughout Great Britain could cooperate in scheduling events, and for publishing race results that quantified the performances of British thoroughbreds.

The Expansion of Written Rulebooks to Other Sports

Wealthy Britons did not confine their gambling habits to horse racing. "Deep play" also drove the patrons of other traditional folk sports to create written rulebooks, to organize clubs, and to standardize their practices to bring order and stability to their wagering. As horse racing modernized, so too did other sports on which the British ruling classes loved to wager. Near the Jockey Club in the exclusive Pall Mall section of London, the Marylebone Cricket Club appeared in 1787. The MCC amalgamated several early clubs devoted to cricket and wagering that had been staples of the neighborhood since the early 1700s—into a new bureaucracy that shaped the modern game. As early as 1728, English aristocrats had developed written Articles of Agreement for cricket matches. In 1744, the London clubs that preceded the MCC had crafted standardized rules for the old British folk sport, rules they dubbed the "Laws of Cricket." When the MCC was established by some of Britain's leading politicians and financiers a few decades later, it took over the "Laws of Cricket," first publishing its version of the rulebook in 1785. The MCC quickly established its "Laws of Cricket" as the ruling constitution for the game as it spread throughout the British Empire, into India and Pakistan, the West Indies and North America, Australia and New Zealand, and South Africa and Kenya.

In addition to cricket matches and horse races, British gamblers also placed large bets on other elite sports, such as yacht races and golf contests. Yacht clubs sprang up in the British Isles in the 1700s to create rules and bring order to the flourishing gambling ventures on boat races. Founded in 1720, the Cork Water Club, headquartered in a thriving Irish port city, is generally recognized as the oldest yacht club in the world—and one of the oldest athletic clubs of any sort. In 1775, under the patronage of one of the major "sportsmen" of the era, the Duke of Cumberland, a community of interest known as the "Cumberland Fleet" took root on the Thames River in London. The exclusive club quickly established itself as the center of English yachting; in 1830, it took a new name—the Royal Thames Yacht Club. British yacht clubs rationalized and modernized the sport, creating special classes of vessels, developing written standards for the sport, and organizing the collection of quantified

An 1849 match at the Lord's Cricket Ground in London—home field of the MCC.

data designed to improve performance in their popular pastime.

Golf clubs emerged in Scotland in the mid-1700s. In 1744, a group of Scottish aristocrats founded the Honourable Company of Edinburgh Golfers. In 1754, another community of interest established the Royal and Ancient Golf Club at St. Andrews. The 13 simple rules established by the Royal and Ancient leadership constitute the first set of written codes for golf—a small starting set that has since grown into an immense code. The Scottish game quickly became a favorite of British elites looking for additional pastimes on which they could wager. In 1766, a group of golf devotees founded the Blackheath Club, the first golfing organization in England. These early clubs standardized and organized the sport, which set the foundation for the rapid spread of golf throughout Britain over the next century.

As horse racing, cricket, yachting, and golf reveal, gambling sparked the earliest efforts to rationalize traditional folk sports and placed them on the path toward modernization. The desire to create stable conditions for wagering by writing rules and creating clubs sparked the rationalization, specialization, quantification, and bureaucratization of these sports. Gambling drove the intense interest that developed in insuring equality of the conditions of competition since such measures provide more rationalized and predictable contests on which wealthy Britons could indulge in their passion for "deep play"—the risking of their fortunes on the outcomes of sporting events.

To review the origins of modern sport in Great Britain and beyond, the irrational desire to bet on sporting events led to the creation of written rules to standardize procedures for competition—a clear first step in the process of rationalization. The rules and procedures were designed to create equality of conditions in competitions and to ensure that matches were "fair." Written rules also gave wagers legal force and allowed bettors to use the court system to enforce collection. In order to handle the process of writing rules, sporting enthusiasts created communities of interest, or *clubs* in the terminology of the 1700s and 1800s. These bureaucratic organizations developed standardized "laws" for games, enforced the new codes, and created social order around the contests. Clubs tended to keep the elites in charge and acted as governing bodies for modernizing sports.

Clubs also promoted gambling, which led to early forms of quantification in sport, especially the numbering and ranking of performances for betting purposes. In horse racing, for instance, by the mid-1700s experts regularly employed stopwatches (invented in 1690 as "pulse watches" to enable physicians to monitor heart rates) in order to compile data about the performances of thoroughbreds. These records comprised the earliest "racing forms"—compendiums of quantified data on which gamblers rely in order to make "rational" wagers. This widespread quantification set the stage for the quest for records. Indeed, in horse racing, it is now possible to compare times at a variety of distances across nearly four centuries of records.

Games for the Common Folk

Wealthy British elites created the earliest modern sports, rationalizing folk pastimes in order to protect their wagering interests in these games. The lower classes soon got involved as well. As the industrial and urban revolutions transformed Britain into a nation of factories and cities, a huge working class arose. Like their wealthier contemporaries who owned the means of production in which they labored, the workers enjoyed both sport and gambling. In the cities, they imported folk games from the rural hamlets they had left and soon remade them, sometimes with assistance from rich allies, into modern commercialized sports.

The rise of prizefighting as a British national pastime in the 1700s illustrates this trend. Folk pugilism had for centuries been a popular entertainment among peasants all over the British Isles. They watched, gambled on, and even participated in fisticuffs at country fairs and at holiday festivals. In the new urban centers of Britain, clever entrepreneurs transformed folk pugilism into a modern sport by crafting rationalized written rules, developing specialized training methods, and standardizing hand-to-hand combat. Prizefights drew large crowds of working-class customers to urban taverns and theaters to watch, drink, and gamble.

Some members of the upper class who could not get enough sporting action at the horse races, yacht races, golf matches, and cricket games where they normally gambled also came to these working-class hangouts to bet large sums on pugilism. The British press labeled the wealthy devotees of prizefighting "the fancy," for the rich clothing they wore to these pugilistic events, eventually shortening the phrase to "fans." By the mid-1700s, prizefighting had become extremely popular among both the working-class masses and "the fancy," thus ranking as Great Britain's original national pastime and developing into a lucrative business.

In spite of the efforts to rationalize prizefighting, however, the large sums of money involved attracted nefarious elements, including early organized crime gangs that fixed fights and corrupted the sport. After a particularly notorious fight in which several members of "the fancy" who also held seats in the British Parliament lost large amounts of money, the British government made prizefighting illegal. Pugilism, however, did not go away. Rather, it moved underground and remained a popular if unsavory pastime, particularly for working-class men, both in Britain and throughout the empire.

The Rise of the Sporting Fraternity

Prizefighting heralded the emergence, in Britain and in its colonies and settlements, of what historians have identified as the "sporting fraternity." This loose association of tavern owners, gamblers, criminals, and sporting promoters staged prizefights and other athletic entertainments for the amusement of the masses in cities ranging from London and Manchester to New York and Philadelphia, Toronto and Montreal, Sydney and Melbourne, and Cape Town and Calcutta. By the late 1700s and 1800s the sporting fraternity stretched around the English-speaking world, promoting a dazzling variety of sporting events on which people could gamble, including not only prizefights but also footraces through city streets (or pedestrianism, as it was known at the time), rowing races, and tournaments of tavern sports such as darts and billiards. Although the middle and upper classes often viewed the sporting fraternity as wasteful, corrupt, and irrational, its locales remained popular as haunts for the working classes and served as the primary early sites for the modernization of sport.

Games, Rule Making, and Political Revolutions

The desire to gamble served as the original impetus for transforming folk games into modern institutions, but other motives soon entered the picture. In the modernizing nations of Europe, and in their colonies and dominions around the world, civic institutions such as sport clubs grew rapidly, especially in new urban environments. These associations of like-minded citizens generally coalesced around a shared interest or passion, such as cricket, literature, religious instruction, philosophical debate, economic investment, or prison reform. In these clubs, both the emerging middle classes as well as the traditional ruling classes learned how to build and navigate new political and social situations where free assembly and the free expression and circulation of ideas flourished. The clubs immersed members in bureaucratic rationalization, in developing codes of conduct and constitutions for their activities, in promoting and disseminating new ideas, and in negotiating roles and identities.

Many scholars have contended that these clubs provided the environment for a series of political revolutions that would modernize governance in many parts of the world, including Great Britain's Glorious Revolution (1688–1689), the American Revolution (1765–1783), and the French Revolution (1789–1799). These events refashioned international politics and marked the decline of traditional authoritarian governments based on customary fealty to aristocratic and monarchical leaders. They ushered in a modern and more democratic era based on representative governments regulated by constitutions that enshrined at the heart of many modern societies such institutions as a free press, freedom of religious conviction, free assembly, and freedom from arbitrary authority. Like modern sport, these developments originated in voluntary associations—the ubiquitous clubs of the early modern West.

From such a perspective, the creation of the "laws" of cricket resembles the creation of modern political constitutions. In both cases, interested citizens gathered to debate and devise rules to govern conduct, whether political or sporting. Thomas Hughes had in mind precisely this link between sport and modern politics when he had Tom Brown and his other fictional characters describe cricket as more than just a game and insist that, in fact, it was an institution that belonged among the birthrights of modern citizens.

The Rationalization of Fair Play

As addressed in chapters 2 and 3, the British were not the first to view sport as a promising tool for teaching important lessons of life and good citizenship. Such concepts date back to the civilizations of antiquity, and they flourished especially in Greek cultures. Still, the British emphasis on rationalization put a new focus on fair play, one of the central tenets of competitive sport. But what exactly does fair play require? And how can it be most reliably assured? As you have seen in this chapter, these were important questions for the 18th- and 19th-century Britons who "irrationally" risked their own money by placing bets on such events as horse races and golfing matches. These questions remain relevant for us—for example, when we enter a game or root for our favorite team to win. Like our predecessors, we want contests to be fair.

Fairness is an ideal, one that is difficult to achieve in sport or in the rest of life. We know that our lives are affected from cradle to grave by both advantages and disadvantages such as birth order, genetic endowment, gender, familial socioeconomic status, and innate intelligence. The variable outcomes of this lottery, some of which constitute significant handicaps, lead to the very reasonable conclusion that life is not fair. As the contemporary American political philosopher Michael Sandel has argued, our existence has an inherent giftedness to it. That is, serendipity or chance has much to do with our prospects for living a good life. Given that human existence is not, and never will be, entirely fair, Sandel suggests that mutual support and a strong sense of fellow feeling are necessities.

Even so, many scholars have followed Thomas Hughes, the British philosopher and apostle of modern sport, in arguing that sport is different, at least in degree. As seen in chapter 1, games can serve as attractive forms of play. They are artificial problems created by and for us. As the authors of these competitive activities, we have an opportunity—indeed, an obligation—to make them as fair as possible. Here is where care, ingenuity, and rationality enter the picture. It would seem that smart individuals such as ourselves, and our comparably intelligent 19th-century ancestors, could construct a contest in which nobody is "playing uphill."

According to the philosopher John Searle, we promote fair play and develop game-playing institutions through the vehicle of constitutive rules for games. As much as possible, game rules neutralize power, privilege, and wealth—three factors that give individuals advantages in daily life. Thus, when we stage races, the rules stipulate a common starting line, clearly articulate the goal and how the winner will be determined, and, perhaps most important, describe the means that are allowed (and disallowed) in getting to the finish line. Thus merit is determined objectively. The fastest runner gets the prize regardless of whether he or she is rich or poor, a ruler or a common laborer, a member of the leisure class or of society's lowest level. If any coach or runner were to find a loophole in these regulations, a new rule could be written to reestablish the level playing field.

We have already suggested that fair play, understood in games as the provision of equal opportunity, remains an ideal that can never be fully realized. In spite of thick rulebooks, absolutely level playing fields never have been, and never will be, a reality.

To this point, we have assumed that fair play is characterized by equal opportunity in the form of the proverbial level playing field, which, since Tom Brown's days, has symbolized the egalitarian promises of sport. We have noted that, in a fair game, each side tries to achieve a commonly

Identifying Factors That Make Game Playing Unfair

Student Exercise

What unearned advantages do some players possess? Do these factors detract from the merit that some athletes claim for themselves when they win or play well? What other factors appear in the course of playing games that might prevent them from being fair? Identify five factors related to players and another five related to events in the game that might produce unfair results.

If your reflections suggest that a perfectly level playing field is more a myth than a reality, is it still worthwhile to try to promote fair play? In other words, should we try to make games as fair as we can? What, specifically, can be done to create the most level playing fields possible?

One recent effort to promote fairness involves using new methods to reverse bad calls made by referees or umpires. Challenges and video replays of contested calls are now permitted in the NFL, in NCAA football, in Major League Baseball, and in other sports. Do you think these high-technology methods for promoting fairness are good practices? Is fairness worth pursuing at all costs, or should it be weighed against other game values? Provide the reasoning for your answers.

---

understood goal by selecting strategies from the same group of available means in conditions where achievement or success is measured objectively and accurately. That is, both sides play by the same rules. Bias and other harmful forms of subjectivity are reduced or eliminated so that those who truly play better receive their just deserts.

Thus, rulebooks do much to promote fair play; they are not, however, sufficient. As a result, many ethics books recommend that players and coaches abide by both the letter and the spirit of the rules. The notion of the spirit of the rules deserves attention for at least three reasons. First, rulebooks, no matter how rationally constructed, are rarely, if ever, complete. The reason is that rule makers can neither anticipate every game eventuality nor remove every ambiguity from the language of the rulebook. Second, many rules need to be interpreted, and this process can be facilitated by cultivating a sense of the spirit of the rules. Third, both rule makers and game players typically have a good sense of what a game is about—that is, what skills a game is designed to test.

According to sport philosophers Bob Simon and John Russell, this sense of what a game is about can help in cases where either no explicit rule exists or vague rules require interpretation. This position, called broad internalism, is generally thought today to provide both the most sophisticated interpretation of games and the strongest foundation for promoting fair play. It has much in common with the recommendation to play by the spirit of the rules because it asks players and officials to consider what the game is ultimately about, what it is designed to test. If we know what a game is designed to test, then we can transcend the rules and make the game fairer.

You read earlier in this chapter that beginning in the 1600s interest in gambling raised the stakes for playing by the letter and spirit of the rules. People who wagered their own good money on various contests had a stake in establishing common objectives, means, and reliable measures of success, as well as methods for policing these sporting agreements. Without such safeguards, cheating, officiating mistakes, and uneven enforcement of rules could be very expensive for a victimized gambler. Thus fairness was essential in the games on which bets were placed—and on which fortunes could be won or lost.

Gamblers also relied on another sense of fair play, one that is analytically distinct from fairness defined as equal opportunity promoted by game rules. This other sense has to do with the opportunity to win or prevail. After all, it is only by winning, or achieving a high finish, that a bettor makes good on his or her wager. Thus gambling presupposes opportunity and uncertainty; gambling on a sure thing, in other words, is a contradiction in terms.

This second sense of fairness is also found outside the domain of gambling. For example, if a professional golfer were to enter a contest with an eight-year-old who had just been introduced to the game, we would intuitively identify the game as unfair. The child would have no chance to win—or even come close to winning. Such a contest would allow for no drama or uncertainty. Therefore, insofar as it involved a quest for victory, the activity would be a bore for the professional golfer and an unhappy exercise in futility for the child. The outcome would be known before the first hole was played. Given these circumstances, we would say this contest was patently unfair.

Understandably, we avoid such contests in our daily lives as sport competitors. Instead, we look for someone who is close to our own ability. We set up leagues in which teams are reasonably well matched. We group competitors by age, height, and weight—all to promote a fair contest, one in which each side will have a chance to win, or at least to finish among the leaders.

The betting community also takes steps to assure that each side in a contest has a chance. In some cases, where one side is a prohibitive favorite, no betting line is offered. In more common situations, where one side is favored but not prohibitively, gambling establishments provide compensatory odds or give points to the lesser competitor. For example, in some horse races, weight is added to the faster runners. In golf, extra strokes are often granted to the weaker player. These practices—finding similarly skilled opponents, establishing betting odds, giving points, and employing handicaps—are all intended to produce the same effect: to assure that each side has a chance to win—that is, that the game is fair in this particular sense.

This analysis shows that at least two distinct notions of fair play are employed in order to construct good competitions. These two species of fair play are mapped in a Venn diagram in figure 6.1. Venn diagrams are used by philosophers to clarify

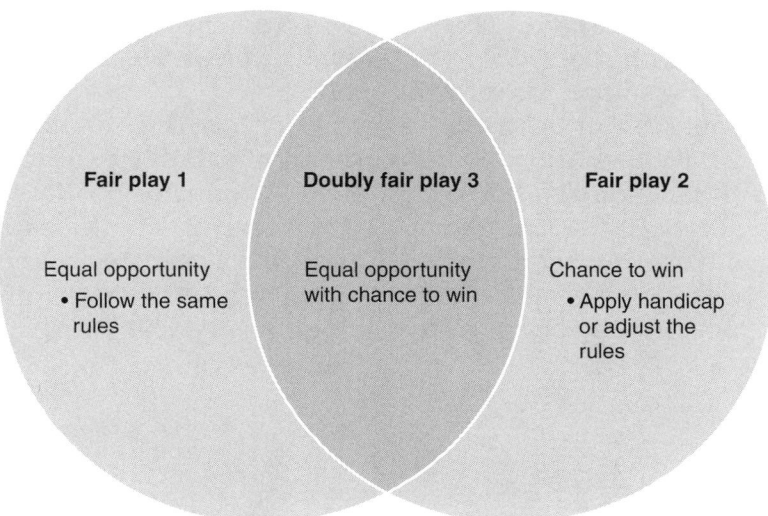

Figure 6.1 Two concepts of fair play and their intersection.

relationships between different things. For our purposes here, we are looking at relationships between two notions of fair contests—the fair game in which all competitors follow the same rules and the fair game in which each party has a chance to win, even if this requires the use of different rules for each side.

In the figure, to the left, under Fair Play 1, the diagram shows a game that is fair in terms of the contest rules and the provision of a level playing field but not fair in terms of providing each side with a chance to win. One example of such a contest is the hypothetical golfing match, discussed earlier, between a professional golfer and a child beginner. Their contest would be fair in the sense that they would both play on the same course under the same conditions, religiously follow the rules, count every stroke, and so on. Thus a final score of, say, 68 to 175 would objectively and accurately reflect the competitive difference between the two. But this game would not be fair in the second sense, because the child would have no chance to win. Thus this part of the Venn diagram houses what we commonly refer to as blowout victories and defeats. Again, they may be perfectly fair games and produce accurate knowledge of differences in skill and strategy, but they are commonly regarded as undesirable because they lack the drama of contests that are fair in the other sense of "having a chance."

The right side of the Venn diagram includes contests that are fair in the sense that all competitors have a chance to win or achieve a high finish but are not fair insofar as lesser competitors are given specific advantages. In other words, the competitors here are not playing by the same rules. The superior player may be handicapped, or the weaker opponent may be allowed to violate or ignore certain rules. Our golfing example could be located here if the professional golfer gave the child a large number of strokes on each hole. Thus, this section sacrifices fairness as equal opportunity, as well as accurate knowledge of relative skill—both of which were realized in section 1—for the benefit of the aesthetic experience of uncertainty and drama, the "sweet tensions" afforded by a close contest, or the wagering delights associated with placing a smart bet.

The middle of the diagram shows the overlap between the two senses of fair play. This is perhaps the best location for sporting contests because such games generate both accurate knowledge and the pleasures associated with close contests. It could be argued that these are what we might call "good games" because they are doubly fair. They do their best to erase unearned advantage (fairness type 1) and to preserve the uncertainties of close contests (fairness type 2). In these games, all competitors play by the same rules *and* have a chance to win. These kinds of games are useful both for players who like to compete on a level playing field and find out how good they are (that is, those who value the epistemological or accurate-knowledge outcome) and for players, fans, and bettors who relish the chance to win and experience a close game (that is, who favor the aesthetic or dramatic-contest outcome).

Even as the development of fair play was important for gambling, it also offered educational value beyond that realm. Therefore, it remained an important ideal as British culture shifted away from gambling and individual activities and toward community and team sports.

CHAPTER WRAP-UP

Wrapping Up and Looking Ahead

The early phases of the modernization of sport developed from the desire of gamblers to make sure that the games they bet on were fair contests. The logic of rationalization soon moved modern sport beyond that goal and began to shape other rationales for justifying the time and energy devoted to such pursuits. When, in the era of democratic revolutions in the late 1700s and into the 1800s, the middle classes discovered sport, they began to think of it not just as an activity for amusement and entertainment but also as an instrument that could teach citizens how to function in a modern society. They soon offered "rational recreation" as a wholesome alternative to the sporting fraternity's raucous playgrounds. They decried gambling as an irrational vestige of the past and moved sporting contests from taverns and theaters into schools and churches. They also turned increasingly from sports that prized individual prowess and skill, such as prizefighting or pedestrianism, to team sports.

Tom Brown and his friends outlined the new, corporate direction that modern sport would take at the end of their conversation about cricket as a modern institution. Their teacher marveled that cricket not only developed individual skills but also demanded teamwork to achieve common goals. "The discipline and reliance on one another which it teaches is so valuable, I think," the teacher observed of cricket. He labeled it "such an unselfish game. It merges the individual in the eleven; he doesn't play that he may win, but that his side may." Tom agreed with his teacher, in the process making the case that team sports provide superior training for modern life." "That's very true," Tom noted, agreeing with the master about the unselfishness taught by cricket. Tom continued, "and that's why football and cricket, now one comes to think of it, are such much better games . . . than any others where the object is to come in first and win for oneself, and not that one's side may win." Just six years after the 1857 publication of *Tom Brown's Schooldays*, in which this conversation was detailed, a "community of interest" met in London and founded the Football Association. The next era in the modern history of sport was beginning.

Study Questions

1. Why did Tom Brown call sport "more than just a game"? In what sense did sport become a critical institution during this period of time?

2. What are the specific features of the cultural revolution described by Guttmann? How did they affect the earlier folk traditions of sport?

3. Why were utilitarian ethics attractive in an age of increased rationalization? What are the key advantages and disadvantages of Bentham's utilitarian ethics?

4. How and why did sport betting emerge during this period? What specific forms did it take?

5. Why, specifically, is the ideal of the level playing field so difficult to achieve, even in modern-day sport?

6. What are the two specific senses of fair play, and how do they relate to the so-called "good game"?

LIBERTY, EQUALITY, FRATERNITY

The Development of Modern Sport

In this chapter, you will

1. learn about early attempts to formulate game rules and standardize sporting contests;

2. see how the French Revolution's values of liberty, equality, and fraternity influenced (and were influenced by) sport;

3. examine the equality-based ethics of Immanuel Kant and their implications both for sporting behavior and for the 19th-century emphasis on sport as a meritocracy;

4. determine the role played by fraternity and increasing nationalism in the development of sport;

5. review the moral assets and liabilities of partisanship—that is, of rooting for one's home team or country—and speculate on the nature of the "ideal fan"; and

6. study the emergence of sport as a commercial product and how it affected the "cult of amateurism."

In the autumn of 1863, a collection of well-educated British professionals including lawyers, journalists, bankers, merchants, military officers, and government officials held a series of meetings at The Freemasons' Tavern in London to draw up a set of "laws" that would codify the game for which they held a great passion—"football." Most of the men in the meeting were "old boys," a designation that meant they were, like the fictional Tom Brown, graduates of one of the elite "public" schools (for more on Tom Brown and these schools, see chapter 6). These schools prepared young men to attend either Oxford University or Cambridge University, then propelled them into the ranks of the growing professional classes who provided leadership for the dominant superpower of the era, the British Empire. The "old boys" led the British military, government, and economy, both at home and abroad.

They had fallen in love with football and other sports during their boyhoods in British boarding schools. They continued to play as they began their professional careers in London and in other capitals of the empire from Manchester, Edinburgh, and Glasgow to Mumbai, Melbourne, and Hong Kong. Their experiences in British schools and in their early careers convinced them that they desperately needed a set of rules for the game they loved. Older folk forms of "farmers' football," which had been a favorite pastime of British peasants for centuries, rapidly declined in the 1600s and 1700s as agricultural laborers left farms in droves and migrated to cities to take jobs in the new industrial factories that revolutionized the economy and the society.

Farmers' football pitted hundreds of combatants against one another in violent encounters fueled by alcohol and local pride. Such a "riot," as football's medieval critics often described these games, could not be replicated in crowded urban societies where authorities felt compelled to control the unruly passions of the masses. In the early stages of the urban and indus-trial revolutions, folk football disappeared from British landscapes, leaving only scant traces in a mere handful of small towns in which anachronistic contests continued to be held as odd remembrances of a distant past.

Even British legal codes confined archaic football to oblivion. In 1835 the British Parliament passed a series of laws that sought to regulate the chaotic conditions that had developed on the growing system of public "highways" for foot and horse-powered traffic, requiring pedestrians and carriages to keep to the left side of roadways in order to unravel the traffic jams that cluttered the system and threatened to damage Britain's commercial vitality. In addition to the provisions that created modern traffic patterns, the Highway Act of 1835 also barred the playing of football on roadways, putting the final nail in the coffin of farmers' rowdy games.

The Emergence of Modern Sport

Only the passion of the "old boys" who devoted themselves to football games at their boarding schools (and off the public highways) kept football alive. More than two dozen of these schools had sprouted in the 17th and 18th centuries in order to educate the sons of the new middle classes and the older gentry and aristocracy for the duties of building and maintaining the empire. Each school developed its own version of football. Fundamental rules such as whether or not using one's hands to advance the ball was permissible as well as playing styles varied widely.

When the boys matriculated at Oxford and Cambridge, they brought with them their passion for games. At these two bastions of higher learning, codes had begun to be standardized in the 1700s for many of the early college sports, such as crew, cricket, and track and field. The multiple varieties of football, however, created a major problem for the social order at

Oxford and Cambridge. "Old boys" wanted to continue the football traditions of their particular alma maters and wrangled ceaselessly, and sometimes even violently, over which football "codes" should reign on campus—the rules of Rugby or Eton or Harrow or Westminster or one of the many other schools from which students had graduated. In the first half of the 19th century, these schools began writing down their own distinctive football "codes," with Eton producing a rulebook in 1815 and Rugby a rather different one in 1845.

In 1848, representatives from many of the schools met at Cambridge University and developed a set of rules designed to satisfy all of the "old boys" with a standardized version of football that drew from the traditions of Eton and those schools that preferred a game centered on kicking the ball. The Cambridge Rules that emerged from that meeting pleased many of the football zealots, though not the graduates of Rugby, who preferred their game that allowed players to hold the ball in their hands and run with it. When the Football Association met at the London tavern in 1863, the participants drew heavily from the Cambridge Rules in creating a game that came to be called association football, or, in the British slang term for an abbreviation of the word *association*, "soccer."

A group of "old boys" from Rugby and allied schools who preferred a different version of football attended the Football Association's founding meetings but grew disenchanted with the constitution for football their comrades created, in particular the bans against running with the ball held in their hands and "hacking" (as tackling opposing players advancing the ball was called). Frustrated that these changes might, as the Rugby alumni put it, "do away with all the courage and pluck from the game," as one of the proponents of hands and hacking complained, they marched out of the Football Association and crafted their own constitution. They held their constitutional convention at London's Pall Mall Restaurant in 1871 and formed the Rugby Union, which codified and promoted rugby football. In similar fashion, over the next few decades, a wide variety of new football codes would appear in other parts of the English-speaking world, as coalitions of football aficionados in other nations called their own conventions to build constitutions for the games they adored.

The process of creating modern constitutions for football—or "codes" or "laws" in the parlance of the people who made them—resembled the process for making new political systems that emerged first in the Western world during the 17th, 18th, and 19th centuries and eventually spread to many other parts of the globe. This resemblance is more than a mere coincidence. The rise of modern team sports and the rise of modern nations emerged out of the same world-changing social and cultural processes. Early modern Western societies manifested a mania for creating communities of like-minded individuals in voluntary organizations rather than relying on more traditional vehicles for social bonding, such as family structures and local attachments to enduring religious, political, and economic institutions.

These interest groups especially attracted the emerging middle classes but also drew members from across the spectrum of class and caste. Scholars have long contended that the mania for rationalization that shaped modernity grew from the fervor for creating codes of membership and organizing and defining how they approached whatever mutual interest created these associations. Scholars have also argued that the free association of like-minded citizens generated the era's many political revolutions, providing places for both criticizing the flaws of old regimes and designing blueprints for new political systems. Finally, scholars have identified these voluntary associations as incubators for modern democracies, noting in particular the democratic interactions between relatively equal members that often prevailed in these groups.

Modern sport thus emerged out of the same social locations and intellectual factories that produced modern ideas about government systems, economic relations, and human nature. The voluntary associations that incubated these ideas—the salons and Sunday schools, the coffeehouses and taverns, the reading clubs and civic fraternities—also created modern sport. The mass public culture that emerged from these associations and spread rapidly around the world carried modern sport along with the multitude of other ideas that it disseminated. The same newspapers, magazines, and books that brought the political, social, and economic ideas of these associations to vast new audiences also promoted and popularized modern sport. Modern ideas about the bonds required to make order out of the chaos of pluralistic mass societies, called "civic virtue" in its classical formulation, or "social capital" in the language of contemporary scholars who describe this force, are inextricably embedded in modern sports. Parks and playgrounds, gymnasiums and swimming pools, and sports teams and physical education classes were designed to create social capital—the essential bonding agent of modern nations among citizens who differed in race and ethnicity, occupation and economic level, and religion and culture.

A famous painting depicting the ideals of the French Revolution illuminates this deep connection between modern sport, modern nation making, and the quest to manufacture social capital. Jacques-Louis David's painting *The Tennis Court Oath* (1791) captures the moment in 1789 during the French Revolution when the members of the Third Estate, the representatives of the common people of France, having constituted themselves as the National

The Tennis Court Oath, by Jacques-Louis David, 1791.

Assembly, moved to seize power from the First and Second Estates—the monarchy and aristocracy. Inspired in part by the American revolutionaries who had created a new United States just a few years earlier, representatives of the Third Estate pledged themselves to the revolutionary motto of "liberty, equality, and fraternity." They wrote a new, democratic constitution that fundamentally reordered the French political cosmos and inspired other revolutionary movements in Europe and Latin America, and, in later epochs, in Asia and Africa.

The site of this pivotal moment in world history—the tennis court at the Palace of Versailles, sacred bastion of royal power that the revolutionary tide was in the process of sweeping into the dustbin of history—represents an important component of the story of the French Revolution. Tennis developed over several centuries in medieval and early modern Europe as the game of the monarchy and the aristocracy, the First and Second Estates of France's traditional social order—a regime not long for the world in 1789. The invasion of the tennis court by the masses, in the form of the representatives of the Third Estate, carried enormous symbolic power. It represented the arrival of the commoners at the center of modern societies as they overwhelmed the elites who for millennia had dominated the landscape. It also signaled that the concepts of liberty, equality, and fraternity were deeply enmeshed in modern sport.

That fact that in their hunt for a site on which to write their new social order into existence, the masses seized control of what the geographer John Bale has labeled a "sportscape," the tennis court at Versailles, was no accident. Perhaps nowhere in the more than two centuries that have transpired since the beginnings of the French Revolution have the hoary platitudes of the motto that animated its makers—liberty, equality, and fraternity—been more inscribed onto the consciousness of modern cultures than on the landscapes of modern sport. Indeed, in sport, the elements of liberty, equality, and fraternity have become immanent—or so the chroniclers of sporting narratives have been telling us for more than 200 years in newspaper articles and scholarly tomes, on radio waves, and through television signals.

Freedom and Leisure Time

The connection between sport and modern ideas about liberty works on several levels. In the most obvious way, as the processes of political and economic modernization have created surpluses of leisure time for citizens and consumers to spend, the world's masses have frequently spent that time on sport. Indeed, the very phrase "spending time" represents a key modern attitude that conceives of time as a commodity, like money, to be used on anything that an individual desires. This notion stands in contrast to more traditional conceptions of time, which reigned in older cultures, as something that merely passed or something that had to be endured. Over the past three centuries, modern people have increasingly chosen to "spend time" playing and watching sport.

In our own contemporary world, watching television rules as the most popular activity on which people around the globe now spend time. The two most highly rated global television programs are the Olympics and World Cup soccer. These events draw upward of five billion viewers and constitute the largest "shared experiences" of the early 21st century. Some observers argue that watching sport on television inevitably reduces the number of people who participate in sporting and recreational activities, thereby turning the globe's masses into sedentary "couch potatoes." However, a host of studies reveals a counterintuitive outcome. Many who watch sport on television are in fact more active than those who do not. Spectatorship drives rather than inhibits the spending of time to participate in sport.

Liberty and the Rise of Social Organizations

Liberty and sport also connect on other levels. The same voluntary associations, the sport clubs (see chapter 6, as well as this beginning of this chapter)—that created modern sport were nurtured by the freedom of like-minded people to gather and organize themselves in societies devoted to a variety of common interests. These societies frequently promoted the idea that the sports they developed provided good environments for making good citizens, a sentiment that sporting clubs shared with the multitude of other religious, civic, economic, and recreational clubs that promoted all sorts of other activities. This notion of liberty linked sport directly to the making of social capital. In addition, the structure of modern games themselves required participants to submit voluntarily to the rules of the game. Those rules, like the constitutions developed for modern political contests, limited arbitrary power and enhanced free consent among the players to the design of their games—an apt analogy for modern understandings of liberty in the broader sense.

Equality and the Rise of Meritocracy

Equality also played a prominent role in the development of modern sport. Equality's two manifestations (as we detailed in chapter 6), in the conditions of competition and in broad access to opportunities to compete are key traits of modern sport. These two forms of equality have made sport into symbolic spaces for promoting meritocracy, the idea that talent and skill—not family status, religion, ethnicity, gender, or any other traditional category—should determine who wins and who loses, who rises and who falls, and who garners status and who loses respect in a modern society. In the 19th century, the English cricket player William Gilbert Grace became, next to Queen Victoria, the best-known figure in the British Empire as a symbol of the rise of the middle classes and their values to power and prominence. In similar fashion, in the early 20th century, the American baseball player George Herman "Babe" Ruth became an iconic symbol of the American belief that people could rise from poverty and obscurity to the top of society on the basis of incredible talent. At the end of the 20th century, Argentine soccer hero Diego Maradona played a similar role in his own meteoric ascension from "rags to riches."

Sport has also provided female symbols of meritocracy in the quest for equality from the French tennis star Suzanne Lenglen and the American all-around athlete Mildred "Babe" Didrikson in the first half of the 20th century to the American mixed martial arts fighter Rhonda Rousey and the South Korean figure skater Kim Yuna in the first half of the 21st century.

The focus in modern sport on both facets of equality—equality of conditions and of opportunity—has made playing fields and gymnasiums into symbolic spaces for promoting meritocracy. Modern societies venerate sport as an institution in which the idea that talent and ability should triumph is more fully realized than in many other domains, including political life and economic exchange. Although the ideal of equality has in fact often proven elusive in modern sport—and racial, social, and gender barriers have sometimes limited opportunities—the prevailing expectation has been that sport should be free of such boundaries. (Recall the chapter 3 exercise titled Is Modern Sport a Meritocracy? that addresses the difficulties of promoting fairness in sport.)

Indeed, athletes have famously become symbols of breaching these barriers. From Jackie Robinson's challenges to racial restrictions in American baseball in the 1940s and 1950s, to Edson Arantes do Nascimento's (better known as Pelé) challenges to racial boundaries in global soccer in the 1960s and 1970s, to the increasing inclusion of women in a wide variety of global sporting activities since the 1970s—ranging from Olympic marathons to professional prizefighting to a World Cup tournament for women's soccer—athletes have embodied struggles for equality. The focus on equality has made it the norm in many sporting cultures, requiring those who promote exclusion to defend their stances rather

THE LIMITS OF LIBERTY AND EQUALITY: CLASS BARRIERS AND COLOR LINES

Historical Profile

When the common folk flooded onto the tennis court at Versailles to swear allegiance to the revolutionary republic of France, it did not mark the end of exclusion and segregation in sport. Indeed, barriers to liberty and equality remain to the present day. Historically, even as many people saw signs of expanding liberty and equality in modern sporting practices, exclusion and segregation sometimes continued to flourish on playing fields.

One example emerged in the 19th-century British invention of amateurism. Although the British claimed that the practice dated back to ancient Greece, it in fact had no precedent in antiquity (see chapter 2). Instead, it served the interests of keeping the ruling classes in power in Great Britain and its empire. An amateur by definition not only received no monetary compensation for playing sport but also did not use her or his body in any fashion to earn a living. Such stark lines meant that to claim amateur status a soccer player or a cricket player or a rower or a golfer not only had to make sure that they did not accept payment for their athletic endeavors but also that they did not use their bodies in any way to earn a living. Every working-class occupation—from factory worker to miner, from bricklayer to stevedore (dockworker)—were disqualified from amateur standing regardless of whether they accepted money when they took the field to play games.

Only the middle classes and upper classes, the wealthy who earned their living from their investments or stockbrokers, lawyers, and teachers (the groups who we now label as "knowledge-workers") could be amateurs—the group that the British promoters of sport identified as the superior sportswomen and sportsmen. Why did the middle-classes and upper-classes construct the "amateur code"? Clearly, they built it in order to exclude the working classes from the upper echelons of British sport.

Battles over amateurism and professionalism also raged in the 19th-century United States, but in a society with greater mobility between social classes a simpler definition of the amateur code labeled as professional only those who accepted payment for their athletic performance. As a result, the American version of the amateur code allowed much wider access to sport among the working classes.

When it came to race, however, Americans of European descent drew color lines that either barred African Americans entirely or severely limited their access to sporting opportunities. For instance, as professional baseball developed after the Civil War, at a time when many Americans celebrated the end of slavery as a signal that the United States had lived up to its ideals, color lines were drawn against black players with increasing frequency. As professional leagues developed, even the small handful of black players who had been allowed in the game found themselves excluded from the emerging national pastime as white players demanded that they not be forced to compete with black athletes for jobs. By 1885, the established professional leagues had hardened the color line and pushed black players out of white baseball. As a result, no black players would take the field at the highest levels of professional baseball, the so-called "major leagues," until 1947, when Jackie Robinson debuted with the Brooklyn Dodgers. Excluded from white baseball, black players built their own separate "Negro Leagues"—where Jackie Robinson began his professional career in 1945 with the Kansas City Monarchs.

than viewing segregation as part of the natural order. Even long-standing all-male preserves, such as Augusta National Golf Club (home of the Masters Tournament), have, after prolonged protest campaigns, relented and allowed women members. Such inclusion does not, of course, signal the dawn of complete equality for women, any more than Jackie Robinson signing with the Brooklyn Dodgers heralded the end of racism. These changes do, however, underscore the fact that the expectation for sport in modern societies has tilted toward normalizing equality on many levels.

Liberty, Equality, and Morality

The concepts of liberty and equality not only animated the emerging modern sport cultures of the world but also attracted the interest of the era's philosophers. One such thinker was Immanuel Kant, one of the most influential moral philosophers in history and a strong proponent of the French Revolution, particularly the concepts of liberty and equality. Like Jeremy Bentham, the utilitarian ethicist introduced in chapter 6, Kant was also a fan of rationality—of using reason to determine right behavior. However, very much unlike Bentham, Kant wanted reason to do something other than calculate maximal utility by identifying the outcomes that would provide the greatest satisfaction for the most people.

Specifically, Kant wanted reason to function above our wants, needs, and particular interests. If we are controlled by our natural desires and preferences, he argued, then we are actually slaves to those things; in other words, we are not truly free. Thus, we need to choose our ends. We need to do the right thing whether it is pleasing to us or not, whether it produces the most favorable outcomes or not. In short, we need to act on the basis of duty, not desire. Thus we need to find principles on which everyone can agree—principles that are not the product of local conditions, enculturation, physics, biological requirements, instincts, or other external conditions.

Moreover, we need to act on those principles, and our motives need to be pure. Paradoxically, then, only those who act out of a sense of duty, who try to do the right thing simply because it is the right thing, are truly free. Our freedom, in other words, is grounded not just in certain political arrangements but more fundamentally in our rational ability to see what is right and true and to act on that information.

Kant was equally adamant about the roots of equality, which are grounded, he believed, in the inherent dignity of every person. People have rights. They should never be lied to and should never intentionally be put in harm's way. More broadly, they should never be used as a means to other ends. This was one way in which Kant expressed his famous categorical imperative: People should always be treated as ends, never as means. Thus Kant stood in diametric opposition to Bentham and, as noted in chapter 6, would reason differently than Bentham when faced with situations such as the hypothetical runaway trolley. Kant would have difficulty either throwing the switch or pushing the man off the bridge, even if doing so would save five other people. His reluctance is rooted in a universal ethical rule never to use a human being as the means to other ends.

Ethicists who follow Kant are called deontologists. Whereas utilitarians such as Bentham, and later John Stuart Mill, argue that the ends justify the means, deontologists suggest that this thinking underplays our ethical responsibilities in at least two ways. First, they argue, it fails to discriminate between outcomes—between competing satisfactions, or pleasures. This failure sells our reasoning powers short. We should, Kant wrote, be able to see what is inherently right and not settle for what is contingently desired. Second, deontologists argue that utilitarian thinking fails

KANT'S CATEGORICAL IMPERATIVE PUTS HUMAN BEINGS FIRST

Philosophical Application

Immanuel Kant (1724–1804) was the founder of German idealism and one of the most influential ethicists in the history of philosophy. Born into a devout but poor family that emphasized the practical and ethical implications of one's faith, Kant experienced a pietistic upbringing that would always influence his ethical thinking. He also believed in the power of reason to get to essential truths about how humans should treat one another. He referred to such truths as categorical—that is, as deserving adherence regardless of circumstances, local conditions, cultural traditions, or other variables. Although Kant acknowledged that human beings do not always act in accord with these imperatives, he held that we can still know what they are and therefore still have a duty to follow them.

Kant formulated his notion of the categorical imperative in multiple ways. First, he said that ethical truths can be universalized. That is, if one is acting ethically, one should be able to recommend the given behavior for others in the same situation without rendering the behavior self-defeating. This formulation was

Immanuel Kant: A German philosopher and central figure in modern philosophy, a defender of dispassionate reason and human rights, and opponent of utilitarianism.

designed to eliminate selfish behavior and to prevent people from making exceptions of themselves. For example, Kant argued that lying cannot be universalized because we cannot recommend that behavior for others without its becoming ineffectual; if everyone lied, Kant reasoned, nobody would benefit from it. His second formulation of the imperative suggested that we should always treat persons (including ourselves) as ends. He believed that there is a fundamental difference between persons and things. Whereas things can be used for other purposes, human beings deserve better.

Kant, whose *Critique of Pure Reason* appeared in 1781, eight years before Bentham's *Principles*, set a very high bar for ethics, one that continues to hold intuitive appeal for many. Although most ethicists today see reason as more fallible than Kant did and do not believe that moral absolutes exist, Kant's emphasis on duty and human rights continues to inform ethical theory. Many still agree with Kant that it is important to be good, do the right thing, and carry out moral duties even if, as Kant wrote, "all the rascals in the world should perish from it."

to take the dignity and rights of other human beings seriously enough. For utilitarians, the well-being of others (any of whom might be harmed or sacrificed for a greater good) is always up for grabs. In contrast, Kant believed that human life is more important than that. Kant's notion of equality is consistent with the second principle of the French Revolution—one that requires that we treat all human beings with respect, no matter their rank in society.

Kant's strong stance against lying or intentional deception carries implications for sport. Of course, the kind of deception at issue here is not the type that athletes skillfully employ to make opponents believe that one thing will happen when another is planned—as when a basketball player fakes right and then drives left or a baseball pitcher disguises a changeup by using a motion identical to the one used for a fastball. In fact, that kind of deception is part of what sport is about, and its use can be universalized according to Kant's formulation. It also respects opponents as ends because we all enter sport just so we can be tested, in part, by such deceptive acts.

Kant would be concerned, however, with another kind of lying or deception that has infiltrated sport. Examples would include athletes faking injuries, coaches pretending to be angry in order to "work the officials" and get the next call, youth and collegiate athletes lying about their age or academic eligibility, and competitors pretending to be fouled when no foul has occurred—that is, "flopping" or "diving." Some sport ethicists believe that such behavior is a form of lying even though it is intended to deceive through body language rather than words. Indeed, effective communication can take place both verbally and nonverbally (as illustrated in the chapter 2 exercise titled Communicating and Cooperating Without Using Verbal Language). It would follow that effective lying can also be accomplished in both ways. Arguably, then, lying, or morally questionable deception, is present in the following account by Alan Burdick, writing in the *New Yorker*, of a crucial international soccer match.

> *In the sixty-ninth minute of the World Cup's opening match, between Brazil and Croatia, with the score tied 1-1, a Brazilian striker went down in front of the opposing goal, seemingly shoved or tripped by a Croatian defender. Players from the Croatian team swarmed the referee to protest, but in vain; the referee . . . awarded the Brazilians a penalty kick. Neymar, a forward, briskly converted it, giving the Brazilians a permanent lead. But by then, even the television commentators were howling, as replays exposed the foul for what it actually was: a spectacular bit of theatre. [The defender] had barely touched [the striker], who nonetheless slid down on a pillow of air, his arms raised in mock protest even before he hit the ground. He'd faked it, to draw the penalty.*

Another way to examine the ethical issue of flopping is to ask the following question: Does this behavior promote sport as a meritocracy or detract from it? Would the revolutionary emphasis on equality—a value that "created symbolic spaces for promoting meritocracy" in sport—recommend in favor of or against faking fouls?

One answer is that diving works against merit. In the soccer example, the Brazilian team won on an undeserved penalty kick. To be sure, the team had to convert the kick, but it did not have to display the far more demanding skills required for scoring a regular goal. Reasonable people could argue that this was a miscarriage of justice. Brazil won because its player effectively lied to the official and, unfortunately for the Croatians, the official fell for it. Can we really recommend that soccer games should be decided in this manner? Does diving make soccer a better game?

Ethics of Flopping

Student Exercise

What do you think about flopping in basketball and diving in soccer? Is it morally acceptable to intentionally present the appearance of a foul in order to deceive the referee, get a favorable call, and thereby gain an advantage over one's opponent?

Defenders of the practice have suggested that it is, in fact, acceptable and have supported it by using some of the following arguments.

1. It is part of the game. Everyone does it.
2. It keeps the playing field level. Because opponents are doing it, I need to do it too—just to keep the game fair.
3. It usually does not cause much harm. Better teams still win.
4. It is a skill that can be (and is) practiced. People who "sell" apparent fouls well should be rewarded for it, just as players are rewarded for passing accurately or displaying other skills.

How solid are these arguments in terms of utilitarian thinking on one hand and Kantian ethics on the other? In terms of utilitarian logic, does flopping promote the greatest good for the greatest number? Remember, this logic does not refer to the greatest good only for oneself. Furthermore, if diving does promote the greatest good, what kinds of goods would those be?

In terms of Kantian ethics and deontological thinking, can flopping be universalized? In other words, if everyone flopped regularly, would this phenomenon undo the advantage gained currently by a few athletes who flop only occasionally? Furthermore, does diving violate the rights of one's opponent? Does it place the official or referee in the role of serving as a means to one's own competitive ends? Is diving a form of lying to an official?

Similarly, in the sport of basketball, is flopping a skill that we want to watch? Do we want ESPN, for instance, to replay the 10 best flops from the day's games?

Kant might argue that this behavior shows lack of freedom because players and fans have capitulated to a "win at all cost" ethic of sport. We have become slaves to current cultural values and pressing psychological needs. In other words, we are not doing what is right. Kant would probably also have concerns on behalf of the referees. Their job is to get the call right, to make sure that the team that played better receives its just deserts, and this task is hard enough under the best of circumstances. Diving, therefore, shows disrespect for these individuals by intentionally making their job more difficult and more likely they will get the call wrong.

Even Bentham might suggest that flopping is wrong—not because it is inherently bad, and not because it treats officials as means to an end, but simply because it introduces more harms than benefits to the game. Sport is more fun to play and watch, it could be said, when it features skillful physical action, not illegal deceit. Sport delights us when it focuses on physical feats of going "faster, higher, stronger" (as the Olympic motto puts it), not on theatrical displays intended to mislead. Thus, the greatest balance of good over harm would exist if players did not dive. This line of thought stands as a utilitarian rational avenue to the same conclusion drawn by Kantians, albeit for different reasons. If these arguments make sense, flopping, or diving, is not morally defensible on either utilitarian or deontological grounds.

The Role of Fraternity in Modern Sport

Although liberty and equality have deep connections to modern sport, the most powerful link—to the ideals of the French Revolution, and to the broader concepts advocated during the Enlightenment and the revolutions it spawned—in athletic domains has been the power of sport to promote fraternity. In contemporary history, fraternity—the sense of community, devotion to the commonweal, the patriotic sentimentalism that functions as the very lifeblood of modern nations—has been animated with the greatest force by two institutions: war and sport. The French Revolution itself provides the lesson that when the power of ideas fails, the machinery of warfare emerges to bind the sinews of nationhood. The revolution in France ended, in its first incarnation at least, not in a democratic utopia but with the arrival of Napoleon Bonaparte and dictatorship; thus military fraternity trumped all other forms of community.

Next to war, no other force binds together modern nations with such energy as sport. In national pastimes and international competitions, the polities of the modern world shape and reshape their identities. As a leading scholar of modern nationalism, Eric J. Hobsbawm argues in modern cultures sport represents "an expression of national struggle, and sportsmen representing their nation or state, primary expressions of their imagined communities. The imagined community of millions seems more real as a team. . . . The individual, even the one who only cheers, becomes a symbol of the nation himself."

Since the French Revolution, sport has animated the fraternal bonds of all sorts of nations with all sorts of governments, from democracies that venerate liberty and equality to totalitarian regimes that practice authoritarian rule. When large groups of people identify the athletes and teams for which they cheer as part of the group to which they belong, when people use the pronoun *we* to talk about a team, even though they are only spectators and not players and thus seemingly have no control over the outcome of the contest—then sport becomes, as Hobsbawm observes, a fraternal epoxy that creates communities. The exhilarated "we won" or the exasperated "we lost" expressed by billions of fans reveals the power of sport to shape the fraternal sinews that bind modern communities together, as neighborhoods, cities, institutions, regions, or, most especially, nations.

British Leadership in Developing National Pastimes

When the devotees of a particular variety of football met at a London pub in 1863 to forge the rules for association football, they laid the foundation for the sport that would, by the 1920s, reign as the most popular national pastime in the world (for

Identifying Fraternity in Sport

Student Exercise

Identify an episode of the fraternal power of sport that you have experienced. When have you cheered as a member of "we" against an enemy identified as "them"? What was your community, and who were your rivals? As a historical exercise, search the web for an example, from before you were born, of athletes symbolizing their nation, city, or school. One example is the "Miracle on Ice," in which the underdog U.S. hockey team upset the mighty Soviet squad at the 1980 Winter Olympics in Lake Placid, New York. (But since we gave this one away, you cannot use the "Miracle on Ice" to fulfill this exercise!)

more on the global spread of soccer and other sports, see chapters 8 and 9). In fact, the very idea of a "national pastime" illustrates the power of sport to shape our ideas about nations. In the 21st century, soccer has become one of the leading vehicles for promoting a sense of nationhood in a huge number of nations. From China to Chile, Germany to Ghana, and Mexico to Myanmar, soccer now stands as the most common national pastime. Nations use national pastimes both to define themselves and to assess other nations. For instance, most people around the world can name more Brazilian soccer stars than Brazilian presidents and can cite Brazil's distinguished list of World Cup performances more easily than they can list Brazil's major economic exports. They identify Brazil with soccer far more than with any other institution.

This global phenomenon of national pastimes evolved from roots in the 19th-century English-speaking world. In Great Britain, the development of cricket, association football, and rugby football from "English" games into "British" national pastimes represented the drive to establish a sense of British nationhood in the new United Kingdom built upon the older nations of Scotland, Wales, Cornwall, and Ireland as well as England. The early adoption of games invented in England such as association football in Scotland and rugby football in Wales represented a triumph of national pastimes in the unification process while simultaneously developing national rivalries based on older fraternal structures, such as Scotland versus England in soccer and Wales versus England in rugby.

In contrast, some nations in the English-speaking world used national pastimes to resist British nationalism—in particular the Irish, who decried the spread of cricket, soccer, and rugby into the Emerald Isle and promoted the alternative national pastimes of Gaelic football and hurling. The Gaelic Athletic Association, founded in 1884 in Ireland, connected resistance to British national pastimes and veneration of Irish national games to the struggle for Irish independence. Similarly, though the Scots were initially more enamored of British team sports, such as soccer, they also invented the tradition of the Highland Games, highlighted by Celtic-themed track-and-field contests, to resist English domination in their corner of the United Kingdom.

National Pastimes in Other Parts of the World

Outside of the British Isles, cricket, soccer, and rugby also reflected struggles over the meaning of nationhood in the British Empire. Playing these three team sports linked the colonies and Dominions to British nationalism. It also provided opportunities for the colonies and Dominions to turn the tables on the so-called "mother country," as when, in the 1870s and 1880s, Australian cricket teams began to regularly defeat English clubs. Like the English language itself, cricket created a sense of nationhood among the heterogeneous peoples of the Indian subcontinent, and today it ranks as the dominant national pastime of India, Pakistan, Bangladesh, and Sri Lanka.

In other realms of the English-speaking world, resistance to British culture proved more intense. Though Australia embraced cricket, rugby, and, to a lesser extent, soccer, it also developed its own football code, Australian Rules football. Interestingly, the Australian version predates the official formalization of both soccer and rugby codes, as clubs in Melbourne met in 1859 to draw up "Aussie rules." Cricket, soccer, and rugby developed niches in Canadian sporting culture, but lacrosse and hockey evolved to become Canada's national pastimes.

In the United States, which had thrown off British political control in the 1770s and 1780s, cricket, rugby, and soccer did make appearances. In the 1850s, cricket was quite popular in certain areas of the United

States, and a tour by the All-England XI, an all-star team of British cricketers, drew tens of thousands of fans to matches in Philadelphia and the New York City area. In the 1860s, in the first intercollegiate football game ever played in the United States, Princeton and Rutgers used the association football rules. In the 1870s, a rugby team from McGill University in Canada introduced that British football code to Harvard, Yale, and Princeton. However, in an era of flourishing American nationalism, Great Britain still loomed in American imaginations as a major threat to the republic, and calls resounded to reject British forms of culture. The novelist Mark Twain, for example, demanded an American literature to replace the English literature canon in the nation's schools. In this atmosphere, British national pastimes proved a poor fit for American appetites.

As a result, Americans ultimately rejected cricket in favor of the homegrown game of baseball, going so far as to claim, falsely, that baseball had no linkages whatsoever to British folk games. In addition, although U.S. college students loved the challenges of rugby-style football, they could not swallow the British import whole and therefore began immediately to refashion the sport into an American football code that eventually diverged significantly from its rugby roots. Thus, two of the original American national pastimes developed out of hyperpatriotic resistance to, and refashioning of, British national pastimes by American sport enthusiasts. Imported into Canada, American football underwent a similar process and morphed into Canadian football, a game shorn of its overt connections to American culture and transformed into a Canadian pastime. In the rest of the English-speaking world, American and Canadian football are known generically as "gridiron football."

By the end of the 19th century, national pastimes flourished in the English-speaking world, both in Great Britain and in every region of the British Empire—from Canada to Australia to the West Indies to South Africa to India to Hong Kong. They also flourished in the United States. National pastimes allowed Anglo-American nations both to define their own identities and to interpret the cultures of other nations. They provided both common rubrics for comparison between nations and unique markers for the expression of each country's particular narratives of nationhood. National pastimes functioned as the clearest expressions of the fraternal bonds generated by sport. Like flags, anthems, military uniforms, and English dialects, sporting pastimes flourished as symbols of modern nationhood. As the 20th century dawned, national sporting pastimes would soon explode beyond the borders of Anglo-American realms and conquer the rest of the world.

Fraternity, Partisanship, and Spectatorship

The billions of partisans around the globe who eagerly embraced the emerging sporting boom were responding to something deeply ingrained in human nature and culture. It seems to be a universal characteristic of human nature to join groups, identify with certain causes, make specific religious commitments, and, as part of this process, distinguish ourselves from "the other"—those who are not like "us." Paradoxically, then, fraternity carries the potential to produce both loyal communities and potentially harmful divisions. Indeed, the two often go hand in hand. In other words, a tension exists between the power of partisan fraternity and the ethics of inclusion and mutual respect.

Our natural tendencies toward fraternity and building communities are related to another part of our human nature—the desire to seek and find meaning. As illustrated in the rise of modern sport in the 18th and 19th centuries, we find meaning in various ways: for example, in belonging;

in group loyalty; in being identified as, say, American, Chinese, or French; in being a fan of the New York Yankees or Manchester United; or, alternately, in despising the Yankees or "Man U" and rooting against them. To be sure, we seek and find meaning in many places. However, situations that are oppositional, agonistic, and competitive—and, therefore, would usually pit one group against another—seem to be particularly powerful in this regard. As noted earlier in this chapter, both war and sport present us with such unusually meaningful dichotomies—us versus them, or the virtuous and pure in contrast to the vile and vulgar.

In light of these human tendencies, it is not surprising that sport partisanship carries a checkered reputation. On one hand, it is the lifeblood of competition. If we did not have favorite teams, if we did not care who won, if we did not delight in seeing a longtime adversary fall on hard times, sport would lose much of its drama, its competitive flavor, and its strong purchase on our emotions. On the other hand, partisanship can lead to all kinds of inappropriate behavior, both on the field and in the stands. Some soccer teams have installed moats and barbed wire fences around their pitches in order to protect successful visiting players and game officials who make unpopular calls.

The need for such measures has led to questions about whether strong partisanship is ethically defensible. Partisanship can also blind us to the beauty of the game and prevent us from acknowledging and appreciating excellent performances by opponents. This pitfall has led to questions about whether strong partisanship negatively affects our aesthetic appreciation of sport. Do we miss out on aesthetic elements by rooting for one side? These ethical and aesthetic concerns raise a final issue: What qualities should we find in the ideal fan?

Possible answers have focused on two extremes conceptualized by some ethicists as existing along a continuum. At one end exists the sport purist who adopts an aesthetic attitude. This individual is interested in the excellence displayed on the court or field and celebrates a close, well-played game regardless of the outcome. The purist is in love with the game and finds meaning in heroic comebacks, last-minute reversals, and memorable plays.

The purist perspective has been given voice by some modern sport philosophers, among them Nicholas Dixon and Stephen Mumford. However, they are not the first to do so. One of the first philosophers to defend this aesthetic point of view was Michael Novak, who expressed it as follows: "I love the tests of the human spirit. I love to see defeated teams refuse to die. I love to see impossible odds confronted. I love to see impossible dares accepted. I love to see the incredible grace lavished on simple plays—the simple flashing beauty of perfect form—but even more, I love to see the heart that refuses to give in, refuses to panic, seizes opportunity. . . . When I see others play that way, I am full of admiration, of gratitude." We might notice that Novak says nothing about who won or lost, about partisan commitments or loyalty, about any sense of disappointment over one team heading home defeated. He focuses instead on the beauty of the game, whatever its source and whoever may be responsible for producing it. Much like a person entering an art gallery or attending a concert, he looks to be entertained, reminded, inspired, and uplifted.

At the other end of the spectrum is the excessively avid partisan. This individual cares nothing about the quality of the play or the drama of the contest but only about whether or not his or her favorite team prevails. It matters little if the strong partisan's team played poorly, if the opposing team was not at full strength, if the game was a boring blowout, even if the game was decided on a missed call or a bad hop. All that matters is the victory of the beloved

WORST CALL IN MAJOR LEAGUE HISTORY? DENKINGER CALLS ORTA SAFE

Historical Profile

In what is perhaps the most controversial call in World Series history, Don Denkinger called the Kansas City Royals' Jorge Orta safe at first base in the last inning of Game 6 of the 1985 World Series against the St. Louis Cardinals. Nearly everyone watching the game, including most Royals fans, realized that it was a blown call, and television replays showed that St. Louis pitcher Todd Worrell had clearly beaten Orta to the bag. Denkinger's mistake set the stage for a two-run Royals rally and a crucial 2-1 victory. Having had its season spared at the midnight hour, Kansas City went on to win the series in the following game, 11-0. An online search of Denkinger's 1985 World Series call brings up video clips and articles you may find interesting.

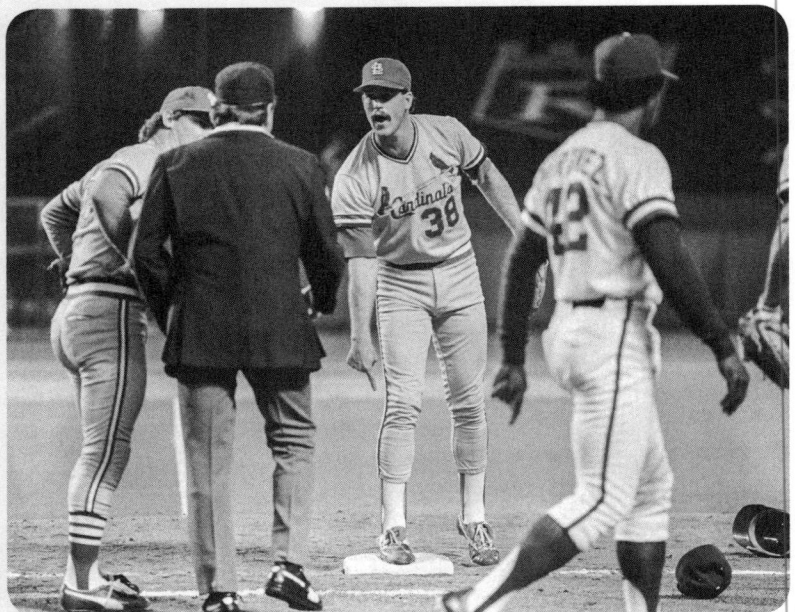

Some philosophers question the ethics of strong partisans who would celebrate a victory that was not earned.

Bettmann/Getty Images

Baseball purists lament this kind of outcome, in which the beautiful skills of the game and the drama of an excellent contest are ruined by an unfortunate incident. The aesthetics of the game are irreparably damaged—no chance of recovery, no reason for anyone who loves baseball to celebrate.

On the other hand, highly partisan Kansas City fans might see their good fortune as some kind of divine intervention. No matter how the victory was achieved, they might reason, the Royals are the World Series champions. Bad calls happen to everyone. In fact, a controversial call earlier in the same game went the Cardinals' way. Thus, Royals fans might say, justice was served. Still, for some more moderate partisans, the way in which the Royals won undoubtedly left a bad taste. It would have been better to win without the unmerited "gift" provided by Denkinger.

Later, Denkinger, a highly respected umpire, would admit his mistake and speak in favor of television replays (then not allowed) for purposes of preserving the game's integrity for purists and more meaningful outcomes for partisans.

team and, correspondingly, the defeat of the enemy.

Most scholars agree that few if any fans are either full-blooded purists or extreme partisans. Most of us are a combination of the two; we reside somewhere in the middle. In fact, our position on the spectrum may change depending on who our favorite team is playing. If we are going against a rival, or if the game carries important ranking or championship implications, we may move toward the partisan end of the scale. Some scholars have even argued that many fans oscillate between more aesthetic appreciations and more partisan perspectives during the course of a single game. A great play by the opponent, for instance, may get our attention and prompt at least a degree of begrudging admiration. As the game nears a crucial point, however, we may oscillate back to our predominantly partisan perspective.

This analysis produces a number of candidates for the ideal fan. It might be the purist who loves the game. This person possesses the virtues of the connoisseur, the one who knows the game, appreciates its excellences, looks for beauty, and treats sport as if it were a form of dramatic art. Alternatively, the ideal fan might be the partisan, who passionately loves his or her team. This person possesses the virtue of loyalty, of sticking with one's team both when it is doing well and when it is not. This individual exhibits constancy and commitment, much like partners in an enduring interpersonal relationship. Or the ideal fan might be the moderate observer who resides halfway between the two ends of the spectrum, exhibiting both loyalty and aesthetic appreciation but not too much of either. Finally, the ideal fan might be alternately purist and partisan throughout the contest. This person possesses both sets of virtues in full bloom and moves back and forth between appreciating and rooting, observing and committing, enjoying excellence and enjoying partisan success.

In another view altogether, sport philosopher J.S. Russell argues that there is no ideal fan. Russell endorses partisanship and the loyalty that often accompanies it but also claims that aesthetic perspectives are defensible. In other words, there are many blends of these two possibilities, many kinds of good fans. However, Russell also argues that spectatorship has a great deal to do with shared stories. He notes that we are born into fraternities of various shapes and sizes—that is, families, tribes, ethnic groups, neighborhoods, religious traditions, nations. We inherit the stories that accompany these people, their places, and their values. As we grow up, their stories becomes our stories. And, Russell argues, as meaning-seeking creatures, we find deep personal meaning in those stories. Moreover, many of our stories are *about* fraternity—that is, about the values that people share and the groups to which we belong.

By its nature, sport (as a species of games), places us in at least two groups. One group encourages partisan values and emotions; the other group encourages more purist sentiments. This claim about the nature of sport and its resources for fraternity provides an example of how and why metaphysics (the study of the nature of things) precedes ethics (the study of what is good). In chapter 2, in our analysis of the structure of games (including sports as physically demanding games), we note that they are fundamentally artificial tests—of lifting, for instance, or of hitting, or moving quickly, or swinging, or climbing, or riding, and so on. Contesting, on the other hand, is fundamentally an attempt to show difference in capability. Differences emerge from testing. This is the case, once again, because contesting (the attempt to show superiority) requires challenges that people meet in more or less successful ways. If everyone always scores the same on a given test—that is, if it is either too easy or too hard—then contesting is impossible. In other words, it makes no sense to try to show superiority where it is impossible to generate differences.

This metaphysical analysis of tests and contests takes us back to the kinds of stories we tell about ourselves, about our favorite athletes, and about our home teams. Some of these stories are about the kind of sporting fraternity that forms around the test. We identify ourselves with different testing grounds and activities—

specifically, those provided by baseball, distance biking, skiing, wrestling, boxing, and other pursuits. We identify with heroes and heroines in these tests and wear clothing bearing their names or jersey numbers. We buy sport-specific magazines, scan websites, join fantasy leagues—in part, because we belong to a game-specific fraternity. You may be a soccer person. I love baseball and table tennis. One of my closest friends lives for golf. The son of one of the authors of this book owns eight bicycles and travels around the country to various gravel and mountain biking events. Each of us is living a story that revolves around a challenging physical test. Each of us may belong to a different testing fraternity. Each of us should feel a kinship with all others who have devoted themselves to playing or watching that particular activity.

The second fraternity forms around the contest and involves individuals of similar skill levels who are dedicated to showing superiority. As argued in chapter 1, in the discussion of the bowling example, testing often leads to contesting. Typically, contesting promotes partisanship, loyalty, and identification with one team or competitor over another. Many of our stories, therefore, are about close contests that "we" won, great comebacks for "our" team, the defeat of "our" longtime rival, or even continued frustrations over "our" team's perennial failures.

The metaphysics of sport suggests that athletes and fans can be members of two communities—two fraternities—at once: the sport community and the partisan community. Either one may dominate, and either one may be a resource for our most meaningful stories. The more purist fraternity typically has the sport at its core, the excellences of that particular game. In contrast, the more partisan fraternity identifies with a person, a family, a tribe, a city, a nation. It cares less about which game is being played or which sporting test is being taken and more about whether the preferred team wins. It cares less about the quality of the contest and more about whether the result is the desired one.

Interestingly, both of these communities provide something more than just spectators who identify with sports or teams. They provide consumers willing to spend

Baron Pierre de Coubertin, the Olympic Games, and Partisanship

Student Exercise

Chapter 9 addresses the revival of the Olympic Games under the leadership of France's Pierre de Coubertin. He has been characterized as an idealist because he had very high (and probably unrealistic) pedagogical aspirations for the Olympics. Many of his hopes and dreams were related to the values of equality and fraternity. When you think of the modern Olympic Games, you may think of values such as excellence, friendship, and respect; or health, beauty, and harmony; or world peace and mutual understanding. The association of such values with the games raises important questions about the place of partisanship, and particularly nationalism, in the Olympic movement. These questions can be addressed at both the historical and the philosophical level. Here, then, are two questions for you to answer after doing some online or library research on Coubertin.

1. Was Coubertin a French partisan? Were French nationalistic motives included in his reasons for reviving the games? What does the historical record show?

2. Are nationalism and Olympism incompatible? For instance, is it logically possible to be strongly partisan (e.g., to hope that your country wins the most medals) and, at the same time, to endorse Olympic values such as mutual understanding and international respect?

both time and money on sports, creating the foundation for thriving sport markets.

Fraternity, Partisanship, and Commercialism

The power of sport to forge communal bonds in modern mass cultures not only strengthened the fabric of nationhood but also provided a new component of economic development. Clever entrepreneurs in the Anglo-American world discovered that patriotic games could generate tremendous profits. The new national pastimes sold easily to eager consumers who would pay handsomely to watch cricket matches, baseball games, and football contests of all varieties.

The development of extensive national railway systems in both Great Britain and the United States beginning in the 1830s and 1840s provided the crucial infrastructure for the development of national spectator sports industries. Trains allowed teams to travel to compete against rival clubs; they also provided transportation for fans to get to games both near to home and in far distant stadiums. The telegraph networks that developed in concert with railroad systems also provided the necessary infrastructure for extensive and timely coverage of sport by the emerging mass media. While tens of thousands of fans attended the games, millions more consumed sport by reading about contests in newspapers and magazines.

National pastimes grew quickly into profitable business ventures in Great Britain and the United States. In cricket, the emergence of a national-pastime industry began with the creation in 1846 of the All-England XI as a touring team that used the train system to play games all over the British Isles. Complex issues of amateurism and professionalism in both Great Britain and the United States often obscures the reality that although the national pastimes of the two nations sometimes paid their players' salaries and sometimes did not remunerate them directly, the touring teams and leagues that developed in cricket and baseball and in soccer, rugby, and American football were always driven by the profit motive. The cult of amateurism—an Anglo-American misreading of the traditions of Greek antiquity (see chapter 3)— revealed much about the class dynamics of both British and U.S. society but never reflected any serious conflict regarding the question of whether clever entrepreneurs should profit from marketing and staging national pastimes.

Indeed, since the 1600s, some English cricket players from the working classes had been paid to play. The upper-class and middle-class "gentlemen" who controlled the sport did not take money for their own play but often did profit from gambling on matches or from writing about cricket or organizing their teams as corporations. The famous Marylebone Cricket Club (MCC; see chapter 6) barred working-class professionals from holding memberships in their august body but hired them to play alongside the MCC's gentlemen members in money-making cricket tours.

After decades of profitable expeditions in Great Britain, the All-England XI and rival clubs began to travel overseas to seek new markets, journeying first, in 1859, to the United States and Canada. Two years later, the outbreak of the U.S. Civil War combined with growing American antipathy to cricket as a British—and not an American—national game led English teams to explore Australia and New Zealand instead. English teams staged numerous tours of the Antipodes from the 1860s through the 1880s. These outings developed the tradition of "test matches" that pitted one nation in the British Empire against another. By the late 1880s, English teams were voyaging to the West Indies, South Africa, and India. In 1887, the development of the County Cricket Council in Great Britain created the foundation for regular league play between cricket clubs. These teams were organized by the older rural geography of counties rather than by the new urban geography of cities that generally shaped other national-pastime industries.

In the United States baseball developed in much the same fashion as cricket. From 1845, when standardized rules for baseball were codified in New York City, through the end of the Civil War, the game was supposed to feature only "gentlemen" amateurs, though under-the-table payments to players from all social classes by clubs eager to best their rivals were not uncommon occurrences. In 1869, the completion of the first transcontinental railroad line—from New York to San Francisco—opened the gates for the first openly professional baseball team, the Cincinnati Red Stockings, to tour the United States from coast to coast. The rise of the Red Stockings represented the arrival of baseball as a national pastime. A game that had originally been the pastime of metropolitan areas in the Northeast became a national institution that helped symbolize the reconciliation of the American South back into the union after the crisis of secession and the disaster of the Civil War.

The Red Stockings had been developed in Cincinnati in order to rebrand the growing city from its identity as "Porkopolis," the nickname it had garnered as the center of the U.S. pig-slaughtering industry, into a more fitting rival for cosmopolitan New York, Philadelphia, and Boston. The Red Stockings bolted Cincinnati for Boston in 1871, joining a new association of professional teams that flourished as railroads knit U.S. cities together. In 1876, the creation of the National League (now the oldest continuously existing professional sport league in world history) cemented baseball's role as both the leading American national pastime and as the country's most lucrative brand in the growing sport industry. It also gave the United States the first professional sport league in world history, predating the rise of British cricket and soccer leagues by a decade or more.

Back in Great Britain, the roster of teams in the Football Association (FA)

expanded rapidly, growing from 50 in 1871 to more than 10,000 by 1900. Beginning in 1871, FA teams competed for the Challenge Cup, which quickly created dazzling opportunities to build a soccer industry. The gentlemen-amateur "old boys" who had founded the FA in 1863 kept control of the sport, and the profits it generated, for about two decades, winning all FA Challenge Cup matches until 1883. By the 1880s, however, working-class enthusiasm for the new game made soccer the national pastime of the British masses and soon sparked the rise of the first professional teams and, in turn, of professional leagues. British factory owners sponsored teams and initially gave workers paid time off from their work duties to practice and compete. The owners also subsidized the teams' travel to contests in an effort to ensure that factory teams could compete with the men of leisure who dominated the rosters of the "gentlemen's" clubs.

The upper-class and middle-class defenders of amateurism objected strenuously to these innovations, but the trend toward professionalism and open payment of players proved too strong to hold back. From 1883 forward, professional teams of working-class players ruled the highest levels of play and won all of the FA Cups. Most of the gentlemen retreated into leagues that played for an amateur FA Cup, created in 1893, while an all-star team of gentlemen known as the Corinthians labored valiantly but futilely from 1900 to 1939 to win back an FA Cup from their professional rivals. The last of the "old boy" teams finally folded on the eve of the Second World War. By that time soccer had become the most lucrative national pastime in the British sport industry.

Meanwhile, American football became a lucrative spectacle on U.S. university campuses beginning in the late 1880s. Unlike British cricket and soccer and American baseball, gridiron football on college campuses never directly paid players—at least not openly. Professional American football leagues date to the 1890s, but until the 1960s, when the National Football League

HOW OLD (AND HOW BIG) IS THE "BIG GAME"?

Historical Profile

Autumn Saturday afternoons on college campuses in the United States sometimes find the libraries empty and the football stadiums full. College football draws crowds in excess of 100,000 at some stadiums and serves as an annual rite of university life for students, alumni, and even fans who never even attended the institution for which they root. You may think that the "big game" on campus dates back to your parents' generation or even to your grandparents' era, but it is in fact much older.

In 1893, leading U.S. journalists described the annual Thanksgiving Day gridiron clash held in New York City between Princeton University and Yale University as a spectacle that drew 40,000 fans and altered holiday traditions. So popular was the game that Manhattan's churches had to move their Thanksgiving services to the morning hours lest they lose all their parishioners to the "big game."

In 1903, Harvard University built a stadium that could seat 30,000. In 1914, Yale opened the Yale Bowl, an edifice seating more than 60,000, while rival Princeton opened a 40,000-seat stadium. During the 1920s and 1930s, dozens of other institutions—including Ohio State University, the University of Illinois, the University of Tennessee, the University of Michigan, the University of Iowa, Notre Dame University, Stanford University, the University of California, and the University of Texas—built monumental football stadiums that held 50,000 or more fans. In the 1920s the Los Angeles Coliseum—designed to win an Olympic bid—emerged on the Pacific Coast. The Coliseum held 105,000 fans for the University of Southern California's home football games.

Some of the stadiums built in that era still loom over college campuses and rank among the largest sport facilities in the United States. In fact, all but one of the fifteen largest stadiums in the United States primarily host college football games, with the exception of the Los Angeles Coliseum that has also done duty as a professional football stadium as well as staging a variety of other events, including two Olympics (1932 and 1984). Topping the list of stadiums that seat more than 100,000 are, in order of seating capacity, Michigan Stadium (the University of Michigan), Beaver Stadium (Pennsylvania State University), Ohio Stadium (Ohio State University), Kyle Field (Texas A&M University), Neyland Stadium (the University of Tennessee), Tiger Stadium (Louisiana State University), Bryant-Denny Stadium (the University of Alabama), and Darrel K Royal–Texas Memorial Stadium (the University of Texas). With the exception of Beaver Stadium, a relative newcomer established at its present location in 1960, all of these stadiums originated in the 1920s and have expanded in the many decades since.

blossomed, the professional version of the game was a minor league affair. From its origins in the 1870s until the 1960s, the collegiate version of football dominated American sporting culture. Utilizing the railroad to play their rivals, a thriving intercollegiate football industry developed in the Northeast during the last decades of the 19th century, then expanded to national dimensions by the early 20th century. Millions of fans paid to watch college football games, and millions more followed the exploits on the gridiron in the pages of newspapers and magazines. In spite of the claim that college football was an amateur affair, the intercollegiate spectacles served as a key commercial component of the growing U.S. sport industry.

To underscore the reality that these national pastimes not only produced patriotic ardor in the Anglo-American world but also served as lucrative industries generating enormous profit, two of the greatest (ostensibly) amateur symbols of middle-class meritocracy in Great Britain and the United States both earned quite a good living from their games. In Great Britain, W.G. Grace, the finest cricket player of his era, had trained as a physician and proudly maintained that he never took even a penny for his efforts on the cricket pitch. Grace, however, rarely put his medical degree into practice, instead earning his living mostly by promoting cricket, garnering prizes from wealthy admirers for his cricket fame, and collecting supposed "expense reimbursements" for his cricket appearances—funds that both critics and admirers alike noted were generally greater than the payments earned by professional cricketers. In 1895, shortly after he retired, Grace became the first athlete to endorse a consumer product, when his image graced tins of Colman's Mustard, making that brand into a British best-seller.

In the United States, Walter Camp played American football for Yale University, then became the longtime leader of the program at his alma mater. He also served as one of the most powerful figures in the process of Americanizing the sport from its rugby roots into its more modern form. Camp preached to his players that they should always remain gentlemen and never take money for their sporting endeavors. However, Camp himself earned a comfortable living from football, commanding a higher salary at Yale than any professors earned and garnering even more revenue by writing about football for the mass media. Though he never advertised mustard, Camp ceaselessly promoted college football and recouped hefty sums for his efforts.

CHAPTER WRAP-UP

Wrapping Up and Looking Ahead

During the 19th century, sport became a crucial component of the political, economic, and cultural orders of emerging modern societies. Linked to a myriad of expressions of the revolutionary values of liberty, equality, and fraternity that suffused many parts of the globe, sport functioned as an emblem of modernity rather than a vestige of the decayed past. Sport became enmeshed in new definitions of freedom, functioning as a mechanism to educate citizens in the responsible exercise of democratic power as well as serving as a product beckoning consumers to spend their hard-earned capital—both money and leisure time. Sport became a proving ground for ideas about equality and meritocracy, a bastion of egalitarian ideals, and a lighthouse that showcased resistance to those ideals. Most significant, sport became a fortress of fraternal patriotism that forged identities, marshaling the masses to bond with their schools, their cities, and especially their nations.

These new sporting trends emerged in their fullest manifestations in the most powerful nations on earth at that moment in world history—in the English-speaking nations that comprised the Anglo-American world. First Great Britain and then the United States served as incubators for the rise of modern sport. When people in the rest of the world looked at Great Britain and the United States, they were struck by the ardor for sport that these nations manifested. In the rest of Europe and North America, and in Asia, Africa, Latin America, and Oceania, admiring and even resentful rivals began to identify sport as the key to Anglo-American power. In order to become prosperous and progressive societies like the Anglo-American nations, they began to deduce that they should emulate the sports and pastimes, and the recreational attitudes and physical education systems of the well-established British Empire and the emerging American empire. Alternatively, they would have to construct successful substitutes. The Anglo-American nations were only too happy to cooperate in the adoption process, as they perceived sport as a tool to spread their cultural values to the far reaches of the globe.

The athletic games of Great Britain and the United States would soon become part of the imperial struggles between the more powerful and less powerful, a part of the wider struggle between assimilation and resistance that would shape the end of the 19th century and the beginning of the 20th century in world history. The incorporation of sport and physical activity into the "civilizing process" would soon raise questions about how plastic these cultural forms were. Were they forces that would transform the rest of the world into Anglo-American shapes? Or were they cultural imports that colonized peoples could use to resist the tides of empires?

Study Questions

1. How did sport participate in the 19th-century process of nation making? At what levels did it help produce "order out of chaos"?

2. What role did the values of liberty, equality, and fraternity play in the power exercised by the Third Estate? Why was it appropriate for these values to be showcased on the tennis court at Versailles?

3. How did equality and liberty form a foundation for Kant's deontological ethics? In what fundamental ways are deontological and utilitarian ethics similar but also radically different?

4. How and why did sport serve as a fraternal epoxy in this period of nation building? What role did partisanship play in this regard?

5. Is rabid partisanship ethically defensible? What alternatives to partisanship exist for sport fans?

6. What was the relationship of partisanship to the increasing commercial value of sport during this period?

GAMES AND EMPIRES

Western Hegemony and Resistance to It

Chapter Objectives

In this chapter, you will

1. examine how and why the British diffused modern sport around the globe;
2. analyze the reasons for the power and popularity of sport;
3. evaluate three theories about what sport looks like in it best light;
4. discover how and why some subaltern cultures resisted modern British sport;
5. consider the historical and philosophical study of sport as a critical lens for understanding human culture; and
6. learn how the United States spread its own modern sporting pastimes.

On May 9, 1867, just four years after a group of British gentlemen met in a London tavern to create the Football Association and provide a set of rules for the game, members of the local British community in Argentina established the Buenos Aires Football Club. For these expatriates, who immigrated to the Argentine capital to help run and maintain the British-owned railway lines in the region, the formation of a soccer club provided an opportunity to play their favorite British sporting pastime in their new homeland. Throughout the 19th century and into the early 20th century, wherever the British went, from Buenos Aires to, Hong Kong, to Cape Town, and Cairo, they took the game with them. Along the currents of imperial power, culture, and industry, British colonial officials, merchants, sailors, educators, and missionaries helped form foreign soccer clubs, establish leagues, and begin to teach basic rules and patterns of play. As a result of this process, soccer, the product of Britain's elite public schools, would soon become a global common language.

Now, in concrete stadiums, on grassy fields, in narrow alleys, on sandy beaches, and even in the impoverished slums of the world's expanding cities, the game is played, understood, and "spoken" by billions of people. "The Esperanto of the ball," as the Uruguayan writer Eduardo Galeano memorably called the language produced by the game, connects all peoples—at least on a superficial level—irrespective of nationality, gender, race, ethnicity, religion, or geopolitical affiliation. Indeed, the game stands as perhaps Britain's most successful cultural export. Soccer has spread farther than the English language, the writings of Shakespeare, and the British legal and judiciary system. It is played by more than 3.5 billion people and in venues still unreached by the Associated Press, Reuters, and religious missionaries. The international bureaucracy that governs the game, the *Fédération Internationale de Football Association* (FIFA), recognizes 209 soccer-playing countries, thus exceeding the 193 member states recognized by the United Nations.

The exact processes by which a game first played and organized by the sons of British elites grew to become known as the "world's game" speak to the economic, political, and cultural power of the British Empire during the 19th and early 20th centuries. Sport formed a vital part of the cultural politics and legitimizing power of the British Empire, a vast transoceanic realm upon which, in a popular phrase, the "sun never set." The British used soccer—and a wide array of other popular pastimes codified and modernized in the British Isles—as tools for expanding their empire, promulgating British culture abroad, training future imperial leaders, and "civilizing" the so-called "natives." As a result, in the Age of Imperialism, modern sport gradually reached beyond the English-speaking world, displaced indigenous cultural practices, and grew to form an integral part of contemporary global culture.

The Paradoxical Power of Sport

The British employment of sport in expanding the empire should strike us as odd. Why sport? Why mere games? Sport seems to have an allure, a power to attract, and a degree of cultural visibility that outruns its apparent merits. A visitor from outer space might be puzzled, if not utterly shocked, at the prominent role played in human life by something as apparently trivial as sport. If we were to list the disqualifying characteristics of sport, they might look like this:

• Sport produces no theory, no insight, indeed nothing that resembles valuable knowledge. It is a practice, a skill, something based in training and habit, both of which traditionally carry less prestige than do education and creativity. Generally, that is, theory trumps practice, and "knowing *that*" beats "knowing *how*." This is so because when we understand something, we can then manipulate that thing for our own purposes. We can teach ourselves. Without understanding, we are condemned to trial and error and thus a high degree of inefficiency. In other words, those who merely know how to do something are blind in an important sense; thus it seems odd that an activity such as skillfully kicking a soccer ball carries so much weight. In a word, then, because sport privileges performance over understanding, we might call it *nonacademic*.

• Even if skills play second fiddle to theory, people still need them. Thus skills are good things, and we can divide them into two basic groups: those that are physical and those (such as writing, calculating, and using deductive logic) that are intellectual. Although this latter type, which involves "knowing how," requires little or no theory or knowledge, it still requires intellectual capability. Such skills are taught in academic courses, such as English composition, calculus, and philosophy. Sport, on the other hand, relies largely on raw strength and physical capability. It is not taught in academic or credit-bearing courses and is usually referred to as "extracurricular." Once again, it seems odd that kicking a soccer ball skillfully and creatively would carry so much weight. Thus, because sport privileges physical skills over cognitive ability, we might also call it *nonintellectual*.

• Some physical practices are considered useful, whereas others are not. Physical skills such as those involved in surgery, exercise, and plumbing are useful because they promote or produce things that we need and value. Sport, on the other hand, is a mixed bag. It has, for instance, some utility for promoting health, certain religious agendas, and various nation-building functions. Most people, however, participate in sport simply because it is fun. Indeed, it seems to have a closer affinity to childhood play and leisure than

to any serious work motive or important social purpose. Thus, here again, it seems odd that a physical activity resembling childhood play or adult recreation would carry so much weight. Because sport privileges serendipity over utility, we might also describe it as *frivolous* and *nonutilitarian*.

• Among all frivolous physical activities, some are categorized as art, or "high culture," others as popular culture or, in the common vernacular, "fun and games." The first category includes such activities as playing the piano, sculpting a statue, and performing a dance, all of which are valued because they inspire us and generate meanings that cannot easily be put into words. They are the products of high culture. Sport meanings, by way of contrast, are simple and partisan. Either our team wins or it loses, and, fundamentally, this is what kicking a soccer ball comes to. For this deficit, we can call sport *parochial*.

This line of reasoning that depicts sport as something of a trivial pastime can be transposed into a tournament featuring a losers bracket with four rounds. Those who defend sport lose all four competitions: Nonacademic loses to academic. Among all nonacademic practices, nonintellectual skills lose to intellectual skills. Among all nonacademic or physical skills, nonutilitarian or frivolous activities lose to those that are demonstrably useful. And finally, among all nonutilitarian cultural activities, parochial pastimes typical of popular culture lose to high culture and art. For a graphic representation of this analysis, see figure 8.1.

As discussed in chapter 5, the kind of Cartesian, dualistic thinking represented in figure 8.1 can place our subject matter in a poor light. Body almost always loses to mind. When we contrast the physical to the intellectual, we get into trouble and typically underestimate the power of sport. This is why, in our public schools, physical education is grouped with other subjects, such as music and driver education, that many perceive as nonacademic.

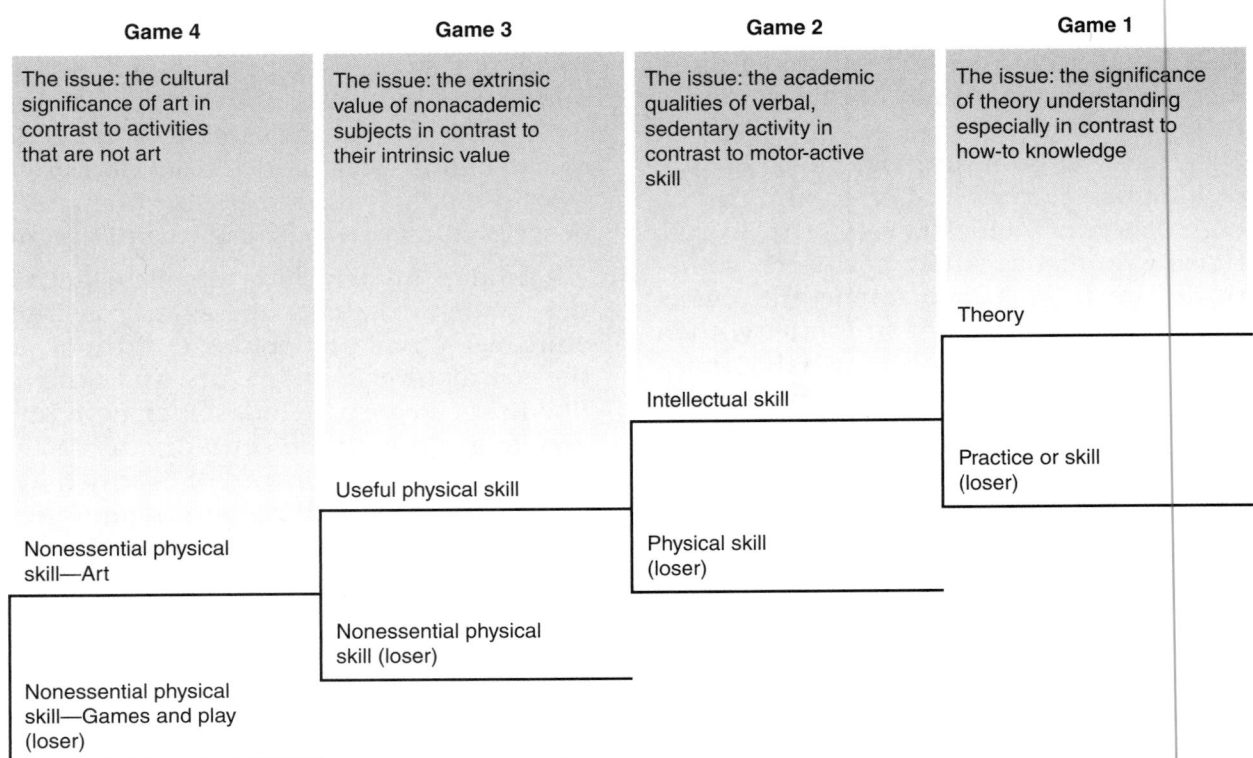

Figure 8.1 Everyone begins on the right side of the bracket in game 1. At each level, the winners stop playing and reap the benefits that go with victory in that particular game. Only the losers in each game move on. Lovers of sport, unfortunately, always advance, and they end up as the only four-time losers.

For decades, physical education has been either dropped or reduced in many educational institutions; time for recess has been reduced in elementary schools; eligibility for high school sports is contingent on academic success and not the other way around. This devaluation is also why some colleges offer performance majors in voice, piano, dance, and theater but not in sport.

As a result of this view, when we educate our youth, physical activity is often treated as less important than intellectual activity, and playful sport as less defensible than useful exercise. At least exercise, as now argued by many people in kinesiology, addresses our national concerns about sedentary living and childhood obesity. Thus jogging and fitness walking replace tennis and basketball, Jump Rope for Heart replaces golf and swimming, and, in some schools, sit-down academic courses related to health and fitness replace any and all movement experiences whatsoever. In other words, talking about movement and understanding physical activity's relationship to health carry more value than moving itself.

Because of our contemporary focus on health, current efforts to defend physical education are aimed at winning game 3 in figure 8.1. The logic behind this strategic decision works as follows: If we have to lose games 1 and 2—that is, if physical activity is categorized as nonacademic and nonintellectual—we should work hard to win game 3. We better jump on the public health bandwagon and advertise ourselves as useful.

History, however, appears to teach us a different lesson. The British did not export exercise. They exported sport! They did so because they understood, or at least intu-

Tournaments and Winning Strategies

Student Exercise

The tournament represented in figure 8.1 presents kinesiologists with what appear to be no-win choices. We are uncomfortable being forced, as it were, to identify with only one side of each dichotomy—with practice not theory, with physical skills not intellectual capability, with frivolity not utility, and with low culture rather than the arts. Perhaps we should play on both teams. Evaluate this strategy by doing the following two things:

1. Give examples of how our field has attempted to play (or could play) on both sides of each game.
2. Evaluate how well this strategy has worked.

In other words, how has it worked to portray ourselves as academic, intellectual, useful, and culturally respectable? How does sport fare when we take this tack?

In contrast, some argue that we should not even get involved in this tournament. That is, playing in these games requires that we adopt a dualistic framework. Perhaps moving in the direction of materialism would be better. Alternatively, as we speculate in chapter 10, holism might be our best option. If we moved in a materialistic direction, the dualistic distinctions represented in figure 8.1 would lose their significance. Moreover, in the new materialistic tournament of atoms and void, we might be able to make arguments about exercise improving brain function. Such causation works from physical antecedents (e.g., increased heart rate) to physical effects (e.g., improved delivery of oxygen to the brain.)

If we moved in a holistic direction, the dualistic distinctions would again lose their significance. In this homogenized world of "bodymind," we might be able to make the more radical argument that positive affect (e.g., joy, alertness) improves health, and vice versa. That is, intangibles and physical reality intermingle, and causation is reciprocal. Intangibles affect health and health affects intangibles, such as meaning. What do you think? Which approach holds the most promise?

---

ited, a fundamental truth: Sport possesses considerable utility because people find the puzzles it poses and the challenges it presents to be inherently intriguing. Anything that is not very meaningful and not much fun would probably not be very useful either. This fact suggests that the tournament outcomes presented in figure 8.1 are invalid. Fun actually trumps utility, and playing games skillfully carries more cultural weight than discussing games theoretically. Those who love sport because it is exciting, interesting, and meaningful are actually the winners, not the losers. Sport as a powerful form of play is the genuine source of sport's cultural power—whether that power is used for fun, utility, or both.

This paradox of sport being most useful only when it is useless creates a philosophical puzzle: How can an activity be both "silly" and "serious" at the same time?

Where should we start when trying to put our finger on the source of sport's virtually universal allure? What can explain the historical fact that religious, political, economic, and other institutions have turned to sport more often than to many other activities in order to further their own ends? Why was the British expansionism of the 19th century aided by exporting British games just as much as (or more than) by sharing Shakespeare, high tea, and Yorkshire pudding?

The quick answer is that sport is fun—a lot of fun! But this response only delays getting to the heart of the matter. Scholars would then ask why sport is so much fun and why it arouses such passion and attracts such intense interest.

Philosophers might look for the answer in any number of places, one of which would likely be the structure of games. Just as the structure of pyramids provides an architecture of stability, the structure of games might provide an architecture of intrigue. The question, then, is this: What aspects of games attract human interest? Several possibilities have been offered, and it is time to evaluate a few of them.

Problems, Uncertainty, Partisanship, and Drama

If nothing else, games seem to be grounded in problems. In sport (and some other places) problems are good things. We love to solve problems. That's why we buy computer games, play cards, try our hand at solving crosswords or Sudoku puzzles, and play basketball. That is why we take jobs that are challenging. Doing something difficult is fun, particularly if the difficulty is just right—that is, not too hard and not too easy. If only all of life were like that! If only life gave us one problem after another that was perfectly suited to our skills and interests. In these conditions, our days would likely fly by on the wings of delight. We would never be anxious; we would never be bored.

If we have any doubts about the allure of problems, all we need to do is consult good literature. Problems or predicaments give stories their life too. Why do we find it hard to put down a good novel? It is because we want to know what will happen to the characters: whether the lovers will get together, who committed the crime, how the hero will escape this time, whether the story's tension will be resolved in happy or unhappy ways for our favorite characters.

The tests or challenges of sport provide two of the greatest gifts ever bestowed by humankind on itself: uncertainty and drama. We invent tests just so we can solve them. We make up sports just so we can play them and experience the sweet tension of uncertainty. How will I do today? If I play well, will I win? Will my team win today? Will my favorite player be a star again this afternoon?

Uncertainty in sport invites us to take a stand, favor one side or another, risk disappointment, put our name on the line. In other words, sport makes it hard not to care. As discussed in chapter 7, the disinterested or aesthetic attitude toward sport is difficult to maintain when something meaningful is at stake. At such moments, *a* team quickly becomes *our* team; *a* difficult climb becomes *my* difficult climb. Sport would be dull if we didn't care, just as a book would be boring if it didn't matter to us whether the hero lived or died! The bottom line for sport and literature is this: Uncertainty coupled with partisanship is a powerful recipe for human engagement.

This engagement is not simply an intellectual assent. It is emotional in nature. In reading a story, we fall in love with a certain character and root for a favorable outcome. Thus, at the end of the story, we excuse any "foolish" tears shed, whether in sadness or joy. In sport, whether or not it is rational to do so, we identify with one side, one team, one town, one nation. Thus we understand those who are emotionally exhausted after watching a close game. This is the way it is with symbolically rich activities. We know, rationally, that the characters in a novel do not really exist; that the death we see enacted on a theater stage does not really happen; and that a loss by our favorite team does not, in the larger scheme of things, really matter. Yet we react as if they do.

Freedom

The pioneering kinesiologist Eleanor Metheny held that part of the magic of sport could be traced to its invitation to give one's all. She argued that rarely in life do we find ourselves in circumstances where we can focus every bit of attention and dedicate every ounce of energy to one simple task. Going all out, seeing what one can do, can be exhilarating and liberating.

Some of this freedom undoubtedly comes from the fact that sport is a relatively safe place to reach for the stars. We construct our sporting tests so that they are unlikely to harm us in any serious way. We wear equipment, follow safety rules, and limit the length of our games. We usually train and prepare before we play, and officials blow whistles when someone has been hurt or the game gets too rough. Where else in life, Metheny wants us to ask ourselves, do we have the freedom to "leave it all on the court," to run as fast as we can and jump as high as our legs will allow?

Agency and Resilience

The philosopher J.S. Russell argued that resilience is the cardinal virtue of sport. Resilience is important because sport is primarily a meritocracy, a crucible that tests our skill, training, dietary practices, and techniques. When we face worthy problems, such as climbing a daunting mountain or taking on a well-matched opponent, it is inevitable that we will experience failure, defeat and disappointment—if not today, then tomorrow. However, if instead we accepted only easy challenges, if we played only weak opponents, sport would be largely meaningless and a dreadful bore.

In fact, the possibility of failure or defeat provides much of the drama that enlivens our games. Just as the hero or heroine of a novel might die, a worthy cause might not be realized, or an impossible dream might remain just that, the same is true in sport. At least some of the blame reflects back on the participant, the athlete, the team. Thus an inevitable question arises: When failure occurs, do we have the gumption, the courage, the energy, to get up and try again?

If fate were in charge—if sport were merely a game of chance—no resilience would be required. It is only when *I* fail that my mettle is tested. It is only when *our* skill is insufficient that we have to muster the strength to go back to the practice field and, eventually, play again. In short, sport gives us multiple opportunities *not* to quit, even when we are down and it would be easy to do so. This dynamic challenges us to our core.

The Flexibility of Sport

As discussed in more detail later in this chapter, cultural and historical analyses portray sport as something of a chameleon. That is, sport takes on the color of its surroundings. For instance, sport takes on one appearance in a capitalist society but looks very different in a socialist society. Thus the British learned at least two things when they exported their favorite sports. First, sport is a universal language that transcends culture. The British loved sport, and the colonists did too. Second, sport meanings are shaped by culture. The meanings that sport carried for the British were not always the same meanings experienced by the colonists and native peoples. Even if British games largely replaced indigenous sports, the British could not control the meanings that others found in these new games. That is the story to which we now turn.

Conquest, Colonialism, and the Spread of Western Sport

During the late 19th century and the early 20th century, the British Empire covered over 12 million square miles. Spanning the globe, this vast transoceanic realm of Dominions, colonies, mandates, protectorates, and other territories comprised a population of more than 430 million people, of whom Great Britain and the white self-governing Dominions (Canada, Australia, New Zealand, and South Africa) made up a mere seventy million. The possession of this massively fragmented empire—with a predominantly nonwhite, non-Christian, and non-English-speaking colonial population—ensured that modern British sport would eventually transcend the Anglo-American world and become a truly global phenomenon.

Beginning at its institutional seedbed in Victorian Britain, modern sport traveled the globe, from the cosmopolitan Dominion cities of Cape Town, Sydney, and Toronto to distant imperial outposts in sub-Saharan Africa, the Indian subcontinent, the Caribbean, Southeast Asia, and beyond. The British diffused modern sport via a series of interrelated mechanisms, notably the public schools; the economic and industrial system; the imperial British army; the evangelical and muscular Christian movements; and a vast literary network of sporting journals, male adventure stories, and imperial tracts. During the Pax Britannica—an age of unrivaled British power in the economic, cultural, and military realms—the British introduced their sporting pastimes to vast regions of the world, established the organizational and bureaucratic framework that ensured their diffusion, and created the conditions that would inspire local traditions and patterns of play. Through their dominance and their control of bureaucratic organizations and private clubs such as the Football Association (1863), the Marylebone Cricket Club (1787), and the Royal and Ancient Golf Club (1754), the British provided the formal codification and the national (and in some cases, international) administration that helped propel the diffusion of modern sport on a truly global scale.

The British did not spread their modern sports and games around the globe as an act of official policy. On the whole, the British state preferred to offer general encouragement and latitude to the vast number of British colonial officials, merchants, soldiers, educators, and missionaries who brought sport to the world. However, despite the absence of an explicit government policy to export sport, political motives certainly help explain why the British brought their games to Africa, Asia, and Latin America. British colonial officials—the vast majority of whom were recruited for colonial service on the basis of their sporting prowess in the public schools—deliberately forced modern sport on colonized peoples as a program of political domination. Sport, the British believed, served as an effective substitute for war. It taught middle-class values and attributes necessary for maintaining an orderly and civilized society; it also reinforced the racial and social hierarchy that placed the white man on top and natives on the bottom of the imperial edifice.

The British-run public schools established in Britain's colonial outposts served as a vital cog in this process of political domination. Generally reserved for the sons of local ruling elites, public schools such as Mayo and Rajkumar Colleges in India and Harrison and Combermere Colleges in the Caribbean, offered a quintessentially elite British education. In these schools, the sons of indigenous rulers and educated elites were reared in the language and ideals of *Tom Brown*. Through participation in modern sport, they were taught bravery, teamwork, morality, fair play, and loyalty to the British crown. After indoctrinating—or more precisely, Anglicizing—the sons of local elites through sport, the British could call on these indigenous rulers to help hold down the so-called "natives" and preserve British rule.

British missionaries, particularly those affiliated with the Young Men's Christian Association (YMCA), a Protestant organization founded in London in 1844, also diffused modern sport to help fulfill their own cultural desires and evangelical duties. Missionaries introduced sports such as cricket and soccer in their tireless efforts to convert native peoples to the Christian faith. By introducing these games, missionaries believed that they were unleashing a civilizing force. The value of sport, they argued, could be found in the moral lessons it taught. In this view, playing modern British sports taught indigenous peoples to respect Western authority, to wear Western-style clothing, follow basic rules and regulations, and learn qualities such as teamwork and fair play. In the languages of social Darwinism and imperialism, missionaries believed that sport would enlighten Britain's "dark" empire and help transform licentious, idolatrous, "wild savages" into civilized, religiously devout, and productive members of British imperial society. From a more benevolent

Sport and Religion

Student Exercise

As you have seen, sport and religion have been partnered through much of history. If nothing else, this fact speaks strongly to the symbolic power of sport, which provides a place where poignant religious meanings can be publicly expressed and rehearsed. The power and visibility of sport also make it a useful tool for religious education and even religious conversion, and this fact was not lost on 19th-century British missionaries.

Is this still the case today? Do religious organizations still use sport to proselytize, educate, and inspire? To answer this question, begin by researching the Fellowship of Christian Athletes. Then look for other organizations that engage in similar activity, as well as journals devoted to sport and spirituality. Based on your findings, what conclusions can you draw? Does the sport–religion connection still exist? If so, is it still robust? Which religions seem most inclined to partner with sport?

---

perspective, some sincere British missionaries also promoted modern sport because they genuinely believed that it contributed to one's health and well-being, diminished religious animosities between rival tribes, and encouraged fortitude.

Their importance notwithstanding, the political and cultural motives of the British colonizers do not tell the full story. To speak of modern sport as if it were merely a mechanism for political, cultural, and religious indoctrination and repression distorts the historical record. Colonized peoples were not duped into caring about sport; indeed, for many people, modern sport provided a genuine source of enjoyment and satisfaction. Like the boys on the playing fields of Britain's elite public schools, colonized peoples recognized the intrinsic qualities of these games. As a result, after overcoming some initial religious and cultural opposition, cricket and soccer matches as well as other British sports grew to become objects of passion for millions and eventually billions of people who were either subjugated under the British crown or subjected to British economic domination. For other colonized peoples, particularly the native Anglophile elites who were educated in British-run public schools, the desire to imitate their masters from Britain—the world's preeminent cultural and economic power—proved particularly alluring. Emulation was a powerful motivator. Thus, reciting Shakespeare, drinking tea, and playing cricket served as badges of social exclusivity and reaffirmed their high status in imperial society.

Whether via coercion, imitation, or a willing embrace, modern British sport diffused rapidly throughout the globe during the 19th century and the early 20th century. Its spread often occurred unequally, however, especially across lines of race, gender, and social class. Although the cosmopolitan sons of local elites—many of whom were educated in British-run public schools—first embraced soccer, it eventually trickled down the social-class ladder and became popular among the masses. The game's inherent accessibility and affordability ensured that it would grow to become the world's game, a sport played and watched in the 21st century by more than 3.5 billion people. Other sports proved far more exclusive. For example, cricket and golf, the preserves of aristocratic British and colonial elites, were often hidden behind the walls of private clubs for those considered to be gentlemen and away from the purview of the lower social strata. Meanwhile, the British largely confined the spread of rugby union to its white-settler Dominions (more on this a bit later).

Like all post-Enlightenment imperial powers, the British Empire had been founded—in part with evangelism and utilitarianism—on a strict ethnocentric hierarchal structure, a racist imperialism rooted in the ostensibly enlightened and chivalrous virtues of progress and liberty. Although a variety of British racial attitudes existed, belief structures rooted in biological determinism, comparative anatomy, Darwinian evolution, and eugenics espoused—often in contradictory ways—the notion that the races had separate origins and were marked by distinct, biologically fixed, and unequal characteristics. Fueled by the late 19th century and early 20th century professionalization of anthropology and the popularization of scientific images through the growth of the modern mass media and cultural exhibitions, a clear color-coded ranking of races emerged with Anglo-Saxons placed on top of the scale and indigenous and non-white peoples at the bottom. Employing this racialist lens, the British believed that Bengalis, Ceylonese, Fijians, Gurkhas, Hindus, Jamaicans, Maoris, Malayans, Punjabis and Zulus lacked the psychological, social, and physical attributes needed to play such an intricate and masculine sport as rugby union.

Despite the layered and uneven diffusion of modern British sport, its introduction on a vast global scale still stimulated the decline of traditional indigenous sports and pastimes. For example, as noted by sport scholar Allen Guttmann, Ibo tribesmen who once wrestled to the beat of tribal drums now harken to the whistle of a soccer referee. British sport proved deeply alluring. It induced indigenous peoples to abandon the cultural and religious games that their ancestors had played for centuries and embrace the secularized, specialized, and quantified excitement of modern sport. Even cultures that passionately clung to their traditional pastimes could not completely resist the allure of modern sport (for more on this subject, see chapter 10). For instance, even though local political and cultural leaders have preserved Afghan *buzkashi*, Japanese sumo wrestling, and Spanish bullfighting into the 21st century, these traditional sports are now laden with modern char-

acteristics. Nowadays, for example, *buzkashi* players are neatly ordered into two evenly matched teams, sumo wrestling is broadcast across international airwaves, and bullfights take place in officially standardized arenas. Thus the rapacious forces of British (and later, U.S.) imperialism irrevocably changed human physical culture. Traditional games and pastimes that once resided at the heart of indigenous social and religious life have been replaced by a far smaller number of modern Western sports.

Sport in Its Best Light

The rise in popularity of Western sports raises questions about their status. Are they better games than the indigenous games they replaced? It is hard to say, because this transition could be attributed to any number of factors, and the quality of the games is only one of them. We might surmise that the Western offerings had to be reasonably good games. Soccer, for instance, seems to be a very good game. But why is this the case? What counts as a good game? Or, as some philosophers have recently put the same question, what is sport like in its best light?

Answers to this question could be important both theoretically and practically. Theoretically, we think we can distinguish sport from other things and this belief should result in an ability to name those characteristics that make this identification possible. Practically speaking, it would behoove us to spend more time in good games than in their defective counterparts. Furthermore, when our friends—or sport governing boards—suggest a rule change, we would like to have criteria for determining whether the change would help or hurt the activity.

In modern times, very few scholars argue that sports have a fixed nature. That is, we now doubt that there is an ideal form of basketball or golf, as Plato might have argued. Rather, we see games as conventions that are invented by us and for us. Therefore, they can change. In fact, rule makers for most of our popular sports meet regularly to consider amendments to current rules. Basketball today is different than it was 70, 40, or even just 20 years ago. Games are never perfect, and modifications are often warranted.

This, however, is where the agreement ends, and we can identify three rival positions regarding sport in its best light: broad internalism, conventionalism or ethnocentrism, and pluralistic internalism. The first position, broad internalism, sees sport forms as relatively stable and worthy of respect. In this view, sport is about physical testing and contesting, and those who display better skills should win. It is a meritocracy featuring a number of virtues but emphasizing physical capabilities—speed, strength, flexibility, and accuracy, among others. It aims for achievement and thus seems to have an affinity with excellence. People do not play sport to lose or see how mediocre they can be. Indeed, sport in its best light benefits all—even losers, who can still play well, learn much, and enjoy the struggle despite their defeat. Thus sport in its best light is mutually gratifying. This interpretation of sport, according to many of its adherents, can be defended on the basis of reason—that is, it makes the most sense.

The counterpoint to this position is conventionalism, or ethnocentrism, which portrays sport as much more plastic or malleable. From this perspective, sport has no best-light set of features; rather, it can take an indefinite number of forms in different cultures. This view still applies limits—for example, defensible versions of sport cannot be harmful, mean-spirited, or divisive—but allows for an unlimited number of good sporting forms. In one culture, individual sports and excellence might be celebrated. In another culture, team sports and self-knowledge may be more highly valued. Moreover, there are no criteria for saying which version of sport is better. As with the broad internalist perspective, this interpretation of sport can

be defended on the basis of reason and observation. After all, multiple versions of sport do exist in the world and are enjoyed by the people who play them. This popularity suggests we need to support culturally shaped diversity in sport forms.

The third position, pluralistic internalism, lies in the middle. Those who take this stance argue that there are several best-light versions of sport and that these versions are produced by a mixture of nature and nurture—that is, by our biology and our socialization. Given our evolutionary history, certain kinds of activities tend to be meaningful. Moreover, certain aspects of human nature are poles or attractors of meaning, and sport can shape itself around these poles differently in different cultures with different histories and political systems. Thus one culture might gravitate toward one pole, whereas another culture might find another pole more appealing. Here are six examples of poles.

1. **Achievement model:** This model portrays humans as achievement-focused problem solvers, makers and doers, competent and creative agents who control their own fate. Its rallying call is "improvement!" Thus it is closely associated with work and its ethic of achievement and dedicated effort. This model features a meritocratic ethic in order to accurately assess excellence and fairly identify victors who show greater degrees of excellence. The achievement of excellence reinforces one's self-image as capable, powerful, even virtuous. In this view, sport is most meaningful when it is understood as a "mutual quest for excellence." This is arguably the most popular model of sport in U.S. culture today.

2. **Serendipity model:** This portrays humans as dependent on at least occasional episodes of grace and good fortune. It notes that not everyone is gifted at birth and that even those who think of themselves as gods are not fully in control. This model is not based on work, achievement, or merit but on play, serendipity, having a chance, and enjoying occasional suc-

cess—whether fully deserved or not. Thus it is a lighter version of sport, one that celebrates what is good about life, not what is missing or still needs to be achieved. This model also provides a more humble version of sport. In this view, a degree of serendipity is always afoot. Thus we look for joy in sport but also count on joy finding us. Success in this model reinforces one's self-image as fortunate, blessed, lucky. Sport does not mimic work or serious play but resides in the world of frivolity and relaxed play.

3. **Epistemological model:** This model portrays humans as insatiably curious, as needing to know who they are and how they are related to the world. In this version of sport, athletes seek understanding, find out what they can do, and learn where they stand in relationship to nature and others. Such self-discovery characterizes many Eastern sports, such as judo and Zen archery. Thus, although the epistemological model is not incompatible with quests for excellence, it places sport in a different light. Specifically, it views winning and losing as by-products of learning who you are. In this view, game rules, instant replays, and other mechanisms are used to better ensure accurate measurement and therefore accurate knowledge. Success in this model is achieved as one's ignorance is replaced by enlightenment. Sport does not mimic work or play but resides in the world of learning and self-discovery.

4. **Aesthetic model:** This model of sport portrays humans as story-loving individuals, as people who are at their best when taking part in a coherent narrative. In this view, sport is experienced as a drama replete with a kind of "sweet tension." Thus, much like a good story line, a good game includes a slow rise in the action, a climax, and a resolution. For both players and fans, story coherence requires connections between past, present, and future. One must be true to one's place, one's history, one's role in life as it relates to sport. From this aesthetic perspective,

close games are far preferable to blowouts, and handicapping makes sense, particularly if it elevates the sweet tension in the contest. Success in this model is marked by living out one's sporting role in a personally meaningful story.

5. **Existential model:** This model portrays humans as individuals who make their own choices, accept responsibilities for those choices, and actualize their freedom. It often has a countercultural flavor and might even question a focus on excellence, particularly in an achievement-oriented, compulsively work-oriented society like our own. This model is home to those who love adventure activities such as parkour, skateboarding, hang gliding, and other sports that are largely unconcerned with status and competition, have few rules, and seem more taken with stretching limits and expressing one's individuality than with winning championships. Success in this model is marked by living one's sporting life authentically and fighting for meaning outside the normal conventions and values of sport.

6. **Communitarian model:** This model characterizes humans as social animals who define themselves and flourish in community. This version of sport is less concerned with the zero-sum features of sport than with its cooperative elements. Athletes in this model celebrate their membership in testing subcultures (as, for instance, skiers, table tennis players, or distance runners) and cluster in contesting subcultures (that is, with individuals at a similar skill level). They celebrate the mutual gratification that comes from engaging in close contests. They push the limits of their sport and honor each other's successes against the common foe presented by the game. Success in this model occurs as athletes join communities, root together, belong together, strive together, share a common set of values.

There could certainly be other models, but this middle position of pluralistic internalism suggests that common tendencies related to human nature—humans as strivers and achievers, as playful individuals, as seekers of self-knowledge, as tension-loving and storytelling people, as fierce individuals, and as social animals—interact with culture to produce a variety of popular sporting forms. In all likelihood, most of our good sporting experiences include elements from more than one model. Once again, philosophers like to analyze the landscape to see what is out there.

The foregoing analysis suggests that a limited number of best-lights versions of sport intrigued both the 19th-century British and the many cultures they influenced (and continues to intrigue us to this day). Of course, favored British models were foisted onto the colonies. However, this process was reciprocal, even if the forces pushing in one direction were greater than those pushing in the other.

The Subaltern Dilemma

In the 19th-century British army, the term *subaltern* referred to a lower-ranking officer, such as a second lieutenant, who was a subordinate cog in the power structure but still wielded considerable power over the common soldiers under his command. The term soon evolved to describe the local ruling elites in British colonies and influence zones who held some power over the lowest-ranking members of their societies but played a subordinate role in the larger imperial system. In colonial history, the term has come to refer to the process through which people who were subordinate—but not powerless—cogs in the political system played an important role in shaping their cultures by accepting yet modifying what the colonizing authorities imported.

The diffusion of modern British sport cannot be simply characterized as a one-way process. Despite the enormity of the British Empire and its global cultural reach, the British were never all-powerful. In turn, Britain's colonies and "dark" dependencies were never completely powerless. The unidirectional model of cultural imperialism simply does not fit the global spread of British sport. Rather, scholars have applied the term "cultural hegemony" to better describe this process. Based on theories of the Italian political philosopher Antonio Gramsci, cultural hegemony theory asserts that cultural interaction is more complex than mere domination of the totally powerless by the entirely powerful. More specifically, the theory acknowledges internal contradictions, accounts for agency, and testifies to the existence of undercurrents of resistance. Through this lens, we observe that sport provided subaltern cultures with an opportunity for self-expression and resistance to British control and influence. These cultures possessed the ability to receive, reject, or even subvert British bat, stick, and ball games.

If a sporting event is—as American anthropologist Clifford Geertz asserted—a tale that people "tell themselves about themselves," then the stories that the British were telling did not always fit with the stories that colonial peoples were telling. The British spread their sports—and the associated middle-class values and model of manhood—in order to win the hearts, minds, and souls of their subjects and to strengthen the bonds of imperial loyalty. But sport often became used as tools of resistance by subordinate groups of colonial and foreign peoples. They applied their own agendas and meanings to sport, developed their own unique sporting practices, and celebrated their own distinctive sporting cultures. Through sport, the dominated turned the tables on their dominators in a myriad of deliberate, often elaborate, and symbolically meaningful ways.

Although soccer traveled the transoceanic waves of British imperialism and steadily grew to become the world's game, subaltern cultures still found inventive ways to claim the sport as their own. In Latin America, countries such as Argentina, Brazil, and Uruguay developed and implemented their own innovative playing styles and techniques that represented a departure from the rigid tactical approaches and physical play of the British. Specifically, Latin American soccer developed a reputation for technical mastery, creativity, adventure, and speed of play. On the fields, streets, alleys, and beaches of Buenos Aires, Rio de Janeiro, and Montevideo, colonials and indigenous peoples alike cultivated a homegrown way of playing the "beautiful game" that reflected the energy and flair of Latin American life. The formal, written laws of the game remained the same, but Latin American peoples imbued soccer with their own unique cultural style and aesthetic. In a similar way, the white-settler Dominions of Australia, New Zealand, and South Africa infused rugby union, another product of the British public schools, with their own distinctive playing styles and practices in an attempt to distinguish themselves and *their* sport from the standard British forms.

In some instances, subaltern cultures also organized and administered modern British sport in an effort to reflect the growing egalitarian realities of life outside of the British Isles. Unlike the elite public school constituency of "old boy" British teams, colonial and foreign teams were, within limits, more democratic in their composition. They took a loose approach to the strict British amateur rules, which often limited participation on the basis of social class and proscribed cash payments, instead adopting more progressive and scientific methods of training and preparation. For instance, "priding themselves on 'outback' egalitarianism," Australian cricket officials eliminated the "gentleman" vs. working-class "player" distinction that traditionally divided British cricket along class lines. In Uruguayan soccer, Juan Delgado and Isabelino Gradín became the first black players in history to represent a national team when they starred at the inaugural South American championship in 1916. In contrast to the British style, colonial and foreign peoples infused their beloved imports with local playing styles and wider opportunities for participation across both racial and social-class lines.

Subaltern cultural resistance also took form in the idea of "beating them at their own game." Vanquishing the British in the arena of competitive sport undermined Britain's leadership claims and, symbolically at least, challenged the colonial order. Australia's cricketers were perhaps the first to recognize the nationalistic value of beating the "mother country" at its own game. In 1882, a team of Australian cricketers made history by handily defeating an All-England XI in an international test match at the Oval cricket ground in London. Australia, a former penal colony of individuals deemed to be undesirable elements of the British Empire, reveled in its remarkable victory, flaunting its superior prowess and skill. In contrast, the British interpreted the defeat as a loss of national and masculine vigor. In a humorous mock obituary, the *Sporting Life* of London described how the ashes of English cricket had been placed in an urn and proudly carried back to Australia. Ever since, English and Australian cricketers have competed in a biennial test match series known as "the Ashes."

Resistance to British Exports: Irish and German Cases

Other subordinate groups embraced sport to help throw off the yoke of British imperial influence in more direct ways. Ireland offers perhaps the most deliberate, politically infused example of using sport as an act of resistance against British imperialism. Irish resentment toward a political union with Britain can be traced all the way back to the Acts of Union of 1800, when King George III incorporated Ireland into the greater British realm. Over the course of the next few decades, the calamity of the Great Famine and the

THE GAELIC ATHLETIC ASSOCIATION

Historical Profile

Founded on November 1, 1884 in the billiard room of Lizzie Hayes' Hotel in Thurles, Ireland, the Gaelic Athletic Association (GAA; or *Cumann Lúthchleas Gael* in Gaelic) would grow into a 500,000-member international organization for amateur sport and culture. From its inception, the GAA has worked to preserve and foster traditional Irish sporting cultural pastimes, including hurling, Gaelic football, rounders, handball, and camogie.

The GAA boasts historic and symbiotic links with the Irish cultural and revolutionary movements. During the late 19th and early 20th centuries, the organization attracted nationalists of all hues, including Home Rule politicians (those who demanded independence from Great Britain), Catholic leaders, and Fénians (those who supported a resort to armed rebellion against the British). Many GAA members were actively involved in Sinn Féin (the Irish Republican political party), and some served in the Irish Volunteers during the 1916 Easter Rebellion in which Irish nationalists sought to end British rule in Ireland and establish an independent Irish republic. In fact, Michael Collins, the prominent Irish revolutionary leader and politician, honed his political skills and fiery rhetoric in the committee halls of the GAA.

Hurling, an outdoor team game of ancient Gaelic and Irish descent, administered by the Gaelic Athletic Association. Players use a hurley (wooden stick) to hit a sliotar (small ball) between the opponents' goalposts either over the crossbar for one point, or under the crossbar into a net guarded by a goalkeeper for one goal.

As part of the popular movement for national and cultural self-expression, the GAA has worked to promote Irish heritage and identity across the globe. Irish immigrants, particularly in the United States, turned to the GAA as an important sporting, cultural, and socioeconomic resource upon their arrival in the new world. Immigrants established GAA clubs and organizations in New York, Chicago, Boston, and San Francisco—the key U.S. hubs of Irish immigration—and began playing hurling, Gaelic football, and other traditional Irish sports.

Throughout its history, the GAA has also sought to foster Irish cultural identity beyond the realm of sport. It has actively supported the preservation of the Irish language, publishing booklets and its annual conference proceedings in Gaelic. During one period in its early history, the GAA even penalized hurlers and Gaelic footballers for using English during a game. The GAA has also promoted other aspects of Irish culture, including traditional Irish music, song, and dance.

rising forces of Anglicization fueled waves of violent political insurrection.

After decades of subordination to the English (the dominant people of the British Isles), Ireland underwent a cultural renaissance. Through the literary, religious, educational, and political realms, the Irish promoted their own distinct national and ethnic heritages, a process that distinguished them even further from the English. Specifically, the Irish established the Gaelic Union (1880) to promote the Gaelic language, established the Gaelic League (1893) to advance the nation's cultural heritage, and spearheaded a political campaign to achieve national independence (for more on this topic, see chapter 7). Irish nationalists also established the Gaelic Athletic Association (GAA) to preserve and cultivate their own traditional sports of hurling and Gaelic football.

Archbishop T.W. Crooke, a prominent religious figure in Ireland during the late 19th century, captured the nationalistic sentiments of the GAA when he angrily denounced "the ugly and irritating fact that we are daily importing from England . . . her games and pastimes to the utter discredit of our grand national spirit." Crooke and his colleagues in the GAA called on Irish men to put down their English cricket bats and soccer and rugby balls and instead take up distinctly Irish sports. In particular, the GAA celebrated hurling and Gaelic football as symbols of freedom. GAA leaders lectured their countrymen that they were bound by duty to revive the games played by the heroes of ancient Irish history rather than fall for the imperialist seductions of British sporting habits. Through the efforts of the GAA, the Irish forged their own sporting identity in direct opposition to that of Britain.

Historically, the most stubborn opposition to modern British sport came from the proponents of German gymnastics, an activity referred to by its adherents as *Turnen*. Made popular by German nationalist Friedrich Ludwig Jahn, *Turnen* achieved popularity during the 19th and early 20th centuries. An avowedly political and nationalistic form of physical culture, *Turnen* represented a regimented version of gymnastics that Jahn and his followers linked back to the ancient Greeks. *Turnen* gymnastics featured communal calisthenic and paramilitary exercises as a means to build and promote the physical and moral character of the German people and, as with the ancient Greeks, to prepare citizens to fight for their homeland.

As the British navy ruled the waves and Britain's economic and cultural influence came to bear on German national interests, *Turnen* represented a symbolic riposte to British imperialism. The *Turnen* rejected modern British (and American) sport, dismissing soccer, cricket, and other popular pastimes for their win-at-all-cost ethos and the insatiable thirst for record breaking. Modern sports encouraged pride and egoism, the *Turners* argued—values deemed destructive to the cultivation of a German national spirit. In contrast, the *Turnen* celebrated the noncompetitive virtues of gymnastics exercises. In *Turnvereine* (gymnastic clubs) and other indoor facilities, *Turners* promoted discipline, obedience, and German nationalistic pride. Thus they were ardent and active supporters in the eventual creation of the German empire, resisting Napoleon's occupation of their region in the early 1800s and providing the core of the military force that defeated Napoleon III in the Franco-Prussian War in 1870 and 1871.

Thanks to the millions of Germans who immigrated to North America and Latin America during the 19th century and early 20th century, *Turnen* also enjoyed popularity outside of Germany. In the bustling streets of New York, Chicago, Philadelphia, Buenos Aires, Rio de Janeiro, and Santiago, German immigrants kept alive their cultural ties to the homeland by founding *Turnvereine* and participating

FRIEDRICH LUDWIG JAHN

Historical Profile

Known as "the father of German gymnastics," Friedrich Ludwig Jahn (1778–1852) was a physical educator and German nationalist who inspired the development of the *Turnen* gymnastics movement. Born in Lanz, Jahn studied theology and philology at the University of Greifswald before joining the Prussian army. Mortified by Napoleon's crushing victory over Prussian forces, Jahn dedicated his life to establishing an independent and united Germany capable of resisting the onslaught of France and other European rivals.

To rid Prussia of French impurities, Jahn counseled schooling in German language, literature, and history. He also turned to Germany's strong background in physical education, a tradition that traces back to Johann Bernhard Basedow (1723–1790) and his *Philanthropinum*, a school dedicated to providing both mental and physical education. Jahn identified physical education as a necessary ingredient in the training of citizens and in the creation of an egalitarian German state free from the vestiges of both foreign and aristocratic rule.

In 1810, Jahn began to teach at a German boys' school, where he wedded

Friedrich Ludwig Jahn: A German gymnastics educator and nationalist who founded *Turnvereine* (gymnastic associations) and promoted physical exercise as a way to restore German identity and pride.

his vision of national liberation with his personal motto: *frisch, fromm, fröhlich, frei* ("fresh, pious, joyous, free"). Setting up his *Turnplatz* (playground) on the outskirts of Berlin, Jahn taught his students to run, climb trees, throw sticks and stones at targets, jump over barriers, and complete other paramilitary-style drills. Soon, adults joined, in growing numbers, and *Turnen* societies sprang up throughout the region. In 1811, Jahn hosted a major *Turnfest* (gymnastics festival), which attracted thousands of spectators. Known as the *Turnvater* (Turnfather), Jahn soon presided over a large-scale nationalistic organization that he hoped to use to liberate Germany from France.

In 1813, Jahn and his followers did in fact participate in the rout of Napoleon's battered forces. However, the reactionary regime that seized power following the defeat of Napoleon branded Jahn a political revolutionary. Rugged, zealous, and argumentative, Jahn and his defiant opinions aroused such fear that Prussia's autocratic rulers imprisoned him in 1819 and outlawed *Turnen* for 20 years. When the *Turnen* eventually reemerged in the 1840s, Jahn's boisterous open-air gymnastics had been replaced by indoor, routinized calisthenic exercises.

in gymnastic exercises. Remarkably, even Germany's enemies embraced *Turnen* gymnastics. Throughout Eastern Europe, Czechs, Slovaks, Poles, and Hungarians appropriated German gymnastics to fulfill nationalistic agendas of their own. Ironically, they embraced a product of German culture and used it in their struggle to liberate themselves from the political shackles of German and Austrian rule.

Trobriand Cricket: Subordinate Subversion

As illustrated by the examples of the German gymnastics movement and the Gaelic Athletic Association, some subaltern cultures openly rejected modern British sports. Instead, they cultivated their own sporting and movement practices as an opportunity for nationalistic self-expression and cultural resistance. In contrast, in the Trobriand Islands—an archipelago of coral atolls off the east coast of New Guinea—indigenous tribes challenged the existing colonial power structure not through rejection but through subversion. Not satisfied with playing "white man's" cricket, Trobriand Islanders modified the popular British bat-and-ball game by incorporating many of their own traditional practices and values in an attempt to repel British control and influence.

A group of British missionaries, led by William Gillmore, introduced cricket to the Trobriand Islands in 1903 as a means to reduce rivalry and fighting between indigenous tribes. Gillmore and his fellow evangelists hoped to use the sport to transmit the muscular Christian and, in their view, civilizing values of discipline, bravery, and respect for authority. In a fascinating twist of irony, the native Trobriand Islanders transformed British cricket in their own image.

Unlike the British version, Trobriand cricket allows upward of 50 players per team (rather than the customary 11) who enter the field in warlike formations with their bodies decorated by military-inspired colors and designs. The players celebrate each out with colorful choreographed dances and chants that mock the unsuccessful batsman and tout the superior skills of the bowling team. Even the equipment differs from the standard British version of the game, including a redesigned bat that is locally handcrafted. Moreover, all equipment is blessed by a local spiritual leader, who is also responsible for ensuring good weather for the competition. In addition, in a remarkable departure from the modern mania for quantification, the Trobriand Islanders always declare the home team the winner (regardless of the score) by virtue of its hospitality. In these ways, despite their position on the periphery of the British Empire, Trobriand Islanders symbolically challenged the colonial power structure by using the master's tool against the master. Thus British cricket became Trobriand cricket.

Sport as a Revolutionary Force

As the preceding discussion shows, there were times when sport—the great bond of the British Empire and agent of British cultural imperialism—served to undermine Britain's global dominance. In the final analysis, then, sport both served as a vehicle for imperial domination by reinforcing the colonial class order and, paradoxically, crystalized anti-colonial sentiment and even occasionally inspired movements for national liberation from British rule. These complex dynamics are addressed forcefully by the West Indian historian C.L.R. James (1901–1989) in his acclaimed autobiography *Beyond a Boundary*, which explores how sport served as a site where the foundational ideologies of British imperialism (i.e., race, nationalism, and masculinity) were reinforced, reflected, contested, and challenged. The book recounts the experiences of James—a black, colonial, classically educated, and self-defined Briton—in growing up on the island of Trinidad in the British West Indies.

James dedicates considerable space to analyzing the role of cricket in the history of the British Empire. Reading cricket through the complexities of life under British rule, he reveals the influence of British sport and culture on the colonialized peoples of the West Indies. On the cricket fields of the British-run public schools in Trinidad, James became immersed in the language of *Tom Brown* and the public school code of rugged masculinity, bravery, and fair play. He vigorously adhered to the ethics of the game, obeying the umpire's authority, subordinating his personal interests to the good of the team, and remaining gracious in both victory and defeat. James even grew to revere British culture—its sports, its literature, and its religion. Through cricket, then, he learned to respect the colonial order, the supposed superiority of his white rulers, and the designated place of the native on the periphery of the British Empire.

James also explores how cricket—an agent of British cultural and political domination—eventually came to reflect the Afro-Caribbean majority's aspirations for freedom to run their own affairs after long subjugation under British rule. Moreover, James asserts that the fortunes of black West Indian players became a metaphor for hope. In particular, the appearance of descendants of slaves representing the West Indies in international test matches (at the expense of white players) forged a sense of colonial unity, confidence, and pride. Reflecting the hierarchical ordering of British West Indian society, however, one position remained unavailable to black cricketers: team captain. In seeing superior black players get purposely overlooked, James grew to perceive the weaknesses

and inadequacies of those who claimed moral superiority. Thus he finally awoke to the insidious realities of British racism and oppression.

James engaged in a long campaign to get the white-dominated executive council that selected the members of the West Indian national team to consider a black captain. James and his supporters found a clearly deserving candidate in Frank Worrell, a highly talented and proven black international cricketer. Fueled by a revolutionary spirit, James spearheaded a campaign in support of Worrell's candidacy, which, he asserted, came to embody a broader anti-colonial movement for decolonization and the establishment of a multiracial West Indian democracy. If a black man was capable of leading his team in the arena of international sport, an enlightened James opined, then could the black majority of the West Indies not also govern their own nation and control their own destinies?

In the preface to *Beyond a Boundary*, James asks, "What do they know of cricket who only cricket know?" Deciphering the riddle, James makes the case that those who know only cricket (that is, only its rules, techniques, and star players)—but do not grasp its power in the greater world beyond the field—ultimately know little of the game. Thus James elevates sport as a lens for understanding history, culture, power dynamics, and social relations. Clifford Geertz in his study of Balinese cockfighting, also reads sport as a cultural "text" for understanding society at-large. On the Indonesian island of Bali, Geertz asserts, cockfights reflected broader social patterns. Specifically, the fights represented a symbolic battle for money, prestige, and status and also served as a safety valve for settling personal disputes and demonstrating prowess against rival social groups (whether on the level of family, clan, or village). The higher the social status of the participants (that is, the owners of the roosters), Geertz discovers, the larger sums of money wagered on the contest and the deeper the meaning of play in the activity. Like C.L.R. James, Geertz encourages students of sport and physical activity to read sport as a critical text for understanding human culture, both past and present.

Sport, Colonialism, and American Imperialism

Although modern sport is, to a large degree, a British invention, one should not overlook the important role played by the United States in popularizing and spreading modern sports and games of its own (see chapter 7 for more on the development of American national pastimes as distinct from British games). By the late 19th century, the United States, itself a former colony, began to peer out from behind its cloak of isolationism and to assert, with increasing aggressiveness, its economic and cultural influence on a global scale. Through various military successes, notably in the Spanish-American War of 1898, the United States soon presided over an empire that included Hawaii, Cuba, Guam, Puerto Rico, and the entire Philippines archipelago. Although U.S. expatriates, teachers, military personnel, businesspeople, and Christian missionaries were among the first to diffuse popular American sports to Asia, the Caribbean, and other strategic trading outposts and naval bases, the acquisition of a global empire made this diffusion possible on a far greater scale.

Following the British example, U.S. imperialists employed modern sport as a tool to assert U.S. dominance; assimilate indigenous peoples; and bridge prevailing differences involving race, gender, class, language, and culture. The U.S. branch of the YMCA, which had gained a strong foothold in the United States during the late 19th century, played a prominent role in this process. Specifically, in Latin America, the Pacific, and East Asia, "the Y" introduced basketball and volleyball—games that it had invented—as well as baseball and track and field to help develop body, mind, and spirit and to support its evangelizing efforts. Wherever U.S. dominion grew, the YMCA found fertile ground for its mission. In the Philippines, for instance, YMCA missionaries established the Manila Carnival, a nationwide championship event that drew thousands of athletes across a variety of American sports. The YMCA also cultivated close connections with U.S. government officials and educators in an attempt to implement interscholastic competitions and regular physical education classes in all U.S. territories. In addition, it published official recreation manuals, trained playground staff, and coordinated sport programs on both the regional and national scales.

Ethnic Sport in America Today

Student Exercise

As you have read, the Turners populated portions of the U.S. Midwest during periods of heavy German immigration. More generally, many U.S. cities in the 19th and early 20th centuries had ethnic neighborhoods, ethnic grocery stores, ethnic churches, and the like. Eventually, however, such cultural strongholds dissipated as diverse ethnic groups, including Germans, were assimilated into the broader American culture. Your assignment here is to determine whether that was the case with the Turner movement. Have the *Turnvereine* disappeared? Is there still a Turner organization in North America? If so, what is its philosophy? How many clubs are still in existence? What activities do they sponsor?

Driven by its desire to save souls and fulfill a Darwinian-inspired concept of manifest destiny in order to "civilize" indigenous peoples, the YMCA spread basketball to Asia in the years immediately following James Naismith's invention of the game in 1891. YMCA missionaries, many of whom starred on Naismith's original basketball teams in Springfield, Massachusetts, first brought the game to China, India, and Japan. Dr. William Lyon nurtured the development of basketball in China. In 1895, Lyon established the first Chinese YMCA, at Tientsin (now Tianjin), and began to introduce athletic competition into Chinese schools. In the following years, a flurry of U.S. missionaries arrived in China and began coordinating athletic programs and modern sport meets. In 1910, the YMCA organized China's first national athletic meet in Nanking. The inaugural event attracted more than 140 Chinese teams for competition in basketball, tennis, track and field, and soccer. Inspired by the event's success, the YMCA later spearheaded the creation of the Far Eastern Championship Games. First held in Manila in 1913, the Games brought athletes from China, Japan, the Philippines, the British East Indies (Malaysia), Thailand, and the British crown colony of Hong Kong to compete in modern U.S. sports such as baseball, basketball, and volleyball.

These efforts to spread the game of basketball notwithstanding, the growing international reach and imperial ambition of the United States during the late 19th and early 20th centuries is best illustrated by the diffusion of baseball. From the crafting of baseball's original rules in New York City, America's favorite pastime first made port in Japan during a period of widespread modernization, under the Meiji dynasty, that included the complete reorganization of the nation's educational system. These changes were overseen by foreign educators, many of whom were recruited from the United States. One such person, Horace Wilson, an English professor at the *Kaisei Gakko* (now the University of Tokyo) and a U.S. Civil War veteran, is credited with introducing baseball to the Japanese, in 1873. The game quickly took hold as the Japanese, releasing older indigenous customs and embracing the patterns and tempo of modern industrial society, swapped the *kendō* sword for the baseball bat. By the end of the decade, a group of local players had established the Shimbashi Athletic Club, the first organized baseball team in Japan. Interscholastic and intercollegiate contests soon followed, as well as nationalism-fueled games against teams of U.S. naval and merchant sailors who regularly docked at Japanese ports, thus furthering U.S. military and economic presence in the region (for more on Japanese baseball, see chapter 12).

Even as baseball quickly became Japan's national sporting pastime, it attained similar popularity in regions of Central America and the Caribbean. Reportedly, Cuban students who were sent to study in the United States brought baseball back to their homeland as early as 1864. Later, Cubans who fled their homeland after failing to oust the Spanish imperialists in the first war for independence (1868–1878) brought baseball to the Dominican Republic. From that point on, periodic U.S. military occupations of the island ensured that the Dominican Republic would become the center of gravity for Caribbean baseball. By the early decades of the 20th century, the consolidation of the United States as a dominant economic, military, and cultural power increased the spread of baseball. In Mexico, for example, U.S. investments and corporate holdings guaranteed that baseball eclipsed British cricket in popularity. Some scholars argue that America's favorite pastime even penetrated the sphere of British cultural influence and made inroads in Australia in the aftermath of World War II.

CHAPTER WRAP-UP

Wrapping Up and Looking Ahead

Just a few years after the modern rules for association football were promulgated in Great Britain, the game popped up in Argentina. Just a few years after the modern games of basketball and volleyball were invented, they debuted in China, Puerto Rico, and the Philippines. As illustrated by these two cases, during the late 19th century and the early 20th century, the sports and pastimes of the world's two most powerful empires, Great Britain and the United States, became coveted international exports. For both British and U.S. exporters, physical activities served not just as commodities to sell but as mechanisms for spreading their ways of life to foreign cultures. They believed that sport would transform the rest of the world into societies in the Anglo-American mold.

For the cultures into which these new forms of physical activity were imported, the games seemed to carry the secrets of British and U.S. success on the world stage. The subaltern groups involved in these processes—those with less power and status—saw sport not simply as a form of flattering imitation but also as a means for subverting the dominant order. At least on the cricket pitch, if not in other realms, Australia could turn the tables on its colonial overlord, Great Britain, by winning test matches. Trobriand Islanders subverted cricket on a deeper level by inserting their own cultural traditions and logics in order to create a radically altered form of the game. In other places, nations resisted imperialism more fiercely by creating their own alternative forms of physical culture, such as Gaelic sports in Ireland and *Turnen* gymnastics in Germany.

As sport and physical education programs spread around the world, critical questions emerged: Do systems of physical activity contain critical ingredients that make the culture that imports them more like the culture in which they were invented? Or are systems of physical activity relatively plastic instruments that can be used by any culture for any purpose? Over the rest of the 20th century and into the 21st century, these questions have remained important but unresolved. In our own historical moment, we might ask the following: Has sport created a more homogenous global civilization in which all cultures have become more alike? Or can cultures use sport to carve their own unique identities among the world's societies?

As the 19th century ended and the 20th century began, the early trickle of sport flowing throughout the world would become a roaring deluge. Increasingly, new international events, such as the Olympics and World Cup soccer, would highlight the fact that sport was not simply a product of Great Britain and the United States but a global property. Indeed, sport would quickly become a major element in forging national identities in every region of the world. But would sport and recreation serve as an Esperanto, a universal language understood by all, that united the globe? Or would they evolve into a discordant babble of hundreds of dialects, each of which being little understood outside the exclusive world of its national tribe? Fascinating yet still-not-final answers would be provided for these questions with the rise of a truly global "sportsworld" in the first half of the 20th century.

Study Questions

1. What motivated British colonial officials, merchants, educators, and missionaries to spread modern sport around the globe?

2. Why is it difficult to understand the power of sport? Why do many people consider sport and games to be trivial activities? What qualities of sport give it such cultural visibility?

3. Why did some subaltern cultures resist the spread of modern British sport? What are some ways in which colonial and foreign peoples mounted resistance?

4. Is there one best version of sport, a vast number of culturally shaped sporting models, or a limited number of models related to human nature and cultural preference?

5. What is cultural hegemony? How is this concept useful for understanding the historical diffusion of modern British sport?

6. How does C.L.R. James' account of cricket in the British West Indies reveal the importance of studying sport as a lens for understanding human culture?

CHAPTER

9

THE RISE OF INTERNATIONAL SPORTSWORLDS

The Olympics, the World Cup, and Other Competitions

Chapter Objectives

In this chapter, you will

1. examine the rise of international sport, including the Olympic Games and the World Cup;

2. learn about the philosophy of Olympism and critically evaluate its role in promoting social policies that are just;

3. review the struggles in international sport to increase the diversity of athletes to include women, people of color, and individuals outside of Western culture;

4. discover how international sport fostered class-based notions of amateurism and became a tool for nationalism and political propaganda;

5. evaluate the ethics of sport and nationalism; and

6. explore how the rise of the print and electronic media supported the selling of international sport to a global audience.

On March 2, 1896, a small contingent of 14 U.S. athletes boarded a steamship from Hoboken, New Jersey, and began the long transatlantic voyage to Athens, Greece. Supported by private donors, the U.S. team—composed mostly of Princeton University students and members of the Boston Athletic Association—joined 241 male athletes from 14 nations to compete across nine sports in the first modern Olympic Games. On board the vessel was James B. Connolly, a 28-year-old Irish American triple jumper, who, only weeks earlier, had quit his undergraduate studies at Harvard University after the school had refused to grant him permission to compete in the Games. Upon his arrival in the Greek capital, Connolly hop-skip-and-jumped his name into the record books by becoming the first modern Olympic champion. Earlier, an estimated 40,000 spectators, including many European and American tourists vacationing in the Mediterranean, had packed into the newly refurbished Panathenaic Stadium (site of the ancient Greek games dedicated to the Goddess Athena) to see King George I of Greece proclaim the official opening of the Games. Thus, after an absence of more than 1,500 years (it is believed that the last ancient Games were held in 394 CE), the Olympic flame was rekindled in the ancestral homeland of physical culture.

Reviving the Olympic Games

French aristocrat Baron Pierre de Coubertin has been credited with leading the movement to re-create the Olympic Games. Born in Paris in 1863, Coubertin grew up in the aftermath of France's surrender in the Franco-Prussian War of 1871. Disheartened by France's humiliating defeat, he became absorbed in finding a solution to the turmoil that gripped his nation. France had fallen behind its imperial rivals in the quest for overseas expansion, its foreign trade had plummeted, crime had

James Brendan Connolly, an Irish American athlete who hop-skip-and-jumped his way into the record books by becoming the first modern Olympic champion at the inaugural Athens Games in 1896. Following his athletic career, Connolly achieved recognition as a prodigious author of novels and short stories.

soared, and the nation's birth rate had declined alarmingly. Coubertin identified a lack of physical training in French schools as a major cause of his nation's rapid decline.

Seeking a solution, Coubertin looked longingly toward Great Britain and the United States, the creators of modern sport and the most powerful nations in the world during the late 19th century. In particular, his fascination with British culture and British competitive sport derived from reading Thomas Hughes' celebrated fictional novel *Tom Brown's Schooldays* (for more on this book and its importance, see chapters 6 and 7). Coubertin mistook Hughes' fictional version of Thomas Arnold, the legendary headmaster of Rugby School and a champion of muscular Christianity, as the person responsible for the significance given to competitive sport in British public schools. After a pilgrimage to Rugby and other leading institutions of British education, he theorized that if France adopted an Anglo-American sporting culture it would regain its status as the leading nation in the world. Thus, rejecting the military, diplomatic, and legal careers expected of a member of France's old aristocracy, Coubertin devoted his life to revitalizing French society through British and American competitive sport and physical education.

Coubertin's educational mission put him at odds with many of his compatriots, who held a strong distaste for the British and their "wild" sporting pastimes. He proved resilient, however, in the face of French prejudice and opposition; in fact, as a keen historian and scholar of ancient Greek culture, he broadened his pedagogical ambitions. Inspired by German excavations of ancient Olympia, as well as his knowledge of a broad series of regional and national Olympic festivals dating to the 17th century, Coubertin sought to promote modern sport through the notion of an international Olympic revival. Using his own vast wealth and political and social connections—as well as a persuasive arsenal of charm, passion, and intelligence—Coubertin traveled across Europe and North America in search of support for his plans to reestablish the Olympic Games. In the winter of 1889 to 1890, he headed to the United States, where he found an ally in William Morgan Sloane, professor of history and politics at Princeton University. Sloane shared Coubertin's passion for a modern Olympic revival and pledged his support by setting out to create the American Olympic Committee (now the United States Olympic Committee).

After British sport leaders expressed their approval of the project, Coubertin organized what was known as the International Athletic Congress. Held in the grand auditorium of Paris' Sorbonne University on June 23, 1894, Coubertin seduced the attendees with modern sporting exhibitions, extravagant banquets, and allusions to ancient Greek culture. His charm offensive worked, and the delegates voted unanimously to revive the Olympic Games and institute the International Olympic Committee (IOC). Blending ancient Greek custom with themes of contemporary internationalism, Coubertin proposed that the Games be staged on a four-year basis and rotate between cultural capitals of the world—this latter idea inspired by the extraordinarily popular world's fair movement. In recognition of Greece's rich sporting heritage, attendees of the Congress voted for Athens to serve as host of the first modern Olympic Games, scheduled for 1896. Over the next century Coubertin's Olympic Games would grow to become the world's largest sporting phenomenon, eventually attracting premier athletes from more than 200 representative nations, as well as global television audiences of more than four billion viewers.

The Olympic Movement Takes Shape

The very idea of a modern Olympic Games reflected the technological progress of the late 19th century. Emerging transoceanic

RIVAL OLYMPIC SCHEMES

Historical Profile

History has showered Pierre de Coubertin (1863–1937) with praise for reviving the Olympics almost single-handedly. Indeed, this French aristocrat, educator, and historian did oversee the establishment of the International Olympic Committee in 1894 and served as its president from 1896 to 1925. However, in spite of his strong tendency for self-promotion, Coubertin was not the first to conceive of an Olympic revival. To the contrary, proposals to re-create the Olympics had been circulating in Western civilization for more than three centuries. Moreover, the Greeks held modern Olympic Games—known as the Zappas Olympics and staged in 1859, 1870, and 1875—before Coubertin even reached adulthood. Thus the Olympic revival movement was decades old before he joined it.

In fact, a number of plans to create a modern version of the Olympics were floating around Europe in the late 19th century. During this era, well-publicized archaeological excavations of the site at Olympia revealed that the grandeur associated with the ancient Olympic Games was not merely an embellishment crafted by ancient fabulists. These excavations inspired both Coubertin and his rivals. In the 1890s, at the same time that Coubertin

Baron Pierre de Coubertin, the man credited for reviving the Olympic Games in the modern era. Coubertin served as the president of the International Olympic Committee from 1896–1925.

was making his major push, John Astley Cooper, a devout imperialist and English minister, promoted an Olympic Games to create solidarity between the colonizers and those who were colonized in the vast reaches of the British Empire. Cooper's scheme eventually paved the way for the British Empire Games, now known as the Commonwealth Games.

The schemes promoted by the Greeks and the British clearly influenced Coubertin. In truth, Coubertin borrowed the idea of developing an international Olympic Games directly from William Penny Brookes, the founder of regional and national Olympic Games in Britain that dated back to 1850. Thus Coubertin was an important cog in an already turning wheel. He used his vast wealth and personal influence to bring about the restoration of the Olympic Games on an international scale. As the Games gradually reached maturity, Coubertin simply rewrote history, erasing any mention of Cooper, Brookes, or the Zappas Olympics, and presented himself as the sole reviver of the Olympic movement.

travel and communication systems created by the opening of steamship lines, the installation of telegraph networks, and the development of the modern media, fueled the mass movement of peoples on an international scale. Free trade, foreign investments, and the broadening scope of global commerce illustrated the greater connectivity and intermingling between nations. It is in this moment of heightened cultural intimacy that the modern Olympic movement was born. Like other international efforts promoting pacifism—for example, the Red Cross (1863) and the Esperanto movement (1887)—the Olympics promised to break down cultural barriers by providing a means of communication and contact between nations. Harnessing a belief in the educational and moral value of sport, Coubertin envisioned a modern Olympic revival as an ideal platform for mitigating international hostilities and promoting peace, justice, and respect among nations. Coubertin later enshrined these beliefs in a humanistic and educational philosophy known as Olympism.

Olympism as a Philosophy

Although many people around the world have become familiar with the Olympic Games, fewer know the philosophical values of Olympism that shaped the Olympic movement. Even so, many who participate in or watch the Olympic Games sense Olympism's continued presence, even if they cannot name it. Olympism emerged as a unique philosophy of sport as Coubertin worked to revive the ancient Greek sporting spectacle. Though Coubertin was hardly a philosopher in the traditional sense, he blended philosophical ideas from ancient Greece, the British educational system, and European Romanticism to create a vision of sport that went far beyond cinder tracks and playing fields.

Like Plato, Aristotle, and other ancient Greek philosophers, Coubertin devoted philosophical thought to the nature of the ideal person and how such an individual can be developed. In answer to this query, he saw sport as a way of life where the struggle and the contest provided the "hammer and anvil" to forge an individual's physical and moral character. Here, Coubertin took inspiration from the cultural, military, and political success of the British Empire and the emerging United States. He knew that the ancient Greeks had valued a physically educated person, and he also concluded that French military defeats and the British and American battlefield triumphs indicated the importance of a nation maintaining its citizens' physical fitness. In other words, successful nations were composed of ideal individuals, and Coubertin adopted the metaphysical position that such individuals possess a balance of body, will, and mind. In this view, they are not only physically strong but also can make difficult decisions under pressure and persist in combative struggle. Such individuals, Coubertin concluded, emerge from competitive sport.

Coubertin's ideal "Olympic" athlete was also an updated version of the Renaissance man—a connoisseur of art, music, politics, and letters who avoids overspecialization while achieving excellence in many areas (for more on Renaissance ideals, see chapter 5). Hence the early modern Olympic Games included arts contests as well as sporting competitions. This philosophical view of a human person was later personified in the 1980s film *Chariots of Fire*, which portrays the British sprinter Harold Abrahams, who performs a musical number in a Gilbert and Sullivan opera and excels as an Oxford University law student while preparing to win a gold medal at the 1924 Olympic Games in Paris. In many ways, Abrahams served as a real-life model of Coubertin's Olympism.

Later, Olympism grew to include more abstract ethical, axiological, and aesthetic components. Coubertin realized that sport provided a tool for improving a participant's character but also believed that sport had a far higher aim. In particular, he embraced the democratic impulse that he believed the ancient Greeks had infused into sport. In this view, all participants,

OLYMPISM

Philosophical Application

According to the Olympic Charter, "Olympism is a philosophy of life, exalting and combining in a balanced whole the qualities of body, will and mind. Blending sport with culture and education, Olympism seeks to create a way of life based on the joy found in effort, the educational value of good example and respect for universal fundamental ethical principles.

The goal of the Olympic movement is to contribute to building a peaceful and better world by educating youth through sport practiced without discrimination of any kind and in the Olympic spirit, which requires mutual understanding with a spirit of friendship, solidarity and fair play."

regardless of birth, wealth, or status, join together at the starting line to compete on equal terms for victory. This philosophy would inspire the Olympic movement to be inclusive of all people and provide the ethical impetus for supporting gender, racial, and differently abled equality in the Olympic Games.

Coubertin also added elements of internationalism and pacifism to Olympism. In the wake of the Great War of 1914 to 1918, during which Europeans witnessed the devastation wrought by modern warfare and suffered 38 million casualties, Coubertin used the ancient Greek idea of *ekecheiria*, or Olympic truce, to promote peace between nations. He believed that sport could break down barriers between athletes, promote mutual understanding and respect, and even prevent war. In this way, sport could transcend national differences and help promote a universalist view of humanity focused on common bonds and shared community. Such principles can be seen today in the closing ceremony of the Olympic Games. After taking part in a fortnight of sporting contests, athletes enter the stadium for a final time, mixed together in the Parade of Athletes, in distinct contrast to the opening ceremony's Parade of Nations.

Critiques of Olympism

Scholars have given the philosophy of Olympism mixed reviews. For starters,

some critics have doubted whether Olympism even qualifies as a philosophy. Philosophers aim to use reason, logic, and personal experience to better understand their subject matter. Their conclusions often prove uncomfortable because they challenge—based on compelling reasons— what we think we know to be true. The ancient Greek philosopher Plato described philosophy as doing violence to our sense of what we know and likened knowledge to freeing oneself from the cave. The philosophy of Olympism does not seem to have this effect. Indeed, the tenets of Olympism seem so obvious that objections are hard to imagine (only a grinch would object to friendship and fair play). In addition, there is no explanation of how or why Olympism is true; thus Coubertin provided an ideal without a foundation.

On the other hand, ideals can be useful, and some philosophers have pointed out that the principles of Olympism have served as a suitable guide for achieving a more ethical vision of sport. For instance, the emphasis on tolerance has helped the Olympic movement embrace diversity in sport by expanding its inclusion across racial, ethnic, and gender lines and providing opportunities for athletes with a disability to compete. By dint of effort, the IOC has abandoned the patriarchal, largely Eurocentric standards that prevailed at the early Games and now enforces rules supporting gender equity, religious and racial tolerance, and a Paralympic Games hosted at the same site as the Olympics. Thus, even if Olympism is not as well defended as the philosopher Immanuel Kant's categorical imperative (see chapter 7), it serves as a valuable reminder of what sport can and ought to be. This ideal is especially useful in sport where social biases as well as commercialism, corruption, fame, and other extrinsically motivated forces can pose ethical challenges. These speculations may frustrate academics looking for more rigor, but that does not mean they should overlook Olympism's role in serving as an ethical ideal for sport.

Olympic Growing Pains

Even as Olympism took hold as a philosophy, Coubertin's Olympic revival itself proved difficult to implement. As globalizing forces transformed Western societies into modern, industrialized nation-states, sport remained in a state of relative infancy. From its organizational birthplace in Great Britain, modern sport traveled the globe on the currents of imperial trade, conquest, and expansion. However, British sport failed to enjoy universal popularity. Traditional movement practices, such as the ferociously nationalistic German Turnen gymnastics movement and the indigenous brand of Trobriand cricket developed in the Trobriand Islands (see chapter 8) stifled the spread of modern sport in some regions. Even in the British Isles, league and cup competitions were few and far between in cricket, soccer, and rugby union. National and international sport federations were also scarce, which ensured that rules and regulations, as well as patterns and traditions of play, remained largely fragmented and inconsistent.

Creating a Truly International Venue

In this environment, international contests between rival nations were virtually nonexistent. A handful of savvy promoters had previously organized commercially fueled international sporting ventures, but they had met with only limited success (see chapter 8). In 1810, African American boxer Tom Molineaux, formerly a slave, traveled across the Atlantic to fight against the white English champion Tom Cribb before hordes of gleeful gamblers. In another example, American media tycoon John Cox Stevens attempted to harness the financial possibilities of international sport in 1851 by launching the America's Cup, an event that would eventually grow to become a yacht-racing world cup.

Some of these efforts involved mounting tours. In 1859, for example, England's cricketers engaged in a highly profitable tour of the United States; they later challenged England's imperial cousin Australia in a biennial test match series known as the "Ashes." In 1888, an unofficial British Isles rugby union team—composed of English, Scottish, and Welsh players—competed against the leading provincial, city, and school teams in Australia and New Zealand. The inaugural 35-match tour, organized by British sporting entrepreneurs Alfred Shaw and Arthur Shrewsbury, laid the foundation for future quadrennial rugby union tours by the British and Irish Lions in the southern hemisphere. The exclusive country-club sports of tennis and golf also boasted international competitions. Wimbledon opened its doors to foreign tennis players in 1877, and the U.S. Open launched its Grand-Slam golf event in 1894. Labeling these early sporting events as "international," however, is really a misnomer, given that the vast majority of the participants were drawn only from Britain (and its white Dominions) and the United States.

Early Editions of the Olympics

The early editions of the Olympics reflected the embryonic state of international sport. Despite Coubertin's lofty vision of a global Olympics, the Games held in 1896 (Athens), in 1900 (Paris), and in 1904 (St. Louis) proved to be rather small-scale affairs, attracting athletes primarily from

Europe and North America. Spread out over many months, these first Olympic installments were remarkable for their sometimes-glaring mismanagement; their relatively low international turnout of elite athletes; their almost exclusively male roster of participants; and their bizarre assortment of events (which often defied IOC parameters), such as underwater and obstacle swimming races, balloon racing, tug of war, and live pigeon shooting.

Nor had the format of the Games been well-defined. They included no Olympic villages, no formal medal ceremonies, and little Olympic symbolism; the Olympic rings and oath, for example, were introduced only after World War I. In a handful of Olympic events—such as tennis, rowing, and polo—athletes were often paired with teammates from a rival nation because the IOC had yet to formulate the bond between citizenship and Olympic representation. In fact, the early Olympics were so disorganized that, in the case of the 1900 Games in Paris, some athletes were shocked to later discover that they had competed in the Olympics. Without money and international support, a beleaguered Coubertin even had to fend off attempts by the Greek government to seize control of the Games and establish them permanently on Greek soil.

Social Exclusion and Other Harsh Realities of the Early Olympics

The haphazard and piecemeal development of the early Olympic Games also illustrated the unequal and discriminatory realities of modern competition in this era. During the late 19th and early 20th centuries, sport remained a preserve organized and enjoyed almost exclusively by men of wealth and privilege from predominately Western nations. Though such practices clearly contradicted the Olympic movement's philosophy of Olympism, few people recognized the stark hypocrisies. Under the leadership of the all-male IOC, the gov-

erning body that oversaw the running of the Olympic movement, the Olympics subordinated groups on the basis of gender, race, ethnicity, and social class despite asserting that sport was a universal moral good for all people.

Such contradictions between ideals and practices provide useful insights into how philosophy can stimulate progress. Specifically, people often develop a philosophical ideal and then fail to realize how broadly it applies. For instance, in leading the effort to draft the 1776 Declaration of Independence, which articulated the right of the nascent United States to divorce itself from Great Britain, Thomas Jefferson famously proclaimed that "all men are created equal" and "endowed by their Creator with certain unalienable Rights," including a right to liberty. In terms of an idea, or theory, Jefferson meant that all men, regardless of race, creed, or color, should be free to enjoy liberty and that slavery had no place in a just society. Yet Jefferson owned slaves. He wanted to abolish slavery but did not know how to do it, and he ended up keeping his own slaves, tolerating slavery in the new nation that he helped to found and lead, and failing to generate practical mechanisms for ending slavery.

Eventually, after enormous conflict, bloodshed, and struggle, the nation did abolish slavery and seek to extend the rights of liberty to former slaves—a labor that many would argue remains unfinished today, more than two centuries after Jefferson penned his famous pronouncement that "all men are created equal." These changes over time were not merely matters of shifting opinion but constituted real philosophical progress. Jefferson's great ideal, which even he could not live up to, has slowly become a foundation for increasing if imperfect guarantees of the fundamental equality of all human beings.

Women Make Their Case

As with the Declaration of Independence, Olympic sport has taken time to catch up with its own ethical principles. On the basis of then-prevailing (though ultimately incorrect) scientific theories of female physiological and psychological vulnerability, Coubertin and his colleagues originally excluded women and later marginalized women from the Olympic arena. Initially, the IOC insisted that sport remain a masculine affair. Over time, women slowly gained entry into the Olympic movement along limited, controlled, and supposedly gender-appropriate lines that conformed to the male leadership's Victorian sensibilities. For example, a group of 22 women competed in a handful of country-club sports such as tennis, croquet, and golf. Thus, Britain's Charlotte Cooper became the first female Olympic champion with her victory in singles tennis at the 1900 Games in Paris. In subsequent editions of the Games, notably in 1908 (London) and 1912 (Stockholm), the IOC granted permission to a small number of women to participate in a few additional sports, including archery, figure skating, and swimming.

ALICE MILLIAT

Historical Profile

Alice Milliat (1884–1957) was a pioneering French sport enthusiast, administrator, and founder of the *Fédération Sportive Féminine Internationale* (FSFI). Under the authority of the FSFI, Milliat spearheaded the creation of the Women's Olympic Games. In its 15-year history (1921–1936), the FSFI and Milliat held a series of four international competitions with Olympic or world status.

Milliat's desire to promote sporting and recreational opportunities for women emerged out of her support for the feminist movement. She believed, as did many feminist leaders of the time, that woman suffrage could help bring about acceptance and recognition for women's sport. She used her feminist convictions, sharp intellect, and multilingualism to forge opportunities for female athletes in the male-dominated world of competitive sport.

Milliat held leadership roles with *Fémina Sport*, the first sport club for women in France, which sponsored matches in soccer, rugby union, track and field, and bicycling.

Alice Milliat, a pioneering French sport enthusiast, administrator, and founder of the *Fédération Sportive Féminine Internationale*.

National Library of France, Prints and Photography Department, EI-13 (700)

She proved to be a highly effective administrator. In recognition of her leadership qualities, she was elected president of the *Fédération des Sociétés Féminines*, an almost exclusively male organization that controlled women's sport in France. After the IOC and the male-dominated international sport federations rejected Milliat's pleas to help promote competitive sport for women, she mobilized female sport leaders from England, France, Italy, Norway, and Sweden to help create the FSFI and establish the Women's Olympic Games.

In the years after World War I, even as the exclusively male ranks of the IOC continued to voice serious concern about the strain of high-level competition for women, interest among female sporting enthusiasts skyrocketed. The growing political assertiveness of the European and North American feminist movements in concert with the introduction of mass public education served as the catalysts for greater female participation in sport. Under the leadership of Alice Milliat, a French authority on women's sport and founder of the *Fédération Sportive Féminine Internationale* (International Women's Sports Federation), the inaugural Women's Olympic Games were held in Paris in 1922, where a crowd of 20,000 spectators watched female athletes from five nations compete in track-and-field events. Six years later, when the IOC finally permitted women's track and field at its Olympics, it allowed only six events. Meanwhile, the Women's Olympic Games, renamed the International Ladies' Games, were held again in 1926 (Gothenburg), as well as in 1930 (Prague) and 1934 (London).

Coubertin and the male sporting establishment initially greeted these rival Games, as well as the broader emancipatory spirit of the feminist movement, with disapproval. They worked to control the development by bringing women's sport clubs and organizations under the authority of the all-male international sport federations and the IOC. Perhaps unsurprisingly, male control of women's sport often hampered progress. For instance, when several competitors fell briefly to the track in exhaustion after the women's 800-meter final at the 1928 Olympic Games in Amsterdam, the International Amateur Athletic Federation voted to prohibit female track athletes from competing in events longer than 200 meters. Remarkably, such restrictions remained in place until the 1960 Rome Olympics, where the 800-meter race for women finally returned. Slowly thereafter, the IOC began to add women's endurance races to the Olympic program, culminating with the addition of the marathon at the 1984 Los Angeles Olympics.

Though Alice Milliat made great strides in carving out space for women in the 1920s, scholars have debated whether separating women from men is beneficial or even necessary in sport. As philosophers constantly work to revise concepts of gender equity, some have argued that having women participate in sport separately from men reflects outdated and indefensible gender biases. On the other hand, some argue that biological differences limit women's success against men and thus require women to have their own classifications in much the same way that weight classes are used to equalize competition in boxing, wrestling, and weightlifting. If sport did not use gender classifications, women's participation would be dramatically reduced. Society would also lack female athletes as role models, and their absence might constitute a step backward in terms of equality in society as a whole. On this line of reasoning, it is not only fairer but far better in the long run to ensure that women and men can compete separately.

Others, however, argue that such divisions are detrimental to women. In this view, separating women from their ostensibly "better" male counterparts relegates women to inferior status while denying them a chance to prove themselves equal. Thus they receive less support, less prize money, and, most important, less respect because their athletic accomplishments are considered inferior to those of men. Alternatively, some argue that, given time, better coaching, and better training, women's performances in many sports would approach those of the men. Women would then be able to benefit from the scarce goods of fame and fortune, which are currently realized mostly in male-dominated sports. In this view, women should be allowed to compete for those benefits without being segregated into "protected"

The Search for Gender Equity

Student Exercise

Efforts to promote gender equity in sport have been complicated both by long-held biases and by challenges related to the development of just policies. At the center of the discussion lies one basic question: Does organizing women and men into separate sporting spaces make sense? In other domains of society, many gender divisions have been broken down on the premise that men and women are equally capable of doing similar tasks. Even militaries now include women alongside men in some combat situations. Yet sport has resisted the larger gender movement toward integration that has taken place in education, the workplace, and at home. At almost all levels, sport is still organized by gender—that is, divided into separate teams for boys (or men) and girls (or women).

Is this practice supported by morally defensible reasons? In working to reach a conclusion, consider the following questions:

- Can separate ever be equal? Does the segregation of girls and women on separate teams from boys and men perpetuate the idea that they are inferior athletes?
- Would creating teams without regard to gender—for example, having a single, coeducational basketball team at school—do more harm than good? Explain your reasoning.
- If gender-specific teams are retained, should outstanding female athletes be allowed to join boys' and men's teams? Conversely, should unusually small men be allowed to join a female team?
- Since popular sports such as American football, basketball, and soccer favor the male physique, should new sports be developed that are more gender neutral or even favor the female anatomy and physiology?

leagues, even if doing so means that fewer women will make the team or otherwise achieve notoriety.

Still others argue that we need new sports that favor a female's physique. Because most popular sports were invented by men and for men, it is no surprise that they tend to highlight such factors as height, weight, raw strength, and explosive power—factors in which, on average, males enjoy a substantial advantage. However, there are some sports that may favor traditional female physiques including ski jumping, open water swimming, and ultra-long distance running. In these sports, elite women have shown themselves superior to elite men. Even if stigmas or disinterest accompany traditional sports at which women can excel or emerging athletic activities such as cheerleading, the sporting landscape should be more balanced in honoring different physical traits. Eventually, adherents of this vision

contend, society will support this broader spectrum of sporting excellence.

Amateurs and Social Class

The IOC not only discouraged women from competing in the early Olympics but also created rules that discriminated along class lines. Reflecting the British sporting culture on which Coubertin based his movement, including its misguided claims about ancient Greek amateurism, the revived Olympics excluded professional athletes. Philosophically, Coubertin sought to restrict Olympic eligibility solely to amateurs who shunned the lure of monetary rewards in favor of pursuing sporting excellence solely for its intrinsic value. In practice, the IOC's defense of amateurism carried ramifications related to social class because Olympic training, travel, and participation required (then as now) significant outlays of time, energy, and money. In an era in which statutory holiday arrangements did not exist, even in industrialized nations, aspiring Olympic athletes were forced to take unpaid leave or even resign from their jobs if their employers refused to compensate them for time away from the workplace.

Let us illustrate the issue by considering the investment of time and money required for an athlete from California to travel to Europe for the Olympic Games. When Californian sprint star Charley Paddock competed in the Olympics in 1920 (Antwerp), 1924 (Paris), and 1928 (Amsterdam), his participation required a transcontinental train journey followed by a transatlantic voyage and two weeks of sporting competition before starting the journey home. Many athletes of this era paid their own way or at least raised funds from family and friends. Those who were unable to secure funding simply could not participate.

In practice, then, amateurism clearly favored wealthy and middle-class athletes who had the necessary time and monetary resources to train and travel to competitions. Amateurism also proved difficult to define and enforce. Faced with the prospect of giving up their dream of competing in the Olympic Games, many athletes looked to circumvent the IOC's amateur regulations. In order to secure money to train, travel, and compete, athletes accepted under-the-table appearance fees, secret cash prizes, and clandestine subsidies. This practice proved to be a calculated risk. For some, the covert monetary payments provided them with the resources to achieve Olympic fame. Charley Paddock, for instance, managed to make financial arrangements that maintained his "shamateur" ("fake" amateur, in the parlance of the time) status and preserved his amateur eligibility. Specifically, he earned money for writing about his athletic feats in the media and even for acting in movies in the role of an athlete, thus skirting the amateur rules of that era.

Those who were unlucky enough to get caught were severely punished. For example, Native American Jim Thorpe, a two-time Olympic gold medalist, violated the amateur code by accepting money for playing baseball in a summer league before he competed in the Olympics. Amateur authorities in the United States stripped Thorpe of his gold medals and barred him for life from competing in international sporting events. Through this kind of policing, amateurism ensured that wealthy athletes from affluent Western nations retained special advantages in Olympic competition that their working-class comrades did not enjoy.

For the first three decades, the revived Olympics remained a highly exclusive sporting event. Although Olympism inspired those in the Olympic movement to dream of a universal, multiracial Games, it largely failed to stimulate the development of sport in Africa, Asia, and Latin America or to facilitate the entry of non-Western nations into the Olympic movement. Indeed, embracing a form of social Darwinism, Coubertin and the IOC believed that most non-Western peoples lacked the requisite psychological and social attributes to compete in international sport. These officials failed to understand how poverty, colonialism, and indigenous sporting cultures factored into the equation. The IOC predicted that most non-Western athletes would never achieve the prowess necessary for world-class competition and decided instead to promote separate, regional games for the "lesser," non-European peoples of Africa, Asia, and Latin America.

Thus Coubertin effectively forced colonized peoples to the periphery of the international sporting community. Under his leadership, the IOC remained dominated by European and North American members, Western-style sports filled the Olympic programs, and Olympic festivals were held exclusively on Western soil. Only later would IOC leaders realize the problematic

JIM THORPE, NÉ WA-THO-HUCK

Historical Profile

Jim Thorpe (1887–1953) was a decorated Native American athlete from the Sac and Fox nation who rose to international prominence following his gold-medal-winning performances in the pentathlon and decathlon at the 1912 Stockholm Olympics. Thorpe had a robust multisport background, which included competing at the collegiate and professional levels in American football, baseball, basketball, and track and field. Though widely credited by the U.S. press as the greatest athlete of the first half of the 20th century, the Oklahoma-born Thorpe is perhaps most infamously remembered as the first Olympic athlete to be punished for violating the IOC's amateur regulations.

Shortly after Thorpe's Stockholm victories, the press uncovered evidence that he had received money for playing in a baseball league in North Carolina during his summer vacation away from the Carlisle Indian School in Pennsylvania. The Amateur Athletic Union (AAU), embarrassed by the revelations and fearing fallout in international relations, convicted and punished Thorpe without a trial, investigation, or hearing. Thorpe had no money, no lawyer, and no opportunity to mount a defense. Numerous other ostensibly amateur collegiate athletes from that era had played with Thorpe in the league and received remuneration for their labors. Thorpe, however, had made the mistake of appearing in the high-profile Southern circuit under his own name, whereas his fellow supposed amateurs had used fake identities. The AAU made an example of Thorpe, in part because he was a working-class athlete and in part

Jim Thorpe, a versatile American athlete and double Olympic gold medalist. Considered the greatest athlete of his generation, Thorpe attained notoriety during his lifetime for violating Olympic amateur regulations.

EMPICS Sport/PA Photos

because he was Native American, by convincing the IOC to both strip him of his two Olympic gold medals and expunge his performances from the record books.

Thorpe persevered, turning his attention from track and field to professional baseball and American football. In baseball, he signed with the major-league New York Giants in 1913 and later did stints with the Cincinnati Reds and Boston Braves. His major-league career lasted until 1919, after which he bounced around in the minor leagues until 1922. In football, he signed in 1913 with the Pine Village (Indiana) Pros and later starred for a string of fledging teams, beginning with the Canton Bulldogs and finishing—in 1928, at the age of 41—with the Chicago Cardinals, the forerunners of today's Arizona Cardinals of the National Football League (NFL). Thorpe even transferred briefly from the playing field to the boardroom, where he served as inaugural president of the American Professional Football Association, which would become the NFL in 1922. He also served as player-coach for several of his teams.

As with many nonwhite athletes in the first half of the 20th century, Thorpe found life after sport to be difficult. Without the economic stability or postcareer opportunities enjoyed by white athletes, Thorpe bounced from job to job, battled alcoholism, and lived his last years in ill health and poverty before passing away in 1953. In 1982, nearly 30 years after his death, years of campaigning by his admirers and family finally convinced the IOC to overturn its 1913 decision and restore his amateur status and his two Olympic gold medals. However, the IOC has yet to reinstate his pentathlon and decathlon wins in the official record book.

ethical issues in such approaches and repurpose the philosophy of Olympism to inspire the organization to support a more diverse group of athletes, international festivals, and more diverse leadership. Once again, Olympism provided an ideal that was not easy to implement.

The amateur bias of Olympic and international sporting competition aroused significant opposition among the emerging communist and socialist movements in Europe. The early Soviet Union, born in the revolutionary ferment of World War I, initially rejected the Olympics as an inherently capitalist and exploitive bourgeois invention that excluded women, members of the working classes, and nonwhites. The Soviets refused to join the Olympic movement; instead, they formed the Red Sport International (*Spartakiad*) in 1921 to promote mass participation in sport, pageants, parades, and military events. The Soviet distaste for Olympic competition also garnered support from socialist groups that emerged across Europe and North America in the aftermath of the Russian Revolution. Reflecting a similar antibourgeois form of radical class consciousness, the workers' sport movement arose to promote the provision of sporting and recreational opportunities to all, irrespective of social class, gender, race, ethnicity, and skill level.

The Globalization of Modern Sport

In spite of the class, gender, and ethnic barriers erected by the early Olympic movement, the decades following the First World War witnessed a tremendous explosion in the popularity of modern sport around the globe. Advances in travel and communication that evolved from the new technological infrastructures put in place during the Great War, stimulated the diffusion of modern sport on a truly international scale. Led by YMCA mission-

aries, who embraced sport as a moral and social good that should not be denied to people due to class, creed, or color, sport expanded its reach in Africa, Asia, and Latin America.

The international spread of sport was paralleled by its soaring popularity across Europe and North America. Following the war, organized sport had been embraced as a way to provide entertainment and maintain national levels of fitness. Throughout the Western world, governments and educators promoted sport for its benefits to health, fitness, and recuperation. Meanwhile, the construction of large sporting arenas—notably, London's Wembley Stadium (1919), the Los Angeles Coliseum (1923), and massive sporting structures in Munich (1924), Frankfurt and Düsseldorf (1925), and Rome (1928)—propelled sports such as soccer, college football, baseball, boxing, and track and field to the level of mass public spectacles. With sport thus embedded in international popular culture, sportsmen and (to a far lesser extent) sportswomen became global celebrities who competed before the watchful eyes of huge worldwide audiences and were promoted by celebrity agents and an expansive global media apparatus.

The Creation of International Federations

The emergence of international sport federations further fueled the rapid post-war growth and diffusion of modern sport. As sport put down roots around the globe, international federations were gradually founded to oversee their regulation. More than a dozen of these federations appeared prior to the Great War, including the *Fédération Internationale de Football Association* (FIFA) to govern soccer. Initially, these federations were politically and financially weak. In the postwar years, however, international federations gained in strength, developed a degree of autonomy and status, and moved to assert their place and their policies in the sporting world. Eight new federations developed between 1918 and 1932. FIFA best exemplified the postwar growth, consolidation, and expansion of international federations. Founded by seven countries in 1904, FIFA expanded its membership by the late 1920s to 43 nations, including the South American states of Brazil, Uruguay, Paraguay, Argentina, Chile, Peru, Bolivia, and Ecuador. Other international federations followed similar trajectories. As a result, despite the persistence of local traditions and practices, a global sporting culture emerged—a lingua franca that aligned modern rules, regulations, and patterns of play.

The postwar development and consolidation of international sport federations heightened the regularity of sporting contests between rival nations. In soccer, rugby union, and cricket, for example, international fixtures flourished during the 1920s and 1930s. The British and Irish Lions rugby tours to the Southern Hemisphere nations of Australia, New Zealand, and South Africa, begun in 1988, also reached maturity and popularity. In cricket, the West Indies (1928), New Zealand (1930), and India (1932) achieved test match status and began to compete on a regular basis against England, Australia, and South Africa. In 1930, the first British Empire Games (later known as the Commonwealth Games) were held in Hamilton, Ontario. Replicating the multisport format of the Olympics, the British Empire Games grew to include Dominion and colonial athletes from across Britain's vast empire. Outside of Britain and the British Empire, the American national pastime of baseball also achieved greater international visibility, especially in Japan. First introduced to Japan as early as the 1870s, baseball reached unparalleled heights there in 1934, when an American all-star team led by New York Yankees sensation Babe Ruth engaged in an 18-game tour of the islands.

The Growing Popularity of Sport

The Olympic Games reflected the growing international popularity of modern sport. The post-World War I participation of Latin American nations (Argentina, Brazil, Ecuador, Mexico, and Uruguay), new European states (Ireland, Lithuania, Poland, Romania, and Yugoslavia), and African and Asian newcomers (Egypt, India, China, and Turkey) transformed the Olympics into an increasingly "global" sporting event. As the 1920 Antwerp Olympics, the 1924 (Paris), the 1928 (Amsterdam), and the 1932 (Los Angeles) Olympics demonstrated, a larger roster of participant nations elevated the standards of performance and challenged the decades of invincibility enjoyed by Britain and the United States. The Olympic victories by Algerian-born marathoners, Argentinean boxers, Finnish long-distance runners, Japanese swimmers and triple jumpers, and Indian field hockey players throughout this period demonstrated the fact that smaller, less experienced nations had begun to catch up. In soccer, a small South American nation, Uruguay, stunned the Old World powers of Europe by winning back-to-back Olympic gold medals at the Paris and Amsterdam Games. Uruguayan star forward José Leandro Andrade, nicknamed the "Black Marvel," dazzled international viewers with his speed and technical ability, showing that sporting ability crossed both national and racial lines.

The Creation of the FIFA World Cup

Boosted by Uruguay's successes, the Olympic soccer tournament established itself as the greatest source of revenue and the most popular spectator event at the Games. The tournaments at the Paris and Amsterdam Games yielded more in gate money than the entire track-and-field program and even exceeded the aggregate receipts of the other popular Olympic sports. Despite this popularity, a backlash arose due to the problematic amateur status, in the eyes of the IOC, of many of the South American players, who often received stipends for the long trips to Europe to battle for national honor. Professional soccer leagues had already been firmly established in many parts of the world, and it had become clear that if the Olympics wanted the world's finest players, those players would be professionals.

In addition, the leaders of soccer's governing body, FIFA, were eager to cash in on the sport's growing riches. Under the leadership of its president, Jules Rimet, FIFA drew up plans to create its own tournament open to both amateur and professional players. In 1930, in recognition of Uruguay's status as the world's leading soccer power, FIFA awarded the inaugural World Cup to the nation's capital city of Montevideo. Held in conjunction with the centennial celebration of the drafting of the Uruguayan constitution, the first World Cup proved only a limited success, as the vast geographical distance kept the leading European nations away. In a tournament involving only 13 nations, including the United States, the host nation clinched the title with a close-fought 4-2 victory against South American rival Argentina. The United States finished in third place, which still ranks as its best result in men's World Cup history.

Despite this relatively inauspicious start, the FIFA World Cup grew in global popularity. From its birthplace on the playing fields of British public schools and universities, soccer thus experienced a rapid diffusion and rose to become the undisputed "world's game" and the favorite pastime among people in the lower social strata. In the years following the Great War, soccer became a near-universal phenomenon that captured the attention of an emerging global mass media. Journalists flocked to both amateur and professional matches, dedicated countless newspaper columns and magazine articles to the sport, and provided live radio coverage. This media coverage transformed soccer stars into national and even international icons who captured the hearts and minds of hordes of passionate fans. Throughout the 1920s and 1930s, more than 100,000 spectators regularly filled London's Wembley Stadium to watch the FA (Football Association) Cup Final—the world's oldest and, at that time, most prestigious soccer competition.

Sport, Politics, and Propaganda

Given the growing appeal of soccer, many powerful nations turned to the World Cup arena as an ideal platform for measuring and trumpeting national stature. Italy, under the grip of its Fascist dictator Benito Mussolini, arose as the first nation to ruthlessly exploit the value of international football for the purposes of propaganda and political gain. Mussolini, himself a competitive athlete and a self-professed model of Italian manhood, embraced soccer as a vehicle for binding the Italian people together, promoting Fascist doctrine, and demonstrating the physical and moral development of Italy under his new regime. As a key piece of his foreign policy, Mussolini aimed for an Italian victory in the 1934 FIFA World Cup, held in Italy, and he stopped at nothing to ensure his nation's success on home soil. Rumors abounded that Mussolini and his Fascist Party stage-managed the entire event by bribing FIFA officials and referees.

Italy also tested the limits of FIFA's rules on eligibility by recruiting the best Argentine players—Argentina had been the runner-up to Uruguay at the 1928 Olympics and the 1930 World Cup—to switch allegiances and compete under Italian colors. The Italian team adopted a physical and intimidating style of play, which, unsurprisingly, went unchecked by the referees, and clinched the Cup by defeating Czechoslovakia 2-1 in extra time. Mussolini reveled in the victory and encouraged similarly brutal tactics at the 1938 FIFA World Cup in France. He allegedly sent a telegram to his players on the eve of the final that read "Vincere o morire!" ("Win or die!"). Fortunately for the Italian players, they held on to beat Hungary 4-2, thus ensuring that they did not have to return home to see if Mussolini and his Blackshirts would back up the brutal threat.

The Italian system of elite, state-run sport would serve as a model for other governments in the years preceding World War II. Born in the ashes of the global economic decline known as the Great Depression, which began in the late 1920s and lasted through much of the 1930s, authoritarian regimes emerged in Europe. In addition to the Fascists in Italy, examples included the Nazis in Germany, Francisco Franco's totalitarian regime in Spain, and authoritarian regimes in Japan and Latin America. These militaristic dictatorships pulled sport under the umbrella of foreign policy, thus transforming major international sporting competition into an affair of state. Ironically, this encroachment by authoritarian governments enhanced the popularity and visibility of sport. Born of industrialization and urbanization, modern sport was initially a private affair. Sports clubs, associations, and promoters, organized, codified, and developed sport for fraternal, social, and commercial reasons. During the 1930s, however, governments brought sport into the public sphere.

As the world descended into the cataclysm of another total war, authoritarian governments devoted enormous resources to national fitness, military preparedness, and cultural propaganda. Ministries of Sport provided the masses with playing fields, sport stadiums, clubs, associations, and leagues. Close governmental interference ensured that international sporting events, such as cycling's *Tour de France* and *Giro d'Italia* grew in importance and popularity. National regimes also pioneered advancements in sport science and medicine by funding experiments in biomechanics, nutrition, and even the effects of tonics, stimulants, and hormones. Driven by nationalism and state sponsorship, modern sport grew to become a powerful force around the globe. The nationalistic focus sometimes cut across class boundaries and even blurred (albeit to a far lesser extent) racial, ethnic, and gender lines.

Official poster from the 1934 FIFA World Cup.

Popperfoto/Getty Images

The Nazi Games

The connection between sport and the state reached new heights at the 1936 summer Olympics in Berlin. The infamous "Nazi Olympics" proved to be a remarkable success. Attracting more than three million people (more than double the attendance recorded at Los Angeles in 1932), the Berlin Games could rightfully claim the title, up to that point, of being the best Olympic Games ever. Berlin won the Olympic bid when it was still part of a democratic republic aligned with Great Britain, France, and the United States. When the Nazis took over in the early 1930s, they initially pondered canceling Berlin's Games. However, despite Adolf Hitler's initial opposition to the Games, Joseph Goebbels, the Nazi minister of propaganda, convinced him of the political value of hosting the Olympics. Goebbels encouraged Hitler to embrace the Games as a platform for national propaganda, an opportunity to dazzle the world with the financial solvency and power of the new militaristic German state. In response, Hitler commissioned the expenditure of lavish sums, estimated by one account at 100 million Reichsmarks (more than $40 million in 1936 U.S. currency, and more than $685 million in inflation-adjusted 21st-century U.S. currency), for the construction of state-of-the-art sporting and media facilities, as well as an Olympic Village—the first time in Olympic history that a state provided substantial resources toward hosting costs.

Only the gold medal victories of American Jesse Owens and his African American teammates, dubbed by the cynical German press as the "Black Auxiliaries," dealt a blow to Hitler and his proclamation of Aryan supremacy. Despite the victories by the African American stars, the three totalitarian nations that would, in 1940, form the Axis alliance—Germany, Italy, and Japan—each bested their democratic rivals. Germany won 89 total medals to just 56 for the United States, Italy nipped France by a count of 22 medals to 19, and Japan won 18 medals to Great Britain's 14. Further complicating the popular American narrative that the "Black Auxiliaries" pushed back racial barriers around the world, the press in both the United States and in many other nations, pointed out that when Owens and his African American teammates returned home they faced segregation and second-class citizenship that deprived them of equal rights in their own nation.

Hitler and Mussolini were not the only national leaders to employ international sport for political purposes. The leaders of Western democracies also used sport to promote their ideologies around the world. Both the U.S. Department of State and the British Foreign Office considered sport in this era to be an instrument of statecraft that could win allies and block the designs of rival states. As many political leaders realized, sport provides a powerful medium for representing a nation to the world and an important tool for a nation's efforts to make sense of itself. For example, Uruguay's successes in Olympic soccer and at the first FIFA World Cup provided the former colony with a sense of national identity. Similarly, Finland's strong showing in Olympic track and field during the 1920s and 1930s made that small nation on the periphery of Europe a star during the era.

Meanwhile, notwithstanding Germany's triumph in the 1936 medal count, the United States fielded dominant Olympic teams during this period, crushing the rest of the world in every other Olympic medal count during the 1920s and 1930s. This run of excellence provided many observers with concrete confirmation of what other comparative data about national strength clearly indicated—that the United States had become the world's leading power. In this way, scholars have noted that an athlete, or a national team, can become a symbol of an entire nation. More generally, the rise of international sport in the period from the end of World War I to the outbreak of World War II reveals that nations saw athletic victories as signs of power and as important elements of foreign policy.

The Ethics of Sport and Nationalism

The powerful influence of international sport has prompted questions about its true value. To answer these questions, many philosophers adopt utilitarian arguments that examine the benefits or harms of international sport. Those who support it often point to its many positive consequences. For instance, when American Jesse Owens sprinted to a record number of victories at the 1936 Berlin Games and when Norwegian figure skater Sonja Henie, a three-time Olympic champion and ten-time World Champion during the 1920s and 1930s, revolutionized figure skating, they became tangible representatives of their respective nations. This relationship promoted national pride and identity through sporting performance; thus, sharing a sense of community and self-respect helps people form a more cohesive society.

In addition, sport competition between nations can promote peace and tolerance by exposing people of different communities to one another through a mutual passion for athletic excellence. It allows nations, regardless of differences in wealth and power, to compete on an equal footing in order to prove their worth, as the formerly colonized nations of Uruguay and Argentina demonstrated in regularly besting the European powers in Olympic and World Cup soccer matches. Moreover, as athletes staying at the Olympic Village (an innovation that dates to the 1932 Los Angeles Games) can attest, these international gatherings can show people how much they have in common and break down prejudices and misconceptions. For all of these reasons, many observers support international sport as an ethically admirable enterprise.

Not all philosophers agree, however, that sport promotes international understanding and good will. Some scholars see the harms of international sport as outweighing its benefits. Critics point out, for example, that nationalism can easily subvert the supposedly harmonious qualities of international competition. Indeed, novelist and social critic George Orwell famously described international sport as "war minus the shooting." Penning these lines in the aftermath of World War II, Orwell noted that the political differences infused into international sport during the 1920s and 1930s drove nations apart rather than producing reconciliation.

For example, the 1938 FIFA World Cup, held in France, followed Nazi Germany's annexation of Austria as well as Italy's development of heightened Fascism under Mussolini. With Europe on the verge of another war, the Italian side performed the Fascist salute before its matches, which provoked whistles and jeers from the host fans. Mussolini, whose anti-French attitude had been on display at numerous sporting contests, further provoked the host nation when the two sides met in the quarterfinals on June 12, 1938. The Italians took to the field in black uniforms (instead of their prescribed white outfits) adorned with the Fascist symbol on the left breast, and this figurative gesture was made unmistakably clear when they gave their Fascist salute. Italy went on to win the 1938 World Cup, and sides likely recalled the gesture almost two years later to the day, when, on June 10, 1940, Germany and Italy invaded France and World War II spread throughout continental Europe.

Of course, not all problems with nationalism are so overt. Scholars have also pointed out that international sport has become a way for powerful nations to assert and remind the world of their domination. Whether it be the Olympic medal count, success in the FIFA World Cup, or being chosen to host an international sporting event, sport-related triumphs can help remind the global community of who is in charge. In this way, the medal count at the 1936 "Nazi Olympics" startled many in the United States, Great Britain, and France, who saw their nations slipping in the standings against the rising totalitarian powers in Germany, Italy, and Japan. Thus, international contests are capable not only of uniting but also of dividing, by reinforcing the "us against them" mentality that international sport is supposed to dissolve. When this dynamic takes hold, fans become further entrenched in patriotic fervor and more easily see the opponent

The Role of Sport in Promoting International Understanding

Student Exercise

We often take for granted the links between sport and national identity. Consider the example of international soccer. As it developed, players represented their nations on the pitch, and national teams became iconic representations of their citizens. But is this a morally defensible practice? Should we create teams along national lines? Did having Italy compete against France at the 1938 FIFA World Cup ease tensions or exacerbate hostilities? Or consider the Olympics, which are organized on the basis of nationality and invite comparisons and competition between nations. Do the Olympic Games increase tolerance and mutual respect between opposing athletes by highlighting their common love of sport? Or does the competitive environment further divide athletes along national lines?

A different approach involves assembling a mixed team of professional athletes from multiple countries. In fact, this model is used by the Union of European Football Associations for the wildly popular UEFA Cup championship series that features the best professional teams from across the continent. It is also followed by Major League Baseball, in which the teams represent North American cities but draw players from around the globe. Does this approach create a richer climate of tolerance and acceptance than do contests that match nation against nation? Or is it possible to avoid adopting an "us against them" mentality when representing one's nation in competition against a rival nation? These important questions speak to the complex relationship between international sport, national identity, and transnational understanding.

Conduct some library research on one of these questions and draw some conclusions. Alternatively, address this issue in a formal class debate. The affirmative position would contend that competition between national sides creates an effective vehicle for promoting peace and cross-cultural understanding. The negative position would argue that competition between national teams does not promote peace and cultural understanding but in fact damages relationships between nations.

---

as an enemy. For these reasons, some philosophers have argued that, despite the commendable ideals, international sport ultimately undermines tolerance and moves us further away from effective global community.

It is important to debate whether sport competition between nations ultimately produces more positive or more negative results. As all philosophers would agree, it is not enough to concede that something is acceptable just because it is the case; the important question is whether it *ought to be* the case. In other words, the mere fact that we have international sport does not mean that we *should* have it. Before supporting such an activity, we should be able to identify sound ethical reasons for doing so. Moreover, both supporters and critics agree that, in the international sporting arena, national symbols, credentials, and protocols produce a highly charged com-petitive atmosphere. National anthems, uniforms, and flags are displayed as cultural symbols to accentuate differences and to focus on comparisons. Political leaders use sport as a tool for asserting their own political agendas—sometimes inflaming national passions and raising ethical concerns. For these reasons, the rise of international sport throughout the 20th century should not be taken lightly or viewed uncritically.

Sport in Black and White and Technicolor

As we have seen, the growth of modern sport from an Anglo-American pastime into an international phenomenon rested on technological and bureaucratic advancements, as well as the rise of nationalism and politics. In terms of technology, transoceanic travel and communication provided the framework to facilitate early international sporting contests between rival nations. In terms of bureaucracy, the post–World War I rise of international sport federations fueled the standardization of sport and created uniform, mutually agreeable playing standards. As a result, basketball players in Los Angeles and Shanghai, cricketers in Mumbai and Brisbane, and baseballers in New York City and Tokyo began playing the same game in accordance with the same international rule book. Nationalism and politics stimulated the global diffusion and popularity of modern sport even further. Passionate fans and opportunistic politicians alike considered victory in international sport to be a matter of national importance, particularly when it came against a neighboring nation or an ideological rival. For instance, French wins against Germany in soccer, like Australian victories against England in cricket, were elevated beyond the realm of sport and translated into broader statements about national strength, identity, and prosperity.

The development of print and electronic communication systems also played a significant role in the global diffusion and popularity of modern sport. The early-20th-century media revolution of print, radio, and cinematic newsreels and films helped elevate sport to a position of global prominence. Admittedly, metropolitan editors had long recognized the power of sport for selling newspapers and journals. Throughout the late 19th century, the public's growing interest in sport had been reflected in front-page stories about prominent sporting figures such as English cricketer W.G. Grace and American boxing champion John L. Sullivan. However, in the years following World War I, a media revolution propelled sport to new heights. The enormous propaganda machinery deployed during the Great War had increased the capacity of the news, radio, and cinematic industries to disseminate information on a mass scale. When the war ended, sport began dominating the front pages and the airwaves to fill the void. Editors dispatched teams of journalists to cover live sporting events, radio networks broadcast play-by-play coverage of games, and cinematic newsreels provided images to the millions of fans unable to watch in person.

The modern mass media not only transformed sport into an international institution but also elevated the status of athletes to unprecedented levels. Athletes became celebrity figures—national and international icons who were recognizable to billions around the globe. In the new consumer-driven economy and consumption-oriented culture, sportsmen and sportswomen represented important commodities. As a result, they were positioned as the lead actors in burlesque aquacades and vaudeville-inspired shows and even recruited to write their opinions in newspapers and popular literary sources. Clever sporting moguls, public relations experts, and publicity agents exploited the commercial potential of sport even further, aggressively pursuing athletes to compete in special exhibitions before gleeful hordes of paying spectators. Advertising and marketing agencies also recruited athletes to lend their names and faces to help sell an expanding range of consumer products. The public's growing fascination with fame, glamor, and youth positioned star athletes as the perfect celebratory pitchmen (and pitchwomen). Their young athletic bodies helped undermine public fears about overspending and even unconsciously urged the masses to embrace the new option of purchasing on credit and through installment plans.

At the forefront of this media and commercial boom stood some of the most decorated athletes of the postwar era. Most notably, baseball star George Herman "Babe" Ruth parlayed his sporting success with the New York Yankees into considerable commercial and financial rewards. Under the skillful guidance of his personal agent, Christy Walsh, Ruth became a lucrative commercial brand. His vaudeville tours, off-season barnstorming circuits, celebrity appearances, and endless list of product endorsements elevated him to the status of first a national sporting icon and then a global one. His name was as recognizable in Tokyo and Havana as it was in New York. Thus Ruth's incredible baseball feats, exaggerated public persona, and expansive lifestyle made him a symbol of a new age of celebrity and consumerism.

In similar fashion, hordes of public relations experts and publicity agents sought talented athletes to make the lucrative transition from the playing fields to the celebrity ranks. Famed American promoters such as George Lewis "Tex" Rickard and Charles C. Pyle raised the art of packaging and valorizing sport figures to unprecedented levels. They promoted and sold athletes as racial and ethnic icons; for example, Olympic sprinter Jesse Owens and heavyweight boxing champion Joe Louis were heroes to millions of African Americans—and, increasingly, to many white Americans. Similarly, baseball player Hank Greenberg and boxer Max Baer were symbols of pride in Jewish communities, and baseball player Joe DiMaggio and boxer Rocky Marciano were embraced by Italian communities.

Media-savvy promoters such as Rickard and Pyle also promoted female athletes—for example, French tennis champion Suzanne Lenglen, U.S. Olympic swimmer Gertrude Ederle, and U.S. golfer and track star Babe Didrikson—by sexualizing them and selling them to the public as icons of desire. Their performances were publicized, their appearances and private lives serialized, and their fashion and makeup preferences broadcast to millions of eager readers and listeners across Europe and North America. Norwegian figure-skating starlet Sonja Henie became perhaps, the most recognizable female sporting icon of the postwar years. Henie cashed in on her newfound global fame by making public appearances and starring in commercially packaged athletic shows and exhibitions.

The modern fusion of leisure, entertainment, and big business elevated sport to a position of heightened prominence and visibility throughout the Western world and even beyond. Soon, Hollywood studios and directors began recruiting athletes to appear on the silver screen. For example, Johnny Weissmuller, five-time Olympic gold medalist and holder of several world records, translated his Olympic success in the pool into the glitz and glamor of Hollywood by starring in *Tarzan the Ape Man*. The attractive and charismatic Weissmuller opened the door for a steady stream of athletes seeking movie stardom. Rival studios—MGM, Paramount Pictures, Warner Brothers, and Fox—began auditioning well-known athletes in search of the next Hollywood lead actor or actress. The long list of star athletes who proved successful as celebrity draws among moviegoers included American Charley Paddock, the first athlete to be dubbed "fastest man in the world," as well as Clarence "Buster" Crabbe and Eleanor Holm, who were gold medalists in swimming at the 1932 Los Angeles Olympics.

Beyond the movie industry, even the organizers of global sporting events capitalized on the power of sport to attract consumers with money to spend. During the 1920s, leaders of the Olympic movement began to recognize that they could make a fortune not only by charging the public for entry into the event venues but also by demanding fees from the media corporations who covered the Olympian spectacles. Beginning with the Paris Olympics in 1924, organizing committees negotiated exclusive contracts with media outlets for the right to create both still and motion picture images of the Games. Thus the IOC became the first major sporting organization to decide that its contests were not just news items that the media could cover for free but entertainment commodities that could produce compelling photographs and motion picture clips for which the media should pay. Media outlets around the world complained loudly about this new policy but ultimately paid the fees demanded by the IOC rather than be restricted to printing stories unaccompanied by pictures or trying to sell newsreels without Olympic footage. The IOC's business innovation increased the power of the sport industry immensely and created a foundation for itself and other sporting organizations, from FIFA to the NFL, to grow into multi-billion-dollar conglomerates.

The burgeoning postwar relationship between sport and the modern mass media reached its most visible and provocative heights during the 1936 summer Olympics in Berlin. The scale of precision, organization, and publicity of the grossly politicized Nazi spectacle were unprecedented. Journalists attended in droves, provided blanket newspaper and radio coverage, and enabled the Games to reach an estimated 300 million listeners worldwide. In addition, closed-circuit television cameras broadcast live images of the Olympics to residents of Berlin and the surrounding areas. As a testament to Hitler's grand propaganda ambitions, the 1936 Games were, at that time, the largest global media event in history. Documentary filmmaker Leni Riefenstahl's cinematic masterpiece *Olympia*, captured the 1936 games in their full aesthetic and politic splendor. Employing groundbreaking motion picture techniques, Riefenstahl's film earned enthusiastic acclaim and accolades around the globe. Although some critics have discredited her work as further evidence of Nazi propaganda, *Olympia* illustrated both the power and possibilities of sport media.

The Ethics of Commercialism

It can be easy to criticize commercialism as a ruinous force in sport—easy to think that if only money, greed, and corporate interests were removed, then sport would flourish as a showcase of human excellence. After all, who enjoys watching a beloved athlete hold out for more money or enduring endless commercials touting corporate sponsors? The same criticisms emerged in the 1920s and 1930s as athletes and promoters capitalized on the growing popularity of sport. Seeing star athletes appear on the silver screen or endorse products in advertisements—or reading about the huge salaries garnered by star athletes—angered some fans who yearned for the halcyon days when athletes supposedly played purely for the love of the game. Although fans provided the consumer base for commercialization, the exploding business of sport often troubled their sensibilities, particularly those who looked to sport for an escape from the daily grind of competition in their own economic struggles.

Even so, philosophers have noted that commercialism brought several benefits to sport. Without the funds created by selling sport as a product, there would be fewer elite athletes for fans to enjoy. Sport needs revenue in order to support such athletes, and it needs fans in order to generate revenue. Thus commercialism allows talented individuals to pursue excellence in ways that we admire. If no one wanted to buy Leonardo da Vinci's statues or pay for Claude Monet's paintings or purchase a ticket to hear Wolfgang Amadeus Mozart's symphonies, the world would probably have lost great artists. Without money to support their genius, how could they have devoted themselves to their crafts? The same is true for athletes. If no money were available to allow athletes to pursue the ultimate in human performance, then the world would have missed out on Sonja Henie, Jesse Owens, Babe Ruth, Babe Didrikson, and the many other purveyors of athletic excellence who have dazzled global audiences for more than a century. Therefore, the money that many decry as a corrupting force is the same revenue that supports athletes in their quests to test the limits of human ability and achievement.

At the same time, companies that profit from sport carry moral obligations to sport. Philosophers have argued that those who benefit from sport cannot merely mine athletic competition like a motherlode in order to line their own pockets. Just as greedy fisheries should not catch too many fish and timber companies should not harvest all of the trees, those who profit from sport have a responsibility to be good stewards of the game. This obligation might involve, for example, forgoing a television timeout that generates revenue but harms the aesthetic value of the game or choosing not to manufacture a piece of equipment (such as an advanced golf club or running shoe) that makes a sport too easy. More important, it means ensuring that sports cherished by communities continue to thrive for future generations, even at the cost of not reaping the maximum profit today.

Unfortunately, the evidence is mixed regarding how many organizations follow a stewardship model. One example can be found in the Amateur Athletic Union, which was the most powerful organization in U.S. sport during the 1920s and 1930s. The AAU was originally created to support, organize, and grow amateur sport throughout the United States. As amateur sport became more profitable, the group used some of its profits to invest in grassroots sport and better support athletes who lived in poverty. This use of funds helped cultivate elite sport even as it benefited individuals who otherwise would not have had access. At the same time, the AAU wielded its power to ensure that the entire financial windfall flowed into its own coffers. With the excess funds and unchecked power, AAU executives traveled first class while athletes received far less support. The AAU also bullied amateur athletes into appearing at certain events in order to ensure that promotors enjoyed large ticket sales even as it prosecuted athletes for receiving under-the-table payments from the same promoters. Ultimately, this hypocrisy led to the AAU's downfall in the 1970s. Thus the organization's story illustrates the complex moral issues that can arise in relation to commercial interests in sport.

CHAPTER WRAP-UP

Wrapping Up and Looking Ahead

During the late 19th and early 20th centuries, the popularity and reach of sport increased dramatically. International events such as the Olympic Games and the World Cup grew from modest roots to become highly visible and prestigious competitions that attracted vast international audiences. For all their successes, these competitions still reflected the social conditions of the times, including the inequities that affected girls and women, ethnic minorities, and members of the lower social classes. At the same time, however, these games sometimes presented new opportunities for many individuals previously excluded from such activities and thus served in those cases to promote social reform. In addition, the growing popularity and symbolic power of sport allowed it to be intentionally co-opted for political purposes, which raised ethical questions about sport's capacity to promote international understanding and good will. The tremendous popularity of large-scale international events also turned sport into a lucrative commercial commodity. This development raised moral concerns of its own, in this case over the potential incompatibility of sport and big business—issues that remain flash points for controversy to this day.

As we have seen, Great Britain, the United States, and other Western nations developed modern systems of physical activity and exported their versions of sport and recreation to the rest of the world. In many cases, the world welcomed these imports, as is illustrated in soccer's emergence as the world's game. In some cases, people used Western sport to Westernize their own culture; in others, they used Western sport to resist Westernization and preserve their own traditions. As discussed in chapter 10, this global exchange did not result in the disappearance of non-Western sporting cultures. To the contrary, some indigenous practices would continue to provide alternative accounts of the importance and value of sport and other forms of physical activity.

Study Questions

1. What were the historical and intellectual roots of the Olympic Games and the World Cup? What were some of the most significant challenges faced by promoters of these two sporting spectacles?

2. Did the idealism and lofty goals of Olympism result in Olympic policies that promoted social justice? How did women, ethnic minorities, and members of the lower socioeconomic classes fare in the early years of the Olympic movement?

3. Are statements of value and purpose, such as those contained in the philosophy of Olympism, useful or not?

4. Did amateurism preserve the purity of the Olympics, or was it used for less ethically defensible purposes?

5. Why did sport emerge as an important political tool? How is it still used for political purposes today?

6. Is the logic of business compatible with the logic of sport? Why or why not? How has the commercialization of sport both helped and harmed our games?

7. How does the notion of good stewardship relate to obligations carried by sport entrepreneurs? What kinds of actions would good stewards undertake?

THE WEST AND THE REST

The Emergence of Critiques and Countercultures

Chapter Objectives

In this chapter, you will

1. examine the ways in which modernization led to the disappearance or transformation of traditional and indigenous sports and games;

2. discover traditional physical cultural practices and folk games that have survived into the modern age and examine their efficacy;

3. learn about the predominantly Western nature of modern sport and games;

4. consider the ways in which modern beliefs have been influenced and shaped by ancient and non-Western ideas about physical activity, health, and well-being; and

5. understand the philosophy of holism as an alternative to dualism and materialism.

In 1907, the renowned German anthropologist Adolf Friedrich, Duke of Mecklenburg, led a major anthropological expedition to the mountainous regions of Rwanda in East Africa. As part of his efforts to study precolonial and early colonial Rwandan culture, Friedrich observed and photographed the Rwandan cultural practice of *gusimbuka*, an indigenous form of high jumping that scholars trace back to the 16th century. Various folk forms of vertical jumping existed at that time in parts of the globe still untouched by European colonialism and imperialism, but Friedrich's explorations brought the Rwandan jumpers and their gigantic leaps to the world's attention. To Friedrich's astonishment, he saw a number of Rwandan Tutsi men clear a 2.5-meter jump, far eclipsing the 1.94-meter modern Western record for the high jump held at the time by Michael Sweeney of the United States. Viewing these remarkable feats through his European colonial lens, Friedrich predicted that African "natives" could—with appropriate training and opportunity—vanquish Western athletes in any modern sporting event.

Despite Friedrich's fascination with the "natural" ability, extraordinary physiologies, and impressive physiques of the Rwandan Tutsi, the *gusimbuka* represented a form of physical culture far removed from the ascribed competitive tenets of modern Western sport. Rooted instead in the social, sacred, militaristic, and carnival spirit of Rwandan body culture, the Tutsi male high jump held layered and complex meanings. Devoid of notions of winning and record breaking, it could be read as a coming-of-age rite of passage or as a symbolic ritual intended either to boost fertility or to prevent miscarriage, heart disease, and other illnesses. Alternatively, it could be understood as an expression of the Rwandan fixation on body-energy dynamics; a successful jump purportedly freed the male body from blocked energy and fluids. The *gusimbuka* also formed a central component of Tutsi military training and served an important social function in the court (the center of government) of the *mwami*, a sacred being revered as the gods' representation of earth. In this dimension of significance, the jump demonstrated the immutability of the Tutsi social elite and the martial prowess of the *mwami's* court.

Comparable to the other Rwandan body-culture practices of dancing, fighting, spear throwing, and running, the *gusimbuka* lacked both the rationalization and standardization of Western sport. Considerable variation existed in both the equipment used and the settings in which the activity took place. Embracing the natural and varied landscape of play, the Tutsi used stones, termite mounds, natural ridges, and large logs (of various sizes, based on topography) as spring boards to aid their jumps. Successful jumps were

German anthropologist Adolf Friedrich, the Duke of Mecklenburg, looks on as a young Tutsi male performs in the Rwandan cultural practice of *gusimbuka*, an indigenous form of high jumping.

measured, but, in stark contrast to modern sport, the Tutsi emphasized participation and ritualistic symbolism.

In an era in which modern, Western-inspired sport grew to dominate the globe, Adolf Friedrich's study of the Rwandan *gusimbuka* illustrated the persistence of traditional physical cultural practices and folk games. As both Western and non-Western peoples were increasingly drawn into a "world system," they fought to preserve and protect their indigenous and traditional pastimes. Inevitably, many of these activities, including Rwandan *gusimbuka*, eventually succumbed to the rapacious forces of Western cultural imperialism and industrialization. However, a few premodern European and non-Western indigenous physical activities survived, in one form or another, into the 21st century. Retaining their spontaneity, vitality, and connection with the rhythms of celebration, ritual, and nature, these traditional physical activities stand today as persistent remnants of a distant past—a contrast to the secularization, rationalization, and achievement orientation of modern sport.

Sport is not an exclusively Western practice but rather the product of a complex patchwork of diverse cultural interactions. Even in the 21st century, it is influenced considerably by premodern and non-Western patterns of play and ideas about human movement, health, and well-being. Whether in pursuit of voyeurism or exoticism, modern (particularly, Western) audiences have celebrated, adopted, and even recently revived aspects of premodern European and non-Western indigenous physical culture. The revival of these traditional pastimes represents a countercultural response to what some perceive as the artificial, commercialized, exclusive, and win-at-all-costs mentality of modern sport. The persistence of these physical cultural practices reveals both a modern nostalgia for the distant past and a fascination with the "other"—the foreign, the unknown.

Traditional and Indigenous Sport in an Age of Modernity

Scholars have long observed that societies are neither perfectly static nor immune to the processes of historical change. Rather, all societies evolve as a result of social interaction. Such interactions, and the accompanying cultural exchanges, have helped produce the forms of sport and physical activity that exist in the modern world. Emerging alongside modern industrial society and fueled by patterns of economic and imperial domination, modern sport is largely reflective of Western cultural practices and values. The particular sports that dominate the global sporting landscape are overwhelmingly Western in origin. These sports are governed and controlled by predominantly Western institutions and played in accordance with Westernized rules, customs, and patterns. Even the defining characteristics of modern sport—quantification, quest for records, rationalization, bureaucratization, specialization, secularism, and equality—are indicative of the Western mania for industrial production, economic productivity, and scientific inquiry, as well as post-Enlightenment and post-revolutionary notions of truth, liberty, and justice (for a fuller account of these trends, see chapters 5 through 8).

The effects of Westernization—by means of industrialization, urbanization, and Anglo-American and European imperialism—have irrevocably changed human physical culture. The myriad traditional games and pastimes that once resided at the heart of both premodern European and indigenous social and religious life have been eclipsed by a far smaller number of modern Western sports. For example, the Jicarilla Apaches of the American Southwest no longer run as part of sacred rituals to boost fertility and ensure a bountiful harvest. Similarly, indigenous Australian people no longer run along their sacred "songlines,"and the descendants of the Maya and Aztec peoples have largely ceased playing *ulama*, the ritualistic Meso-american ball sport of their ancestors. Colonialization led to the forced introduction of alien (Western) sporting practices and the mass extinction of indigenous games linked with religious or pagan celebrations. Preindustrial folk games suffered a similar fate, succumbing to the forces of industrialization and urbanization because they were deemed incompatible with social and economic modernization and with the temporal and spatial limitations of modern urban societies.

By the end of the first half of the 20th century, a predominantly Westernized and monolithic sporting culture had taken shape. By this point, the power of modernization appeared all-consuming. Even practitioners of traditional and indigenous games and pastimes that had appeared to survive the onslaught of imperialism and industrialization ultimately compromised the integrity of their ancestral customs by embracing some aspects of modern sport. The religious significance of these contests gradually waned in favor of a symbolic gesture to the gods. In addition, players and teams were quantified on the basis of skill level and other objective measures of performance, and equipment and playing facilities were rationalized under the direction of newly formed bureaucracies.

For example, Afghan *buzkashi*, Japanese sumo wrestling, and Spanish bullfighting are now laden with modern characteristics disguised by traditional patterns; thus they represent what scholar Allen Guttmann labels as "hybrid sports" (for more on the tensions between indigenous sports and modern Western sport, see chapter 8). The traditional sport of *buzkashi*—which once involved as many as a thousand mounted Afghani tribesman vying, sometimes over the course of many days, to seize control of a decapitated goat or calf—now bears some of the hallmarks of modernity. In today's version, players are neatly ordered into two evenly matched teams who struggle within a regulated play space to make off with a symbolic carcass made of cloth or leather in timed contests governed by the National Olympic Committee of Afghanistan.

Japanese sumo, whose roots can be traced back to prehistoric times, has also taken steps along the path toward modernity. The mighty wrestlers still wear traditional garb, perform the ancient Shinto rituals, and stomp their feet to expel evil spirits, but they now do so before the eyes of an international television audience of millions. Concessions to modernity have also been made in Spanish bullfighting. In keeping with historical Spanish custom, the colorful capes and costumes remain intact, as does the matador's repertoire of stylized motions. However, Spanish designs to preserve the cultural authenticity of this traditional pastime mask the fact that bullfights now take place in regulated arenas, are marked by timed conditions, and are performed by matadors officially sanctioned by a national governing body.

In various parts of the world, political and cultural leaders intervened directly to repel the forces of modernization and the deleterious effects of Western cultural imperialism. For instance, eager to protect their historical sporting pastimes and preserve their local cultural identities, the Arab governments of Morocco, Algeria, and Tunisia mandated that their people participate in the traditional sports of *al kora* (a ball game) and *haih a deux* (a game similar to the British sport of prisoner's base). In another example, in the face of centuries of Danish colonial suppression, the Inuit peoples of the Arctic kept alive their drum dance, a combination of sport, physical contortion, laughter, music, dance, poetry, and magic. Some cultures that deliberately isolate themselves from the incessant pressures of modernization have also succeeded in preserving their ancestral games and pastimes. In the United States, for instance, Pennsylvania Dutch communities continue to play the historic Amish folk game of corner ball (*eck balle*), in which

BRAZILIAN CAPOEIRA

Historical Profile

The Brazilian martial art of capoeira, a traditional combat sport infused with elements of dance, acrobatics, and music.

The Brazilian martial art of capoeira—a traditional combat sport infused with elements of dance, acrobatics, and music—has been transformed under the unrelenting weight of modernization. Rooted in Brazil's colonial past, capoeira emerged from the descendants of West African slaves who first developed this unique martial art as a form of resistance to the oppressive and inhumane realities of life on Portuguese slave plantations. Combining native Brazilian influences and agonistic elements of striking and immobilizing an opponent with one's hands, feet, and hips in a rhythmic, dancelike fashion, capoeira symbolized a desire for liberation from slavery, poverty, and class domination. The *capoeiristas* (combatants) fought to music played on distinctive, sacred instruments that corresponded to the Yoruba gods of West African religious origin.

Some scholars date the sport back as far as the 16th century; whatever its exact time of origin, capoeira spread rapidly during the 19th century as Brazil underwent a period of widespread urbanization. Forced to power Brazil's new manufacturing industries, slaves brought capoeira from the plantations to the cities, where it rose to prominence. Although colonial governments suppressed capoeira—because it was often used against the colonial guard—the sport experienced a further resurgence following the abolition of slavery in 1888.

Capoeira exists today in a considerably modernized (Westernized) form. The many regional variations of capoeira have been reconciled into one standardized martial art that is now practiced in many parts of the world. Under the guidance of a *mestre* (teacher), *capoeiristas* take exams, earn diplomas, and wear colored belts signifying their skill levels. Although some of the musical and religious associations remain, modern-day *capoeiristas* have largely jettisoned tradition; they are now generally consumed by the quest for victory and record breaking.

Historical Games

Student Exercise

Find a game from a non-Western culture—either a historical game that is no longer played or one that still exists in a non-Western location or culture. Then do the following:

- Identify the game's name, its origins (e.g., country, religion, culture), and the time period of its popularity.
- Describe how the game was, or is, played and identify the skills or capabilities tested by it (e.g., strength, dexterity, cooperation).
- Describe the fate of the game—for example, its current popularity or why it died out, when and why it has been dramatically modified, and whether or not it has been affected by Western influences.

---

two teams of six players try to eliminate the opposition by hitting opponents with a small, handmade leather ball.

In addition, a few traditional forms of mob or folk football, which were played by peasants across Britain and France as part of medieval festival celebrations, have survived the tumult of industrialization and modernity. In other words, even though the modern codes of football—soccer, rugby union, rugby league, American, Australian rules, Canadian, and Gaelic—enjoy global visibility and popularity, the traditional antecedents of these sports have, in some isolated communities, been preserved and protected. In Kirkwall, located on the Orkney Islands off the northern shores of Scotland, residents spend Christmas and New Year's Day playing the Kirkwall Ba'. Dating to the 12th century, the Ba' is a rough-and-tumble affair in which the two sides of this quaint port town (the Uppies and the Doonies) compete for control of a hand-stitched round ball. Victory is attained by the team, consisting upwards (and often, unevenly) of one hundred local residents, that manages to advance the ball, in a series of violent scrums and chaotic melees, toward its end of the town. In a similar vein, the residents of Ashbourne in Derbyshire, England, have kept alive their own distinct medieval ball game, Royal Shrovetide football. Replete with local customs, dialects, and anthems, the Royal Shrovetide game is played annually on Shrove Tuesday and Ash Wednesday.

Undoubtedly, the most successful and hardy traditional sport is wrestling. Hundreds of styles of traditional folk wrestling and grappling—including Breton, Cornish, Cumbrian, Congolese, Ethiopian, Icelandic, Iranian, Mongolian, Turkish, Indian, and Swedish—have survived into the 21st century. In contrast to the specialized, standardized, and secularized nature of modern wrestling, the premodern European and indigenous variants that have survived are rooted in the festivities, rhythms, rituals, and spirituality of daily life. They celebrate local identities and pride, are inclusive (often across gender and age boundaries), and are democratically governed from below. These traditional styles of wrestling stand as persistent reminders of distant pasts—and as proof that alternative models of sport still exist even in the modern world.

Western Appropriations of Eastern Muses

The survival of some traditional physical cultural practices and folk games into the 21st century should not obscure the dominance and overrepresentation of Western-inspired modern sports. A brief glance at the modern Olympic Games—the world's largest and most popular multisport event—reveals this truth. Though portrayed as a global phenomenon, the Games have long privileged modern Western sports and ideologies. The Olympics, in the words of founder Baron Pierre de Coubertin, were intended to be open to "all games, all nations." However, it was only in the aftermath of World War II that Coubertin's vision of a multiracial and universal Olympic Games would begin to take shape, as impoverished and unindustrialized nations in Africa and Asia—driven by decolonization, non-Western solidarity, and anticolonialism—slowly entered the Olympic Movement. Beginning with the entrance of Nigeria for the 1952 Helsinki Olympics, 19 National Olympic Committees from Africa and 18 from Asia received accreditation from the International Olympic Committee (IOC) in the years leading up to the 1964 Tokyo Olympics.

Although this development constituted progress, the integration of Asian, African, and other non-Western nations into Western imperial sporting structures reproduced the old colonial power dynamics. For example, the IOC imposed a policy of cultural assimilation rather than reconciliation. The predominantly Western officials that governed the IOC never entertained the idea of incorporating indigenous African and Asian sporting and movement practices into the catalog of Olympic events. As a consequence, the daily sports of the non-Western peoples of the world are—with the exceptions of judo (from Japan) and taekwondo (from Korea)—entirely absent from the program of Olympic events. Thus the Olympic docket ignores such sports as aikido, Muay Thai boxing, Southeast Asian ball games such as *sepak raga* and *sepak takraw*, and the Indonesian martial art of *pencak silat*. Even more surprising, the Olympics do not yet include the enormously popular forms of Wushu martial arts practiced today by billions of people all over the world, including tai chi, *shaolin*, and kung fu (for more on the origins of Wushu, see chapter 4).

In truth, then, the modern Olympic array of sports is by no means representative of a unified global physical culture; rather, it exists as the result of centuries of West-

ern domination in the social, economic, and colonial realms. As a result, in order to participate, African and Asian nations have been forced to assimilate themselves, often quite literally, on foreign fields of play. Even in the rare instances when the Western-controlled IOC has conferred Olympic status on non-Western sports, these activities have eventually been forced to shed almost all traces of their cultural origins. This fact raises an important question: Just how non-Western are these additions to world sporting events? The special case of judo is revealing.

Founded in 1882 by Japanese educator and athlete Kanō Jigorō, the modern sport of judo is a full-contact form of grappling in which a practitioner seeks to throw or take down the opponent, to immobilize the opponent, or to force the opponent to submit by means of a hold or chokes. Rooted in the philosophical tenets of Confucianism, judo was originally conceived not as a competitive sport but as a pathway toward self-improvement and a tool for contributing to the betterment of Japanese society. In Jigorō's words, judo was envisioned as "a principle of life, art, and science . . . a means for personal cultural attainment" (quoted in Brousse and Matsumoto). After Jigorō's death in 1938, judo began to gain widespread international recognition. Steadily Jigorō's traditional Japanese martial art adapted to the dictates of modern competitive sport. As a result, the competitive form of judo found in the Olympics—added in 1964 as a demonstration sport and elevated in 1972 to permanent medal status—bears little resemblance to Jigorō's original design.

Though Jigorō drew inspiration for judo from Japanese traditions, he also had been among the late-19th-century and early-20th-century advocates for the modernization and Westernization of Japan that dramatically reformed the country during the Meiji Restoration (for more on the role of sport in the modernization of Japan, see chapter 6). In this context, perhaps it is unsurprising that with judo now stripped

CONFUCIUS

Historical Profile

Confucius was born in Qufu in 551 BCE in the northeast part of China. His full name was K'ung-fu-tzu, which means "K'ung the Philosopher." By the age of 22, Confucius had become well known for his keen intellect and insightful wisdom. In spite of his youth, he ventured into his profession of founding a school and becoming a teacher. Coincidentally, this was precisely the time that Socrates was teaching in Greece. Just as Socrates attracted his well-known student Plato, Confucius attracted a gifted pupil named Mencius, a disciple who would expand on and explain many of his master's teachings.

Among other things, Confucius was known for his deep humility. He did not regard himself as a brilliant philosopher but more as a translator of preexisting cultural wisdom. His sayings are consistently directed toward the promotion of virtuous behavior in this life. This focus placed his work in diametric opposition to the thrust of many other mystical religions from the East (such as yoga, from India) that are designed to provide an escape from common experience. Confucius, therefore, opposed Lao-tzu, who would have students achieve a trancelike state and thereby escape from the body.

In another contrast with Lao-tzu, Confucius was not an ascetic. Rather, he was a sportsman who enjoyed hunting and

Confucius: A philosopher, teacher, and political leader respected for his wisdom in promoting positive social interactions and known for the many aphorisms collected in his *Analects*.

fishing. He was also a lover of music. He preached an ethic of humility, kindness, sincerity, conscientiousness, courage, and respect for others. In addition, he was a respected political leader. Confucius, in short, preached an egoless, this-world philosophy. In his *Analects* (book VIII, chapter VIII), we read the following: "1. The Master said: 'Let the character be formed by the poets; 2. Established by the laws of right behavior; 3. And perfected by music.'"

Later in life, Confucius exiled himself from his native state, due to political unrest, for 13 years. He moved about the countryside with his band of disciples. He returned home at age 68 and died five years later, in 479 BCE. Days before his death, in a weakened condition, he sang one of his favorite odes: "The great mountain must crumble; The strong beam must break; And the wise man wither away like a plant."

of its philosophical and humanistic foundations, it bears all the hallmarks of modernity. Official judo competitions today are governed on a global scale by rules and regulations disseminated and enforced by the International Judo Federation. Even the distinctive system of wearing colored belts to quantify and signify skill level is a modern Western invention. Thus, as noted by sport scholar Allen Guttmann, the case of judo reaffirms that non-Western athletes compete "on Western terms in sports which either originated in or have taken their modern forms from the West" (*Games and Empires*).

The historic Indo-Persian game of polo stands as another example of a non-Western sport that has been stripped of its unique cultural origins in the East and subjected to the transformative effects of modernity (for more on the diffusion of polo in ancient and medieval Asia and the Middle East, see chapter 5). During the late 19th century, British colonists in India reconceptualized and transformed this indigenous folk pastime in keeping with the rationalized standards of modern sport. Although Persian and Indian elites had historically engaged in equestrian ball-and-stick games, the practice had been largely forgotten by the time the British imposed imperial rule over the Indian subcontinent; indeed, only a few folk variations of polo had survived. In the traditional game, an indeterminate number of riders on small ponies propelled a ball, often in a chaotic fashion, around a loosely defined playing field. In contrast, the British, with an eye toward their broader imperial mission of, in their view, civilizing India, sought to infuse the unruly game with conformity and order. To this end, the British penned official rules, standardized the field dimensions, limited the number of players per team, established a governing body, and organized official tournament and cup competitions. In this way, the modern Western game of polo emerged from Eastern roots to become the favorite pastime of Indian maharajahs, British military officers, and country gentlemen alike.

Aside from appropriating and transforming non-Western indigenous sports and folk games in its own image, the Western world has more recently borrowed non-Western philosophies and beliefs and applied them to elite-level, modern sporting competition. In one striking example, Phil Jackson, 10-time NBA champion as coach of the Chicago Bulls and then the Los Angeles Lakers, revolutionized the game of basketball in the 1980s by applying Zen Buddhist philosophies and forms of meditation to help transform team dynamics and maximize team performance. Specifically, Jackson introduced a form of sitting Zen meditation known as *zazen* to help his players clear their minds of negative thoughts, enhance concentration, and "trust the moment." He also grounded the famous triangle offense, which powered both the Bulls and the Lakers to such remarkable success, in the Zen Buddhist attitudes of self-sacrifice and self-awareness. His championship teams sacrificed *me* for *we* by buying into an offensive system that emphasized the equal and free-flowing movement of the ball rather than the star-studded individualism that had long dominated the NBA landscape.

The Effectiveness of Folk Psychology and Folk Medicine

In hindsight, the hegemony wielded by the West over the nature of sport, how it is practiced, and what it means has produced mixed results. On one hand, our science, education, technology, and advanced coaching techniques have allowed athletes to perform at levels never seen before. (Later in this chapter, we review the Anthropology Days experiments that exploded myths about the supposed athletic superiority of native athletes.) But one has to wonder if anything has been lost in this move from folk coaching and folk psychology to our more scientifically grounded versions of these practices. More broadly, one has to wonder if anything has been lost in the parallel move from folk medicine and folk exercise to modern health care and exercise science.

It turns out that many people, including professional coaches such as Phil Jackson, wondered about these very things. For instance, some physical education instructors have rediscovered time-honored methods for improving their students' ability to focus in laser-like fashion on the skill at hand and relax while they engage in the learning process. Some professional teams have hired sport psychologists trained to promote flow, peak experiences, playing in "the zone," and the superior performances that often go with these phenomena. And a number of health practitioners now look to the East for "new" therapeutic interventions that range from yoga, tai chi, chigong, quiet meditation, and counting one's breaths to acupuncture, deep message, and herbal therapies.

This elevated interest in cultural traditions suggests that something indeed has been lost. In other words, at least some forms of folk coaching, psychology, and medicine—largely through trial and error across the centuries and after careful observation of successes and failures—may have been onto something. That something may have been lost in our rush for new knowledge found primarily through the powerful methods of reductionist science.

Reductionist methods, as you learned in the Introduction and will revisit later in this chapter, attempt to understand and manipulate the small, the part, or the micro element in order to predict and improve the large, the whole, the athletic performance, or one's health. Eastern approaches, in contrast, place no priority either on the small or on the large. Instead, they hold that interventions to improve performance or health may occur anywhere—from the chemical level to spirituality and everywhere in between.

These potential losses notwithstanding, people such as Phil Jackson are not interested returning to "the good old days" and turning their backs on important scientific advances in athletic performance. Rather, they hope to complement current practices and thereby make them more effective. This complementation is based on a philosophy that views the world (including us) as a product of interactive, dynamic systems. In the common vernacular, these interactive elements are described as holistic, as in "holistic coaching" or "holistic medicine." Later in this chapter, we take a closer look at this inclusive view of life and see how it differs from two other dominant philosophies that you have already encountered—dualism and materialism.

Here, however, we need to examine the ways in which Eastern practices have been co-opted by the West and whether or not this translation has been faithful. If not, then we need to examine how this state of affairs may affect the utility of these interventions. To answer these questions, we consider two examples—one in the domain of athletic performance, the other in the area of health promotion.

Zen and Athletic Performance

One common Western method for teaching and coaching consists of what is known as direct instruction. In this approach, the teacher or coach typically explains verbally how an action should be performed—for instance, how to grip a racket, how to take a backswing, how to position one's feet, and where to hit the ball. In some cases, the verbal instructions are supplemented by a brief demonstration. In any case, the learner's head is loaded up with facts, including a list of dos and don'ts—and perhaps too much information to process at one time. In contrast, Eastern approaches attempt to avoid information overload.

In addition, a considerable amount of ego and tension is often found in this direct form of instruction. Having been told what counts as success, beginners are often worried about the outcome and thus insufficiently attentive to the process. They frequently try too hard, often with unhappy results. A negative spiral ensues, characterized by trying harder and failing again, which produces more tension and utter frustration. This pattern prompted some instructors and coaches to look for a technique that diminished the ego, reduced stress, and avoided information overload. As mentioned in chapter 4, this kind of approach is offered by Zen Buddhism. Specifically, the four truths of Buddhism speak directly to the issues of ego and the stresses related to desire:

1. All life is suffering.
2. The cause of suffering is ego-desire.
3. To eliminate suffering, one must eliminate ego-desire.
4. To eliminate ego-desire, one must follow the way of the Buddha.

This sounds relatively straightforward and easy. All a person has to do is follow the way of the Buddha—whatever that means!

Many Western coaches and trainers do not appreciate the demands entailed in following the way of the Buddha. The problem is this: Removing the ego is not an easy process, which means that it is also not easy to remove the stress and distraction that come with ego-oriented living. Thus, the authentic tradition of Zen Buddhism offers a holistic solution to the problem of skill development, but it is not an easy one. For example, as described in chapter 4, Eugen Herrigel was engaged in the spiritual discipline of archery for years before he was able to experience the arrow shooting itself—that is, experience the acts of aiming and shooting with no ego and without the need to rely on more and more information.

This near impenetrability of Eastern experience has not deterred western practitioners from attempting to adapt Zen philosophy and techniques to local cultural tolerances. Even if a full dose of Buddhist-inspired interventions cannot be delivered, perhaps partial measures still do some good. In fact, according to many reports, faith in this halfway approach has born some fruit. Here are three examples of Eastern-inspired interventions:

1. **Bounce-hit and concentration:** Tim Gallwey gained notoriety years ago when he published a book titled *The Inner Game of Tennis*, in which he argued that in the West we set up a battle between Self 1 and Self 2. Self 1 is the analytic, judgmental self that talks to us, tells us what we did wrong, and reinforces the importance of success or victory. This is the seat of the ego. Self 2 is the intuitive, automatic self that is in charge when we accurately attend to something and react appropriately without any gap between the two. Self 1 tells us to *make* it happen. The result is stress, effort, trying too hard, and sometimes a forced or constructed movement. Self 2 simply *lets* it happen. The result is peace, rhythmic action, relaxation, and natural movement.

Gallwey correctly observed that Self 1 typically fills the player's head with too many ideas—so many, in fact, that most of his students were unable to focus on the ball and watch it make contact with the racket. In order to counter the excess tension and lack of focus, he employed a simple technique called "bounce-hit." He told his learners that they needed to watch the ball, even to the point of seeing the ball's seams. When the ball hit the ground, they were to say "bounce." The moment the ball hit the racket, they were to say "hit." Gallwey reported that, instantaneously and almost without exception, performance improved dramatically through the use of this simple concentration technique.

2. **Meditation and transfer:** Some coaches, including Jackson and some skill instructors, require their athletes and students to meditate. Some do this formally at the start of practice or before an instructional session. Others require it as a homework exercise. In most Zen

GAUTAMA BUDDHA

Historical Profile

Mystery and uncertainty surround the person called Gautama Buddha, Siddhartha Gautama, or simply Buddha. The exact dates of his birth and death are unknown, but he lived sometime during the 6th century to the 4th century BCE—more specifically, according to some traditions, from 563 to 483 BCE. He traveled and taught in the eastern parts of India in what is now Nepal. What we know about his life and teachings was originally passed down by oral tradition and not put to writing until hundreds of years after his death.

Siddhartha Gautama was born into a noble family and was said to have been shielded from the harsh realities of life by his father. He was provided with all the material luxuries he could want, but he came to realize that wealth, comfort, and security were not valid objectives for life. Some traditions say he left his father's palace at the age of 29 and observed, for the first time, profound suffering in the world. He became an ascetic—that is, a person who forsakes worldly pleasures and commits to a rigorous practice of meditation.

Gautama Buddha (also known as Siddhartha Gautama): an ascetic and sage whose life and writings served as the foundation for Buddhism.

This zeal for enlightenment through self-mortification almost led to his death. After nearly drowning in a river while bathing, and after having been restored to health, Siddhartha Gautama realized that the practice of extreme self-deprivation and self-imposed suffering was not a path to mystical wisdom. Thus he discovered the so-called Middle Way, a path that requires self-discipline and ethical living but not extreme deprivation or self-mortification. (This characteristic distinguished his approach from those of many Yogis who promoted spiritual growth through difficult and painful physical postures.) It is said that, shortly thereafter, while seated beneath the Bodhi tree, Siddhartha achieved full enlightenment—a mystical awareness or wisdom that cannot be fully explained by words or theories. In Buddhist terms, he achieved Nirvana, a condition of an empty mind, no thought, perfect peace, final wisdom. The name *Buddha*, in fact, means "Enlightened One."

Across the centuries, Buddhism evolved from more modest goals of enlightenment (Hinayana Buddhism) to more ambitious religious objectives (Mahayana Buddhism), but both of these versions of Buddhism have common roots in the life and teaching of the Buddha. Fundamental to Buddhism is the belief that all beings are Buddhas or have Buddha nature in them. However, one's Buddha nature remains hidden—because humans are deceived by apparent wants, needs, or desires and because human minds are naturally cluttered with worries and other thoughts—unless one adopts a rigorous practice of meditation designed to focus attention and strengthen one's powers of concentration.

This practice typically involves sitting in a lotus posture and meditating in a number of different ways, such as counting one's breaths, focusing on a physical object, or solving paradoxical puzzles called koans. This practice tends to be arduous and lengthy. But if enlightenment is achieved, one's life changes dramatically. The world is seen through new eyes. Truths that cannot be put into words or theories or propositions are experienced directly. One's mystical interest in unity is satisfied. All is experienced as One!

traditions, *zazen*, or sitting zen, is regarded as the most direct and efficacious route to the elimination of ego-desire and the resulting enlightenment. One common technique requires the practitioner to sit in a lotus posture (or some posture that approximates this stable tripod position) for an extended period of time, often 30 minutes to an hour, while counting one's breaths—one on inhale, two on exhale, three on inhale, and so on up to 10 before starting again at one. The sitting is to be motionless, utterly peaceful, with nothing in one's thoughts except the numbers.

Once again, some athletes and coaches report a positive transfer from the meditation hall to the athletic or practice field. Players are more focused and relaxed and thus too, more effective.

3. **Process and achievement:** Gallwey argued that much frustration and failure in sport result from thinking too much and trying too hard. Instead, one must quiet or empty the mind in order to allow one's natural abilities to show themselves.

This approach was once tried by one of the authors of this book in a kinesiology class with a group of 15 undergraduates, all of whom were reasonably accomplished distance runners. The coach noticed that before each day's run, the students exhibited considerable anxiety about how far he would have them go and at what pace. During the runs, he noticed individuals looking ahead from time to time to see what distance remained. Self 1, in other words, was speaking loudly and clearly inside their heads, and they were distracted by, among other things, their aching bodies, their demanding running coach, the upcoming hills, and the competition with their classmates. Their minds were anything but quiet or empty.

One afternoon, the coach mentioned that the class would be running differently. The runners would negotiate the usual five-mile loop but this time would run from their *hara* (according to Zen traditions, a place in one's abdomen, roughly three finger widths below the navel) rather than

from their heads. He told them to imagine a string pulling them forward from the belly, or, alternatively, a wave continuously breaking on their backs and pushing them forward. They were to focus on the ground, about three yards ahead of themselves, for the entire five miles. During the run, the coach would occasionally remind them: "Run from the *hara*; focus on running from your belly; concentrate on the ground in front of you!"

When the group finished, the coach asked them how they felt. "Terrific," they said, virtually in unison. One person added, "But it was one of the easiest runs we had all semester." Others nodded in agreement. Unbeknownst to them, the coach had timed the run. He pulled the stopwatch out of his running shorts and showed them that it was in fact their fastest time of the semester for that loop.

What are we to make of these anecdotal accounts and of Phil Jackson's success in the NBA? It is probably safe to say that a considerable amount of wisdom can be found in many Eastern traditions—whether from Hindu roots, Buddhist traditions, the *Analects* of Confucius, or other sources. Their philosophies, in other words, make sense and contain more than a kernel of truth. Moreover, the wisdom found in these traditions can carry very practical ramifications. Psychologists, neurophysiologists, sociologists, anthropologists, and others have done enough research on the meditative and wisdom traditions to show effects that can be measured in the brain, in hormones and other body chemicals, in day-to-day behavior, and in experiences that impact our quality of life.

We must also recognize, however, that important differences exist between these Western adaptations and their original cultural sources. Most Eastern religious traditions are designed to change one's life in profound ways. The Zen focus on eliminating ego-desire is a case in point. Except in very rare cases, enlightenment comes neither quickly nor easily. When it does arrive, it is decidedly life-changing. Everything is new. Everything is different.

The more modest gains from the diluted Western versions of Zen practice show up in a number of ways. First, improvements in the ability to concentrate are modest. Focus of attention usually lasts only moments. Backsliding is common. Second, no serious damage is done to the power of the ego. It may be pushed to the background for a while, but it typically reemerges just as healthy and intrusive as it was before the intervention began. Third, performance improvements are tenuous and unreliable. Self 1 may be quieted during lower-pressure performances but is likely to reemerge when the stakes are high. In short, the more authentic profile of pursuing Eastern transformation provided by Herrigel leaves us with an important lesson: Compromised methods beget compromised results. Even so, they may provide a glimpse of what lies in this direction. The occasional peak experiences we have—those times when a difficult sporting activity is beautiful, effortless, and spontaneous—are unforgettable.

Yoga and Improved Health

Yoga is now a fairly common intervention in the West, where it is intended primarily to improve posture and reduce stress. However, it is advertised and often presented as an exercise, a therapy, a mere means to better health. Connections to its religious roots have been effectively severed. Yoga traditions can be traced to India and date back to about the 5th century BCE. One of the most popular forms in the West is hatha yoga, which is said to have been introduced by the deity Shiva. Traditionally, hatha yoga was an ambitious spiritual practice that included a variety of "limbs" or disciplines: postures (*asanas*), purification procedures (*shatkriya*), subtle energy and breath control (*pranayama*), gestures (*mudras*), and meditation (*dyana*). Many believe that hatha yoga was an ascetic practice designed to lead to self-realization.

Most Western versions of yoga now focus exclusively on only one of the limbs of this tradition—namely, the *asanas*, or postures. Similarly, the benefits now said to accrue from yoga are almost exclusively related to physical health: improved sleep, increased energy, improved muscle tone, improved flexibility, reduced muscle soreness, reduced levels of stress and blood pressure, and improved heart rates. As impressive as these gains may be, they fall short of the mystical experiences and other forms of enlightenment said to emerge from the full practice. As a result, many Eastern yogis argue that this curtailed version of yoga is little more than a faint shadow of the genuine practice. As noted by Johanna Michaelsen, "There is a common misconception in the West that hatha-yoga, one of about ten forms of yoga that supposedly leads to self-realization, is merely a neutral form of exercise, a soothing and effective alternative for those who abhor jogging and calisthenics. . . . You cannot separate exercises from the philosophy."

One way to interpret the West's fascination with Eastern traditions—whether for the purpose of improving athletic performance or improving one's health—is that it hinges on their promises of success. That is, they work, at least to a degree. This efficacy, however, is interpreted in the West largely in terms of extrinsic benefits, such as better and faster learning, more victories and championships, less stress, and better health. Such outcomes, like the focus on outcomes in and of itself, fit Western logic. They fail, however, to capture the more comprehensive, holistic hopes and aspirations embedded in these Eastern approaches to life. Traditionally, one's commitment to Zen Buddhism, or yoga, or the teachings of Confucius, was intended to affect not just one's mind or body or skills or fitness, but the whole person. From this point of view, the focus on victories, championships, good health, or even longevity misses the broader point about quality of life. Thus, Eastern sages might argue that there is something crass and shortsighted in our selective employment of many non-Western practices and philosophies.

Encounters With the "Other"

The contemporary fascination with applying Eastern philosophies and spiritualistic principles to elite sporting performance and health-related contexts mirrors an emerging Western appreciation of colonial and native traditions. The sedentary, industrialized, and technology-assisted realities of 21st-century life have stimulated calls for a return to simpler, more primitive lifestyles and customs. In fact, citing modern fears about rising obesity levels, sedentary lifestyles, processed foods, and the harmful effects of labor-saving devices, some cultural commentators argue that modernity has weakened and infantilized Western civilization. In contrast, in this view, primitive men and women were rugged, virile, healthy, and naturally gifted as athletes. As a result, some physical activity experts, convinced that primitive peoples enjoyed a higher quality of life and well-being, have advocated a return to supposed ancient traditions such as the "Paleo" diet, which is based on the types of foods presumed to have been eaten by early humans and thus excludes dairy and grain products and processed food. Others sell "primal" or "primitive" workout routines aimed at re-creating the predatory movement practices of prehistoric hunter-forager peoples.

Perhaps the most celebrated ancient custom to enjoy popularity in the modern era is that of barefoot running. In his 2010 bestselling book *Born to Run*, journalist Christopher McDougall revealed the ultramarathon prowess of a remote tribe of barefoot runners, known as the Tarahumara or Rarámuri, from Mexico's deadly Copper Canyon. McDougall describes this "near-mythical tribe of stone-age superathletes" as capable of running ultra-endurance races in the blistering heat over harsh and rocky terrain and steep canyon trails. All members of the tribe, not only adult men but also women and children, participate in these races wearing nothing but thin-soled sandals to protect their feet.

To McDougall's surprise, the Tarahumara suffer none of the common foot, ankle, and knee injuries that often afflict modern-style runners. In fact, these runners are trim and powerful and enjoy near-perfect health. McDougall hypothesized that the running prowess of the Tarahumara derives from their primitive simplicity. He consequently rejects our modern dependence on heavily padded and rigidly constructed running shoes, as well as artificial treadmill running environments, and calls for a return to an age of natural running—even advocating barefoot marathons through the wilderness.

Modern Western audiences have long displayed a deep-rooted admiration for indigenous lifestyles and customs. As early as 1926, Mexican sporting officials recruited members of the Tarahumara tribe to participate in a 100-kilometer (62-mile) footrace from Pachuca to Mexico City. Excitable sport officials dreamed of using the Tarahumara to help bring gold-medal glory to Mexico in the Olympic Games. The German anthropologist Adolf Friedrich, Duke of Mecklenburg, harbored a similar belief in the natural athleticism of the "native" when he first encountered the Rwandan Tutsi high jumpers in 1907. Through these romantic lenses, modern Western observers have sometimes believed that the vices and excesses of modernity have produced harmful effects on human physical capabilities and lifestyles. Hardy indigenous peoples—with their pristine diets, supposedly uncivilized customs, and extreme primitivism—enjoyed an existence unspoiled by the technological advancements of the modern era. These beliefs, of course, tend to reflect the anxieties of our modern age rather than the realities of the past. In actuality, rigors such as widespread famine, malnutrition, diseases, dysentery, and high child mortality rates in the ancient world testify to the fact that the past was not the pristine utopia that some imagine.

Much of the modern fascination with the supposed natural athleticism of indigenous peoples is rooted in late-19th-century

ANTHROPOLOGY DAYS

Historical Profile

The 1904 Olympic Games in St. Louis captured the modern, Western admiration for native physicality and the perceived natural athleticism among the so-called "exotic" and "primitive" peoples of the world. The Games were held in conjunction with the St. Louis World's Fair, a grand cultural exposition marking the centennial celebration of the Louisiana Purchase that included a "human zoo" of so-called "primitive" peoples. For their part, the St. Louis Olympics are infamous for the inclusion of an anthropological sideshow pitting the supposedly "uncivilized" tribes of the world against one another in a series of modern and indigenous athletic events. Anthropology Days (as the event became known) granted curious onlookers the opportunity to gaze at the sight of Navajos, Sioux, Pawnees, Apaches, Pygmies, Patagonians, Ainu, Eskimos, and members of tribes from the recently acquired Philippines as they competed in 18 events—including, running, jumping, throwing, archery, pole climbing, tug-of-war, and mud fighting—over the course of two days.

These "Savage Olympics," as local newspapers called them, constituted an attempt to quantify and measure human morphology and physical performance. Viewing the events as a scientific experiment, Dr. William McGee, chief of the anthropology department at the St. Louis exhibition, aimed to discover whether Western industrial civilization produced athletes who could match the natural speed and raw prowess of the so-called "primitive" peoples of the world. The results, McGee opined, would be used to determine the effects that industrialization and technological advancements produced on athletes from more advanced and civilized cultures.

Lacking any formal experience and training in modern sport, the performances of the "uncivilized" and "primitive" peoples predictably paled in comparison with those of the Western athletes. In effect, the results contradicted the deeply ingrained belief that indigenous peoples occupied a low plane on the evolutionary totem pole and therefore must embody animal or savage athletic prowess. In spite of these so-called experiments, however, ideas about "primitive" superathletes did not disappear, as revealed by the success of McDougall's *Born to Run* among 21st-century readers.

and early-20th-century scientific thinking about race. Although a variety of Western racial attitudes existed, the concepts of biological determinism, the study of comparative anatomy, and the embrace of a simplistic "survival of the fittest" version of Darwinian evolution and eugenics generated the widespread belief that the so-called "human races" derived from separate origins and featured characteristics that were distinct, biologically fixed, and unequal. A clear, color-coded ranking of races emerged that placed people of European descent (especially Nordics and Aryans) at the top of the scale and indigenous non-European peoples at the bottom. On this evolutionary scale of social Darwinism, the "dark-skinned" races were associated with the initial evolutionary stages of savagery and barbarianism. In contrast, Europeans occupied a position of full enlightenment and complete superiority—mental, physical, and moral. When people of European descent dominated athletic events, it proved scientifically that they possessed not only superior bodies but also superior brains.

The emergence of anthropology as a recognized form of scientific study, as well as the popularization of scientific images through the growth of the modern mass media and cultural exhibitions, consistently and broadly reinforced these flawed ethnological theories and typologies of race. These ideas became immersed in Western popular culture and influenced the ways in which Western audiences read and perceived the sporting performances of nonwhite athletes. Tellingly, if not surprisingly, when people of African or

Asian descent won victories over whites, many scientists changed their scripts. For example, when the African American boxer Jack Johnson held the heavyweight crown (1908–1915) or Jesse Owens won a record four gold medals (at the 1936 Olympics) or Jackie Robinson broke the color line and integrated Major League Baseball (1947), their feats were often interpreted as the triumph solely of primitive physical prowess and frequently assumed to indicate a lack of mental acuity on the part of their race. Thus white audiences rationalized the emerging success of black athletes through the use of pseudoscientific notions that, for example, black athletes were insensitive to pain, or possessed thicker skulls, or ran faster thanks in large part to longer heel bones.

These racialist ideas have all been effectively debunked by contemporary science, sociology, history, and philosophy; even so, they continue to influence 21st-century sporting culture. In particular, the predominance of African American athletes in basketball and American football—along with the unprecedented success of Jamaican sprinters and Kenyan and Ethiopian long-distance runners—has preserved the notion of the supposedly natural black athlete who triumphs through genetic fortune alone rather than hard work, persistent training, or intelligent strategy. This notion persists in spite of persuasive sociological arguments that highlight, for instance, the pivotal role played by geography, local culture, coaching, access to facilities, and role models in promoting sporting opportunities across racial groups. Such arguments are often overlooked in favor of outmoded and flawed interpretations of genetic and evolutionary assumptions.

For some thinkers, the old fight over nature and nurture has been settled by admitting that both play an important role in shaping human life but that neither one completely determines the qualities of a person or predicts future behavior with absolute certainty. Human life is affected, as Eastern philosophers would argue by both yin and yang—that is, interpenetrating influences that affect the indivisible

Nature and Nurture in Health and Athletic Performance

Student Exercise

The interplay of nature and nurture is complex. Even though both are always involved in producing both good health and athletic success, health and sporting domains are unique. For some health issues and some athletic feats, physiological endowments, biology, and genetics play the major role. In other cases, culture, opportunity, and socialization largely explain the outcome.

For this exercise, first identify either a sporting role (e.g., playing center on an NBA team) or a health condition (e.g., high cholesterol) and develop an argument for identifying the cause as either nature over nurture, nurture over nature, or a mixed or variable relationship between the two.

Second, evaluate the merit that we typically assign to athletes who exhibit dedication, practice longer, and care more about achieving excellence. Is that merit deserved? Is it possible that a good "work ethic," as it is commonly called, is a product of both nature and nurture? And if such an ethic is due, at least in part, to being born in the "right" family or culture, or with the "right" genes, then how much credit do such athletes deserve?

Third, evaluate the influence exerted by supportive sociocultural conditions on athletic performance. Look up historical records of women's athletic achievements in the days before Title IX, when good coaching, proper facilities, and social support were often denied to girls and young women (Title IX was passed in 1972). Compare those records with records of more recent women's sporting achievements. Two good sports for making this comparison are running and swimming. Are the improvements dramatic? Do the top women today outperform even some well-trained male athletes in the same sport?

whole. As you may recall, we have symbolized this concept in this book by using a tilde, or squiggle, to represent ideas such as nature~nurture, mind~body, and genetic advantage~cultural advantage; we can now expand the list by adding yin~yang.

Holistic Kinesiology

Holism cannot be traced to any single cultural tradition, though it is typically associated with Eastern philosophy. Nor is dualism owned by any single tradition, but it took root in the Western world. Two of the most famous dualists—Plato and Descartes—are discussed in earlier chapters of this book. Descartes, who was a great mathematician as well as a philosopher, noticed a significant difference between physical stuff (matter) and mental stuff (ideas). Physical things operate according to laws based in math and physics. The body, in other words, is essentially a machine. The mind, on the other hand, obeys rules that have nothing to do with physics. These are the rules of logic, clarity, and coherence—in other words, the rules that govern effective thinking. Physical stuff can be weighed, divided in half, and carried from one place to another, whereas it makes no sense to describe

ideas in this fashion. After all, how much does love weigh? Or how would one divide the idea of justice in half? Many in the West thought these ideas made a great deal of sense. How could one even begin to challenge these apparent truths?

Holists thought they found a way to do so. The basic principle of holism is fairly simple: The whole is always greater than the sum of its parts. That is, if you were to add up all the pieces that constitute a live person—the chemicals, organs, bones, brain tissue, circulatory system, and so on—you would still not get the whole person. What would be missing? Lots of things—including the person's values, dreams, and ethics, as well as the story of his or her life. To put it bluntly and simply, holists noted that one cannot find ethics in a muscle or a brain. However, holists noticed another truth. We never find ethics *apart* from muscles or brains either. Somehow, therefore, we need a philosophy that acknowledges the fact that muscles, brains, and ethics are intimately related and affect one another in a reciprocal fashion. Some Eastern philosophies acknowledge this intimacy in the terminology of "bodymind."

Some of the principles of holism are explained in figure 10.1. This representation is an adaptation of analyses by one of

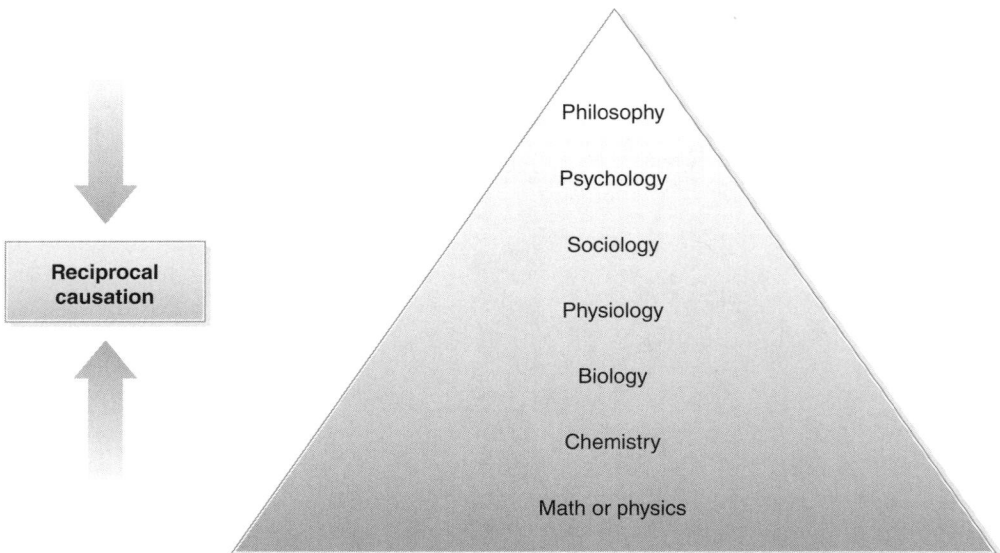

Figure 10.1 Philosophy of holism.

Holistic Causation

Student Exercise

As you may recall, this book's introduction includes an exercise addressing the importance of cross-disciplinary research. Holists are strong supporters of this kind of inquiry because they believe that problems and solutions can be found at the cell level, the cultural level, and everywhere in between. See if you can find scientific support for causation that works from the small to the large and for causation that works from the large to the small.

For the first relationship you might consider ecological issues, such as the quality of the air, the water, the soil, or the food we eat. Can you find evidence that poisons in these places can affect, for instance, our body chemicals, which in turn affect our intelligence or how we can think? Conversely, see if you can find research showing that positive ideas such as happiness, optimism, and joy can affect our chemicals—or, if you want to look on the negative side of the ledger, showing that depression, anger, and hopelessness can affect our muscles and maybe even how our genes express themselves.

---

the great holistic philosophers of modern times, Maurice Merleau-Ponty. Some of this material is not easy to grasp, so you will need to put on your thinking cap in order to get your intellectual arms around holism.

The triangle shown in the figure symbolizes whole persons and their functions. The different shades of gray, and the absence of lines from the base to the top of the triangle, symbolize one of Merleau-Ponty's central points—namely, that human functions are ambiguous. They are affected both by physical particles and chemicals (the bottom of the pyramid) and by ideas and values (the top). As you can see, as you move toward the bottom of the pyramid, you move in the direction of physical stuff and machinelike principles. As you move toward the top, you move in the direction of ideas and thoughtful principles. However, the important point that makes this holistic and not dualistic is that they are internally related. Somehow, chemicals, genes, and other small things affect hopes, dreams, and other big things. The reverse is also true. That is, we can see ideas, hopes, and other big things in chemicals, genes, and other small things. This two-way relationship is symbolized by the two arrows at the left side of the diagram—the upward arrow from cells to ideas and the downward arrow from ideas to cells.

We might stop here to consider the evidence for this supposed intimacy. If the holists are right, we should be able to verify this two-way causation empirically.

If you completed the exercise titled Holistic Causation, then you now have one piece of evidence suggesting that a holistic philosophy of the person has advantages over dualistic visions. This is so because, as you may recall, one of dualism's problems involves explaining how something that is not physical can affect something that is. Mind and body would seem to exist in two radically different worlds. In principle, mind cannot affect body, and body cannot affect mind. In the holistic conception of bodymind, however, they interact continuously because they are different aspects of a unified whole.

Materialism as an Alternative to Dualism

You may recall that materialism developed, in part, to overcome this problem of mind–body relationships. In materialism, there is no problem, because everything is body. Humans are, according to materialists, complex machines, and the principles that affect physical objects are sufficient for understanding human behavior. Figure 10.2 presents another triangle that can be used to see how materialism differs from holism.

Notice how different this triangle is from the holistic diagram. First, everything is physical. "Cells and void" describes the content of the entire person and has the potential to explain all behavior. The difference between the bottom and top of the triangle can be captured by the twin notions of simplicity and complexity. Because all animate life is viewed as nothing but a machine composed of cells and void, differences between single-celled animals and multi-celled, large-brained beings like us must be attributed to complexity—that is, different organizations of cells and void. For materialists, then, our brains are very complex machines.

Similarly, causation, for materialists, is limited to physical interactions. This is why experience, ideas, hopes, cultural values, and the like are listed outside of the triangle, to the right side. The question marks underline the fact that even though we experience these things, they do not do any work. In other words, as will be explained, nonphysical elements play no role in causation. For materialists, causation occurs from physical to physical in two directions—from lesser to greater complexity (e.g., from chemicals to altered brain states) and from greater to lesser complexity (e.g., from brain states to altered chemicals).

The two arrows are not, however, equal in size. In materialism, because the part can explain the whole, it stands to reason that attention will be focused on the parts. For instance, if the whole is in any way defective, the cause of the defect must be related to one or more of its parts. In other words, problems should be traceable to simpler elements. Scientists express this reductionist tendency when they say they are searching for "underlying mechanisms."

This mentality leads to an oddity in reductive science. What we commonly see, observe, or otherwise encounter in our daily lives is said to lack reality. Rather, it is the invisible underlying mechanisms that are responsible for everything we know—from rocks to trees and from the behavior of honeybees to the actions of people. For instance, when we see an apparently solid, immovable table, micro-technologies inform us that we have been deceived. The table is in fact neither solid nor motionless.

This oddity aside, reductive techniques have proven to be powerful and effective strategies. In fact, it is at the micro level

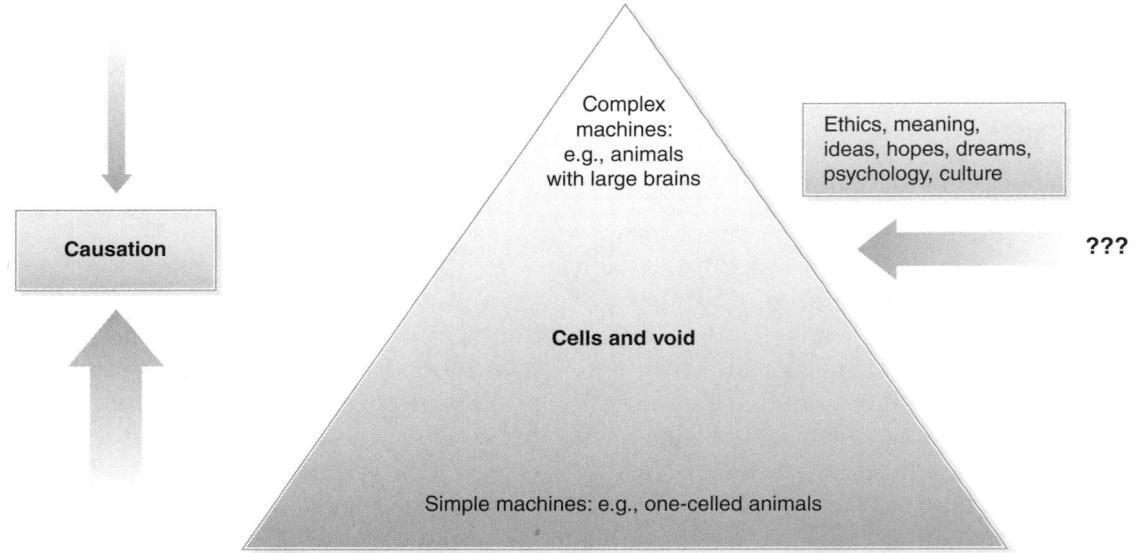

Figure 10.2 Philosophy of materialism.

that many scientists hope to find cures for cancer, prevent birth defects, solve problems such as world hunger, and unravel the deepest secrets of the universe.

Holists, however, argue that this materialist view of the world contains only partial truths. To be sure, human beings are like machines in many ways. For instance, our forearms, upper arms, and elbow joints constitute a lever system that can be understood in terms of the Newtonian physical principles that govern all levers, whether human or otherwise. But the regularities found in machines, according to holism, cannot explain the entirety of what it is to be a person; nor can they account for all human behavior. Holists level several charges at materialists that, if valid, point to both theoretical and practical problems with materialist philosophy.

The theoretical problems are revealed in the new laws or rules that emerge in the holistic triangle as one moves from the bottom to the top. Logically stated, if higher-level rules emerge that cannot be explained by lower-level rules, then the whole is necessarily greater than the sum of its parts. Examples of such emergent rules are provided in table 10.1. Notice that each lower-level rule permits, but cannot predict or explain, the higher-level rule. For instance, rules related to chemical compounds allow for, but cannot predict or explain, biological rules related to homeostasis. That is, nothing in chemistry tells us how complex, chemically grounded systems need to be balanced. Likewise, biological rules of homeostasis allow for, but cannot predict or explain, social rules related to family bonding.

This dynamic is easiest to see when we look at the extremes. Specifically, in terms of the examples presented in table 10.1, nothing in the rules of chemistry can predict or explain the emergence of ethical guidelines such as the Golden Rule. In other words, you can study all of the rules of chemistry from every angle possible and never find rules of ethics in them. Here again, these arguments provide evidence for the claim that the whole is greater than the sum of its parts.

Table 10.1 Emergent Rules at Different Levels of the Triangle

Level of the triangle	Principle	Example of a rule from that level
Chemistry	Rules of bonding	A bonding of one sodium ion with one chloride ion produces a compound called salt or halite (NaCl).
Biology	Laws of homeostasis	Saline level affects the health of an organism. This level is regulated by organisms through homeostatic mechanisms.
Physiology	Overload principle	Muscles need to be stressed beyond normal levels of resistance if hypertrophy is desired.
Sociology	Bonding principle	Kin relationships are stronger than those among unrelated humans. Maternal bonding with one's own children is particularly robust.
Ethics	Golden Rule (reciprocity)	We should treat others as we ourselves would like to be treated.

A second problem with materialism is related to the issue of causation. Once again, holism regards emergent rules as real—so real, in fact, that they have the power to cause changes both upstream (toward the top of the pyramid shown in figure 10.1) and downstream (toward the bottom of that figure). In contrast, materialism does not regard nonphysical states—or the rules that go with them— as real or as having any causative power. Thus, in the materialist diagram (figure 10.2), all nonphysical levels are outside of the triangle in a kind of strange neverland. It can be characterized as strange because these lived experiences are vivid in our daily lives and seem to cause all kinds of changes in our behavior, our physiology, and our chemistry. They can be said to reside in a kind of neverland because materialists relegate them to the status of an ineffectual sideshow. Materialists do not deny that we have experiences of love, hope, and fear, for instance, but they do deny that these experiences do any work. Only brain states, they assert, cause things to happen.

Common sense, however, suggests that ideas do in fact play a significant role in changing future behavior. For instance, if we are tired of studying and decide to go outdoors to play soccer, it seems that our memory of soccer, the ideas associated with good times, and the values we associate with the game are responsible for getting us out of the chair. Likewise, if I plan to raise my right hand in a salute to the flag, and then do so, it is clear that meanings related to patriotism or duty had something to do with my physical actions. Materialists would say that common sense is misleading us and that it is really a series of brain states that do the work. What we experience as the cause of our behavior is, once again, a kind of sideshow that parallels behavior but does not affect it.

Modern holists do not deny brain states, physiology, or chemistry. They agree that ideas do not come from nowhere. As noted in discussing basic tenets of holism, no ideas exist apart from chemicals, brains, or the influences of evolution, learning, and socialization. All human experience— from the most basic drives to the loftiest ideals—is physically~socially tethered, yin and yang at the same time. But ideas (the whole) cannot be explained simply by appealing to chemicals, brains, and a cultural tradition—that is, to some of the parts. Most important, chemicals, brains, and cultural mores are shaped and otherwise affected by ideas. After all, ideas expressed through language across thousands of years have reconfigured the human brain. Specifically, the parts of the brain that process language have grown larger. Some would argue that this is proof positive of culture affecting physiology, of ideas causing changes in physical things— even brains.

In the holistic diagram (figure 10.1), the downward arrow is robust, which indicates that holists can explain, for example, the success of the coaching and teaching interventions used by Phil Jackson and Tim Gallwey. Ideas associated with relaxation and focus can change the nature and quality of physical movements. Similarly, holists can explain the even more dramatic performance conversions of a person such as Herrigel, who could hit archery bull's-eyes effortlessly. Holists can also explain the surprisingly good health benefits provided by yoga even when it is practiced outside of its full spiritual context. Causation works both up and down. Exercise affects attitude; conversely, attitude, emotion, and stress affect health. This is a relationship of intimacy between ideas, emotions, culture, and flesh. It is what one would expect if people like us are bodymind.

Living From the Body, Not Toward It

Merleau-Ponty's philosophy of ambiguity had another important implication for physical activity and health. He argued that we can have our body in two ways—as an object and as a subject. We have ourselves as an object when we look in a mirror, when we feel self-conscious while others are staring at us, or when we tend to a body part—say, when we scrape a knee and put a bandage over it. In sport, this objectification happens, for instance, when we are not performing well and look at our stance, grip, or another physical element in search of a remedy.

Objectification of the body is normal and often helpful, but it can also cause us trouble. For example, some students do not like physical education because they are not comfortable having others watch them, particularly if they are not skilled. Some adults do not like to move much because they are overweight, uncoordinated, or otherwise at odds with their own body. In addition, due to socialization and unrealistic standards related to appearance, many people, particularly girls and women, care more about how they look than what they can do. All of these individuals suffer from what might be called excessive objectification.

Merleau-Ponty was more a philosopher than a psychologist, yet he had an important psychological insight. He understood that it is not much fun to live self-consciously *toward* one's body. Fixation on self as body puts one in a kind of self-imposed jail. In contrast, a well-adjusted, happy person typically lives *from* his or her body. In other words, the person gets interested in what he or she is doing and pushes the body to the background. Forgetting the body provides a way to escape; thus, in this sense, the "forgotten body" is the good body.

This thought serves as a second important insight from holism. When we are functioning well, we are on automatic pilot, and our intelligence is embedded in our actions. We see what we need to see, we feel what we need to feel, we recognize what we need to recognize—and we respond quickly, seamlessly, and effectively. Earlier in this chapter, we referred to this state as experiencing flow, having a peak experience, or playing in the zone. In our daily lives, we would probably just call it exciting or wonderful. It is fun to forget one's body, stop talking to oneself, quiet Self 1, and just react correctly. It is wonderful when Self 2 takes over and we are able to just let it happen.

John Dewey (1859–1952), an American pragmatist and holist philosopher, understood the paradox of objectifying one's body in order to grasp the subjective reality of it. He wrote about the importance of developing good habits in all aspects of life—habits of thinking philosophically, thinking scientifically, promoting good character, playing musical instruments, and playing sport. To be sure, during the process of developing such habits, people have to objectify their bodies, their actions, or their thoughts from time to time in order to improve a sequence of logic or correct a movement. However, with enough repetitions, good habits form and the habits take over. A person with good habits can perform a task, as we sometimes say, "without thinking." Of course, this is not entirely true, but that is the way it feels. Our reflective self (Self 1) is not thinking, but our automatic self (Self 2) is.

People with good movement habits and other resources that promote self-confidence are, as a common phrase puts it, "comfortable in their own skin." They live from their bodies unconsciously toward an interesting world. Again, a body that lives in the background is, for holists like Merleau-Ponty and Dewey, a good body. It is an automatically minded body or a bodymind.

Holistic insights such as these are still being worked out, studied, and applied in practice. Traditional dualistic and materialistic approaches continue to be challenged. Folk traditions and non-Western practices can be expected to continue serving as counterpoints to contemporary values and patterns of behavior. This process can be seen in the emergence of various countercultural practices.

The Emergence of Countercultural Movement Practices

According to sport scholar Henning Eichberg, the modern Western desire to seek answers to the riddles of human physical performance and well-being in both the distant past and the non-Western present illustrates a growing dissatisfaction with the dominant patterns of modern sport. Eichberg contends that the artificial, exclusive, and hypercompetitive nature of modern Western sport—as well as the ecologically damaging effects of modern global sporting mega-events such as the Olympics and the World Cup—have stimulated the emergence of a countercultural movement designed to revive traditional forms of sports and games. All around the globe, local cultures and communities have begun reclaiming their past and restoring the physical cultural practices, folk games, and dances of their ancestors.

Eichberg situates this movement in the context of modern anxieties about the loss of ethnic and cultural identities in the wake of incessant globalization. In post-Franco Spain, the Basques launched movements to restore the traditional folk games that had long served as markers of regional identity. Dozens of regional sports that had been suppressed under Franco's fascist rule—including the *pelota* ball game, folk acrobatic gymnastics, numerous feats of strength, and traditional forms of wrestling—have been restored and promoted to commemorate and celebrate the rural and maritime traditions of the Basque people. Similarly, the Inuit peoples of North America (Alaska, Canada, and Greenland) established the World Eskimo-Indian Olympics in 1961 in an effort to preserve indigenous practices and tra-

ditional survival skills essential to life in circumpolar areas. These activities, long disregarded as vestiges of a premodern and non-Western world, include tug-of-war, one-foot kick, canoe racing, drum dancing, igloo building, and the greased pole walk. In another example, in the 1960s, a *volkssport* (people's sport) movement began in Germany that promoted noncompetitive recreations such as hikes and runs. *Volkssport* quickly spread across Europe and into North America.

In fact, efforts to revive traditional and regional sports, or even to resist the dominant presence of Western-inspired modern sports, also flourished in even earlier times. In the late 1800s, the Highland Games developed in Scotland to revive and promote traditional aspects of Celtic culture, including music, dance, and feats of strength. Today, against the backdrop of bagpipe players clad in traditional Scottish kilts, 21st-century competitors still vie for victory in ancient Celtic strongman events such as the caber toss, the stone put, and the weight over the bar.

During the 1920s and 1930s, communist and socialist groups developed rival physical cultural festivals in direct opposition to modern Western sport and its focus on individualism, specialization, commercialism, and record-breaking achievement. In 1921, the Soviet Union formed the Red Sport International (*Spartakiad*) to promote revolutionary class consciousness through mass participation in Soviet-style sports, pageants, parades, and military events. In a similar vein, socialist groups across Europe and North America launched the workers' sport movement to provide sporting and recreational opportunities to all willing participants, irrespective of social class, gender, race, ethnicity, and skill level. Favoring the mass participation of less-privileged national and social groups, the global nexus of workers' sport federations even united to stage a series of "Worker Olympics," held on three occasions between 1925 and 1937.

CHAPTER WRAP-UP

Wrapping Up and Looking Ahead

Following decades of physical cultural revivals around the globe, the United Nations Educational, Scientific, and Cultural Organization (UNESCO) launched a major international initiative in 1983 designed to formally protect traditional physical practices, folk games, and dances. UNESCO's focus on promoting cultural awareness and sensitivity and preserving national heritages in an increasingly global community has led Eichberg and other scholars to predict that modern Western sport will become less popular in the future. The concrete stadiums and secularized, commercialized, and artificial modern sporting environments will be replaced, they imagine, with natural landscapes of play as the masses in diverse cultures, nations, and regions continue to promote their own historical sporting patterns and cultural traditions.

In spite of the vision of Eichberg and his followers that modern sport will somehow melt away, a look at the second half of the 20th century and the beginning of the 21st century reveals that a modern Westernized sporting culture is in fact growing in power and influence around the world. One need only look at the soaring popularity of association football, or what Americans call soccer. The world's version of football now boasts more than 3.5 billion players spread across more than 200 nations. Telecasts of World Cup soccer rank as the most popular shared experiences that everyone around the globe watches—ranking alongside the Olympics at the top of the global ratings chart. This brief glance at contemporary global soccer culture reveals that modern Western sport continues to dominate the globe.

Study Questions

1. Why did some Western and non-Western cultures seek to preserve and protect their traditional and indigenous games?

2. How and in what ways do traditional and indigenous sports and games differ from modern sports?

3. Are major modern sporting events such as the Olympic Games truly representative of global culture? Explain why or why not.

4. How faithfully have Western cultures adopted Eastern practices designed to improve athletic performance or health? What effect has this had on the utility of these practices?

5. How has late-19th and early-20th-century Darwinian thinking about race shaped contemporary ideas about the sporting prowess of nonwhite and ancient peoples?

6. What are the three or four most important principles that distinguish holism from dualism and materialism?

7. Why are issues of causation and the objectification of the body important for kinesiologists?

THE GOLDEN AGE OF MODERN SPORT

Global Dramas and Global Influence

Chapter Objectives

In this chapter, you will

1. learn about how sport reflected the politics of international conflict during the Cold War;

2. examine the philosophical discipline known as phenomenology and its influence on kinesiology;

3. discover the role played by the Cold War in shaping modern attitudes toward science and sport;

4. examine the philosophical debate over banning performance-enhancing substances;

5. examine the ways in which discontented nationalities and minority groups used sport to broadcast their demands for equal rights and opportunities;

6. examine the ways in which racism and sexism have created barriers for the ethics of inclusion and empowerment;

7. consider the influence of television in shaping and spreading modern sport; and

8. explore the post–Cold War dimensions of global sport.

World War II brought unprecedented calamity and destruction as more than 60 million people died in a conflict that truly spanned the globe. The grim realities of total war destroyed the Axis powers and left the Allied powers disoriented and bitterly fragmented. Even before the war ended, it became clear that the two most powerful nations emerging from the conflagration—the United States and the Soviet Union—had mutually exclusive goals and objectives that would almost instantaneously turn them from allies into enemies. This divide produced a Western bloc, led by the United States, and an Eastern bloc, led by the Soviet Union, that faced off at flash points around the globe and soon armed themselves with stores of nuclear weapons which promised that another world war would annihilate humanity.

The maelstrom of war sparked new geopolitical considerations about the polarization of West and East as Germany and Korea divided into mutually hostile fragments, China convulsed into a civil war that divided the nation into opposing communist and anti-communist factions, and the Soviet Union intensified its grip over Eastern Europe. In an effort to contain and confront the emergence of the communist world system, the United States engineered plans to spread democracy and free-market capitalism and rally the Western bloc. The subsequent formation of the North Atlantic Treaty Organization (NATO) and the implementation of the Marshall Plan led communist and capitalist rivals into an all-out battle for the hearts and minds of the world.

Since both the Soviet Union and the United States possessed a nuclear deterrent, the Cold War largely played out in the diplomatic and cultural arenas. Beyond the United Nations—in which the United States and the Soviet Union both served as founding members—international sport provided the most public and symbolic cultural forum for Cold War rivals seeking to affirm the superiority and vitality of their respective ways of life. Sport took on greater levels of political and cultural importance throughout the Cold War, attracting the interest of political leaders on both sides of the Iron Curtain that separated East and West and spurring nations to devise policies for promoting national fitness and ensuring victories in elite international sporting events. Indeed, as observed by one of the most insightful chroniclers of Cold War tensions, the British novelist George Orwell, international sporting contests served as "war minus the shooting."

Fueled by Cold War politics, as well as advances in land and air travel and the advent of television, modern Western sport entered into its final phase of globalization in the decades following World War II. The transformation of modern sport into a wildly popular and globally televised phenomenon began to erode the racial and gender boundaries that had long made the sporting world mainly the province of white men. Amid the countercultural and revolutionary spirit of the post–WWII years, black and female athletes and activists joined forces in demanding greater access, opportunities, and equal rights in all facets of society. Thus sport grew to reflect the politics of both international and domestic conflicts. It became a battlefield where political superpowers, discontented nationalities, and minority groups contested, challenged, and asserted their agendas and ambitions—a truly global form of Orwell's "war minus the shooting."

Phenomenology

Post–World War II experiences of disorientation and discontent speak to the importance of quality of life and the factors that promote good living. What we feel, how we think, what values we espouse, and what emotions drive us forward all make a difference. The conditions that prevailed after World War II called for a new philosophical method that would take seriously both experience and the contents of consciousness. The work by German philosopher Edmund Husserl offered just such a solution with a novel philosophical method known as phenomenology, which focuses on investigating things through first-person lived experience. Phenomenology originated in the work of Husserl prior to World War I but came to flourish in the aftermath of World War II as philosophers such as Maurice Merleau-Ponty, Jean-Paul Sartre, and Martin Heidegger further developed this method.

All of these philosophers agreed that phenomenology begins by interrogating lived experience—that is, by reflectively looking at the phenomena or "things" that consciousness is about. These experiences can vary from perception of colored things (e.g., what it is to perceive a red ball) and memory of a childhood experience (what it is to remember a childhood toy) to bodily awareness (what it is to sense your feet) and embodied action (what it is to encounter an oncoming tennis ball with an intention of returning it). The most important concept in phenomenology involves what Husserl called "intentionality," or how we direct either our reflective or actual gaze toward something. We can direct our reflective gaze, for example, toward a childhood toy and thus remember the toy; or we can direct our actual gaze toward an oncoming tennis ball and thus have the ball as something to be intercepted and returned.

Phenomenology, and especially the works of Maurice Merleau-Ponty (addressed in chapter 10) and Martin Heidegger, exerted a profound influence on kinesiology. Both of these thinkers examined the kinesthetic awareness of embodied action and intentionality of movement, thus expanding philosophy from the world of mental reflection and abstract ideas into the world of physical action. Indeed, Heidegger claimed that Descartes had presented the world to us "with its skin off," like a cadaver, to reveal the muscles below. If we want to get back to the human person (not just the body), we have to know the person as the person really is (*not* with the skin off). Merleau-Ponty also stressed the

Using the Phenomenological Method

Student Exercise

In order to practice reflecting on conscious experience like a phenomenologist does, consider each of these first-person statements that characterize an experience one might have in everyday life:

- I remember that summers were longer when I was a child.
- I intend to go for a long run after my class.
- I see the earth rushing toward me right before I pull my parachute.
- I walk across the balance beam while staring at my feet.
- I stroke a backhand crosscourt with a dipping topspin.

Each of these sentences captures, in simple language, a phenomenological description. In each, the *I* shows that this is a first-person experience, the verb indicates the type of intentional activity described (e.g., memory, thought, perception), and each sentence includes an object of awareness (e.g., summers when I was a child, a long run). Of central importance, however, is the way in which we *conceive* of the objects of awareness. Notice that some of these claims are not factually true—the summers were no longer in the past, nor does the earth rush toward us—but they are true as subjective lived experience.

Take a moment to create your own phenomenological description of a lived experience that includes a first-person experience, an intentional activity, and an object of awareness. Describe an experience that was subjectively true as a lived experience but objectively false.

importance of the lived body in contrast to thinking about our bodies as "objective bodies" explained only through scientific knowledge and empirical facts. He points us to the "other knowledge which we have of our bodies [i.e., the body], in virtue of its always being with us." The lived body is how we exist in the world, which led Merleau-Ponty to conclude ultimately that "we are our body."

Such claims were important for those studying human movement. Particular branches of kinesiology—such as motor control, motor learning, and sport psychology, as well as philosophy—would eventually seize on phenomenology's focus on the intertwined nature of embodied thought, a perspective that provided Western philosophers with alternatives to dualism and materialism. For example, this intertwined concept was used in gerokinesiology, the study of human movement in aging adult populations, to show how the combination of declining eyesight and reduced nerve sensations in a person's feet contributes to the loss of balance. Phenomenology emphasizes that the person's lived experience of movement changes because that individual is feeling and seeing the world differently. This change can be disorienting because the sensory-movement patterns that a person has learned and habitually embodied since birth have now changed.

The focus on lived experience makes sense for those working in clinical and pedagogical settings. These phenomenologically oriented practitioners balance objective explanations that they read about in journal articles and lab reports with the values, hopes, goals, and experiences of their patients and clients. Because phenomenology focuses on subjective experience, this approach allows practitioners to relate better to people as they live their experiences. For example, a sport psychology consultant does better with a client who is experiencing anxiety if the client talks about feeling tightness in the chest and rapid, shallow breaths rather than

talking about increased brain activity in the neural substrate and the release of cortisol. Of course, all of these characteristics—the subjective experiences and the objective physiological conditions—are present during anxiety, but the first two (the chest tightness and rapid, shallow breaths) are lived experiences. Emotions and sensations, as well as cultural conditions, seem closer to our concerns about quality of life and self-understanding than do electrochemical explanations of our brain functioning or biochemical descriptions of our physiology.

Cold War Sport

While phenomenology restructured the postwar philosophical landscape, the Cold War geographical restructuring of the world's political and economic balance transformed the Soviet Union into a superpower. This shift created a major change in the Soviet Union's attitude toward participation in modern sport. Before World War II, the Soviets had generally refused to take part in what they labeled as bourgeois sport. Reflecting Joseph Stalin's contempt for the West, Soviet leaders declined to affiliate with international sport federations and, in most instances, boycotted direct competition with the Western, capitalist nations. Soviet leaders considered sport a subsidiary affair, subordinate to the intellectual, moral, and physical education of the communist worker. Rejecting the quantified, record-driven sport of their Western rivals, the Soviets favored mass participatory (*massovost*) sport, pageants, and military parades designed to promote national defense, social integration, health, hygiene, and nutrition.

The political realities of the Cold War, however, required the formulation of a different approach to sport. Acknowledging its symbolic and cultural power, Soviet leaders rejected the traditional model of mass collective physical culture in favor of modern, Western sport. Desperate to ensure propaganda victories, the Soviets developed a scientific and highly specialized system designed to prepare their athletes both physically and politically for their duties in international sporting competition. Under close supervision by state medical personnel and KGB (Soviet intelligence service) officers, talented Soviet athletes received financial payments for fictitious work—in order to maintain the amateur status then necessary for international competition—in the armed services or state industries. Many athletes were also state-supported full-time students (and would remain so throughout their athletic careers) who attended one of a network of 42 elite sport-performance boarding schools.

In these ways, Soviet leaders transformed their athletes into "ambassadors for socialism" tasked with the responsibility of bringing international prestige to the Soviet Union by triumphing over bourgeois states—especially the United States. Remarkably, the Soviets achieved immediate success in international competitions, especially the Olympics. At the first Olympics they entered, the 1952 summer games in Helsinki, they finished a close second behind the United States in the overall medal count by a score of 76 to 71. Thereafter, they dominated the standings at both the winter and summer Olympics, leading the medal count at Cortina and Melbourne in 1956, Squaw Valley and Rome in 1960, Innsbruck and Tokyo in 1964, Sapporo and Munich in 1972, and Innsbruck and Montreal in 1976, before the U.S.-led boycott of the 1980 Moscow Games followed by the Soviet-led boycott of the 1984 Los Angeles Games disrupted the head-to-head competition. During the Soviet era of domination, the United States managed only one overall medal-count victory, at Mexico City in 1968.

The sight of communist athletes challenging their ideological foes from the capitalist West provided modern sport with a dramatic appeal that enhanced its global popularity. Scholars have observed that the Cold War (East-versus-West) narrative enhanced modern sport as a mass public spectacle in three major areas: viewership, event size, and commercialization. Amid the Cold War clamor for international victory, high-performance sport dominated the landscape. In this atmosphere, athletes, coaches, and governments alike became increasingly results oriented, demanding victories over their Cold War rivals. Winning conferred prestige, and prestige enhanced power. Just as Cold War nations turned to their scientists in the race to put a human on the moon, they also used scientists in their race to the top of the Olympic podium and the World Cup charts. As a result, exercise physiologists, biomechanists, and psychologists became, in effect, coaches in lab coats. Their knowledge of human physical capabilities generated new standards of human performance. Indeed, modern audiences now take for granted the fact that international sport in the 21st century took its shape under the weight of the Cold War political and cultural battle for supremacy.

Modern Science and Sport

The application of science to sport and human performance predates the Cold War era. During the late 19th century, scientists turned to the modern sports of cycling and track and field as a laboratory for exploring the human capacity for endurance. Sport science and sports medicine later emerged as viable fields based on their military application during World War I. The pioneering advancements made in the human physiology laboratories at Harvard University, Yale University, and the University of Chicago helped to further legitimize scientific investigations into sport and human performance. Sport science witnessed another explosion of research in the years following World War II. Scientists in this era focused on endurance capacity, training adaptation, the effects of altitude, the maximum volume of oxygen that the body can use, work economy, and muscle velocity. They also explored whether sport performance could be boosted by pharmacological means such as anabolic steroids, blood transfusions, and amphetamines.

Coaches in Lab Coats

Although athletes had always striven for triumph, the seriousness with which elite competitors approached their craft increased dramatically during the Cold War years. Athletes, coaches, and governmental officials on both sides of the East–West divide flocked to sport science as a tool for improving performances and boosting national and ideological prestige. The field of sport science—including exercise physiology, biomechanics, pharmacology, and even psychology—became essential for athletes seeking to meet elite-level standards of performance. The latest technological, physiological, and pharmacological innovations found their way, often through state funding, onto training grounds and into locker rooms. Athletes enjoyed the benefits of specialized sport scientists, high-quality training facilities, and better coaching. Political leaders allocated more state resources to the science of high-performance sport in the hope that national sporting success would play well to audiences both at home and abroad.

State-Sponsored Doping

The Soviet Union and its satellite states pioneered advances in pharmacological interventions. Lavish state support extended beyond specialized coaching and training facilities to state-funded research on oral creatine for the purpose of enhancing muscle function and blood transfusions for the purpose of boosting aerobic endurance. As elements in a political institution, all Soviet sport facilities and clubs came under the absolute control of the state, which devised methods for discovering, nurturing, and harnessing sport talent. With the Kremlin overseeing

illicit doping and enhancement programs, cash-reward and subsidy schemes, and state-funded elite training schools, the Soviet Union dominated Olympic medal counts until the empire unraveled in the late 1980s and early 1990s. During the Cold War era at the Olympics, from 1952 through 1988, the Soviets won 393 gold medals and 1,009 total medals at the summer and winter Games as compared with 315 gold medals and 774 total medals for the United States.

In the German Democratic Republic (GDR), a Soviet satellite state in East Germany, politicians took the Soviet model of sport to greater extremes. There, they diverted sizable sums of state money and infrastructure toward scientifically identifying talent, developing youth into elite athletes, training coaches, and optimizing training routines. Under the joint direction of minister of sport Manfred Ewald and physician Manfred Höppner, the GDR initiated State Plan 14.25, a systematic state-sponsored doping program. From 1974 to 1988, the clandestine East German doping program provided Oral Turinabol, an anabolic steroid developed by the East German pharmaceutical company Jenapharm, to an estimated 10,000 athletes. The results were staggering. Through its state-controlled laboratories, the GDR—with a much smaller population than its rivals—became a global sporting powerhouse, achieving top-three finishes in the medal count at every summer and winter Olympic Games from 1972 to 1988.

The Soviets and their allies were not alone in applying governmental resources, scientific knowledge, and pharmacological substances to boost sport performance. The growing political currency of international sport victories also prompted the United States Olympic Committee (USOC) to establish a panel of experts to explore medical, nutritional, and pharmacological approaches considered taboo in training and performance. Eager to erode the governmental and pharmacological advantages enjoyed by athletes from communist countries, USOC staff member Ed Burke even facilitated blood transfusions for his cyclists at the 1984 Olympic Games in Los Angeles in the hope of securing victories on home soil. Although, with that singular exception, no evidence exists of a state-sponsored program of pharmacological drug enhancement in the United States, some U.S. athletes certainly used a variety of substances on an individual basis in an effort to remain competitive at the elite level.

Sport and the State

Over time, the growing failure of the United States to defeat the Soviet Union and its communist allies at the Olympics motivated the U.S. government to intervene directly in sporting affairs. On the surface, the state use of sport conflicted with the traditional U.S. belief that Olympic sport should be run by private, voluntary associations composed mostly of unpaid individuals and free from government interference. However, fears of national degeneracy and a perceived loss of physical vigor prompted the presidential administrations of Dwight D. Eisenhower and John F. Kennedy to formulate a sport policy focused on the mass participation and wellness of the entire U.S. citizenry. The recharging in 1963 of the President's Council on Physical Fitness (founded in 1956 as the President's Council on Youth Fitness and known today as the President's Council on Fitness, Sports, and Nutrition) signaled an attempt to address the falling standards of national fitness. Sport-for-all governmental initiatives, however, failed to stem the advances made by the Soviet Bloc.

The increasing regularity with which the Soviets stood atop the Olympic medal stand during the 1970s inspired the U.S. government to reevaluate its role in the country's domestic preparation for the Olympic Games. U.S. vice president Gerald Ford acknowledged the growing political currency of Olympic victory in a 1974 interview with *Sports Illustrated*: "It is not enough to just compete," Ford opined. "Winning is very important. Maybe more important than ever." Still, federal legislation awaited until 1978, when U.S. president Jimmy Carter signed the Amateur Sports Act, which comprehensively reorganized the U.S. elite-sport establishment and handed USOC the incredibly lucrative commercial rights to the five-ring Olympic logo in domestic markets. As a result of this unprecedented federal legislation, hundreds of millions of dollars were poured into the preparation and administration of U.S. Olympic efforts.

Science and governmental policies in the Cold War era pushed elite sport to dangerous, dehumanizing levels. As world and Olympic records fell, observers expressed concern about the health and well-being of elite athletes, who were viewed as victims in a grossly politicized race for medals. Indeed, the East German and Soviet doping programs administered drugs without the consent, or in some cases even the knowledge, of the athletes who took them. In the midst of widespread abuses, international sport federations tried to restore order and some semblance of respectability and fairness to elite sport. In 1961, the International Olympic Committee (IOC) created an anti-doping commission (which became the Medical Commission in 1968), published a lengthy list of prohibited substances, developed testing, and dispensed bans for those who violated its anti-doping rules. By the end of the of Cold War, the IOC's Medical Commission had established itself as a leading authority in anti-doping efforts and wielded a growing budget as well as increasingly sophisticated laboratory techniques for detecting prohibited substances.

The IOC's efforts had little effect on the practice, however, until the very end of the Cold War, when Soviet Bloc nations concluded that in the long run the West had a tremendous advantage in medical research and resources. That realization pushed the East to consent to more effective enforcement policies, although most experts agree that far fewer athletes were caught doping than engaged in the practice. As the Cold War ended, the IOC handed over responsibility for screening for impermissible performance enhancement to the World Anti-Doping Agency (WADA), a quasi-independent body founded in 1999 to monitor drug testing both in and out of competition.

The Ethics of Performance Enhancement

Cold War sport—with its results-oriented focus and increasing reliance on science and medicine for producing favorable results—provided the necessary ingredients for widespread use of performance-enhancing substances such as anabolic steroids, amphetamines, and blood transfusions. These drugs were banned by most sporting organizations, including the IOC. However, ethicists have debated whether doping bans are justified. Despite nearly universal agreement among sport institutions to ban doping, the ethical justification for such bans is much more complicated than many realize; in fact, these prohibitions raise fundamental philosophical issues.

First, philosophers point out that we must start by considering the right question. Questions such as "Is it unethical to use performance-enhancing substances?" and "Is doping cheating?" are misleading because the vast majority of sporting organizations *do prohibit* a common set of substances that can enhance an athlete's performance. Thus, the obvious answer to both questions is yes. So long as the rules prohibit their use and no extenuating circumstances exist, no persuasive case can be made for covert use.

At the same time, many philosophers stress the need to avoid circular reasoning in the doping debate. For example, arguments that doping is unethical sometimes seek to justify the claim by asserting that doping is unfair or constitutes "cheating." Naturally, philosophers might then ask, "Why is it cheating?" Most people would respond, "Because there are rules prohibiting doping." When pressed to explain why there are rules prohibiting doping, the critics may respond, "Because doping is unethical." This response completes the circle, and we are right back where we started.

This argument is circular and falls apart because it assumes (without saying so) that its own evidence is persuasive—namely, that doping is wrong. Circularity can be avoided by asking a better question: *Should* sporting organizations prohibit certain performance-enhancing substances? By asking whether sporting organizations *should* prohibit certain substances, ethicists can explore the doping question without assuming that the rules must exist. This new conversation produces two options: (1) Certain performance-enhancing substances can be ethically prohibited, and (2) certain performance-enhancing substances cannot be ethically prohibited. Either choice is potentially defensible and places the obligation on philosophers to provide justification for their recommendation.

Justifying the Bans on Doping

Many who argue in favor of such bans point out the health risks associated with the use of performance-enhancing substances. These risks seem inappropriate for sport, a recreational activity that is seemingly far less important than forms of work that are dangerous but necessary. Given that unnecessary health risks should be avoided, some ethicists argue that the bans reflect reasonable choices. Other ethicists, however, point out that banning performance-enhancing drugs over health concerns is inconsistent. All sports involve some degree of health risk, especially at the elite level. For example, why ban anabolic steroids due to a risk for heart disease while allowing NFL football in spite of risks for concussions and other serious health problems?

Some philosophers also reject doping bans on the grounds that such bans do not respect peoples' autonomy to make choices for themselves. That is, the bans are indefensibly paternalistic; they improperly restrict a person's freedom to make decisions even when those decisions may not be in their own best self-interest. After all, adults are allowed to make decisions about riding motorcycles, smoking cigarettes, and consuming alcohol—all of which carry significant risks. Why, then, should they not be allowed to make decisions about performance enhancement?

Of course, paternalism can be acceptable when protecting children, those who are uninformed, or those who are coerced, but these conditions do not necessarily apply to adult athletes. Philosopher John Stuart Mill argued that infringing on an adult's ability to make a free and informed decision—even if one suspects that the decision is not in the person's self-interest—places an unethical limit on his or her freedom. In this view, as long as one's behavior does not harm or infringe on the rights of others, that person should be free to choose his or her own course in life. In short, freedom lies at the heart of the good life.

Rejoinders to arguments about paternalism and autonomy run in two directions. First, the decision to use performance-enhancing substances may not meet Mill's standard of being fully informed and freely chosen. Because we do not know the long-term health risks for many substances, it is difficult for an athlete to be fully informed about them. Also, we know that if some athletes choose to use enhancements, then otherwise reluctant athletes may feel pressured to use them as well in order to continue competing on a level playing field. This choice is hardly free in the sense that Mill imagined.

Second, philosophers point out that sport is filled with rules that restrict what

people can do. Playing a sport means voluntarily agreeing to follow the rules, and if one of the rules prohibits doping, then players must follow that rule as well. Because we are free to choose to play the sport or not, anti-doping rules hardly constitute an unfair restriction of a person's freedom. It can also be argued that athletes are not coerced in any strong sense into taking enhancers. They are free to stay "clean," work harder, and compete in those conditions.

Doping and the Spirit of Sport

Finally, some philosophers have argued that doping violates what has been referred to as the "spirit of sport." This argument holds that something about the nature of sport is simply at odds with athletes using performance-enhancing substances; this position is taken by the World Anti-Doping Agency. Critics point out, however, that the spirit of sport is conceptually vague and may not really be so out of step with doping. What, in fact, is the spirit of sport? By what authority is something like this determined?

WADA asserts in its *World Anti-Doping Code* that the spirit of sport is characterized by the following elements:

- Health
- Excellence in performance
- Character and education
- Fun and joy
- Teamwork
- Dedication and commitment
- Respect for rules and laws
- Respect for self and other participants
- Courage
- Community and solidarity

Philosophers note some obvious problems with this statement. First, not all sports require teamwork. Second, some of the elements, such as respect for rules

Ethics of Banning Performance Enhancers

Student Exercise

We have outlined several arguments for and against the current bans on performance-enhancing drugs, but these are hardly all of the reasons that can be rallied in regard to this issue. List four arguments for each side—the strongest pro and con arguments mentioned in this text and two additional arguments that you identify on your own. Then weigh the strengths of the arguments to decide whether sporting organizations should prohibit certain performance-enhancing substances for adult athletes. Explain the reasoning behind your conclusion.

and laws, run into the problem of circular argument. Third, as revealed by the Cold War clashes, elite sport hardly seems to be about fun, joy, or health. Most important, it can be argued that an athlete who is willing to risk his or her health by using performance-enhancing substances demonstrates commitment to excellence, courage, and dedication rather than detracting from those ideals. To be sure, if any substance were a "magic bullet" or otherwise served as a substitute for dedication and hard work, then the spirit-of-sport argument might be stronger. However, no such enhancer is yet available, and some athletes who have used steroids, for instance, have noted that such use allows them to recover faster from practice regimens and thus work even harder than other athletes.

So, do performance-enhancing substances belong in sport? Most ethicists argue that they do not, though some disagree. Both sides acknowledge that the debate is far more complicated than it may at first seem. And even if the prohibition of certain performance-enhancing substances is supported, many philosophers argue that current anti-doping policies should be improved to better protect athletes' rights to due process and medical privacy.

Breaking Gender Barriers

The intensity of the Cold War sporting conflicts between East and West posed new ethical challenges for sport in the second half of the 20th century and into the 21st century. The propaganda value of victories also increased opportunities for certain groups, especially women, to compete in what had historically been a bastion of male privilege. Governments and sport officials on both sides of the Iron Curtain came to the realization that the victories of female athletes held the same weight as those of men in the medals race for national supremacy. From a propaganda perspective, both the communists and the capitalists argued that the participation and success of female athletes reflected the ideological superiority of their respective ways of life.

Having this gender logic in mind from the outset, the Soviet Union expended considerable resources to bolster the size of its female contingent. At the 1952 Helsinki Olympic Games, the Soviet Union selected 40 females, who composed 13 percent of the team. By the 1988 Seoul Games, the number of women ballooned to 162, who made up 32 percent of the team. The United States also recruited female athletes to defend American pride against a growing wave of Soviet sporting victories by women. From a mere 41 female athletes, who made up 14 percent of the team in 1952, the U.S. delegation grew to include 195 women in 1988, accounting for 32 percent of the team.

In terms of race, although the United States had historically (since the 1930s) bolstered its Olympic success by including black male athletes even as they faced racial discrimination at home, the Cold War rivalry expanded opportunities for black female athletes on the U.S. Olympic team. Still, these opportunities continued to reflect racial divides, as white American women flocked to sports that were considered "feminine," such as diving and swimming, while women of color filled the void in the widely perceived "masculine" sport of track and field. Thus, even as black female athletes served their nation by earning medals and scoring points, their triumphs were used to reinforce stereotypes of African American women as less feminine than their white counterparts. Still, through Olympic prowess, a number of African American women became Cold War heroines, including Alice Coachman in the 1940s; Willye White in the 1950s; Wilma Rudolph in the 1960s; and Evelyn Ashford, Jackie Joyner-Kersee, and Florence Griffith Joyner in the 1980s.

The Intersectionality of Race and Gender

Women of color have long faced biases in sport that highlight the important need to appreciate how intersectionality influences discrimination in sport. Intersectionality involves the interconnected nature of social categorizations such as race, class, sexual orientation, religion, and gender as they are applied to a given individual or group and create overlapping and interdependent systems of discrimination or disadvantage. Thus, whereas white women have faced sexism in their efforts to claim their rightful place in sport, black, Asian, Native American, and Latina women have faced not just sexism but racialized sexism, which includes not only racism and sexism but also discrimination compounded by their racialized gender.

In the case of black women, American assumptions about race long precluded their entrance into many traditional feminine sports, such as gymnastics, diving, tennis, and golf. One notable counterexample was tennis great Althea Gibson, who dominated women's tennis in the 1950s and broke many racial barriers while facing persistent discrimination in the United States. She became the first black athlete—man or woman—to play in the U.S. Open, then broke another barrier by winning the tournament in 1957. However, it was only after a 42-year gap, when Serena Williams won the U.S. Open in 1999, that Gibson's feat would be duplicated by another African American woman.

From Gibson's perspective, not even her talent or the nascent civil rights movement erased discrimination against her. "When I looked around me, I saw that white tennis players, some of whom I had thrashed on the court, were picking up offers and invitations," she wrote in her autobiography. "Suddenly it dawned on me that my triumphs had not destroyed the racial barriers once and for all, as I had—perhaps naively—hoped. Or if I did destroy them, they had been erected behind me again." That Gibson's white colleagues received better sponsorship deals than their more talented peer illustrates how intersectionality can compound discrimination for women of color. Female athletes in the 1950s and 1960s already received far less prize money and fewer endorsement opportunities than did their male counterparts, and black women such as Gibson received only a fraction of the sponsorship payments offered to white women in that era.

More than 50 years later, both female and male African American athletes continue to face similar challenges. Although a handful of black male athletes, beginning with Michael Jordan and Tiger Woods in the 1990s, have come to earn as much as or more than their white counterparts in off-the-field endorsement contracts, black women are only beginning to break through. For example, in spite of winning considerably more major tennis titles in the past two decades than her white rival Maria Sharapova, Serena Williams earned

Intersectionality and Discrimination

Student Exercise

Ethicists have argued that sport has a moral obligation to be an inclusive space. Yet it has been the scene of discrimination against, among others, women of color and other intersectional groups. What other examples can you identify where overlapping social categorizations can make sport seem like an unwelcoming environment for some people? Consider aspects of identity beyond gender and race, including ethnicity, social class, sexual orientation, religion, and disability. Next, have you ever felt that you did not belong in a certain sport because of your identity? What does it say to you when no one who shares your identity is playing a particular sport?

---

less in endorsement contracts until she finally topped Sharapova's off-the-court income in 2016.

In addition, although sport has made great strides toward inclusion, women of color still face discrimination in many traditionally feminine sports. For example, in 2013, Simone Biles became the first black woman to win the all-around title at the World Gymnastics Championships (and she would go on to win Olympic gold at the 2016 Rio Games). Biles' success at the World Championships was derided by some. After Italian gymnast Carlotta Ferlito made a poor joke about needing to paint her skin black in order to beat Biles, an Italian gymnastics official defended Ferlito by saying, "Carlotta was referring to a trend in gymnastics at this moment, which is going towards a technique that opens up new chances to athletes of color (well-known for power) while penalizing the more artistic Eastern European style that allowed Russians and Romanians to dominate the sport for years" (quoted in Hersh).

Such claims, which embody racialized stereotypes as well as culturally constructed notions of femininity, serve as a harsh reminder of the fact that women of color still face both explicit and tacit forms of racism. Elite female athletes of color such as Williams and Biles face racialized assumptions that tie their strength and power to their skin color rather than to their talent (for more on this topic, see the discussion of the book *Darwin's Athletes* later in this chapter). At the same time, vague critiques about lacking style and grace—especially in sports where subjective judging plays a role, such as ice skating, diving, and gymnastics—diminish the femininity of women of color while sending the covert message that they do not belong in these supposedly white sports.

Expanding Sport, Increasing Challenges

During this era, female athletes competed not only in greater numbers but also across a broader range of sport disciplines as the Cold War opened the door for the addition of new events for women to the Olympic program. From 1952 to 1988, 13 events for women were added, including volleyball (1964), basketball (1976), and field hockey (1980). The inclusion of a marathon event for women at the 1984 Olympic Games in Los Angeles signified another step on the slow march towards gender equality. Inspired by the trailblazing feats of Kathrine Switzer, who had registered for the 1967 Boston Marathon under the alias "K.V. Switzer" and completed the arduous 26.2-mile (42.2-kilometer) course much to the disgust of the male meet officials, an entire generation of female long-distance runners pressured the IOC to include the women's marathon on the program in Los Angeles.

Unfortunately, the increased participation opportunities for women during the Cold War failed to translate into full equality. Women still endured second-class status. They were subjected to demeaning

TOO SEXY FOR MY COURT

Historical Profile

Women's sexuality in sport has often raised social concerns, especially in regard to the uniforms worn by women during competition. Historically, sporting organizations (often controlled by men) have passed uniform rules requiring modest dress for women. At the same time, the uniforms prescribed for women often differ from those worn by men in order to highlight women's gender; examples include skirts in women's field hockey and lacrosse. More recently, controversy has emerged as women's uniforms have increasingly highlighted female athletes' sex appeal. Many have noticed the increase in women wearing sport bras and spandex in fitness and track-and-field events. Similarly, in beach volleyball, women often wear bikinis, whereas men typically opt for basketball-length shorts and tank tops.

Bikini uniforms are not a matter of performance or function but rather one of aesthetics, which in this case highlight women's sexuality. Though many acknowledge that the revealing bikinis have increased the viewership for women's beach volleyball, some have argued that it has also drawn attention away from the athletes' talent while objectifying their sexuality for the male gaze. In addition, women from cultures where customs and laws require more modest dress—in

© Goran Bogicevic/fotolia.com

Current clothing trends, in contrast to more conservative 1950s uniforms, have raised ethical questions about ways to promote women's sport.

particular, a group of Muslim nations—have complained that the bikini requirements excluded them from beach volleyball. At the same time, many female professional beach volleyball players wish to keep the bikini. Even though the *Fédération Internationale de Volleyball* (FIVB) removed its bikini requirement in 2012, the vast majority of women still wear that type of uniform. As explained by decorated Olympian Misty May-Treanor, "People might come out to our sport at first because they see the bikinis . . . but they change their tune when they see our athleticism."

However, it is easy to see how the culture of bikinis in beach volleyball might draw criticism beyond that of unwanted sexual objectification of women. For instance, seeing only athletes wearing bikinis, some women who might wish to play beach volleyball may choose not to do so because of cultural or religious reasons. Other women may fear receiving comments about their body or being subject to "fat shaming." And even with FIVB loosening the rules, some women may wish to play in other clothing but fear sticking out for their choice if bikinis remain the norm.

Proper Dress for Sport

Student Exercise

How should sporting organizations decide what attire athletes can wear? Explore this issue by answering the following questions.

- Should some clothing be considered too sexy for the court, pool, or field?
- Is it ethical for sport leaders to market athletes' sex appeal in order to build a fan base?
- What ethical difference, if any, exists between the scanty swimsuits worn by male divers and the "uniforms" worn in women's beach volleyball?
- Who should decide what uniforms athletes wear? Sport officials? Athletes themselves? Why?

conversations and stereotypes concerning race, femininity, and sexuality. The sight of a strong, athletic woman exposed deep-seated cultural anxieties and struck at the heart of male dominance in Western society. As a result, women continued to face cultural prejudice and wrestle with sexual discrimination. Invoking historical stereotypes, male observers, coaches, officials, and media scribes branded female athletes with the pejorative "lesbian label"; disparaged those who fell short of a traditionally feminine, sexually alluring appearance; and accused those who achieved feats of remarkable athleticism and success of biological abnormality. In particular, the pursuit of excellence by muscular and bulky Soviet sportswomen elicited deep consternation and ridicule among Western audiences who celebrated petite builds and grace as signifiers of athletic femininity. Cultural commentators in the West decried the victories of "strong Red ladies" and cast muscular Soviets as suspicious cheaters. The success of the masculine female "other" even aroused fears that the communists had employed male imposters to invade women's events.

Responding to mounting Western accusations, the then-named International Amateur Athletics Federation (IAAF; called now the International Association of Athletics Federations) ruled that all female competitors must prove their womanhood prior to participation. In 1966, to satisfy this standard, the IAAF implemented what came to be known as the "nude parade," which required women to submit to visual inspection in front of a mostly male panel of supposed experts. Soon afterward, the IAAF replaced visual inspection with a chromosome check, and Cold War anxieties persuaded the IOC to follow suit in 1968. This introduction of sex testing, or gender verification, offered reassurance to Western audiences that only "real" women—that is, those who upheld normative notions of heterofemininity—could compete.

Ethics of Gender Verification

The use of sex testing, or gender verification, originally intended to combat the fear that some countries might try to sneak men into women's events quickly gave way to concerns that certain women might have an unfair advantage due to their naturally elevated levels of testosterone. These concerns relate both to the complicated biology involved in sex differences between males and females and to the dominant cultural assumption about gender—namely, that people fit neatly into the rigid binary categories of male and female, when in fact some individuals defy such simple categorization. Sport often follows this cultural tendency in dividing events by gender.

Gender is defined as a cultural construction based loosely on sex traits tied to reproduction, as well cultural norms, characteristics, and behaviors. In contrast, a person's sex is often considered in relation to biology, which is expressed by sex chromosomes, often as XX or XY. However, nature is much more complicated than this mere binary can accommodate. Roughly 1 in 100 people qualify as intersex, meaning either that their chromosome makeup is XXY, XYY, XXX, or another variation or that they have a naturally occurring condition such as androgen insensitivity syndrome (AIS), which makes a person unreceptive to male androgens. Many females with AIS have elevated levels of testosterone, yet their cells are unable to bind with the androgen, thus maintaining a typical female physiology.

In sport, the issue of elevated testosterone has driven unfounded concerns that intersex women might have an unfair advantage that should disqualify them from competing as women. The use of chromosomal sex tests to remove women from competition has threatened to leave some women on the sidelines. Two examples are Spanish hurdler Maria José Martínez-Patiño and South African middle-distance runner Caster Semenya. In particular, Semenya's case provoked widespread criticism of gender verification policies. Critics stressed that Semenya, who has identified as a female her entire life, should be allowed to compete in her gender category.

More broadly, scholars argued that the focus on intersex women with elevated testosterone is flawed. Evidence indicates that many intersex women are insensitive to the androgen and therefore do not benefit from elevated levels of testosterone. Yet sporting authorities have debated whether, in order to be eligible to compete, such women should be required to undergo medical procedures such as hormone therapy or surgery—deemed unnecessary since the women's health is not at risk—or should simply be asked to compete in the men's category.

The focus on women's testosterone levels is also inconsistent. Even if it did confer an advantage, the advantage would fall within the normally accepted range of advantages offered to athletes. For example, many female athletes benefit from being tall, yet no one argues that a woman who is 6 feet 4 inches (1.9 meters) tall—and thus taller than 99 percent of men—should be prohibited from competing as a woman. It would be equally absurd to ask a woman who has a larger-than-average lung capacity or higher-than-normal hematocrit to compete as a man. Yet these latter examples are all by-products of genetics that confer a sporting advantage.

The vast majority of scholars have concluded that sporting organizations should not be in the business of deciding who is a woman and thus should do away with gender verification tests. Few see any substantial threat from men trying to compete in women's sport; nor do there seem to be compelling reasons for preventing intersex women from competing against other women. More to the point, the debate highlights how anxieties about gender and misunderstandings of science can disenfranchise some women from participating in sport. It also provides a powerful example of how philosophy grounded in kinesiology can contribute to the handling of practical issues in sport.

The Battle of the Sexes

During the Cold War, women gained more opportunities to participate in sport but continued to face a variety of challenges. Women's sport continued to suffer under the governance of patriarchal sporting bodies and outmoded assumptions about gender, femininity, and physical capability. However, women were not passive victims; to the contrary, female athletes rallied behind the banner of gender equality and opportunity in sport during the second half of the 20th century. The fight for financial parity emerged as a marquee issue among an increasingly self-confident band of women's rights advocates. The discrepancies in pay between the sexes were stark. For instance, during the late 1960s, female tennis players competed in professional tournaments that offered only 10 percent of the prize money offered to their male counterparts.

California-born female tennis player Billie Jean King spearheaded the fight for fair and equal pay. Over the course of a legendary professional career, in which she amassed 12 major singles titles and reigned as the world number one, King demonstrated a remarkable degree of resilience and determination. She organized mass boycotts of low-paying professional events, persuaded the Philip Morris tobacco company to finance the creation of the Virginia Slims tennis circuit for women, and, in perhaps the defining moment of her professional career, defeated former men's Wimbledon singles champion Bobby Riggs in a famous match that came to be known as the Battle of the Sexes. On September 20, 1973, before a sold-out crowd of 30,000 spectators at the Houston Astrodome, as well as more than 48 million television viewers, King defeated the self-professed "male chauvinist pig" Riggs in straight sets to the acclaim of female athletes around the globe.

King's victory, and the publicity it generated, enticed a number of commercial sponsors to begin funding women's sporting events, including women's golf. During the 1980 season, the Ladies Professional Golf Association (LPGA) staged 21 tournaments boasting a combined prize total of $5 million—a dramatic increase from the $435,000 offered just 10 years earlier. Still, despite the efforts of King and a generation of female activist-athletes to narrow the pay gap, women's sport in the 21st century continues to lag far behind men's competition with regard to publicity, media exposure, funding, coaching, and playing opportunities.

At the same time that King and her allies were fighting for equality in professional tennis, the U.S. Congress passed a landmark bill known as the Education Amendments of 1972. The legislation did not primarily target discrimination in sport but focused broadly on discrimination in educational opportunities. Addressing the issue of sex discrimination, one part of the law, commonly known as Title IX, declared that federally funded U.S. educational institutions could no longer discriminate on the basis of sex. Here is the crucial text, quoted from the Women's Sports Foundation:

> *No person in the United States shall, on the basis of sex, be excluded from participation in, be denied the benefit of, or be subject to discrimination under any educational program or activity receiving Federal financial assistance.*

Although the law did not mention athletics, U.S. educational institutions had for decades sponsored sporting activities. Therefore, it soon became clear that Title IX carried profound implications for interscholastic and intercollegiate athletics programs that had historically marginalized and neglected women's sport. As a result, Title IX almost immediately sparked a revolution in women's sport.

Transgender Athletes

Among the many credits due to Billie Jean King for her activism, her effort to make sport inclusive for transgender athletes has often passed unnoticed. In 1976, the United States Tennis Association (USTA) moved to block Renée Richards, who had previously undergone gender reassignment surgery, from playing in the U.S. Open. Richards, who had transitioned in 1975 from male to female at the age of 40, entered a tennis tournament in 1976. While her tall frame and powerful left-handed serve drew attention to her talent, a reporter received a tip from a fan that she had previously lived as a man. The story became a national headline—"Women's Winner Was a Man"—and sparked the USTA's decision to require a genetic test for

TITLE IX: ASSESSING THE ATHLETICS REVOLUTION

Historical Profile

The passage of the Education Amendments of 1972 by the U.S. Congress ushered women's sport in the United States into a dramatic new period of opportunity and growth. Although it took years to settle the law's exact meaning, Title IX stipulated that federally funded educational institutions must prohibit discrimination in all educational programs and activities, including sport. By a 1979 determination of the then-named Department of Health, Education, and Welfare (the agency designated to oversee the law's implementation), complying with Title IX means that schools must pass at least one element of a three-pronged test: (1) offer sport opportunities for men and women in proportion to the populations being served, (2) meet demonstrated need and interest, or (3) show improvement in developing a gender-equitable athletics program.

Despite widespread opposition from the National Collegiate Athletic Association (NCAA), which opposed the ruling on the grounds that it would negatively affect profitable and prosperous male athletics programs, Title IX sparked surging rates of female participation. For example, since 1972, female participation in high school sport has increased by more than 900 percent. Aided by athletics scholarships, women's intercollegiate sport has also grown at an exponential rate. Women now account for 34 percent of all intercollegiate athletes and receive about one-third of all college athletics scholarships.

Despite enjoying the financial benefits, enhanced media exposure, and increased participation opportunities afforded through the NCAA's governance of women's sport, scholars caution that Title IX has also fallen short in meeting some of its objectives. For instance, more than 40 years after its passage, women still make up only one-third of all high school and collegiate varsity athletes, even though they account for more than half of the students at all levels of education, from elementary school through college. More alarming still, men's athletics programs receive twice as much scholarship money as women's programs, three times more in operating funds, and five times more in recruiting expenses. Yet widespread Title IX violations and failure to meet gender equity standards are rarely met with NCAA sanctions.

Title IX and the subsequent NCAA takeover of women's intercollegiate athletics has also had a deleterious effect on the number of women holding leadership positions in sport. In the years prior to Title IX, 90 percent of women's intercollegiate teams were coached by women. Today, that number stands at less than 50 percent, as male coaches have embraced women's sport as a viable and profitable career option. Women sport administrators have fared even worse. Today, women hold only 31 percent of all administrative positions—a stark contrast to the pre–Title IX era, when women held almost sole authority over women's sport.

For these reasons, scholars contend that the promise of an athletics revolution for women has not yet come to fruition. Therefore, the fight for full gender equality in sport continues to be waged at many levels.

all of its women entrants. Richards, who had not planned to enter the U.S. Open, balked at the idea that she would be tested and potentially prohibited from entering women's tournaments. She took her case to court, and physicians supporting her claim explained to both the court and the public the nature of gender reassignment surgery. They testified that Richards' physique was within the normal female range and that her hormones had decreased her muscle mass and altered her muscle-to-fat ratio so that it also fell within the typical female range.

At the same time, the proceedings made Richards the first professional athlete to identify publicly as transgender. Many believed that she still had advantages from having been a male, and quite a few women players in tennis felt uncomfortable about her joining their ranks. Richards eventually won a landmark decision in 1977 from the New York State Supreme Court that both ensured her right to participate and provided legislative cover for the transgender athletes that followed in her footsteps. Although the merits of the case supported Richards, many still believe that it was the signed affidavit from Billie Jean King, the greatest women's tennis player in the world at the time, that swung the case in Richards' favor. King also went to great lengths to ensure that the women on the tennis circuit welcomed Richards, who eventually played five seasons and reached a top-20 ranking in the world.

Like many women, Richards describes herself as a reluctant pioneer; she is ambivalent about her status as a transgender icon and often wishes she had opted for a private life of anonymity. Still, her groundbreaking efforts blazed the trail for another American sporting icon. The same year that Richards took up her case against the USTA, a U.S. athlete who competed with the name Bruce Jenner won a gold medal with a world-record performance in the decathlon at the 1976 Montreal Olympics. Some 40 years later, long after completing a sterling career as an elite athlete, Jenner transitioned to female and changed her name to Caitlyn. Jenner's transition and her activism on behalf of transgender people has increased public knowledge about gender-nonconforming people. It has also highlighted ethical considerations related to bias favoring cisgender people (individuals whose birth sex matches their gender identity) in sport.

Efforts to make sport inclusive for all people have generated concerns about issues ranging from locker-room access to one's eligibility to compete in one's desired gender category. Some of these challenges are amenable to easy solutions. For example, physical education instructors can choose to divide students by ability rather than by gender in order to avoid asking gender-nonconforming students to choose between playing as a boy and playing as a girl. In addition, sport facilities could include private, gender-neutral changing rooms to accommodate all athletes who desire privacy, regardless of their gender identity.

Yet ethicists have noted that one's choice of gender for participation in sport is a complicated question. Of course, this would not be a significant matter if sport did not separate participants by gender. However, men and women often compete separately in order to ensure that both have fair competitions. Men tend to have certain biological attributes that, in some sports, give them an advantage over women. Female athletes have raised concerns, similar to those made against Richards, that transgender women have an unfair advantage when competing in the women's category.

Some sport organizations, most prominently the IOC, have created rules to establish minimum levels of time for which a person must have lived as a woman with hormones typical of women before competing as a woman. Some sports require sex-reassignment surgery, though in 2015 the IOC jettisoned this requirement from its guidelines. Although such policies are intended to promote inclusion, they may set up barriers. The fact that as of 2016 no openly transgender athlete has yet competed at the Olympics suggests that these policies create a de facto barrier that cisgender athletes do not face. For an athlete to transition, he or she must often spend a year away from sport, thus losing a year of competition and training time. Regulations regarding testosterone stoke concerns similar to those raised about intersex athletes. In addition, many athletes, especially during adolescence and college, wish to continue playing sport while wrestling with their gender identity.

Therefore, many philosophers have argued that the only criteria for competing in a given gender classification should be one's self-identification as a member of that gender. Another recommendation is for more sports to be conducted as gender-neutral competitions. For example, it seems unnecessary to mount separate competitions for men and women in sports such as curling, shooting, archery, and ultra-endurance running and swimming (where women have some potential physiological advantage over men). Still, many observers acknowledge that at certain elite levels, imbalances between genders may make gendered competition preferable. In such events, ethicists might argue that the desire to ensure a level playing field needs to be taken seriously. They might claim further that sex-related differences must be measured without bias and that policies related to differences between athletes must be consistent. As addressed in chapters 3 and 6, unearned advantage poses a threat to the very purpose of sport competition.

The Cold War and the Politics of Race in American Sport

During the second half of the 20th century, powerful movements developed in the United States not only to advocate for the equality of women but also to champion equal treatment of nonwhites. The rallying cries for Americans to sacrifice during World War II had included the contention that Nazi Germany and Imperial Japan promoted racist ideologies while the U.S.-led allies championed racial and ethnic equality. The rhetoric did not match reality. Even at the end of the war, the U.S. military remained a racially segregated fighting force, and, in many parts of the United States minority groups were denied—either by law or by custom—basic rights such as the ability to vote. In the American South, a myriad of laws provided legal cover for racial discrimination, and in other regions various traditions and habits excluded many people, especially African Americans, from the full promises of citizenship. From the war emerged a powerful civil rights movement that pushed to end segregation against blacks and other minority groups and challenged racism in every facet of American life.

Important opportunities to advance the cause of civil rights arose during the Cold War. In the struggle between the United States and the Soviet Union for the allegiance of the developing world, American racism offered a powerful opening for Soviet propaganda efforts. When African, Asian, and Latin American diplomats found themselves excluded from many hotels in the U.S. capital, it became even more difficult to defend the claim that the United States stood for democracy and equality around the world.

In response, the U.S. government devised initiatives to defuse the global criticism of racism in the United States. In this propaganda counteroffensive, sport played a prominent role. In particular, the U.S. State Department regularly recruited leading black athletes as cultural ambassadors and sent them on goodwill tours around the globe. Among the most prominent figures were internationally famous Olympians such as Jesse Owens and Wilma Rudolph, as well as tennis champion Arthur Ashe and the Harlem Globetrotters basketball team. Federal bureaucrats calculated that the recruitment of black athletes would enable them to transmit images of a democratic and equalitarian America to global audiences and thus help counter the supposedly fallacious propaganda espoused by the communists.

Despite the U.S. government's carefully scripted version of the United States as a land of democracy, the realities of inequality and racial discrimination remained. Segregation and racism pervaded postwar American sport. In college football, for example, with the exception of "Negro colleges" and a handful of universities outside of the legally segregated South, black players were few and far between. The National Football League also remained a whites-only enterprise until Kenny Washington and Woody Strode broke the long-standing color barrier during the 1946 season.

The quest to erase color lines in American sport took place most prominently in what was then the nation's most popular pastime: baseball. For decades, Major League Baseball (MLB) had maintained and enforced a rigid policy of racial segregation that traced back to the mid-1880s and the implementation of a gentleman's agreement among team owners not to hire African American players. Several tentative plans to integrate MLB had earlier faltered under the weight of racist sentiment, but the changing racial climate of the early Cold War era provided an opportunity for significant change. In this context, Branch Rickey, president of the Brooklyn Dodgers, aspired to succeed where others had failed. He devised a plan, a "great experiment" of sorts, in which he would cast one pioneering black player in the role of racial integrator. He sought a player with the temperament and maturity to withstand the racial venom that the integration of baseball would surely unleash.

Rickey found his man in 26-year-old Jackie Robinson, a multisport star at the University of California, Los Angeles (UCLA), and a military officer during World War II. Rickey promptly signed Robinson to a professional contract and sent the California native on a year's stint with the minor-league Montreal Royals during the 1946 season. Robinson's impressive .349 season batting average earned him a call-up to the majors for the following year. Robinson's entry into the major leagues led rather than reflected the civil rights movement that began to gather steam in the aftermath of World War II. When Robinson took his position in the infield for the Dodgers, all of the other monumental achievements of the civil rights struggle remained in the future—the desegregation of the U.S. military, the dismantling of legalized discrimination, the integration of most public arenas of American life, and the Congressional acts that would shore up voting rights and other legal guarantees for all citizens regardless of race. Thus baseball, the American national pastime, provided a crucial site in the struggle to change hearts and minds both at home and abroad.

Jackie Robinson embodied a rare blend of athletic ability, versatility, intelligence, maturity, youthful promise, and fierce tenacity. He needed to call on these attributes on April 15, 1947, when he broke the unofficial color barrier in professional baseball. Despite Robinson's ability to perform exceptionally in the face of a torrent of racial abuse, physical intimidation, and threats to his life from rival fans and opposing players, the role of racial pioneer was a heavy burden. Robinson experienced loneliness, isolation, anger, and resentment. Segregated from his teammates on the road, in the team hotel, and in restaurants—and stirred by rumors that opposing players were mobilizing to strike in protest of the appearance of an African American in the majors—Robinson fought off despair in order to shine between the chalk-white lines of the baseball diamond.

Transcending the barriers placed in his path, Robinson's equanimity and calmness under pressure inspired a legend. His on-field intelligence, competitive flair, and combination of base-stealing and bunting skills both intimidated and demoralized opposing players and fans. Robinson's league-leading batting average and Rookie of the Year honors in the 1947 season revealed to all but the most recalcitrant observers that he belonged in the majors. During his 10-year professional career,

Robinson helped win six National League pennants and compiled a .311 lifetime batting average, earning him a place in the National Baseball Hall of Fame.

Through his professionalism, poise, and talent, Robinson blazed a trail for other young black athletes to follow. By the time he retired in 1956, major league rosters included a considerable number of black players, including Willie Mays and Hank Aaron. In other sports, the Cleveland Browns' Jim Brown was about to transform the NFL with his repertoire of powerful running and unprecedented speed, and basketball player Bill Russell was beginning the Hall of Fame career during which he would lead the Boston Celtics to 11 NBA titles.

Even with these successes, the road to full racial equality—both in sport and in wider society—was long, difficult, and strewn with obstacles. Baseball's great experiment proved difficult to implement not only in the larger American society but even in the arena of sport. Although the landmark 1954 ruling by the U.S. Supreme Court in *Brown v. Board of Education of Topeka* prohibited the enforced segregation of schools, racism persisted. On the field, black athletes faced the harsh realities of racial bias and systematic racism. They were tracked, or "stacked," into less central positions with fewer decision-making responsibilities (e.g., running back and wide receiver in football), received considerably smaller professional salaries than their white counterparts, and were denied opportunities to hold leadership positions both on and off the field (e.g., team captain, coach, administrator). Slowly, over decades, some of these barriers began to erode, but racial conflicts persist even in the 21st century in both sport and society.

The Debate Over the "Sports Gene"

In the past, the success of black athletes such as Jackie Robinson led to numerous theories that linked athletic success to genetic aspects of race (for more on the origins of these notions, see chapter 10). Such notions persist today. For example, people often try to tie Jamaican dominance in sprint events or Kenyan excellence in distance running to some biological foundation coded in racial genetics. Others point to the supremacy of black athletes in professional basketball and football as proof of the notion that a "sports gene" possessed by certain ethnic groups accounts for their dominance in particular athletic pursuits.

However accurate such claims may appear, the evidence does not support the purported links between race and athletic talent. First, both philosophers and scientists have argued that the concept of race itself is difficult to pin down. Scientists cannot find common genetic threads that could form an essence or basis for such a category. In addition, from a genetic point of view, our species is very young (originating about 150,000 years ago) and not particularly diverse as compared with many other species. In fact, we are far more alike in our DNA than we are different. Indeed, DNA researchers have argued that humans—all seven billion of us—are descended from a common ancestor, dubbed Mitochondrial Eve, who lived in Africa about 150,000 years ago.

Moreover, the factors commonly thought of as marking race—for example, skin color, hair texture, eye shape, and geographical origin—have proven to be so nebulous and widespread that asserting discrete boundaries between races becomes impossible. Even so, people with mixed racial backgrounds, such as Tiger Woods, often get assigned to one race by their culture, which ignores their complex heritage. These complexities have led scholars to argue that race is a social construction that takes its force from the beliefs and values that societies read into it. As a social construction, it is no less real and painful for the people who suffer discrimination based on this human-made category, but it does not have a foundation in our fundamental biology.

A particularly useful example of this point can be found in the claim that a so-called sports gene explains the current sporting prowess of people of African descent. Scientists have largely debunked the notion that what we commonly refer to as "race" plays any role in athletic talent; in fact, the biological variations that make great athletes appear to be unconnected to any sort of racial genealogy. Scholars have also noted that the particular links purported to exist between race, intelligence, and athletic talent have played to racialized stereotypes held by particular groups. For example, Western Europeans used to explain black athletes' lack of success against white athletes as proof of white racial superiority. Later, as black athletes defeated their white counterparts, new claims emerged that black athletes had certain advantages over white athletes that explained their success.

Yet, as historian John Hoberman notes in *Darwin's Athletes*, these narratives often focus only on black athletes and often work to perpetuate the myth of race and racial stereotypes. Few try to explain Scandinavians' dominance in Nordic skiing on the basis of their whiteness, and no one tries to explain Chinese dominance in table tennis on the basis of the players' "Asianness." Moreover, linking an athlete's talent to race is particularly disturbing because it diminishes the athlete's ability to take credit for his or her achievements. Jackie Robinson did not become a great baseball player *because* he was black; rather, he became a great baseball player *despite* the fact that he was black at a time when black people faced systematic discrimination and disadvantages in the United States. This is a reason, then, that we should avoid linking athletic success to race.

Black Power

By the 1960s, the growing demands from civil rights leaders and liberal politicians for full racial equality exposed the prevalence of racism in American sport. Influenced by the countercultural spirit of the era, black organizations and black athletes challenged social norms and the social order, often through radical and subversive efforts. They broke free from the shackles of conformity and raised their collective voices in the name of equality and fairness. For example, world heavyweight boxing champion Cassius Clay led the "revolt of the black athlete," which challenged exploitation and threatened the status quo through a blend of passion, protest, and vocal defiance. Clay joined the Nation of Islam, changed his name to Muhammad Ali, defied the Vietnam draft, and angrily decried police brutality and racial injustice. Ali became an emblem of self-assertion and a spokesman for black America, Black Nationalism, and antiwar sentiment.

Ali inspired an entire generation of black athletes and black sport leaders to join the fight against racial prejudice and inequality, both in sport and in wider society. In particular, Ali raised the consciousness of college athletes and students on campuses across the United States. In October 1967, students at San Jose State College, led by sociology professor Harry Edwards, formed the Olympic Project for Human Rights (OPHR) as a response to what they perceived as discriminatory practices prevailing at college campuses nationwide. A number of prospective African American Olympic athletes joined Edwards in threatening to boycott the forthcoming 1968 Mexico City Olympic Games unless officials met their demands for, among other things, fair on-campus housing, multiracial fraternities, the hiring of black coaches and athletics administrators, and the introduction of courses in African American history and literature.

The proposed boycott generated fierce opposition, and, with the exception of UCLA All-American basketball star Lew Alcindor (who soon thereafter completed his conversion to Islam and took the name Kareem Abdul-Jabbar) and a few of his fellow collegians, most black athletes reluctantly agreed to compete in Mexico City. Undeterred, the OPHR altered its goal from boycott to protest. Most notably, when 200-meter sprinters Tommie Smith and John Carlos took to the Olympic podium to receive their gold and bronze medals, they stunned the world with a powerful gesture of racial defiance. Disregarding Olympic protocol, the students from San Jose State University lowered their heads during the playing of the "Star-Spangled Banner" and each raised a defiant, black-gloved fist in a protest seen and felt around the globe.

S&G and Barratts/EMPICS Sport/PA Photos

Tommie Smith and John Carlos stunned the world with a powerful gesture of racial defiance during the 200-meter medal ceremony at the 1968 Mexico City Olympic Games. Smith and Carlos' "Black Power Salute" represents one of the most overt political actions in the history of modern sport.

The Global Dimensions of Race and Sport

Reflecting the broader aims of the civil rights and Black Power movements, Carlos and Smith's iconic protest in Mexico City sought to expose the plight of people of color at home in the United States and throughout the world. During this period, other black athletes from the United States also became global icons. In the 1970s and 1980s, for instance, Muhammad Ali, who was as famous for his challenges to the U.S. power structure as for his masterful skills in the boxing ring, became the most well-known person on the planet. He also symbolized both the new challenges being made to old racial hierarchies and the power of the underdog to rise in struggles against the establishment. Ali drew huge crowds of devoted fans not only in his hometown of Louisville but also in cities in Asia, Africa, and Latin America as he fought in rings around the globe, including cities as diverse as Manila (capital of the Philippines) and Kinshasa (capital of Zaire, now the Democratic Republic of the Congo).

In addition to Ali, a growing legion of athletes of African descent made their mark on the global stage during the second half of the 20th century. Abebe Bikila of Ethiopia, for example, won marathon victories at the 1960 Rome Olympics and the 1964 Tokyo Games, thus becoming the first African-born Olympian to win a gold medal for his home nation—K.K. McArthur, an immigrant of European descent born in Northern Ireland, won Olympic marathon gold for South Africa in 1912, and Boughera El Ouafi, born in French colonial Algeria, won marathon gold for France in 1928. In 1968, at the Mexico City games where Smith and Carlos raised the black-gloved fists, Kipchoge "Kip" Keino took Olympic gold in both the 1500-meter race and the 3000-meter steeplechase, signaling the dawn of the age of East African

"THE RACE GAME"

Historical Profile

The call to boycott South African sport originated in the mid-1950s as the all-white Afrikaner National Party developed and implemented a barrage of racist legislation that left South Africa's black majority segregated, impoverished, and disenfranchised. Under apartheid law, blacks were limited from owning land and property and—except in a service capacity—from visiting white residential areas. The all-white South African government also prohibited interracial marriage, criminalized interracial sexual contact, and segregated the races in all public areas—including schools, colleges, universities, and sport clubs.

In response, for more than three decades—until the abolishment of apartheid and the tumultuous transition to a democratic South Africa—a global coalition of advocacy networks, multinational corporations, churches, and foreign governments targeted the South African government. The anti-apartheid movement employed a wide spectrum of strategies that included financial sanctions, disinvestment campaigns, visa refusals, boycotts of South African exports, and embargos (military, nuclear, and oil). Drawing invaluable media coverage, the anti-apartheid movement soon began rallying around specific issues, including sport.

A global nexus of anti-apartheid organizations employed a wide spectrum of strategies that included sports boycotts to condemn South Africa and the all-white Afrikaner National Party for its racist, discriminatory apartheid laws.

Throughout the Northern and Southern Hemispheres, anti-apartheid demonstrators deployed an arsenal of disruptive tactics. In international cricket matches starring the all-white South African team, protestors dug up wickets and strewed buckets of glass and fishhooks across the field. The national pastime of white South Africa, rugby union, and their cherished Springbok team became the concentrated focus of similar anti-apartheid attacks. Commando groups infiltrated team hotels to keep players awake. Protesters blew whistles, used mirrors to flash light in players' eyes, and detonated smoke and paint bombs. As a result, wherever South African athletes traveled, they faced an atmosphere akin to that of a police state; behind barbed wire and heavy police protection, they were typically met by a torrent of abuse. As a result, tours were canceled or diverted to more hospitable venues, but protesters still found ways to disrupt events.

The anti-apartheid movement stoked one of the most ferocious controversies in the sporting world, but its efforts bore fruit. One by one, international sport federations, including the IOC and soccer's governing body (FIFA), revoked South Africa's membership and expelled the apartheid state from international competition. The anti-apartheid movement also garnered global political support. The United Nations passed a series of resolutions condemning apartheid, and the British Commonwealth signed the Gleneagles Agreement, which precluded Commonwealth nations from competing against South Africa in sport. Although a small of number of nations and "rebel" players broke the blockade, many scholars conclude that the anti-apartheid movement succeeded in isolating the South African government and stimulating a democratic transition in which apartheid was dismantled.

dominion in Olympic endurance running that continues today.

African Olympic victories emboldened African nations to use their sporting prestige to challenge white supremacist regimes in Rhodesia (modern-day Zimbabwe) and South Africa. In those nations, people of color had long suffered under a system of discriminatory laws, disenfranchisement, poverty, and police brutality that came to be known as apartheid. In sport, they were denied access to facilities, overlooked for national team selection, and denied the opportunity to serve on national and international governing bodies. Inspired, however, by the courage of champion black athletes in the United States and on their own continent, black African sport leaders united to combat the scourge of racism in Rhodesian and South African sport.

Through the formation of the Supreme Council for Sport in Africa (SCSA), which harnessed an emerging post–WWII pan-African identity, black Africans threatened a mass boycott of the 1968 Mexico City Olympic Games unless the IOC reversed its decision to readmit South Africa into the Olympic movement. Fearing both the political fallout of a boycott and the subsequent loss of significant television revenue, IOC president Avery Brundage bowed to the SCSA's threats and promptly revoked South Africa's Olympic membership. The battle over South Africa's Olympic participation in 1968 represented just one in a series of chapters in the international battle against apartheid in South African and Rhodesian sport and in wider society.

Sport in Living Color

The struggles over racial discrimination in sport and the rise of athletes of African descent around the world played out in people's living rooms on the new medium of television. This technology represents one of the most important technological inventions in the history of sport and physical culture. As a mass-communication medium, television stimulated the global popularity and reach of sport by convening the essential elements of sporting competition. It provided intimacy and image, detail and analysis. Through the use of multiple cameras, slow-motion replays, and close-ups of players and spectators, television remade sport into an accessible, first-rate, and respectable form of family entertainment for the world's billions of consumers. With live broadcasts becoming available in color, international sporting events such as the Olympics and the soccer World Cup began reaching viewers in villages, towns, and cities across the globe.

In the United States, televised coverage of sport brought athletes into the homes of nearly every U.S. citizen on a daily basis. By 1960, a staggering 90 percent of U.S. households owned a television set. During the 1960s, eager to exploit untapped television audiences and compete against its more powerful rivals, the American Broadcasting Company (ABC) hired television guru Roone Arledge from the rival National Broadcasting Company (NBC). Throughout his tenure, Arledge proved adept at producing, packaging, and selling sport as a form of mass entertainment. He implemented a series of innovative entertainment techniques, including dynamic halftime shows, instant replays, split-screen views, and directional and remote microphones. He also conceived of the idea of placing cameras on cranes, blimps, and even helicopters in order to provide viewers with optimal game coverage.

Arledge's signature sport programs included *Monday Night Football* and *Wide World of Sports*, as well as productions of the Olympics. These offerings reached millions of people who were not traditionally sport fans, transforming ABC into the country's top-rated television network. Together, Arledge and ABC propelled sport events into the highest-rated programming on television—a status retained by sport in the 21st century. For instance, television transformed the Super Bowl of American football into the nation's newest holiday, an event that represents the largest shared experience in contemporary U.S. culture.

Soaring viewership sparked a bidding war between the leading U.S. television broadcasters for the rights to major sporting events. The escalating payments for television rights constituted a windfall of financial riches for the Olympic Games and other events. As interest in the Cold War Olympic spectacle heightened, ABC brokered a $4.5 million deal with the IOC for broadcast rights to the 1968 Mexico City Games. Spiraling technical and production costs coupled with higher advertising demand and competition between U.S. broadcasters, drove television fees to previously unimagined levels. As a result, in 1984, ABC signed a $91.5 million contract for U.S. broadcasting rights to the Sarajevo winter Olympics and an eye-popping $225 million contract for the Los Angeles summer Olympics.

Fees also skyrocketed for the rights to broadcast American football. In 1964, the Columbia Broadcasting System (CBS) paid $14 million to cover the National Football League (NFL) season. By 1985, each of the NFL's 28 teams received $65 million from the profits garnered through a multinetwork television package. Despite paying astronomical television rights fees, broadcasters recorded windfall profits. The soaring profitability and popularity of televised sport inspired the creation in 1979 of the Entertainment and Sports Programming Network (ESPN), a 24-hour cable television station offering wall-to-wall coverage of a wide range of domestic and international sporting events.

Through such developments, televised sport developed into a huge industry not only in the United States but around the world. The largest international audiences have been drawn by the Olympics and the World Cup soccer tournaments. Outside of the United States, televised soccer has drawn passionate audiences and made the game's greatest players into global icons. During the 1960s and 1970s, the Brazilian soccer savant Edson Arantes do Nascimento, better known to the world as Pelé, rivaled Muhammad Ali as the world's most well-known person. In a multiracial Brazil that, like the United States, carried an enduring history of slavery and racism, Pelé became a symbol—beamed by television into homes around the world—of integrationist hopes and egalitarian dreams.

As the 20th century neared its close, television represented the most important advertising medium for the sport industry. By the beginning of the 21st century, sport ranked as one of the 10 most lucrative businesses in the world. Corporations and marketing agencies embraced televised sport as a platform for showcasing their range of products to both national and global audiences. Athletes became virtual billboards as marketing agencies sought sportsmen and sportswomen to endorse their products. Basketball stars sold sneakers, snowboarders peddled fast food, and decathletes danced with the stars on prime-time television. And multinational corporations, such as McDonald's, Coca-Cola, and Visa, paid exorbitant sums to be recognized as the "official" sponsor or partner of major international sporting events and organizations.

Thus sport became a multibillion-dollar global industry, and herein lay the final ingredients in the global spread of modern sport: commercialism and television. These two factors combined to bring sport to the farthest reaches of the globe, transforming athletes such as U.S. basketball player Michael Jordan and English soccer star David Beckham into international celebrities and turning modern sport into a global celebration of human physical culture.

CHAPTER WRAP-UP

Wrapping Up and Looking Ahead

The historical dimensions of the Cold War propelled sport into world history in new and important ways. In the struggle to convince the world of the superiority of the American way of life as opposed to the Soviet system, women and racial minorities found new opportunities for decrying oppression both in sport and beyond. Sport served on the front lines of the civil rights movement and in the vanguard of campaigns for women's equality. The fact that Olympic stadiums served as sites where the world could examine competing claims about inclusion, opportunity, and quality of life redoubled the social power of sport.

At the same time, sport continued its evolution as a commodity craved by consumers around the world. The new technological medium of television vastly expanded the markets and influence of sport in every region. Television allowed the Cold War Olympic dramas and World Cup clashes between nations to captivate the imaginations of people throughout the world. As a result, sport became the new medium's signature form of content and leading revenue generator. When the world gathered in electronic communion, it was sport that played on the screen. In the global village that some scholars insisted television created, most of the sets were tuned in to sporting events.

In this context, sport provided more than entertainment and amusement. It highlighted more than just what the famous opening line of ABC's *Wide World of Sports*" promised as a globe-spanning look at "the thrill of victory . . . and the agony of defeat . . . the human drama of athletic completion." That human drama involved not only a chronicle of sport winners and losers but also the politics of international relations, the struggles of women and people of color to claim equal status, the assertions of exceptionalism made by a host of nations, the quest to test the boundaries of human performance, and debates over the ethics of scientific enhancement.

In 1999, news broke that Chinese schoolchildren had ranked Michael Jordan as the second-most important historical figure of the 20th century, behind only former Chinese premier Zhou Enlai and ahead of such world-changing people as Adolf Hitler, Henry Ford, Winston Churchill, and Mahatma Gandhi. Jordan, an African American with a huge portfolio of endorsements, had, in the estimation of many observers, crossed over racial lines in the United States and become the first black American to appeal as much to white audiences as to black audiences. By the dawn of the 21st century, Jordan had replaced Ali and Pelé as the most famous human on earth and had become not only a national but a global brand.

Though the Cold War had evaporated a decade earlier with the collapse of the Soviet Union, the fascination with sporting contests and superstar athletes in the decades of symbolic battle between East and West—"war minus the shooting," as George Orwell had dubbed it—left a thriving global sporting culture in its wake. That global culture was primed and ready to focus on new dramas for a new age. China emerged to replace the old Soviet Union in Olympic battles with the United States, and Chinese school children were captivated by Michael Jordan. Soccer also captivated the Chinese, and they knew David Beckham and other icons of the world's game just as they knew Jordan—as stars of the world's most popular television programs.

Since the end of World War II, sport has become a global phenomenon that appeals to people in vastly different circumstances: in communist and capitalist economies, in democracies and dictatorships, in small homogenous societies and in vast and diverse ones. It's no wonder people developed a philosophical method, phenomenology, to make sense of it all by taking into account the lived experiences of people in different political systems and different economic conditions, as well as in the common conditions of humanity—that is, as embodied individuals sharing many of the same concerns, hopes, and ideals. Sport itself stood as a phenomenon that attracted keen interest across cultures and nationalities; in fact, it represented perhaps the most shared phenomenon on the globe. The power of sport in global contexts was highlighted by the fact that sport's most adept practitioners—the likes of Ali, Pelé, and Jordan—were also the globe's most admired figures.

Study Questions

1. What is the focus of phenomenology, and how does it affect kinesiology?

2. Why, and in what ways, did the Soviet Union and the United States strive to achieve international sporting success during the Cold War?

3. What is meant by "paternalism" and how does the concept apply to the debate about the ethics of banning performance-enhancing substances?

4. What role did performance-enhancing substances play in Cold War sport?

5. What roles did Jackie Robinson and Billie Jean King play in advancing the interests and opportunities of African Americans and women in sport?

6. Why should we resist the temptation to use racialized ideas, such as the notion of a "sports gene," to explain black athletes' success? Why did black athletes "revolt," in one observer's description, and how did sport challenge racial conceptions around the world?

7. What is Title IX, and how has it affected women's sport at the high school and collegiate levels in the United States?

8. What role did television play in transforming sport into a global spectacle?

SNAPSHOTS FROM OUR TIMES

Comparing the Globe's Multiple Sportsworlds

Chapter Objectives

In this chapter, you will

1. examine the ways in which sport has been globalized while remaining tied to national and regional communities;

2. understand how sport shapes community and individual identity in the 21st century and reflect on its global, national, and local significance;

3. learn about the origins of lifestyle sports, including action sports and e-sports, and their implications for human movement;

4. reflect on the role of risk taking and the importance of health as they relate to promoting meaningful forms of movement; and

5. consider ways in which contemporary sportsworlds can both unite and divide humanity in the 21st century.

We inhabit a world in which global connections seem paramount. These connections are highlighted in sport perhaps more than in any other aspect of our 21st-century lives. For example, you can easily find jerseys representing LeBron James and other NBA stars in not only every metropolis and hamlet in the United States but also on city streets anywhere from Mongolia to Mozambique. In fact, some of the NBA's most brilliant stars grew up in nations other than the United States, including Hakeem Olajuwon (Nigeria), Dirk Nowitzki (Germany), and Manu Ginobili (Argentina). Just as easily, you can find jerseys representing the world's leading soccer clubs, from Manchester United to Real Madrid to Bayern Munich, far from their home nations of England, Spain, and Germany—adorning strollers in Uganda, Ukraine, the United Arab Emirates, Uruguay, and even the United States.

Do Global Connections Create Global Identities?

Over the past century, a truly global sporting culture has emerged. In addition to the worldwide popularity of various jerseys, one of the clearest signs of the power of sport in creating a global village, as it were, can be found in the fact that the two most popular shared experiences in the world—events that regularly draw upwards of five billion viewers—are broadcasts of World Cup soccer and the Olympics. This duo of sporting events accounts for the most highly rated television programs on earth, which serve as gold mines generating billions of dollars of revenue. Indeed, by at least one count, the world of sport now counts more members than the world of politics. The United Nations now lists 195 member states, whereas the International Olympic Committee (IOC) lists 206 and the *Fédération Internationale de Football Association* (FIFA) lists 209.

Common Ground or Dividing Line?

For keen observers such as sport scholar Allen Guttmann, this global adoration of sport portends the prospect of creating identities that transcend the local, regional, and national connections that have historically shaped human societies. "If sports are an occasion for the expression of *communitas*, which they can be," declares Guttmann, "let them express the human community as well as the tribal one." Guttmann's optimistic transcendentalism seems at odds with much of what transpires at global events such as the Olympics and the World Cup, where tribal conflicts often appear to overshadow universal human interchanges. Indeed, modern sporting events have always provided occasions for clashes of clannish loyalties.

During the many decades of the Cold War, for instance, the United States and the Soviet Union regularly fought out their struggles for supremacy through the Olympics (for more on this subject, see chapter 11). In 1972, the Soviets rejoiced when, in an Olympic miracle, their men's basketball team gave the U.S. team its first loss since the sport's debut at the 1936 Olympics by winning a gold-medal game marked by a highly controversial finish. In 1980, the United States reveled in patriotic celebration when its men's hockey team upset the heavily favored Soviets on the way to a gold medal now memorialized as the "Miracle on Ice." Since the Soviet Union's collapse in the late 1980s and early 1990s, the United States has found a new Olympic foil in the rise of China to global power in the military, economic, and athletic realms.

World Cup soccer features a similar history of national encounters in which countries have proclaimed their virtuosity with World Cup victories and touted their

National Identities and Sport

Student Exercise

Search online for images of some of the nationalistic sporting contests mentioned in this chapter and in other chapters of this book. Collect five historical images (e.g., photographs, paintings, statues, film clips, posters, advertisements) that capture the nationalism that can erupt at the Olympics, the World Cup, or another sporting event. Think about your own experiences with global sport mega-events such as the Olympics and the World Cup. How has nationalism shaped your viewing of and reading about these events?

wins or lamented their losses in battles with rival powers. Indeed, some matches have heightened tensions between nations already at odds over other issues. In 1969, a World Cup qualifying match between El Salvador and Honduras sparked a brief war between the two rivals. In another example, matches between Argentina and England turned into supercharged events in the aftermath of their brief military engagement in 1982 over the contested island chain in the Atlantic that the English refer to as the Falklands and the Argentines call *las Islas Malvinas*. Other sporting encounters register similar struggles between rival nations; for instance, international cricket tests between India and Pakistan have become flash points for nationalistic displays in the midst of ongoing disputes between these neighboring Asian powers.

Global Sport and Ideological Struggles

Sport can also highlight disputes between larger aggregations than nations—that is, between "civilizations" or "blocs," as they are labeled in international politics. The Cold War struggles between the United States and the Soviet Union pitted not only the two main combatants but also U.S. allies from the Western Bloc and Soviet allies from the Eastern Bloc, thus pitting a divided Germany against itself in Olympic stadiums as West Germans competed against East Germans. More recently, conflicts have routinely erupted in international contests between sides framed as representing Western civilization and Islamic civilization based on deep divisions related to religious beliefs, gender practices, and power relations.

Enduring struggles over Israel have also become flash points for conflict. After decades of Israeli participation in the Asian Football Confederation's competitions for spots in the World Cup, a cabal of Islamic nations voted Israel out of its geographic group. Nearly two decades of exile ensued before the Union of European Football Associations admitted Israel into its tournaments in the 1990s. More generally, since the 1970s, Islamic nations and athletes have sometimes refused to compete against Israelis, thus sparking numerous incidents at the Olympics and in international soccer competition. Most dramatically, at the Munich Olympics in 1972, a Palestinian terrorist group known as the Black September Organization seized and killed 11 Israeli athletes and coaches in what remains the deadliest terrorist incident in the history of international sport. The Munich Massacre, as the tragedy came to be known, illustrated the type of tribal fractures that continue to divide the world and pose daunting obstacles to celebrating the universal connections of humanity through sport.

Movement as Meaningful Narrative

Sport sparks intense ideological or tribal passions through its deep associations with meaning and identity. In the 1970s, anthropologist Clifford Geertz studied how sport reflects and shapes specific values, perceptions, and narratives through shared physical activity. In his study of Balinese cockfighting, Geertz explained that this activity's "general function, if you want to call it that, is interpretive: it is a Balinese reading of Balinese experience; a story they tell themselves about themselves." Many scholars have adopted Geertz's original idea that sport—as well as dance, martial arts, and other forms of physical activity—creates stories through which cultures define themselves and make sense of their worlds. At the social level, sport provides opportunities for individuals to live out their cultural stories, which both reflect and help form a community's identity. Thus, when Brazilians play a particularly imaginative and fluid style of soccer, or when Americans play "streetball" (an outdoor variation of basketball that expresses urban African American aesthetics), they are telling a story about themselves to themselves—and often to others as well. These stories create identities for communities that express their shared values, history, and experiences. Just as the Balinese used cockfighting to demonstrate family and social ties, the rituals of Friday night football in Texas or big-wave surfing on the North Shore of Oahu reflect important aspects of collective identities.

In this sense, sport constitutes one important form of social scaffolding that expresses collective values. Once Geertz learned to "read" Balinese cockfighting as a sort of text, he could see how the Balinese expressed their particular blend of values through their sport. "In the cockfight," he explained, "the Balinese forms and discovers his temperament and his society's temper at the same time. Or, more exactly, he forms and discovers a particular face of them." Geertz insisted that the same type of reading of a culture could be done with regard to American football, British cricket, or the shared forms of physical activity in any human society. In other words, we do not need to be anthropologists in a strange land in order to appreciate how humans make sense of their communities and themselves. We can do so instead by attending to sport, which is created and shaped by communities to provide individuals with explanatory accounts about certain meaningful characteristics in publicly demonstrable activities.

At the individual level, people who participate in sporting institutions cannot help but form their own meaningful narratives as well. For example, as discussed in chapter 3, the Greek hero Odysseus used his sporting prowess with the discus to reveal his virtuous character to King Alcinos. Since athletic talents could not be faked, Odysseus knew that his prowess revealed to the Phaeacians something deep about himself that words could not convey. In our own lives, as discussed in chapter 2, we often describe ourselves in terms of our playgrounds; rather than merely engaging in certain activities, we *become* skiers or runners, for example, as we deepen our involvement with a chosen sport.

We begin using sport to write these meaningful narratives even at the youth level, in the same way that we start forming who we are as people. Were you one of the many people who spent a misty autumn morning in a swarm of 7-year-olds trying to kick a soccer ball into a goal as part of a youth soccer league? Perhaps or perhaps not. Either way, you likely realize that having, or not having, such experiences influenced the ways in which you see yourself in relation to your peers. As you grew older, you might have experienced being a star athlete on a high school varsity team, or you might have been cut from the team during your first year and never returned to the sport. Either way, whether you played the role of starting forward or left out, that experience became, for better or worse, part of your identity. It reflects who you were and, when placed against who you are now, forms part of your story.

Your stories, of course, are constantly being written and rewritten throughout your lifetime. In part, we each write the story through the way we play our sports. Consider, for a moment, two individuals playing one-on-one basketball. One player is wearing the latest pair of Air Jordan sneakers, compression sleeves, and name-brand sweatbands. The other player is wearing a pair of canvas Chuck Taylor All-Stars, knee-high gym socks, and a mesh jersey. Both players, whether or not they fully appreciate it, reveal through their clothing some of their identity as basketball players. We do not need to wait to see the skyhook or the between-the-legs dribble to piece together how the two individuals imagine themselves within the larger culture of basketball.

More important, others who also know the game of basketball can read these clothing choices and say something about each individual's identity. If asked, both individuals might casually respond that these just happen to be the outfits they found in their closets. But that answer obscures the fact that this was what they had to wear. At some point, they acquired these articles, and the fact that they not only chose to wear them but also chose to play basketball reflects much about how they view themselves. They could just as easily have said, "No, that's not me. I am not that kind of basketball player." Or they might have simply decided that they did not belong in basketball at all. Perhaps an extreme sport, such as skateboarding or mountain climbing, would have been a better fit for their self-expression. Thus, not only do people's choices about which sports to play (or not play) say something meaningful about them, but also the way in which they play a given sport reveals important elements of their individual story within their larger community's narrative.

Reading Your Story?

Student Exercise

Clifford Geertz offered the following observation:

> Yet what [the Balinese cockfight] says is not merely that risk is exciting, loss depressing, or triumph gratifying, banal tautologies of affect, but that it is of these emotions, thus exampled, that society is built and individuals put together. Attending cockfights and participating in them is, for the Balinese, a kind of sentimental education. What he learns there is what his culture's ethos and his private sensibility (or, anyway, certain aspects of them) look like when spelled out externally in a collective text.

Extending Geertz's claim about Balinese cockfighting to sport in general, the view of sport as a text indicates a durable aspect of the nature of sport and other physical activities. Specifically, sport and recreation are inherently laden with meaningful experiences that are intentionally introduced and shaped by culture. When, for example, members of New Zealand's rugby team, the All Blacks, perform the traditional Maori war dance known as the *haka*, their performance reflects a unique fusion of British sport with indigenous culture. The presence of specific culture can also be seen in Japanese sumo wrestling, which reflects Japan's Shinto religious tradition, and in beach volleyball, which reflects Southern California's laidback lifestyle of sun, sand, and surf.

Now, identify similar movement texts that are familiar to you. How might a sport, a martial art, or a style of dance in your life reflect your culture's values or identity? How might global sports such as soccer take on specific meanings for different communities while remaining universal? How might the answers to these questions inform our philosophical, ethical, or aesthetic considerations when thinking about sport?

We assemble these meaningful experiences into narratives that explain why we participate in sport and other physical activities. Such activities have spoken to people throughout history, in diverse times and places, because they provide meaningful narratives that allow us to both receive and write stories about ourselves and others. Participating in sport (or not participating) is one way in which individuals make themselves socially intelligible in relation to a community's collective text. People shape their personal identities not only in terms of which sports they play but also in *how* they play them. Competitors also have a say in each other's narratives because they provide one another with challenges that can reveal individual limitations, weaknesses, and unique attributes. As philosopher Alisdair MacIntyre reminds us, "We are never more (and sometimes less) than the co-authors of our own narratives. Only in fantasy do we live what story we please."

Moreover, the "storied" nature of sport is illustrated by contemporary society's use of sport as a tool for measuring, ranking, and comparing athletes and teams. If sport's comparative tests compel and captivate modern sporting communities, it is because we find these rankings and measurements meaningful. Separating winners from losers and drawing ever-finer distinctions between finishers or direct competitors is one way—the presently fashionable way—to appreciate athletic performance. Yet, even today, this comparative-test interpretation of sport exists alongside (and occasionally in opposition to) other meaningful narratives. The meaning derived from an interpretation of sport (such as the comparative-test premise) is directly proportionate to and dependent on the force of the narrative that drives it. Circumstance has created an environment in which the comparative test supports meaningful ways to interpret sport, but sport was hardly wanting for meaning before this interpretation became entrenched, and sport will remain meaningful if (or when) the narrow focus on measuring and ranking competitors fades away. The narratives may change, but the narrative power of sport endures.

Global Consumer Culture

The globalization of sport over the past several decades has created international connections and bonds. People can now watch telecasts or stream feeds of sporting events from every part of the globe. Spectacles such as the Olympics and the World Cup link the world into a common global culture, even if sport provides only superficial and transitory bonds. A global marketplace sells sport and recreation in a myriad of forms, from the games themselves to sporting equipment to sport-inspired fashions to every imaginable accessory that consumers might desire. As a result, sport now ranks as one of the 10 largest commercial sectors in the global economy, producing enormous revenues not only through the sale of tickets and broadcast rights but also through the provision of the standard uniforms of the globe's vast youth culture—that is, the sport-branded t-shirts, hoodies, sweatpants, shorts, and athletic shoes that clothe and shod the masses in every nation and culture.

As a result, tremendous profits can be reaped by corporations that tap into the seemingly universal modern desire to admire excellence and to find joy in meaningful movement. Nike, for example, originated in Oregon in the 1960s by importing Japanese running shoes as a budget-conscious alternative to fashionable European brands such as Adidas and Puma. In the ensuing years, of course, the brand has become a multinational industrial leviathan that rakes in billions of dollars in annual revenue by making all sorts of sporting apparel. Nike rose to power not by simply producing unique products but by relentlessly promoting its brand with cleverly crafted advertisements that tap into the universal human fascination with sport performance—for example, the iconic "Just Do It" campaign, a brilliant promotion ranked by some economists as the most creative and successful advertisement of all time. Nike's success illuminates the emergence of a sort of global village united by the consumption of sporting events and sporting goods.

This global consumer culture tied to sporting goods allows us to display our identities by purchasing and wearing products. Show us your shoes, and we can identify the tribal affinities you want to herald. If you sport Vans, you tell the world that you have an affinity for lifestyle sports, such as skateboarding and surfing. Wearing the latest running shoes tells the world that you are interested in fitness. Trail-running shoes signal that you are interested in both fitness and the outdoors. Unlaced basketball shoes hint that pick-up basketball is a regular activity for you. Antique sneakers mark an affinity for hip-hop culture. River-rafting sandals announce a strong potential affinity for environmental activism. Wearing your five-toed pseudoshoes around campus indicates an inclination toward a Paleo diet or vegan commitment. Once upon a time, half a century ago, wearing Chuck Taylor All-Stars meant that you played on your high school basketball team; now it means that you are a millennial hipster. Although this shoe list wallows in stereotypes, wearing symbols of these stereotypes frequently means that you are trying to give the people who inhabit your social universe important cues about your perception of your own identity. You can project multiple identities through your sporting attire, and you can even confuse your peers by matching a Philadelphia Eagles jersey with a Dallas Cowboys cap or a NASCAR t-shirt with an expensive pair of golf pants.

In the world we inhabit, sport can create a seemingly endless variety of identities in every niche and at every level, from the homogenized global to the idiosyncratic local. As an individual, you can use sport to signal your loyalties to multiple identities that function at many levels. What do these myriad options for creating identity through sport explain about the world we inhabit at this moment in history? Clearly, they tell us that we live in a world shaped not by one "sportsworld" but by many "sportsworlds," as both critics and promoters label these cultures built around sport. By examining a series of snapshots of the sportsworlds that exist in our own time, we can develop an understanding of both current trends and future possibilities in our ideas about the role of sport, recreation, and physical activity in our lives. What emerges from our survey of contemporary practices are three major

Catalog the Power of the Sport Industry Among Your Classmates

Student Exercise

Look around the room. What percentage of your classmates are wearing some form of sport fashion, whether it be shoes, shorts, a shirt, a hat, a hoodie, or a jacket? What variety of identities have they adopted in their attire? Is your classroom filled only with the colors of your own institution's teams, or do you see signs of other schools, professional teams, or even other types of sport beyond those your school sponsors? Similarly, is the room filled only with sporting insignias from the United States, or do the emblems of other nations and cultures appear? In most U.S. classrooms, a majority of the students wear sport fashions of some sort. Discuss with your classmates what this means, and what the wide range of identities that they "sport" reveals about their connections to their locality, their region, their nation, and other nations.

developments: the persistence of local cultures, the continuing power of nations, and the emergence of new global forms.

The Persistence of Local Cultures

For all the talk of globalization in our present historical moment, much of human experience remains rooted in the particular dimensions of local habits. Consider, for instance, the unique sportsworld that appears in many parts of the United States on Friday evenings during autumn. For close to a century now, the darkness of fall Friday nights has been lit by the glow of electric lights shining over high school football fields throughout the country. High school football remains a popular ritual that showcases the pride and passion of local communities in urban, suburban, and rural areas. "Friday night lights," as high school football rituals are popularly known, burn especially bright in certain locales—in small towns in the American hinterlands, perhaps in Texas or Pennsylvania, where there is little else to do in isolated desert hamlets or rusted former mill towns where the factories have been shuttered. High school football games in these localities draw almost every member of the community. Grandparents root for their grandchildren who play football, perform in the marching band, or chant support as cheerleaders. Residents fill the stands and exchange gossip or talk business while reminiscing about their own glorious (or not so glorious) exploits under the lights in generations past. Young children dash and play just beyond the sidelines of the electric-lit gridiron, dreaming of a near future in which they will perform under the lights. On the field, in the band section, and among the cheer squads, teenagers enact common rites of passage that fuel community pride and determine status in the adolescent hierarchy of their tribes.

The phenomenon of Friday night lights represents a fundamentally local endeavor in spite of the fact that some American cable networks now broadcast high school games and that most players wear equipment manufactured by Nike and other multinational corporations. The interests and identities created by high school football are rooted in local cultures and express local allegiances. The most important rivalry for the residents of any two given towns may be unknown to the Friday-night-lights communities in the next county over. Bragging rights for victories over neighboring communities represent the continuing power of local identification for many Americans. Thus high school football of the American variety is a highly parochial sport, though a Canadian variant has emerged beyond the northern border. Friday night lights do not burn anywhere else in the Americas, or Asia, or Africa, or Europe. They burn with a particular intensity, however, in rural hamlets and small towns throughout the United States.

Whether they will continue to burn brightly for another century, however, is an open question. As much as those of us who grew up with Friday night lights may believe that they are an eternal local ritual, signs abound that this era may soon end. The specter of serious injury and even death from the violent collisions that seem essential to football have begun to raise questions about the wisdom of playing the game at any level, from professional to intercollegiate to high school to youth. As evidence mounts of the potential for serious brain injury from repeated blows to the head, an increasing number of American parents may well prohibit their children from suiting up for Friday night lights. Indeed, participation rates in American high school football have shrunk steadily over the last half century. In the 1950s, joining the high school football team was a rite of masculine passage that most American boys felt compelled to undertake, whether or not they were interested or skilled. Now, teenage boys have a wide variety of alternative activities, and some high schools struggle to find enough players to field a team. Thus, fear of injury represents only one of several factors in this decline in participation; equally or even more important seems to be the proliferation of other youth sporting activities (such as soccer and lacrosse) and nonsporting activities (such as video gaming, though debates about whether these electronic games should fall under the general umbrella of sport remains an

WILL ASSOCIATION FOOTBALL (SOCCER) EVER REPLACE AMERICAN FOOTBALL IN U.S. CULTURE?

Historical Profile

In the 21st century, the most popular sport in which Americans participate is soccer; the most popular sport that Americans watch, however, is American football. This dichotomy—that more American children, youth, and even adults play soccer but far more Americans in every age category follow American football—has led some observers to predict that we may be near a tipping point in which soccer replaces football as America's national pastime. The reasoning behind such claims derives from studies of national pastimes around the world, which reveal that people rarely develop intense fandom for games that they do not grow up playing. Will the demographics of participation soon mean that more Americans watch the World Cup than the Super Bowl?

Contrary to popular notions, soccer is hardly a new import to the United States. In fact, the game that most historians point to as the first intercollegiate football contest in American history, an 1869 match in which Rutgers defeated Princeton by a score of 6 to 4, was played with rules inspired by soccer codes. Soccer teams, both professional and amateur, have been playing their games in the United States ever since, particularly in areas where immigrant groups have fostered the association football game. Thus the hotbeds of American soccer have ranged from the mill towns of New England to the urban neighborhoods of Philadelphia and St. Louis. The United States also sent soccer teams to the early Olympic and World Cup tournaments. Still, for the first century of American soccer, the game was mainly identified as an interest of immigrants and foreigners that was popular around the world but did not rank among the national pastimes of the United States.

Meanwhile, American football originated in the 1870s from revisions of the British rugby codes intended to create a distinctly American game that reflected the patterns and practices of American nationalism. This alternative form of football enjoyed a century as a game that the vast majority of people in the United States both played and watched. During the 1970s, however, soccer became increasingly popular in the United States as a game for children and youth. In the ensuing decades, as participation in soccer has risen, participation in American football has declined. The recurrent concerns about the dangers of American football have diminished the zeal with which some parents approach the game as an introduction to athletic competition for their children. The shift in participation rates has also resulted in part from the general lack of opportunities for females to compete in American football.

As the number of children playing soccer began to rise, entrepreneurs began to launch new professional leagues with the idea that soccer would become the next national pastime in the United States. In spite of a half century of such predictions, however, American football still dwarfs soccer as a spectator sport. Although more and more of us play soccer and pass our knowledge of the game on to our children, most of us also continue to pass on to our children a passion for watching, if not always for playing, American football. Will these patterns change if current trends continue and future generations play even more soccer and less American football? Entrepreneurs who have bet on soccer have high hopes, but American football continues to dominate ticket sales and television ratings by wide margins—at least for now.

open question, as you will read later in this chapter).

Another inherent problem with the Friday-night-lights phenomenon is that it virtually limits participation in the feature attraction—the football game itself—to boys. More than a million boys still participate in high school football every year, and, though over the last few decades a small number of girls (about a thousand per year) have joined them, playing football remains an almost entirely male endeavor. Thus, although females can find numerous roles in the ancillary activities that add to the pageantry, such as cheerleading and band, the event's leading roles are reserved for males. Perhaps Friday-night-lights spectaculars that provide more equivalent opportunities for boys and girls—such as soccer doubleheaders featuring both teams or even contests featuring co-ed squads—will someday replace football, as the egalitarian logics of modern sport continue to evolve and develop with regard to gender.

Perhaps the most difficult trend facing Friday night lights is the increasing marginalization of small towns and rural areas in both U.S. and global life. For a couple of centuries now, urban areas served as the engines of economic, social, and political innovation—and as the destination of migrants from the countryside. Today, population continues to flow from rural to urban areas, making modern global societies overwhelmingly urban in character and structure. In contrast, though high school football certainly has a foothold in American cities, it is hardly the only game in town in those locations. As a result, in order to serve as sources of identity formation, high school programs in urban and suburban areas must compete with a wide variety of other entities, including intercollegiate programs and professional franchises. Although predictions of the extinction of local identities in an urban age have been vastly exaggerated, metropolitan domination has heightened the trend toward an increasing concentration of power in national and global connections.

The Continuing Power of Nations

Japan now stands as the most urban nation on the earth. Although Japanese culture still venerates rural traditions, the vast majority of Japanese live in large urban centers. As a result, the Japanese version of Friday night lights manifests a more national focus than the tradition of interscholastic American football. Since the early part of the 20th century, when Japan was a more rural society, Japanese high school teams have participated in two national baseball championship tournaments, a Summer Kōshien that began in 1915 and a Spring Kōshien that started in 1924. These tournaments pit local schools against one another in a nationwide bracket that ends not with a local or state championship but a national one. Over the course of the 20th century, the tournaments grew to rank among the most popular sporting events in Japan, eclipsing even the highest levels of professional baseball. From the 1920s through the 1960s, radio networks broadcast the tournaments to enthusiastic listeners. Since then, the tournaments have become the focus of hugely popular television shows—the equivalent of the March Madness frenzies surrounding the NCAA basketball tournaments every spring in the United States. Japanese students, parents, and alumni follow their schools zealously, and, since the 1920s, the championship clashes have drawn capacity crowds at the 55,000-seat Kōshien Stadium in Kobe, which is home to the Hanshin Tigers of the Japanese major leagues except during the weeks in which the high school tournaments force the professional team into extended road trips.

Although tournaments featuring high school baseball in Japan certainly provide sites for celebrating the local identities of competing teams through a national ceremony, the particularly nationalistic elements embedded in Japanese baseball reveal that these competitions focus more on the identity-making processes of nationhood than on locality. In 1872, in the midst of the Japanese effort to rapidly transform the nation's traditional feudal society into a modern industrial dynamo, a U.S. educator hired to aid in that process introduced baseball to his high school students in Tokyo. At the same time, Japanese students who had studied at U.S. colleges brought the game back with them. Baseball quickly became a symbol of national innovation, progress, and modernization in Japanese culture. The game spread through elite schools and colleges, where modernization plans were most fully embraced. Students emulated the American national pastime to showcase their embrace of U.S.-style modernization (for more on the spread of baseball and other modern sports, see chapters 6 through 11). Games pitting Japanese squads against teams of U.S. sailors, merchants, or students on Far Eastern tours became events in which Japan could measure itself against its mentor and rival.

By the 1920s and 1930s, a flourishing professional baseball industry developed in Japan. In 1934, the great American slugger Babe Ruth headlined a team of all-stars that toured Japan and took on Japanese teams, including one game played before a packed house at Kōshien Stadium—the hallowed site of the high school national championships. Over the next decade, as Japan moved into a totalitarian militaristic state, baseball was suspended for the duration of the Second World War. After Japan's 1945 defeat, U.S. military occupiers quickly resuscitated baseball at all levels as part of their design to turn their former enemies into a U.S. ally in the Pacific and reestablish a more pacific Japanese nationalism.

Baseball has continued to thrive ever since, as Japan has grown from the devastations of the war into an economic global power. In spite of the fact that baseball originated as a U.S. import, it has reigned for close to a century as Japan's leading national pastime. Japan has grafted this import onto a multitude of traditional cultural customs. For example, legions of

ōendan, or organized cheering groups, fill the stands at Japanese baseball games and beat traditional drums while wearing traditional Japanese garb, including *hachimaki* (headbands) that represent folkloric symbols of courage and perseverance and are emblazoned with team logos, inspirational sayings, and the names of star players. By incorporating such traditions, the Japanese have transformed baseball into an elemental feature of their national narratives and an essential component in the projection of their national identity, both to themselves and to the rest of the world. Thus, just as it once did in the United States, baseball serves as a common language for the expression of Japanese national identities. As the official website of the Japan National Tourism Organization declares, "If there is one country that takes baseball more seriously than the United States, then it is without question Japan."

One country that might dispute this claim is Cuba, where baseball arrived even earlier than it did in Japan. The game was planted in the Spanish colony in the 1860s, both by Cuban students returning home from their studies in the United States and by U.S. sailors visiting the island. For Cubans disgruntled with colonial rule, playing and watching baseball represented a rejection of Spanish culture's fascination with bullfighting. In addition, New York City, a hotbed of early U.S. baseball, served as a safe harbor for Cubans who sought to organize and motivate a revolutionary uprising. Political ideas and baseball zealotry flowed back and forth between New York and Havana as resistance to Spanish rule began to inflame Cuba. In response, Spanish authorities sought to embargo not only "Yankee" revolutionary rhetoric but also the game of baseball.

In spite of this opposition, or perhaps because of it, *béisbol*, as it was translated in Spanish, took root in Cuban soil. In 1878, in the midst of this political turbulence, the first organized Cuban baseball league was founded. In 1887, the Philadelphia Athletics, a top U.S. club, made a well-received tour of the island. Spanish colonial authorities continued to discourage baseball as a fomenter of rebellious attitudes. By the 1890s, Cuban insurrectionaries, many of them also *béisbol* aficionados, were engaged in armed rebellion, and Spanish authorities banned the game as a seditious pastime. Soon thereafter, with the support of U.S. military intervention, Cuba gained independence, albeit under heavy U.S. influence. Baseball's role in these revolutionary struggles made it one of the most important symbols of early Cuban nationalism.

Throughout the 20th century and into the 21st century, baseball has served both as Cuba's national pastime and as a key element in projections of Cuban identity. During the first half of the 20th century, Cuban professional baseball flourished. Cuban teams regularly toured the United States and sometimes defeated major league squads. Cuban players also earned roster spots on professional U.S. teams, and a handful played in the major leagues. In addition, U.S. players sometimes migrated to Cuba. Two Cuban franchises even joined U.S.-based leagues—the Havana Sugar Kings, who spent several seasons in the International League, one of the top minor leagues in North America (which also included Canadian teams), and the Cuban Stars, an Afro-Cuban squad, which joined the Negro National League.

Cuban baseball had admitted black players beginning in 1900, and African American stars from the U.S. Negro leagues frequently wintered in Cuba in order to play for Cuban squads, where they joined their white major league counterparts. In Cuban winter league contests, the African American stars made a mockery out of Major League Baseball's hollow claims that no color line existed in the United States and that the lack of black players in the sport was due solely to a lack of talent. Below the highest professional leagues in Cuba, a thriving and interconnected network of teams flourished with sponsorship by amateur social clubs, local businesses, and sugar plantations.

Unlike the professionals, however, many of the amateur clubs drew strict color lines against including black players, though the sugar-mill teams and their rivals remained open to blacks.

In 1959, a revolution led by Fidel Castro and his communist comrades overthrew the government and took control of Cuba—and of Cuban baseball. Castro abolished professional baseball as a capitalist apostasy and shut down the export of Cuban players to the United States. However, as a former player himself and a lifelong fan of the game, he sagely continued to promote it as a key national symbol of his new Marxist regime. Castro and his fellow revolutionary leaders played exhibition games to cement the link between their regime and Cuba's history of struggles for independence. The new government also built a state-controlled system that continued to promote baseball as the national pastime and funneled considerable resources to the Cuban national team. Cuba's national squad soon became a powerful symbol of Castro's regime and of Cuban patriotism. When baseball was on the Olympic roster as a medal sport from 1992 to 2008, Cuba dominated the competition, winning three gold medals and two silver medals. Cuba also ruled baseball at the Pan American Games and in other international competitions. Although the United States and Cuba broke diplomatic ties shortly after Castro came to power—and the United States waged a long economic boycott against Cuba's government—baseball contests between Cuba's national side and Major League Baseball teams have occasionally been played. In addition, since the 1960s, scores of Cuban players have also fled the island in search of political asylum and a baseball career in the United States.

Sport Without Borders

The defection of Cuban players seeking the much more lucrative opportunities available in the United States illustrates the fact that the future of sport as an emblem of national identities faces considerable challenges. If current trends continue and the United States and Cuba normalize relations, then the best Cuban players will undoubtedly flow in even larger numbers from their homeland to the richer opportunities on the North American mainland. Look ahead even further and perhaps a Major League Baseball franchise will be located in Havana in order to capitalize on Cuba's love for baseball while profiting from the league's expansion, thus bringing baseball's labor migration full circle.

As exemplified by the exodus of baseball talent from Cuba to the United States, the migration of athletic labor (in a variety of sports) from underdeveloped areas to the wealthy centers of the global economy is already under way. This movement is blurring the boundaries of national identity. Soccer players from Africa and Latin America routinely star on teams in the best and wealthiest European leagues—the English Premier League (EPL) in Great Britain, the *Bundesliga* in Germany, the *Primera División* in Spain, and *Serie A* in Italy. Indeed, only about a third of the players in the EPL were born in Great Britain. The global migration of athletic talent not only produces fantastic games in the top leagues but also sparks tremendous controversy. In the poorer nations that produce players for the wealthy leagues, fans complain that they get few opportunities to see or cheer for their national stars. In the wealthy nations that import players, critics complain that immigrants have smothered the development of homegrown talent and threatened the World Cup prospects of national sides. In addition, though some fans cheer imports to their favorite clubs, old animosities related to race, ethnicity, and nationality often resurface between fans of opposing teams, thus indicating that the cosmopolitan composition of top European clubs evokes national tribalism and as much as tolerant universalism.

Though less intense than the backlash against globalization seen in soccer, comparable divisions appear in a wide variety of other sports. Similar complaints can be heard, for instance, about player movement patterns in international cricket and about the importation of hockey, basketball, and baseball players to North American markets. Analogous responses are also evoked by the recruitment of foreign nationals for U.S. intercollegiate teams. In the affluent regions that receive these talented imports, critics maintain that their nation's citizens are deprived of developmental opportunities due to the flow of foreign prospects who take their roster spots. Meanwhile, voices in the home nations of these athletes decry what they see as colonial exploitation of their athletic talent. Moreover, some wealthy nations—ranging from Bahrain, Qatar, and the United Arab Emirates to Australia, Norway, and the United States—have been accused of luring foreign stars to their shores with guarantees of citizenship and riches in order to bolster the talent pool of their Olympic squads.

Nationalism and International Mega-Events

In addition to the migration of athletic talent, global tensions are also registered in the quest to host international mega-events, particularly the Olympics and the World Cup. The current process for selecting Olympic host cities reveals another dark side of the role of nationalism in contemporary sport. The willingness of nations with authoritarian governments to spend enormous sums to win Olympic bids—as well as the inevitable resistance to these economic outlays that emerges among the populaces of more democratic societies—has troubled observers who argue that the Olympics are in danger of pricing and politicizing themselves out of existence. In the 21st century, for example, China spent at least $50 billion to stage the 2008 Summer Games in Beijing, and Russia spent a similar amount to put on the 2014 Winter Games in Sochi. In contrast, some hosts have minimized costs by taking advantage of existing facilities and infrastructures; for example, Great Britain (2012 Summer Games), the United States (2002 Winter Games), and Canada (2010 Winter Games) each spent less than 10 percent of what China and Russia spent, respectively, in 2008 and 2014.

Even so, recent bidding competitions have revealed the difficulty faced by democratic societies in these increasingly intense battles for hosting rights. Despite the daunting political challenge of persuading taxpayers of the value of supporting such expensive endeavors at the cost of other public works projects, even a whiff of local opposition generally leads the IOC to frown on a bid. Indeed, in the last decade, cities ranging from Oslo to Boston have withdrawn bids due to concern about cost and local opposition, whereas Beijing and Almaty, Kazakhstan—both governed by regimes that tolerate little opposition—have promised huge sums in their campaigns to host future games.

Similar problems have emerged in World Cup soccer, including claims that nations have bribed FIFA officials and that selection processes have been rigged. In the two most recent bid scandals, soccer authorities and investigative journalists—both in Great Britain, which lost the 2018 World Cup to Russia, and in the United States, which lost the 2022 World Cup to Qatar—have charged that their rivals effectively bought these mega-events from a corrupt FIFA. Legal investigations, indictments, and arrests related to these and other issues have rocked FIFA and led to major upheavals in the sport's ruling elite. It remains to be seen whether a more open, transparent, and democratic FIFA will emerge. The same can be said about the IOC following a similar series of scandals surrounding the bidding process for the 2002 Winter Olympics. Finally, in Brazil, which recently hosted back-to-back World Cup (2014) and Olympic (2016) mega-events, expenditures on these opportunities to market the nation to the world have contributed to a financial and political crisis that has sunk Brazil's economy into

peril not seen since the global depression of the 1930s.

For more than a century, nations have been the focal point for the production of identities through sport. International competitions and global mega-events have provided worldwide stages for the expression and advertisement of national aspirations and national dreams. Though such events have been promoted as mechanisms for ameliorating national tensions, most observers admit that in many instances they have done as much or more to exacerbate national hostilities. Some worry that the occasional "soccer war" like the 1969 skirmish between El Salvador and Honduras or Olympic quarrel will, in the future, mushroom into a more destructive conflict. Such possibilities leave us to wonder whether sporting nationalism will continue to be the potent force that it has been since the end of the 19th century. In seeking to enhance the prospects for creating a universal community of humanity, some observers have asserted that sport might contribute to the diminishing of identification with nations and nationalism rather than stoking the fires of patriotic fervor. However, such rosy predictions seem overly optimistic when viewed from historical and philosophical perspectives.

The Emergence of New Global Forms

In spite of signs to the contrary, some observers have continued to argue that in the last few decades, new forms of sport have emerged that animate the universal human community rather than reinvigorating the existing power of nationalism in defining human experiences. These observers welcome these new sports as signs that in an age of ever-increasing globalization, the problems that nationalism creates might recede into the dustbin of history. Supporters argue that these new sports transcend national boundaries and link people together through common interest in novel pastimes. Moreover, they argue that, unlike older forms of sport whose historical origins lie in particular nations (especially Great Britain and the United States) or in particular civilizations (especially in the West), the new sports are the property of all humankind. From this perspective, all of the various football games and bat-and-ball games that now dominate the world are ultimately expressions of Great Britain, the United States, or, more broadly, Western civilization. In contrast, these newly invented sports, born in an era of rampant globalization, seem to belong to Asia, Africa, and Latin America as well as to Europe and North America.

Lifestyle Sports

Lifestyle sports, sometimes called action sports, comprise a wide variety of activities that include surfing, skateboarding, and windsurfing; snowboarding, freestyle skiing, and extreme skiing; triathlon, parkour, and ultra-endurance running; and BASE jumping, mountain biking, and wingsuit flying. These extraordinarily diverse activities are linked by several shared features. First and foremost, in terms of the identity-forging power of sport, lifestyle sports reject mainstream ideas and promote alternative ways of understanding and doing sport. Many adherents of these activities openly reject the standard versions of modern sport, from team games such as baseball and cricket to individual contests such as golf and tennis. Instead, they promote countercultural communities devoted to pastimes that the majority perceives as odd or even dangerous. For example, the evolution of a skateboarding counterculture over the last few decades includes alternative music and clothing that combine with the sport's alternative physical activities to promote the idea that skateboarders are different or even unique. In fact, that sense of difference has contributed to mainstream efforts to ban or limit skateboarding in many public spaces in the United States and other nations.

The alternative ethos of these sports is connected to powerful ideas about individuality, risk taking, and social responsibility. Lifestyle sports frequently reject the fascination with welding individual talents into corporate goals that resides at the heart of modern team sports in favor of highlighting individual creativity and expression. In fact, devotees of lifestyle sports revel in their individuality and often adopt anti-sport outlooks in which sport is defined as consisting of the widely accepted team games that shape much of the standard practice of physical activity around the globe. This radical individualism is often associated with a corresponding devotion to risk taking and thrill seeking, particularly when the mainstream sees the risks involved as excessively dangerous to both individuals and society. For instance, the mortality rates in wingsuit flying and BASE jumping dwarf those of many other sports. Though reliable statistics remain murky, one study by a physician who flies and jumps found that 72 percent of practitioners had personally witnessed at least one death or serious injury in these lifestyle sports.

In one dramatic example, wingsuit flyer Jeb Corliss has estimated that he has lost 50 percent of his close friends to the sport; he has also predicted that he himself will probably die in an accident. Corliss embraces the risk and has asserted that he wants footage of his death, if it comes in this manner, to be posted on the web as soon as it happens. "This is not golf," Corliss scoffed, when questioned by journalist Matt Rudd about the risks involved. When efforts have been made to ban such sports in order to protect enthusiasts from themselves, they have articulated a libertarian devotion to their perceived right to decide what risks they will take without government or society limiting their freedom unless their activities would cause harm to others. Although lifestyle sports vary widely in their degree of risk for serious injury or death, their adherents maintain a consistent devotion to the idea

HOW EXTREME IS TOO EXTREME?

Philosophical Application

Consider the following scenario: Your friend announces that she has just heard about a new sport and excitedly shows you a brochure advertising "extreme no-parachute skydiving." Promising a "once-in-a-lifetime thrill," the brochure makes clear that, after signing a waiver, your friend will in all likelihood plunge to her death. On one hand, you might assume that your friend has gone crazy, but for the purpose of this exercise let us assume that she is of sound mind. Do you have a moral obligation to intervene?

The philosopher John Stuart Mill's influential work *On Liberty* outlined the argument that an individual is free to do as he or she wishes so long as his or her actions do not harm others. In this view, we should not limit other people's freedom, even if we find it distasteful or irrational. In a similar vein, individuals who pursue highly dangerous sports often cite their personal right of freedom to take risks with their own lives.

Returning to our scenario, assuming that your friend does not land on anyone, you cannot find a way in which her actions might be harmful to anyone else. This raises sharp-edged questions: At what point can we limit another person's freedom? Can we ethically prevent a friend from going "extreme no-parachute skydiving?" Can we ethically permit it?

Many argue that principles of personal liberty should prevail. They say that, in a sense, we own our own bodies and should be given maximal freedom to choose the lifestyle (even a dangerous one) that we desire. Opponents argue that we have an obligation to our bodies and, as a result, we have responsibilities to care for our bodies in certain ways. Moreover, undue risk taking and premature death would likely harm our network of family and friends. It might also influence others (including those who lack the maturity to make sound judgments) to act similarly.

that society should not limit their choices and that, as individuals, they have a right to manage their own risk-taking behaviors.

The Value of Risk Taking

The increasing popularity of lifestyle sports highlights important philosophical considerations about the nature of risk taking and the value of dangerous activity. We often consider physical activity, including competitive sport, to be a healthy endeavor that promotes overall wellness. Clearly, we can indeed promote health with low levels of risk by engaging in recreational activities such as jogging, yoga, and hiking. In contrast, serious competitive sports and extreme sports often involve considerable health risks. For instance, torn ligaments, broken bones, and concussions are common in football, basketball, and soccer even at the high school and youth levels.

Even greater risks, potentially including death, are posed by activities such as whitewater kayaking, downhill skiing, skydiving, and BASE jumping.

The contradiction between health promotion and risk taking in sport presents a philosophical problem for practitioners in kinesiology. Many may promote risk-taking activities, whether as a coach, guide, or instructor. Others may help patients return to their risk-taking sports in their professional role as a physical therapist or medical professional. Some may even choose to participate in these dangerous activities. Often, however, those in the field of kinesiology argue for their profession's value by citing the fact that physical activity promotes health across the life span. Without a doubt, physical activity does provide an antidote to many diseases associated with a sedentary lifestyle. An overwhelming amount of empirical evidence demonstrates that regular physical activity offers both physical and cognitive benefits. Still, many of the specific activities defended as beneficial to health may ultimately do harm.

Risk Versus Reward

When debating the value of high-risk activities, one question worth considering is whether the risk of a bad outcome outweighs the reward of a good one. In this approach, we consider whether the risk of an injury from playing a sport outweighs the health benefits offered by the sport. In order to understand a risk, we must consider both the probability of experiencing a negative outcome (that is, whether it is more or less likely) and the degree of possible harm (from moderate discomfort to death). A hard workout in the gym, for example, may result in a strained muscle, whereas skydiving can result in death. We can also weigh the health benefits, which may lead us to conclude that the resistance workout at the gym offers more benefit than is provided by using gravity to fall back to earth.

To perform a risk-versus-reward analysis in a real-world setting, consider an average person who starts running with the aim of completing a marathon. The health benefits of moderate running are clear: weight control, stress reduction, improved blood pressure, and lower cholesterol. Not only are these benefits associated with positive health, but also research has shown that runners live, on average, three years longer than their nonrunning peers. However, training for and running a marathon, as opposed to merely taking a regular 30-minute jog, also presents health risks. Although one study put the risk of a person dying in a marathon at only 0.5 to 1 per 100,000 people, the negative effects of marathon running may erase all of the positive health benefits. For instance, high-intensity exercise sessions that last longer than an hour have been linked to thinning of the heart tissue, irregular heartbeat, and sudden cardiac arrest. Add to this the risk of dehydration, exhaustion, and heat stroke, as well as orthopedic injuries (such as stress fractures, shin splints, and tendonitis), and the balance of risk to reward is far less certain. In fact, one study showed that high-mileage runners have shorter life spans than their counterparts who run moderate distances.

In terms of health benefits, the risk-versus-reward evidence indicates that health benefits peak with moderate levels of exercise and then begin reversing as activity gets more intense. This reversal would likely rule out most serious competitive sports in which athletes train intensely for more than five hours per week. It would also rule out many extreme sports, such as skydiving, in which the physical activity does not reach the beneficial level of moderate exertion but the risks are greater.

Safety First?

If the health risk outweighs the reward, should kinesiologists adopt for a safety-first approach? Many of us may bristle at this idea. The thought of giving up the sports that we love in order to add a few years to our lives may seem depressing. However, intellectual honesty requires that we face compelling evidence, even if it means having to do something that we do not want to do. How, then, can we justify our risk-taking activities if we know that they ultimately do more harm than good?

Useful answers have been provided by a handful of philosophers. In an article titled "The Value of Dangerous Sport," philosopher J.S. Russell argues that the glorification of risk and injury is misguided. No one likes the fact that dangerous sports present a risk of injury or serious impairment. However, we intuitively sense that nondangerous sport is missing something vital. Is running on a treadmill the same as trail running on an uneven mountain path? Is riding an indoor spin bike nearly as exciting as mountain biking? Even climbing an indoor rock wall of equivalent difficulty to an outdoor one does not provide the same experience. Although the former activities offer safer versions of their more dangerous counterparts, they also lack some of the element of excitement that motivates enthusiasts. For Russell, the more dangerous versions of these sports are more satisfying because they "incorporate a challenge to capacities for judgment and choice that involves all of ourselves—our body, will, emotions, and ingenuity—under conditions of physical duress and danger *at the limits of our being.*"

In many ways, Russell's point illustrates the culmination of many themes developed in this text. For example, we have studied how sport emerged from natural problems in hunter-forager societies, how we evolved to enjoy solving good tests, the holistic idea of human embodiment, and even the anthropological and evolutionary roots of physical activity. Each idea supports Russell's claim that "by confronting serious physical danger through our own choice and actions," dangerous sports challenge us "to the very limits of what it is to be an embodied rational being." Therefore, while we need not glorify risk, we would be misguided to try to remove all risk from our sporting experiences certainly seems misguided.

Meaning in Movement

Returning to the idea of health and physical activity, the preceding discussion about risk taking and the value of dangerous activity reveals an important truth about health that many people in the field of kinesiology miss. Although supporting health is important, it may not be the most important thing we do. Instead, we should consider how physical activity contributes to meaningful lives. Focusing on meaning instead of on health flies in the face of the traditional health-oriented rationale that is popular in the allied health professions. The almost dogmatic reference to health in professional settings mirrors popular culture's valuation of physical activity for its health benefits. Certainly, it is true that

we often promote health through physical activity. However, if health were all we wanted, we could not endorse risk-taking activities that put people's health at risk. Instead, we would encourage our clients to take up indoor spinning instead of mountain biking and recommend that they use a rowing machine rather than go whitewater kayaking. After all, these indoor versions take place in supervised, climate-controlled environments and present little risk to the participant yet still provide reliable health benefits.

Yet such watered-down forms of sport hardly provide the moments that we treasure. More often, they feel like placeholders until we can return to the real thing. Moreover, professionals who focus on meaning rather than on health are far more likely to succeed in achieving desired health outcomes for their clients and patients—despite the added risks. The thrill of mountain biking can keep us returning to the sport, as can the challenge of improving and the desire to seek new adventures. In this way, focusing on movement as a meaningful activity acknowledges its risk-taking component while still placing it firmly among the other elements essential to living a good life.

Nature, Technology, and the Ethics of Environment

Meaningful activity, especially in lifestyle sports, often merges an interest in technology, or the universe of human-made implements, with a strong devotion to natural environments. Many lifestyle sports require sophisticated technological equipment, from deftly designed surfboards to well-crafted mountain bikes to high-tech flying suits. At the same time, these technological tools are often employed in spectacular natural settings, such as breathtaking beachfront surf or majestic mountain peaks. A paradoxical interest in both artificial things and natural landscapes animates lifestyle sports.

An additional paradox fuels lifestyle sports. Many of these disciplines reject mainstream sport not only as an impediment to the expression of individualism but also as overly commercial activities. In lifestyle sport, participants seek an alternative to the rampant consumerism and materialism fostered by globalization. In spite of this anti-commercial rhetoric, lifestyle sports have created their own consumer niches in the global economy. Devotees buy expensive gear to pursue their pastimes. Their "extreme" sports are frequently employed by the very mass consumer culture they reject as a way to sell everything from soft drinks to retirement funds. Indeed, consumers can dabble in lifestyle sports by purchasing emblems of these activities without engaging fully in them. Corporations sell far more pairs of Vans to nonskateboarders than to skaters and far more pairs of board shorts to nonsurfers than to surfers. The fact that lifestyle sports have created alternative subcultures that mainstream consumers perceive as "cool" means that they are frequently drawn into the global markets that their practitioners ardently seek to reject.

The image of the "surf bum" inhabiting an idyllic beachfront shack in an effort to escape the perils of modern life while enjoying sun-kissed days and answering to no one with authority—no boss, spouse, parent, or supervisor of any sort—underscores the individualistic and contrarian dreams embedded in the lifestyle sports boom. That image certainly sells products in global markets—not so much actual surfboards but sunglasses, Hawaiian shirts, beachwear, t-shirts, surf music, and all manner of other accoutrements. Ironically, the vast majority of people who buy these products and identify with the lifestyle are not "surf bums" (whose lack of employment and disposable income would make such purchases problematic) but urban and suburban folk who commute in traffic jams, watch too much television, and answer to bosses, spouses, parents, and supervisors of all sorts. Creating desire for a particularly attractive lifestyle and creating the conditions for broad enjoyment of such a lifestyle remain very

different endeavors. Clearly, in our times, the former task is far easier than the latter.

For those who do engage in such lifestyle sports, their pursuit of the wilderness as a playground necessitates ethical considerations for the environment. Environmental ethics as a branch of applied ethics grew in importance in the 1960s and 1970s as philosophers realized that most ethical considerations were anthropocentric; that is, they considered only the ways in which actions affected other humans. The realization that humans have a moral obligation to their environment and to nonhuman species not only advanced environmental ethics but influenced ethical reasoning in other areas of philosophy. Although philosophers in environmental ethics have developed a variety of positions, many concern themselves with wilderness and its preservation. Wilderness refers to landscapes untouched by human civilization. Not only do we appreciate the great outdoors for its aesthetic beauty, but we also realize that experiencing nature is good for our mental well-being. Moreover, it offers the possibility of many exciting sporting adventures that cannot be re-created in built environments.

At the same time, the very desire to enjoy the wilderness threatens its preservation. The increasing disappearance of wilderness due to urban sprawl and agricultural development, coupled with the increasing human population, has reduced the opportunities for many people to access natural playgrounds. At the same time, the waves of lifestyle enthusiasts venturing into the wilderness on ski vacations and mountaineering excursions creates ecological strains that threaten the very wilderness they seek. Consider the irony in the carloads of skiers driving their SUVs to the mountains only to find parking lots dotting the majestic peaks and climate change leaving their ski areas barren of snow. Or consider the fact that, in 2015, Major Ranveer Singh Jamwal of the Indian Army referred to Mount Everest's base camp as "the world's highest junkyard" after leading a mission to remove an estimated 8,000 pounds of garbage left there by climbers attempting to summit the world's tallest peak. In fact, mass access to many wilderness places for the purpose of lifestyle sport raises ethical questions about whether such sports can be morally endorsed. The economic conditions required, and the fact that affluent lifestyles have contributed to the reduction of wilderness, have provoked sharp criticism of the environmental impact of these new forms of sport.

On the other hand, limiting access raises a new range of moral questions because it requires denying people the chance to enjoy areas of natural beauty and limiting individual freedoms that are central to liberal democracies. How can people come to appreciate and preserve the wilderness if they have no connection with it? In fact, human estrangement from the wilderness has contributed to environmental exploitation and destruction, whereas hikers, skiers, and other lifestyle sport enthusiasts—who maintain connections to wilderness—have sometimes led conservation efforts to preserve such areas. This contrast introduces two key ideas from environmental ethics: stewardship and sustainability. Stewardship draws on feminist ethics to note the historical link between the "logic of domination" and ecological exploitation. Rather than putting humans in charge of the environment and seeing it merely as something for humans to use or consume, stewardship emphasizes taking care of the environment. Sustainability requires that the needs or desires of the present not compromise the ability of future generations to meet their own needs. Thus the ethical models of stewardship and sustainability not only seem compatible with lifestyle sport but also may place higher levels of moral obligation on those who enjoy the wilderness in this manner.

Californization

In addition to the numerous aforementioned paradoxes that have arisen as life-style sports have bloomed in the past few decades, the claims that these activities are truly transnational and truly novel begin to dissolve under closer inspection. Although affluent people in nations around the globe covet the lifestyles associated with these sports, thus producing a clearly transnational devotion to these activities, they were not invented or incubated simultaneously at multiple spots around the globe. In fact, lifestyle sports have a particular lineage rooted in a regional and national context rather than a mystical origin in a murky pan-humanism. Specifically, the vast majority of lifestyle sports—from beach volleyball, mountain biking, and triathlon to surfing, snowboarding, and skateboarding—were developed, refined, and perfected in California.

Since the early 20th century, California has led the world in the production and sale of "cool" consumer goods and enticing lifestyles, generating a global industry not only in lifestyle sports but also in other popular culture products, such as cinema, television, music, personal computing, fashionable clothing, and a host of other lifestyle-enhancing merchandise. These California-based industries have mastered the art of selling not only things but also the expectation that certain lifestyles will emerge from possessing these things, promising us an existence rich with health, youth, beauty, and an unending supply of meaningful movement—if only we buy the right products. From this vantage point, the emergence of transnational sport looks more like the Californization of the world—a particular brand of Americanization.

Nationalism remains a powerful force in these allegedly transnational sports in other ways as well. As lifestyle sports have been exported from California to the world and enjoyed increasing global popularity, they have been incorporated into the existing international sporting structures in which nations remain at the center of the organization of international competition. As lifestyle sports have invaded the summer and winter Olympics in recent years—generating new fan bases and increasing television ratings, especially among the coveted global youth demographic—the transnational veneer has largely disappeared since action-sport athletes compete as members of national teams, celebrate their victories with national anthems, and provide new opportunities to weave narratives of national identity.

Shaun White, a native Californian who has become the brightest global star among lifestyle sport fans for his snowboarding feats, ultimately symbolizes the power not of transnational communitarianism but of American prowess when he wins half-pipe gold medals on Olympic slopes, as he did in Torino in 2006 and Vancouver in 2010, and drapes himself in the "Stars and Stripes" for billions of television viewers to witness. Should skateboarding make the Olympic program, a quest that lifestyle sport promotors are pushing, White's proficiency with this other board may catapult him to even greater fame as the most stellar summer and winter Olympian of all time should he add a gold medal in skateboarding's half-pipe. White's career demonstrates that beneath the emergence of new global forms of sport, the forces of nationalism, regionalism, and even localism continue to thrive.

E-Sports

California's influence on sport has extended even into the virtual world as well. California has also become a leader in digital technology. From San Francisco's "Silicon Valley" to Los Angeles' "Silicon Beach," California has put its unique stamp on internationally recognized companies such as Google, Apple, Facebook, and the multi-platform video-game design firm Electronic Arts. As part of the ongoing development of digital technology, the success of multiplayer online gaming has given rise to a phenomenon known as e-sport. Also known as electronic sport, cybersport, online gaming, or virtual sport, e-sport is taking the blend of technology and competition to a level never before seen. There are now professional gamers who win large sums of prize money and lucrative

Are E-Sports Really Sports?

Student Exercise

Throughout this book, we have examined the history and philosophy of sport and physical activity. You have seen how sport has evolved from its Neolithic roots to become religiously and culturally significant. You have witnessed the decline of traditional sports such as the Mesoamerican ball game, medieval jousting, and, let us not forget, cheese rolling. You have also seen how new sports, such as snowboarding and skateboarding, have fused modern technological advances in carbon fiber, polyurethane, and various plastics with human-made ramps and half-pipes. These activities illustrate the fact that sport often blurs the lines between what is natural and what is artificial.

By now, you are well versed in arguments about what constitutes a sport. With that knowledge in mind, consider whether e-sport should be considered a form of sport by the broader society. Use what you know to debate the issue with a partner. To make things interesting, flip a coin (or use a virtual coin-flipping app!) to determine which side of the argument you will take. Then, depending on your assigned side, consider what characteristics e-sport possesses or lacks that are common to other activities commonly referred to as sports. As part of your analysis, attend to the roles played by competition and physical skill, as well as patterns of rationalization, bureaucratization, and history.

Though this debate may seem trivial at first, consider how questions about what is artificial and natural, about the role of physical skill, and about the future of artificial intelligence relate to deeper questions about what it means to be human in an increasingly technological world.

endorsements for their ability to maneuver a virtual Lionel Messi or destroy an enemy's virtual assets. Several U.S. universities have even begun awarding athletic scholarships after including e-sport alongside football and basketball as recognized intercollegiate varsity sports.

Although we have no crystal ball, it seems clear that e-sport will not go the way of the hula hoop or the yo-yo any time soon. Moreover, ongoing investment in virtual reality promises to extend the e-sport experience. Already, it is clear that online gaming has reduced the distance between players. Today, Korean business professionals can stay up late into their night playing League of Legends against 12-year-olds sipping chocolate milk after arriving home from school in France; similarly, a nephew in Poland can beat his uncle in California at a quick game of virtual FIFA. These kinds of connections could scarcely have been imagined just a generation ago, and they illustrate the fact that sporting communities can be transformed in unexpected ways in the digital age.

CHAPTER WRAP-UP

Wrapping Up and Looking Ahead—and Back

In spite of the enduring power of local, national, and regional identities, there are signs that we are becoming more alike than different. We share an evolutionary heritage as "super-endurance predators" (see chapter 1) that has designed our bodies and minds for meaningful movement. Increasingly, we also share a global economic and social system that has created technological and cultural patterns that inhibit our opportunities to engage in meaningful movement. At the same time, several centuries of agricultural revolutions have produced a strange new reality in which the vast majority of us are no longer at risk from periodic shortages in our food supply but in which a superabundance of food in most parts of the world threatens us by making too many calories too easily available. Even as famine remains a tragic reality in some parts of the world, the wealthier parts have more than enough food to feed everyone yet lack the ability (or the will) to distribute the surplus. In addition, the worldwide spread of modern transportation and communication systems, modern manufacturing industries and markets, medical advances, and sanitary improvements has produced a global urban culture that continues to expand dramatically. It took the entirety of human history for the human population to reach 1 billion people, a mark we hit in about the year 1800. It took less than two more centuries for that population to triple (we reached the milestone of three billion people in 1960). In just a half century, that population more than doubled. In 2010, the human population mushroomed to a total of seven billion human beings.

Increasingly, we are not only more numerous but also more affluent than were our ancestors. Even in previously underdeveloped areas of East Africa, where running cultures have long flourished due to a lack of modern transportation systems, cars and minivans are rapidly replacing human locomotion as the main mode of movement. In years past, generations of Kenyan children grew up running to school, a tradition that many scholars speculate when combined with the high altitude of many parts of Kenya accounts for Kenyan dominion in distance running at the Olympics. Now, however, more and more Kenyan children, like children in the United States and many other nations, ride to school in their parents' minivans, or on school buses. Affluence alters the environmental necessities that required us to rely almost entirely on human locomotion in everyday life in the past. Affluence also creates much richer diets, which, when viewed from the perspective of the history of human famine, certainly represents a general improvement in our condition even as it threatens us with easy overindulgence. Affluence has even, as some critics have suggested, produced "affluenza," a global epidemic of "rich" diseases in which caloric abundance and a lack of exercise have contributed to the leading illnesses of our affluent era—hypertension, heart disease, diabetes, many forms of cancer, and the other physical maladies of wealthy and well-developed societies.

This struggle against the challenges with which our current environment confronts us will require us to expand and increase our understandings of and commitments to meaningful movement. Although local, national, and regional identities will no doubt remain important components of our lives for the foreseeable future, perhaps a new global community might emerge in the common human battle against the scourges that affluence has unleashed in our particular time and place in human history. This quest for meaningful movement remains, in the long view of human history, a consistent dilemma; it faced our ancestors, and now it faces us.

More than 100,000 years ago, we emerged from the savannahs of East Africa as "super-endurance predators" fitted by necessity and nature to move nimbly across long distances. Although the necessities of survival no longer force us to run, the search for meaningful forms of movement remains a compelling and complex challenge in our 21st-century lives. In a field devoted to the study of human movement, the question of how to make movement meaningful resides at the core of our endeavor. We hope that the history and philosophy of that quest for meaningful movement, to which we have introduced you in this text, inspires you to think more knowledgeably and deeply about the nature and practice of human movement. We also hope that it impels you to move in ways that are meaningful to you.

Study Questions

1. How do sports enable the creation of meaningful identities for nations, communities, and individuals?

2. How has sport in the 21st century both reinforced national identities and blurred lines between national borders?

3. How are lifestyle sports part of the evolution of physical activity traced throughout this book?

4. What ethical questions must we consider in regard to risk taking and the wilderness in relation to extreme sport?

5. In what ways have companies marketed images of lifestyle sport to global audiences?

6. How do contemporary trends in physical activity illustrate human culture's ongoing fusion of technology and sport?

FURTHER READING AND REFERENCES

Introduction

Aristotle. *The Nicomachean Ethics.* Translated by J. A. K. Thompson. Harmondsworth, Middlesex: England: Penguin Classics, 1953.

Cannadine, David. *What Is History Now?* New York: Palgrave Macmillan, 2002.

Carr, E.H. *What Is History?* Cambridge, UK: Cambridge University Press, 1961.

Elton, Geoffrey R. *The Practice of History.* New York: Crowell, 1967.

Gaddis, John Lewis. *The Landscape of History: How Historians Map the Past.* New York: Oxford University Press, 2002.

Henry, Franklin, M. "Physical Education: An Academic Discipline." *Journal of Health, Physical Education, and Recreation* 35, no. 7 (1964): 32-69.

Kelso, J.A. Scott, and David A. Engstrøm. *The Complementary Nature.* Cambridge, MA: Massachusetts Institute of Technology Press, 2006.

Massengale, John D., and Richard A. Swanson, eds. *The History of Exercise and Sport Science.* Champaign, IL: Human Kinetics, 1997. (See chapter 5, "History of Sport," by Nancy Struna and chapter 6, "Philosophy of Sport," by Scott Kretchmar.)

Newell, Karl M. "Kinesiology: The Label for the Study of Physical Activity in Higher Education." *Quest* 42 (1990): 269-78.

Sage, George H., Mark S. Dyreson, and Scott R. Kretchmar. "Sociology, History, and Philosophy in *The Research Quarterly.*" *Research Quarterly for Exercise and Sport: Supplement* 76, no. 2 (2005): S88-S107.

Snow, C.P. *The Two Cultures: And a Second Look.* Cambridge, UK: Cambridge University Press, 1963.

Wise, Gene. *American Historical Explanations: A Strategy for Grounded Inquiry.* Minneapolis: University of Minnesota, 1980.

Chapter 1

Bekoff, Marc, and John Byers, eds. *Animal Play: Evolutionary, Comparative, and Ecological Perspectives.* Cambridge, UK: Cambridge University Press, 1998.

Blanchard, Kendall. *The Anthropology of Sport: An Introduction.* Rev. ed. Westport, CT: Bergin & Garvey, 1995.

Bramble, Dennis, and Daniel Lieberman. "Endurance Running and the Evolution of *Homo.*" *Nature* 432 (November 2004): 345–52.

Burghhardt, Gordon. *The Genesis of Animal Play: Testing the Limits.* Cambridge, MA: MIT Press, 2005.

Carroll, Douglas. *An Interdisciplinary Study of Sport as a Symbolic Hunt.* Lewiston, NY: Mellen Press, 2000.

Darwin, Charles. *Origin of the Species by Means of Natural Selection and The Descent of Man And Selection in Relation to Sex.* New York: The Modern Library, 1872/1936.

Diamond, Jared M. *The World Until Yesterday: What Can We Learn from Traditional Societies?* New York: Viking, 2012.

Falk, Dean. *The Fossil Chronicles: How Two Controversial Discoveries Changed Our View of Human Evolution.* Berkeley, CA: University of California Press, 2011.

Fink, Eugen. "The Ontology of Play." Translated by Sister M. Delphine. *Philosophy Today* 4 (Summer 1960): 95–110.

Fry, Douglas P. *War, Peace, and Human Nature: The Convergence of Evolutionary and Cultural Views.* New York: Oxford University Press, 2013.

Gould, Stephen Jay. *Punctuated Equilibrium.* Cambridge, MA: Harvard University Press, 2007.

Guttmann, Allen. *Sport: The First Five Millennia.* Amherst, MA: University of Massachusetts Press, 2005.

Heinrich, Bernd. *Why We Run: A Natural History*. New York: Ecco, 2002.

Huizinga, Johan. *Homo Ludens: A Study of the Play Element in Culture*. Boston: Beacon Press, 1950.

Keeley, Lawrence H. *War Before Civilization: The Myth of the Peaceful Savage*. New York: Oxford University Press, 1996.

Leakey, Richard. *The Origin of Humankind*. New York: Basic Books, 1994.

———. *Origins Reconsidered: In Search of What Makes Us Human*. New York: Doubleday, 1992.

Morris, Desmond. *The Soccer Tribe*. London: Cape, 1981.

Pearson, Geoff. *An Ethnography of English Football Fans: Cans, Cops, and Carnivals*. Manchester, UK: Manchester University Press, 2012.

Pinker, Steven. *The Better Angels of Our Nature: Why Violence Has Declined*. New York: Viking, 2011.

Sansone, David. *Greek Athletics and the Genesis of Sport*. Berkeley: University of California Press, 1988.

Schiller, Friedrich. *On the Aesthetic Education of Man in a Series of Letters*. Translated by Elizabeth M. Wilkinson and L.A. Willoughby. Oxford, UK: Oxford University Press, 1967.

Schmitz, Kenneth. "Sport and Play: Suspension of the Ordinary." Paper presented at the annual meeting of the American Association for the Advancement of Science, Dallas, TX, December 1979.

Suits, B. Words on Play. *Journal of the Philosophy of Sport, IV*, (1977), 117-131.

Tomasello, Michael. *Origins of Human Communication*. Cambridge, MA: MIT Press, 2008.

Zimmer, Carl. *Smithsonian Intimate Guide to Human Origins*. New York: Smithsonian Books/Harper Perennial, 2007.

Chapter 2

Aristotle. *The Ethics of Aristotle: The Nicomachean Ethics*. Translated and with an introduction by J.A.K Thomson. Middlesex, UK: Penguin Books, 1958.

Baker, William J. *Sport in the Western World*. Rev. ed. Urbana, IL: University of Illinois Press, 1988.

Crowther, Nigel B. *Sport in Ancient Times*. Westport, CT: Praeger, 2007.

Decker, Wolfgang. *Sports and Games of Ancient Egypt*. New Haven: Yale University Press, 1992.

Dishman, R. (Ed.) *Advances in Exercise Adherence*. Champaign, IL: Human Kinetics, 1994.

Golden, Mark. *Sport in the Ancient World from A to Z*. London: Routledge, 2004.

Guttmann, Allen. *From Ritual to Record: The Nature of Modern Sports*. New York: Columbia University Press, 1979.

———. *Sports: The First Five Millennia*. Amherst, MA: University of Massachusetts Press, 2004.

Huizinga, J. *Homo Ludens: A Study of the Play Element in Culture*. Boston: Beacon Press, 1950.

Kaufmann, Walter, ed. *Existentialism From Dostoevsky to Sartre*. New York: World, 1956.

Kelso, J.A. Scott, and David A. Engstrøm. *The Complementary Nature*. Cambridge, MA: MIT Press, 2006.

Kretchmar, S. "Moving and Being Moved: Implications for Practice." *Quest, 52*, 260-272, 2000.

Kretchmar, S. "Ten More Reasons for Quality Physical Education." *Journal of Health, Physical Education, Recreation, & Dance, 27*, 9, 6-9, 2006.

Kretchmar, S. "The Increasing Utility of Elementary Physical Education: A Mixed Blessing and Unique Challenge." *The Elementary School Journal, 108*, 3, 161-170, 2008.

Mandell, Richard. *Sport: A Cultural History*. New York: Columbia University Press, 1984.

Miller, Stephen G. *Arete: Greek Sports from Ancient Sources*, Second Edition. Berkeley: University of California Press, 2004.

Miller, Stephen G. *Ancient Greek Athletics*. New Haven, CT: Yale University Press, 2004.

Poliakoff, Michael B. *Combat Sports in the Ancient World: Competition, Violence and Culture.* New Haven, CT: Yale University Press, 1995.

Reid, Heather L. *Athletics and Philosophy in the Ancient World: Contests of Virtue.* London: Routledge, 2014.

Roberts, G. (Ed.) *Advances in Motivation in Sport and Exercise.* Champaign, IL: Human Kinetics, 2001.

Chapter 3

Christesen, Paul. *Sport and Democracy in the Ancient and Modern Worlds.* Cambridge, UK: Cambridge University Press, 2012.

Holton, Gerald James. *The Advancement of Science, and its Burdens.* Cambridge: Harvard University Press, 1998.

Kyle, Donald G. *Sport and Spectacle in the Ancient World.* 2nd ed. Malden, MA: Blackwell, 2014.

Lehmann, Clayton Miles. "Early Greek Athletic Trainers." *Journal of Sport History* 36, no. 2 (2009): 187–204.

Miller, Stephen G. *Ancient Greek Athletics.* New Haven, CT: Yale University Press, 2004.

———. *Arete: Greek Sports from Ancient Sources.* 2nd ed. Berkeley, CA: University of California Press, 2004.

Poliakoff, Michael B. *Combat Sports in the Ancient World: Competition, Violence, and Culture.* New Haven, CT: Yale University Press, 1995.

Spivey, Nigel. *The Ancient Olympics.* Oxford, UK: Oxford University Press, 2012.

Whitehead, Alfred North. *Process and Reality: An Essay in Cosmology.* New York: Free Press, 1978.

Xenophanes. *Fragments.* Trans. James Lesher. Toronto: University of Toronto Press, 1992.

Chapter 4

Almond, Steve. *Against Football: One Fan's Reluctant Manifesto.* Brooklyn, NY: Melville House, 2014.

Baker, William J. *Sport in the Western World.* Rev. ed. Urbana, IL: University of Illinois Press, 1988.

Barton, Carlin A. The Sorrows of the Ancient Romans: The Gladiator and the Monster. Princeton, NJ: Princeton University Press, 1995.

Christesen, Paul. *Sport and Democracy in the Ancient and Modern Worlds.* New York: Cambridge University Press, 2012.

Cooper, Andrew. *Playing in the Zone: Exploring the Spiritual Dimensions of Sports.* Boston: Shambhala, 1998.

Crowther, Nigel B. *Sport in Ancient Times.* Westport, CT: Praeger, 2007.

Csikszentmihalyi, Mihaly. *Flow: The Psychology of Optimal Experience.* New York: Harper Perennial, 1990.

Davis, William Stearns. *Readings in Ancient History.* Vol. 2. Boston: Allyn & Bacon, 1913.

Gallwey, W. Timothy. *The Inner Game of Tennis.* New York: Random House, 174.

Golden, Mark. *Sport and Society in Ancient Greece.* New York: Cambridge University Press, 1998.

Guttmann, Allen. *Sports: The First Five Millennia.* Amherst, MA: University of Massachusetts Press, 2004.

Herrigel, Eugen. *Zen in the Art of Archery.* 1953. With an introduction by D. T. Suzuki; translated by R.F.C. Hull. New York: Pantheon Books, 1964.

Hopkins, Keith. Death and Renewal. Vol. 2. Cambridge: Cambridge University Press, 1985.

Kyle, Donald G. *Spectacles of Death in Ancient Rome.* London: Routledge, 1998.

———. *Sport and Spectacle in the Ancient World.* Malden, MA: Blackwell, 2007.

Pinker, Steven. *The Better Angels of Our Nature: Why Violence Has Declined.* New York: Viking, 2011.

Chapter 5

Baker, William J. *Sport in the Western World.* Rev. ed. Urbana: University of Illinois Press, 1988.

Birley, Derek. *Sport and the Making of Britain.* Manchester, UK: Manchester University Press, 1993.

Brailsford, Dennis. *British Sport: A Social History.* Lanham, MD: Barnes & Noble, 1992.

Colón Semenza, Gregory M. *Sport, Politics, and Literature in the English Renaissance.* Newark: University of Delaware Press, 2003.

Descartes, Rene. *Discourse on Method and Meditations.* Translated with an introduction by Laurence J. Lafleur. New York: Bobbs-Merrill, 1960.

Gillmeister, Heiner. *Tennis: A Cultural History.* Washington Square, NY: New York University Press, 1998.

Guttmann, Allen. *Sports: The First Five Millennia.* Amherst: University of Massachusetts Press, 2004.

McClelland, John. *Body and Mind: Sport in Europe from the Roman Empire to the Renaissance.* London: Routledge, 2007.

Midgley, Mary. *The Ethical Primate: Humans, Freedom, and Morality.* London: Routledge, 1994.

Chapter 6

Baker, William J. *Sports in the Western World.* Urbana: University of Illinois Press, 1988.

Bentham, Jeremy. *An Introduction to the Principles of Morals and Legislation.* London: T. Payne, 1789.

Fraleigh, Warren. *Right Actions in Sport: Ethics for Contestants.* Champaign, IL: Human Kinetics, 1984.

Geertz, Clifford. *The Interpretation of Cultures: Selected Essays.* New York: Basic Books, 1973.

Guttmann, Allen. *From Ritual to Record: The Nature of Modern Sport.* New York: Columbia University Press, 1979.

———. *Sports: The First Five Millennia.* Amherst: University of Massachusetts Press, 2004.

Habermas, Jürgen. *The Structural Transformation of the Public Sphere.* Cambridge, UK: Polity Press, 1989.

Holt, Richard. *Sport and the British.* New York: Oxford University Press, 1989.

Hughes, Thomas. *Tom Brown's Schooldays.* 1857. Glasgow, Scotland: Blackie, 1968.

MacAloon, John J. *This Great Symbol: Pierre de Coubertin and the Origins of the Modern Olympic Games.* Chicago: University of Chicago Press, 1984.

Mangan, J.A. *Athleticism in the Victorian and Edwardian School: The Emergence and Consolidation of an Educational Ideology.* Cambridge, UK: Cambridge University Press, 1986.

Russell, J.S. "Are Rules All an Umpire Has to Work With?" *Journal of the Philosophy of Sport* 26, no. 1 (1999): 27–49.

Sandel, Michael J. *The Case Against Perfection: Ethics in the Age of Genetic Engineering.* Cambridge, MA: Belknap Press of Harvard University, 2007.

Searle, John R. *Speech Acts: An Essay in the Philosophy of Language.* Cambridge, UK: Cambridge University Press, 1969.

Simon, Robert L. "Internalism and Internal Values in Sport." *Journal of the Philosophy of Sport* 27, no. 1 (2000): 1–16.

Szymanski, Stefan. "A Theory of the Evolution of Modern Sport." *Journal of Sport History* 35, no. 1 (2008): 1–25.

Taylor, Matthew. *The Association Game: A History of British Football.* Harlow, UK: Pearson Longman, 2008.

Tranter, Neil. *Sport, Economy, and Society in Britain, 1750–1914.* Cambridge, UK: Cambridge University Press, 1998.

Chapter 7

Baker, William J. *Sport in the Western World.* Urbana, IL: University of Illinois Press, 1988.

Bale, John. *Sportscapes.* Sheffield, UK: Geographical Association, 2000.

Burdick, Alan. "Cheating the Beautiful Game." *New Yorker,* June 16, 2014.

Collins, Tony. *Rugby's Great Split: Class, Culture, and the Origins of Rugby League Football.* London: Frank Cass, 1998.

Dixon, Nicholas. "The Ethics of Supporting Sports Teams." *Journal of Applied Philosophy* 18, no. 2 (2001): 149–58.

Hobsbawm, E.J. *Nations and Nationalism since 1780: Programme, Myth, Reality.* Cambridge: Cambridge University Press, 1990.

Holt, Richard. *Sport and the British.* New York: Oxford University Press, 1989.

Kant, Immanuel. *Critique of Pure Reason.* 1855. Translated by Norman Kemp Smith. New York: St. Martin's Press, 1965.

Kirsch, George B. *The Creation of American Team Sports: Baseball and Cricket, 1838–72.* Urbana, IL: University of Illinois Press, 1989.

Levine, Peter G. *A.G. Spalding and the Rise of Baseball: The Promise of American Sport.* New York: Oxford University Press, 1985.

Mumford, Stephen. "Moderate Partisanship as Oscillation." *Sport, Ethics, and Philosophy* 6, no. 3 (2012): 369–75.

Murray, Bill. *The World's Game: A History of Soccer.* Urbana: University of Illinois Press, 1996.

Novak, Michael. *The Joy of Sports: End Zones, Bases, Baskets, Balls, and the Consecration of the American Spirit.* New York: Basic Books, 1976.

Oriard, Michael. *Reading Football: How the Popular Press Created an American Spectacle.* Chapel Hill, NC: University of North Carolina Press, 1993.

Russell, J.S. "Ideal Fan or Good Fans?" *Sports, Ethics and Philosophy* 6, no. 1 (2012): 11–23.

Smith, Ronald A. *Sports and Freedom: The Rise of Big-Time College Athletics.* New York: Oxford University Press, 1988.

Taylor, Matthew. *The Association Game: A History of British Football.* Harlow, UK: Pearson Longman, 2008.

Tygiel, Jules. *Baseball's Great Experiment: Jackie Robinson and His Legacy.* Rev. ed. New York: Oxford University Press, 1997.

Chapter 8

Arbena, Joseph. *Sport and Society in Latin America: Diffusion, Dependency, and the Rise of Mass Culture.* New York: Greenwood Press, 1988.

Cronin, Mike, Paul Rouse, and William Murphy, eds. *The Gaelic Athletic Association, 1884–2009.* Dublin: Irish Academic Press, 2009.

Fraleigh, Warren. *Right Actions in Sport: Ethics for Contestants.* Champaign, IL: Human Kinetics, 1984.

Galeano, Eduardo. *Soccer in Sun and Shadow.* New York: Verso, 2003.

Geertz, Clifford. "Deep Play: Notes on the Balinese Cockfight." In *Interpretation of Cultures,* 412–54. New York: Basic Books, 1973.

Guttmann, Allen. *Games and Empires: Modern Sports and Cultural Imperialism.* New York: Columbia University Press, 1994.

James, C.L.R. *Beyond a Boundary.* Rev. ed. Durham, NC: Duke University Press, 1993.

Kildea, Gary, and Jerry Leach. *Trobriand Cricket: An Indigenous Response to Colonialism.* London: Royal Anthropological Institute of Great Britain and Ireland, 1974.

Mangan, J.A. *The Games Ethic and Imperialism: Aspects of the Diffusion of an Ideal.* New York: Viking, 1986.

Metheny, Eleanor. *Connotations of Movement in Sport and Dance.* Dubuque, IA: Brown, 1965.

Patrick F. McDevitt, *May the Best Man Win: Sport, Masculinity, and Nationalism in Great Britain and the Empire, 1880–1935.* New York: Palgrave Macmillan, 2004.

Russell, J.S. "Resilience." Warren Fraleigh Distinguished Scholar Lecture. *Journal of the Philosophy of Sport* 42, no. 2 (2015): 159–83.

Simon, Robert, Cesar Torres, and Peter Hager. *Fair Play: The Ethics of Sport.* 4th ed. Boulder, CO: Westview Press, 2015.

Van Bottenburg, Maarten. *Global Games.* Urbana, IL: University of Illinois Press, 2001.

Chapter 9

Dyreson, Mark. "Aggressive America: Media Nationalism and the 'War' Over Olympic Pictures in Sport's 'Golden Age.'" *International Journal of the History of Sport* 22, no. 6 (November 2005): 974–89.

———. *Crafting Patriotism for Global Domination: America at the Olympic Games.* London: Routledge, 2009.

———. *Making the American Team: Sport, Culture, and the Olympic Experience.*

Urbana, IL: University of Illinois Press, 1998.

Goldblatt, David. *The Ball Is Round: A Global History of Soccer.* New York: Riverhead Books, 2008.

Guttmann, Allen. *Games and Empires: Sports and Cultural Imperialism.* New York: Columbia University Press, 1994.

International Olympic Committee. *Olympic Charter.* Lausanne, Switzerland: International Olympic Committee, 2014.

Llewellyn, Matthew P. *Rule Britannia: Nationalism, Identity, and the Modern Olympic Games.* London: Routledge, 2012.

MacAloon, John. *This Great Symbol: Pierre de Coubertin and the Origins of the Modern Olympic Games.* Chicago: University of Chicago Press, 1981.

Morgan, William J. *Why Sports Morally Matter.* London: Routledge, 2006.

Murray, Bill. *The World's Game: A History of Soccer.* Urbana, IL: University of Illinois Press, 1996.

Orwell, George. "The Sporting Spirit." *London Tribune,* December 1945. (Reprint: Orwell, George. *Shooting an Elephant, and Other Essays.* London: Secker and Warburg, 1950.)

Young, David. *The Modern Olympics: A Struggle for Revival.* Baltimore: Johns Hopkins University Press, 1996.

Chapter 10

Brousse, Michael, and David Matsumoto. *Judo in the U.S.A: Century of Dedication.* Berkeley, CA: North Atlantic Books, 2005.

Brownell, Susan, ed. *Bodies Before Boas: The 1904 St. Louis Olympic Games and Anthropology Days.* Lincoln, NE: University of Nebraska Press, 2008.

Confucius. *The Analects, Or the Conversations of Confucius With His Disciples and Certain Others.* Translated by W.E. Soothill. London: Oxford University Press, 1910.

Coubertin, Pierre de. *Pierre De Coubertin: Textes Choisis, Volume 1.* Zurich: Weidmann, 1986.

Dewey, John. *Human Nature and Conduct: The Middle Works, 1899–1924, Volume 14.* Edited by Jo Ann Boydston. Carbondale, IL: Southern Illinois University Press, 1988.

Dyreson, Mark. "American Ideas About Race and Olympic Races From the 1890s to the 1950s: Shattering Myths or Reinforcing Scientific Racism?" *Journal of Sport History* 28, no. 2 (summer 2001): 173–215.

———. "The Foot Runners Conquer Mexico and Texas: Endurance Racing, Indigenismo, and Nationalism." *Journal of Sport History* 31, no. 1 (spring 2004): 1–31.

Eichberg, Henning. *Body Cultures: Essays on Sport, Space, and Identity.* London: Routledge, 1998.

Epstein, David. *The Sports Gene: Inside the Science of Extraordinary Athletic Performance.* New York: Penguin, 2013.

Gallwey, Tim. *The Inner Game of Tennis.* New York: Random House, 1974.

Guttmann, Allen. *From Ritual to Record: The Nature of Modern Sports.* Rev. ed. New York: Columbia University Press, 2004.

———. *Games and Empires: Modern Sports and Cultural Imperialism.* New York: Columbia University Press, 1995.

Hoberman, John. *Darwin's Athletes: How Sport Has Damaged Black America and Preserved the Myth of Race.* Boston: Houghton Mifflin, 1996.

Jackson, Phil, and Hugh Delehanty. *Sacred Hoops: Spiritual Lessons of a Hardwood Warrior.* New York: Hyperion, 2006.

McDougall, Christopher. *Born to Run: A Hidden Tribe, Superathletes, and the Greatest Race the World Has Never Seen.* New York: Vintage, 2011.

Merleau-Ponty, Maurice. *The Structure of Behaviour.* Translated by Alden L. Fisher. Boston: Beacon Press, 1963.

Michaelsen, Joanna. *Like Lambs to the Slaughter: Your Child and the Occult.* Eugene, OR: Harvest House Publishers, 1992.

Chapter 11

Baker, William J. *Sports in the Western World.* Rev. ed. Urbana, IL: University of Illinois Press, 1988.

Barney, Robert K., Stephen R. Wenn, and Scott G. Martyn. *Selling the Five Rings: The International Olympic Committee and the Rise of Olympic Commercialism.* Rev. ed. Salt Lake City: University of Utah Press, 2004.

Booth, Douglas. *The Race Game: Sport and Politics in South Africa.* London: Cass, 1998.

Cahn, Susan. *Coming on Strong: Gender and Sexuality in Twentieth-Century Women's Sports.* 2nd ed. Urbana, IL: University of Illinois Press, 2015.

Epstein, David. *The Sports Gene: Inside the Science of Extraordinary Athletic Performance.* New York: Penguin, 2013.

Ford, Gerald R. "In Defense of the Competitive Urge." *Sports Illustrated*, July 8, 1974, p. 17.

Gibson, Althea, and Richard Curtis. *So Much to Live For.* New York: Putnam, 1968.

Guttmann, Allen. *Games and Empires: Modern Sports and Cultural Imperialism.* New York: Columbia University Press, 1995.

Hartman, Douglas. *Race, Culture, and the Revolt of the Black Athlete: The 1968 Olympic Protests and Their Aftermath.* Chicago: University of Chicago Press, 2004.

Heidegger, Martin. *Being and Time: A translation of* Sein und Zeit. Translated by Joan Stambaugh. Albany: State University of New York Press, 1996.

Hersh, Philip. "Italian Gymnast, Federation Spokesman Apologize for Racial Remarks." *Chicago Tribune*, October 9, 2013. http://articles.chicagotribune.com/2013-10-09/sports/chi-italian-gymnast-federation-spokesman-apologize-for-racial-insensitivity-20131009_1_gymnast-simone-biles-federation.

Hoberman, John Milton. *Darwin's Athletes: How Sport Has Damaged Black America and Preserved the Myth of Race.* Boston: Houghton Mifflin, 1997.

Hunt, Thomas. *Drug Games: The International Olympic Committee and the Politics of Doping, 1960–2008.* Austin: University of Texas Press, 2011.

LaFeber, Walter. *Michael Jordan and the New Global Capitalism.* New York: Norton, 1999.

Merleau-Ponty, Maurice. *Phenomenology of Perception.* Translated by Colin Smith. London: Routledge, 2003.

Mill, John Stuart. "On Liberty." In *A Selection of His Works.* Toronto: Macmillan, 1966.

Murray, Bill. *The World's Game: A History of Soccer.* Urbana, IL: University of Illinois Press, 1996.

Nauright, John. *Sport, Culture, and Identities in South Africa.* London: Leicester University Press, 1997.

Orwell, George. "The Sporting Spirit." *London Tribune*, December 1945. (Reprint: Orwell, George. *Shooting an Elephant, and Other Essays.* London: Secker and Warburg, 1950.) Here is the larger quotation: "Serious sport has nothing to do with fair play. It is bound up with hatred, jealousy, boastfulness, disregard of all rules, and sadistic pleasure in witnessing violence: in other words it is war minus the shooting."

Roberts, Randy, and James Olson. *Winning Is the Only Thing: Sports in American Society Since 1945.* Baltimore: Johns Hopkins University Press, 1989.

Schultz, Jaime. *Qualifying Times: Points of Change in U.S. Women's Sport.* Urbana, IL: University of Illinois Press, 2014.

Thomas, Damion. *Globetrotting: African American Athletes and Cold War Politics.* Urbana, IL: University of Illinois Press, 2012.

Women's Sports Foundation. "A Title IX Primer." www.womenssportsfoundation.org/home/advocate/title-ix-and-issues/what-is-title-ix/title-ix-primer.

World Anti-Doping Agency. *World Anti-Doping Code 2015.* Montreal: World Anti-Doping Agency, 2015.

Zang, David. *Sportswars: Athletes in the Age of Aquarius.* Fayetteville, AR: University of Arkansas Press, 2001.

Zirin, Dave. *What's My Name, Fool? Sports and Resistance in the United States.* Chicago: Haymarket Books, 2005.

Chapter 12

Dyreson, Mark. "The Republic of Consumption at the Olympic Games: Globalization, Americanization, and Californization." *Journal of Global History* 8, no. 2 (July 2013): 256–78.

Dyreson, Mark, and Jaime Schultz, eds. *American National Pastimes—A History*. London: Routledge, 2015.

Geertz, Clifford. "Deep Play: Notes on the Balinese Cockfight." In *The Interpretation of Cultures*. New York: Basic Books, 1973.

Guthrie-Shimizu, Sayuri. *Transpacific Field of Dreams: How Baseball Linked the United States and Japan in Peace and War*. Chapel Hill, NC: University of North Carolina Press, 2012.

Guttmann, Allen. *Games and Empires: Modern Sports and Cultural Imperialism*. New York: Columbia University Press, 1995.

———. *Sports: The First Five Millennia*. Amherst: University of Massachusetts Press, 2004.

Heinrich, Bernd. *Why We Run: A Natural History*. New York: Ecco, 2002.

Japan National Tourism Organization. "National Pastime." http://us.jnto.go.jp/adventure/national_pastime.php?np=1.

MacIntyre, Alisdair C. *After Virtue: A Study in Moral Theory*. 2nd ed. South Bend, IN: University of Notre Dame Press, 1984.

Mill, John Stuart. *On Liberty and Other Essays*. New York: Kaplan, 2009.

Rudd, Matt. "The Fall Guys." *Australian*, December 1, 2012. www.theaustralian.com.au/life/weekend-australian-magazine/the-fall-guys/news-story/977f8538e6a42bf7c21326b39e05aee0.

Russell, John. "The Value of Dangerous Sport." *Journal of the Philosophy of Sport* 32, no. 1 (2005): 1–19.

Sandel, Michael. *Justice: What's the Right Thing to Do?* New York: Farrar, Straus & Giroux, 2009.

Wheaton, Belinda. *The Cultural Politics of Lifestyle Sports*. London: Routledge, 2013.

Note: The italicized *f* and *t* following page numbers refer to figures and tables, respectively.

Image courtesy of Penn State.

R. Scott Kretchmar, PhD, is a professor emeritus of exercise and sport science at Penn State University in University Park, Pennsylvania. Kretchmar, a fellow in the National Academy of Kinesiology, is a former president of the International Association for the Philosophy of Sport and previously served as editor of the *Journal of the Philosophy of Sport*. He has been named an Alliance Scholar by SHAPE America (Society of Health and Physical Educators) and a Distinguished Scholar by the National Association for Kinesiology and Physical Education in Higher Education (NAKPEHE).

Image courtesy of Patrick Mansell, Penn State.

Mark Dyreson, PhD, is a professor of kinesiology and an affiliate professor of history at Penn State University in University Park, Pennsylvania. Also a fellow of the National Academy of Kinesiology, he is a former president of the North American Society for Sport History (NASSH), an academic editor for the *International Journal of the History of Sport*, and the coeditor of the Sport in the Global Society: Historical Perspectives book series (Routledge Press).